LATIN AMERICAN STUDIES
SOCIAL SCIENCES AND LAW

Edited by
David Mares
University of California, San Diego

T0347656

A ROUTLEDGE SERIES

LATIN AMERICAN STUDIES: SOCIAL SCIENCES AND LAW

DAVID MARES, *General Editor*

OBSERVING OUR *HERMANOS DE ARMAS*
U.S. Military Attachés in Guatemala,
Cuba, and Bolivia, 1950–1964
Robert O. Kirkland

LAND PRIVATIZATION IN MEXICO
Urbanization, Formation of Regions,
and Globalization in Ejidos
María Teresa Vázquez Castillo

THE POLITICS OF THE INTERNET IN THIRD
WORLD DEVELOPMENT
Challenges in Contrasting Regimes with
Case Studies of Costa Rica and Cuba
Bert Hoffmann

CONTESTING THE IRON FIST
Advocacy Networks and Police
Violence in Democratic Argentina and
Chile
Claudio A. Fuentes

LATIN AMERICA'S NEO-REFORMATION
Religion's Influence on Contemporary
Politics
Eric Patterson

INSURGENCY, AUTHORITARIANISM, AND
DRUG TRAFFICKING IN MEXICO'S
"DEMOCRATIZATION"
José Luis Velasco

THE POLITICS OF SOCIAL POLICY CHANGE
IN CHILE AND URUGUAY
Retrenchment Versus Maintenance,
1973–1998
Rossana Castiglioni

AN INDUSTRIAL GEOGRAPHY OF COCAINE
Christian M. Allen

STATE AND BUSINESS GROUPS IN MEXICO
The Role of Informal Institutions in the
Process of Industrialization,
1936–1984
Arnulfo Valdivia-Machuca

STATE AND BUSINESS GROUPS IN MEXICO

THE ROLE OF INFORMAL INSTITUTIONS IN THE PROCESS OF INDUSTRIALIZATION, 1936–1984

Arnulfo Valdivia-Machuca

Routledge
New York & London

Published in 2005 by
Routledge
Taylor & Francis Group
270 Madison Ave,
New York NY 10016

Published in Great Britain by
Routledge
Taylor & Francis Group
2 Park Square,
Milton Park, Abingdon,
Oxon, OX14 4RN

Transferred to Digital Printing 2009

International Standard Book Number-10: 0-415-97405-4 (Hardcover)
International Standard Book Number-13: 978-0-415-97405-9 (Hardcover)
Library of Congress Card Number 2004030629

Library of Congress Cataloging-In-Publication Data

Valdivia-Machuca, Arnulfo.
  State and business groups in Mexico : the role of informal institutions in the process of
  industrialization, 1936-1984 / Arnulfo Valdivia-Machuca.
     p. cm. -- (Latin American studies : social sciences and law)
  Includes bibliographical references and index.
  ISBN 0-415-97405-4
  1. Industrial policy--Mexico--History--20th century. 2. Policy networks--Mexico--History--
  20th century. 3. Industrialization--Mexico--History--20th century. I. Title. II. Latin
  American studies (Routledge (Firm))

HD3616.M43V354 2005
338.0972'09'04--dc22   2004030629

ISBN10: 0-415-97405-4 (hbk)
ISBN10: 0-415-80570-8 (pbk)

ISBN13: 978-0-415-97405-9 (hbk)
ISBN13: 978-0-415-80570-4 (pbk)

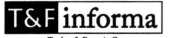

Taylor & Francis Group
is the Academic Division of T&F Informa plc.

Visit the Taylor & Francis Web site at
http://www.taylorandfrancis.com

and the Routledge Web site at
http://www.routledge-ny.com

Publisher's Note
The publisher has gone to great lengths to ensure the quality of this reprint
but points out that some imperfections in the original may be apparent.

To my family, Mami, Chino, Linda, you are everything.
It is because of you and for you that I am here.

To all those who are not here, but have still been with
me along the way, I miss you and love you.
Thank you.

Contents

Acknowledgments

I am much indebted to all those who supported this project. First to Dr. Christel Lane, who shaped the scope of this work from the start, always making the right questions, suggesting alternative directions, and kindly giving me all her encouragement in every step of the way. The comments, ideas, and constructive criticism from Dr. David Lehmann, Professor Laurence Whitehead, Professor Colin Hay, Professor Asdrúbal Baptista, Professor Geoffrey Hawthorne, Mr. Filip Saelens, and Mr. Derek Hanssens Birch were also vital to the completion of the book. Thank you all.

I am also obliged to the many organizations that, through their generous contributions for academic and traveling purposes, made this project financially viable. In alphabetical order, I would like to thank The British Government for their *Chevening Scholarship* scheme; the Cambridge Political Economy Society; the Cambridge Overseas Trust of the University of Cambridge; Clare Hall College at the University of Cambridge; the *Consejo Nacional de Ciencia y Tecnología* (CONACYT); and the *Gobierno del Estado de México*.

This book would not have been possible either without the help of innumerable organizations and individuals that allowed me to compile the information here presented. I would like to thank the Central Library of the University of Cambridge, the Latin American Library of the University of Cambridge, the Social and Political Sciences Library of the University of Cambridge, the Marshall Library of Economics of the University of Cambridge, the Daniel Cosío Villegas Library of the *Colegio de México,* the Central Library of the National Autonomous University of Mexico (UNAM), and the *Archivo General de la Nación* in Mexico for letting me use their fantastic facilities and giving me access to their resources. I am also in debt with ex-president Luis Echeverría Álvarez for giving me unrestricted access to his personal library and archives. I must also thank Héctor Rangel Domene, Pedro Zorrilla Velasco and Carlos Castillo Schütte at the Mexican

Bankers Association, as well as Jorge Espina Reyes and Gabriel Funes at Coparmex. They were all key people in giving me access to the private archives of those two organizations. Equally, I would like to thank all my interviewees for their time and insights. Meeting all of them was a learning experience in itself. I particularly would like to thank José Ramón López Portillo-Romano and Captain Báez for the extensive amount of interviews that they helped me obtain. Without you, this book would not have been possible.

My special gratefulness also goes to the Stone Center for Latin American Studies at Tulane University, and to the European University Institute in Florence, Italy, where I revised substantial sections of this book during my respective stays as a research fellow in those great institutions. Your financial, educational, professional, and personal support was enormous and so is my gratefulness. Thank you Tom Reese, Jimmy Huck, Sue Ingles, Hellen Wallace, Philippe Schmitter, Filipa de Sousa and Pandelis Nastos. Finally, I would like to thank Clare Hall, my beloved Cambridge College, in which I spent some of the best years of my life, and met some of the best people in this world. Gillian Beer, Eckhard Salje, Terry Apter, Hugh Whittaker, Bobbie Wells, Ed Barron, Martin Alridge, and all the rest of the staff: thanks for putting up with me and, mainly, for not letting me leave Cambridge. You all know what I mean.

I would also like to thank my editors at Routledge. Dr. David Mares, thank you for your constructive and useful comments. Kim Giunta and Ben Holtzman, I have deeply appreciated your support and guidance in this new and exciting experience.

Last but not least, I would like to thank all my family and friends for the support they have given me throughout this project. You are too numerous to mention individually, but be sure that if you get a copy of these acknowledgements, you are included in the list of those I keep deep in my heart.

Abbreviations

ABM	Mexican Bankers Association
AMCB	Mexican Association of Stockbrokerage Houses
AMCHAM	American Chamber of Commerce—Mexico
AMIS	Mexican Association of Insurance Institutions
ANIERM	National Association of Importers and Exporters of the Mexican Republic
BANCOMEXT	National Bank for International Trade
BM	Bank of Mexico
BNCE	National Bank for Agricultural Credit
BOP	Balance of Payments
BUOP	Bank for Urban and Public Works
CAMCO	Mexico City Chamber of Commerce
CANACINTRA	National Chamber of Transformation Industries
CCAIIP	Coordinating Committee for the International Affairs of the Private Sector
CCE	Business Coordinating Council
CEIMSA	Exporting and Importing Mexican Company
CEMAI	Mexican Business Committee for International Affairs
CIA	Central Intelligence Agency of the United States of America
CMHN	Mexican Businessmen Council
CNT	National Tri-partite Commission
COLMEX	Colegio de México
CONCAMIN	National Confederation of Chambers of Industry
CONCANACO	National Confederation of Chambers of Commerce
CONCANACOMIN	National Confederation of Chambers of Commerce and Industry
COPARMEX	Employer's Confederation of the Mexican Republic

DHIAC	Integrative Human Development Civil Association
FDI	Foreign Direct Investment
FICORCA	Trust Fund for the Coverage of Exchange Risk
GATT	General Agreement on Tariffs and Trade
GDP	Gross Domestic Product
ICA	Associated Civil Engineers
ICES	Informal Consultation and Exchange System
IF Model	Informal-Formal Model
IMF	International Monetary Fund
INEGI	National Institute of Statistics, Geography and Informatics
ISI	Import Substitution Industrialization
ITESM	Technological and Higher Studies Institute of Monterrey
IVA	Value-Added Tax
KGB	Intelligence and Internal Security Agency of the former USSR
LIBOR	London Inter-Bank Offered Rate
MLN	National Liberation Movement
NAFINSA	National Financial Society
NAFTA	North American Free Trade Agreement
NGOs	Non-Governmental Organizations
OAS	Organization of American States
PAN	National Action Party
PEMEX	Mexican Petroleum Company
PIRE	Immediate Program of Economic Recovery
PNR	National Revolutionary Party
PRI	Revolutionary Institutional Party
PRM	Party of the Mexican Revolution
SARH	Secretariat of Agriculture and Hydraulic Resources
SCT	Secretariat of Communications and Transportation
SECTUR	Secretariat of Tourism
SEPAFIN	Secretariat of the National Patrimony
SHCP	Secretariat of the Treasury and Public Credit
SIC	Secretariat of Industry and Commerce
SLT	Structure Laying Technique
SOP	Secretariat of Public Works
SP	Secretariat of the Presidency
SPP	Secretariat of Programming and Budget
STYPS	Secretariat of Labor and Social Provision

U.S.	United States of America
UNAM	National Autonomous University of Mexico
US$	United States Dollars
USEM	Social Union of Businessmen
WWII	Second World War

"We can forgive a man for making a useful thing as long as he does not admire it. The only excuse for making a useless thing is that one admires it intensely."

Oscar Wilde, *The Picture of Dorian Gray.*
(Chancellor Press Edition, 1991)

Introduction

The objective of this book is to investigate the relation between informal institutions and economic stability during the period of industrialization in Mexico. The work covers the 48 years between 1936 and 1984 and is divided into three parts.

The first part is divided into two theoretical chapters. The first starts with a detailed critical review of modern neo-institutionalist theory and then analyzes the processes of emergence, persistence, and change of institutions. Chapter 2 narrows the scope of enquiry, by focusing on informal institutions. Policy network theory is the framework that guides this second chapter. Accordingly, a review of the literature on policy networks is presented first. I then move to link policy network theory and neo-institutionalist theory in analytical ways, to prove that policy networks may be regarded as informal institutions. The chapter then analyzes the processes of emergence, persistence, and change of informal institutions. I conclude by challenging the view that informal institutions necessarily foster phenomena such as corruption, corporatism, and clientelism.

The second part of our enquiry is the more extensive and vital. It presents a study of the patterns of informal relations between the public and private sectors in 20th Century Mexico, guided by the theoretical framework developed in the first part of the work. It is divided into three chapters. Chapter 3 introduces the Informal Consultation and Exchange System (ICES), which was a system of policy networks that developed in Mexico between the private and the public sectors, during the industrialization period (1936–1984). The chapter describes the participants of the ICES and then, in line with the theoretical part, presents a historical account of the ICES in terms of its emergence and persistence. Chapter 4 analyses the process of change of the ICES. This process is analyzed separately because of its length and complexity. The analytical model of institutional change developed in the theoretical part of the book is tested in this chapter. Chapter 5 analyzes the structure of the ICES and the functional connections between its participants. It uses a graphic approach to describe the different policy networks that made up the ICES. The relations between the participants and the system as a whole are also presented in visual form. To my knowledge, this is the first time that a system like the Mexican ICES has been examined and presented graphically. The methodological framework and tools used for this empirical chapter are presented in appendices 1, 2 and 3.

Chapter 6 constitutes the final part of our investigation and it presents both theoretical and empirical conclusions. The work concludes that economic stability is highly influenced by informal social structures, but only in conjunction with formal structures. The general features of an early model of formal and informal economic governance are presented. I also summarize the specific policy-making lessons offered by this study, not only for Mexico but with regard to other countries where informality might be equally common.

Part One
Theoretical Framework

"The art of progress is to preserve order amid change
and to preserve change amid order."

Alfred North Whitehead, British Mathematician and Logician. *

"Change does not necessarily assure progress,
but progress implacably requires change."

Henry S. Commager, American Historian.

"It is not the strongest of the species that survive,
nor the most intelligent, but the one most responsive to change."

Charles Darwin, British Scientist.

"If we want everything to remain as it is,
it will be necessary for everything to change."

Giuseppe Tomasi Di Lampedusa, Italian Novelist.

"There is nothing permanent except change."

Heraclitus, Greek Philosopher.

"When you are finished changing, you are finished."

Benjamin Franklin, American Writer, Scientist, and Statesman.

Introduction to Part One

Attempts to formulate a theory of institutions have been pervasive throughout the history of Western political tradition. From the Greek study of the state to the philosophical treaties of the eighteenth century, the sources and changing nature of social order and co-ordination have been recurrent subjects of enquiry for thinkers and policymakers alike.

In the second half of the 20th century, this interest in social, economic and political institutions inspired an ample and sophisticated body of work that has come to be known as neo-institutionalist theory. Similarly, the study of complex organizations led to the academic study of the pervasive social phenomenon of informality. This more recent body of work is known as policy network theory. Although these two academic currents have grown separately, in reality they seem to be closely related. While neo-institutionalism studies institutions in general, policy network theory appears to deal with a particular type of institution that is informal in nature.

The broad objective of this theoretical part is to analytically link these two branches of study in ways that may ultimately help us understand the operation, impact, and interrelations of formal and informal social structures. This in turn will allow us to develop a theoretical framework to interpret institutionalized informality in the 20th century Mexican economy, which is the fundamental objective of this work.

This section comprises two chapters. The first deals with the general theory of institutions. Firstly, the historical background of three main neo-institutionalist schools is presented. Secondly, the concept of "mediated rationality" is introduced, as a device for partial reconciliation of the different schools. Finally, the processes of institutional emergence, persistence, and change are discussed in detail.

The second chapter presents an analysis of informal institutions. Borrowing heavily from policy network theory and linking it to neo-institutionalist theory, this chapter is divided into three parts. Firstly, a review of the literature on informal institutions is presented. Secondly, I point out the particularities in the processes of emergence, persistence, and change in informal institutions. Finally, polemic issues that surround informal institutions are discussed, namely corruption, corporatism, and clientelism.

The theoretical framework developed in this part of the work will then be used to study informality in public-private relations in Mexico, during the 1936–1984 industrialization period.

Chapter One
Understanding Institutions

1. APPROACHES TO THE STUDY OF INSTITUTIONS

From its origins, the academic analysis of institutions has been addressed from the standpoint of distinctive theoretical perspectives. Although some authors identify as many as seven strands of institutionalism (e.g. Peters, 1999), modern institutionalist writers agree (see for example Hall and Taylor, 1996; Scott, 1995) on the pre-eminence of three schools: historical institutionalism, rational choice institutionalism and sociological institutionalism. This section will attempt to summarize the historical development of these three institutionalist outlooks during the 20th Century.

1.1. "Historical Institutionalism" or the Political Science Approach

According to Peters (1999:4–13), the roots of modern historical institutionalism can be traced back to the constitutional law and jurisprudence analyses of the late 19th and early 20th centuries. This approach was strongly based on the study of formal structures, and thus tended to neglect the relevance of human input into policymaking processes. This tendency posed serious limitations on the analysis of institutions. For one thing, it lacked an explanation why certain institutions were chosen over others. Nor could it clarify why institutions evolved and affected (or were affected by) actors in different ways and in different circumstances.

In an attempt to complement this descriptive tradition, from the mid-1930s to the beginning of the 1960s, political scientists shifted their interest from the study of formal institutions to that of informal structures of behavioral nature (Scott, 1995:7). Political processes and outcomes were often considered a result of varying distributions of power and disparity in individual behavior, rather than a product of established social structures.

Theorists such as Harold Lasswell (1936), Everett Hughes (1936), David Truman (1951) or Daniel Bell (1965) strove to go beyond the case-specificity that characterized traditional institutionalism, and searched for concepts of universal application. This method, in turn, led to the "grand-theorizing" that marked the behavioralist era (Thelen and Steinmo, 1992:4).

Despite valuable contributions by behavioralists, who highlighted the influence of motive on political outcomes, their approach was increasingly criticized. As Shepsle (1986:52) argues, their emphasis on behavior usually distracted attention from the institutional context where that behavior took place. Moreover, with Scott (1995:5), "grand-theorizing" often overlooked the relevance of the intermediate structures that influence policymaking. Indeed, the radicalization of behavioralism seems to have carried an implicit contradiction: it tried to reconcile human behavior, specific by nature, with grand theorizing, an inherently aggregate and unspecific task. It was in response to these evident inconsistencies that, in the early 1970s, a neo-institutionalist current emerged in political science (Hall and Taylor, 1996:936). These new theorists sought to rescue and build upon the two previous waves of historical institutionalism. They reassigned importance to formal institutions while they tried to discern why particular types of institution matter specifically for those individuals that abide by them. They hoped in this way to capture the complexity of institutional operation and ultimately to explain the distinctiveness of national political outcomes (Eckstein and Apter, 1963).

For neo-institutionalist political scientists, institutional organization is the main factor structuring individual and social behavior. Institutional organization, therefore, also determines the way in which different societies deal with group struggle for scarce resources that lies at the heart of politics (Hall and Taylor, 1996:937). This point is central to policymaking processes because it is through policy decisions and outcomes that one can explain–and later try to predict–different trajectories in political, economic, or social development. Another salient characteristic of this group of theorists is the emphasis they place on "path dependency" (Hall, 1986, 1992). For them, policy outcomes are strongly influenced by the institutional structure in which they were negotiated. This structure, in turn, is dependent on the past decisions made within the same system: it is "path dependent."

Historical institutionalism also relies upon the state as a central actor in the policy-making process (cf. Evans, Rueschemeyer, and Skocpol, 1985; Steinmo, Thelen, and Longstreth, 1992). For historical neo-institutionalists, the state has its own goals, objectives and needs. It must thus negotiate with other societal actors to pass its initiatives. This state influence is precisely one of the factors that dampens policy-making with historicity: public institutions "filter" decisions, in order to make them compatible with the existing framework which is itself the result of past policies. In the words of Skocpol (1985:21), the state is important because "its organizational configurations . . . encourage some kinds of . . . collective political actions (but not others), and make possible the emergence of certain political issues (but not others)."

For an institution actually to shape the behavior of individuals, it must influence their preferences in a way that makes them comply with the objectives of the institution. In terms of compliance mechanisms, historical institutionalism is the most eclectic of all schools. It tends to favor what Scott (1995:35) calls the regulative and the normative approaches. The regulative approach gives prominence to the existence of formal and informal rules, enforced through punishment for non-compliance and reward for compliance. Meanwhile, the normative approach is related in behavioral terms to the notion of structured social expectations and self-constraint as the basis of social order (Parsons, 1951). In other words, for historical institutionalists, institutions elicit compliance through law, written rules, agencies, and policies (see Thelen and Steinmo, 1992:2; Kiser and Ostrom, 1982:179), but also through self-enforced obligation, embedded in the participants of the institution (see Hall and Taylor, 1996:938).

Undoubtedly, historical institutionalism has limits to its explanatory power. As Peters (1999:75) asserts, historical institutionalism lacks clear basic premises that can be used to predict human behavior. By stressing the processes of inertia and path-dependency, historical neo-institutionalists often fail to explain the unexpected creation or change of an institution, as in the case of a Revolution that might wipe out the existing institutional structure. This may be pervasive in many political environments and though successfully analyzed by some historical institutionalists (see the work of Skocpol, 1992 or Thelen, 1991), it is not adequately covered by the general method of the school. More recent works (see Hall, 1992 and 1999; Immergut, 1992) attempt to combine individualistic (rational) and structuralist elements in systematic and somewhat dynamic models. Although the level of integration is still moderate, these studies support what this book will aim to prove later: that both individual deliberation and socially constructed factors contribute to the formation, persistence, and change of institutions.

1.2. *"Rational Choice Institutionalism" or the Economic Approach*

The origins of modern economic institutionalism also lie in the early twentieth century, when the reductionist assumptions of traditional economic theory were challenged. In those years, a group of economists led by Gustav Schmoller in Germany (Balabkins, 1988), and by Veblen, Commons, and Mitchell in the United States (Scott, 1995:2), attacked the view that economics could be reduced to universal laws. Their main argument was that, in mainstream economics, individuals were unrealistically assumed to be calculating, fully informed decision-makers, free of historical, social, or psychological influences. In their opinion, this oversimplified reality and left ample room for erroneous forecasting. They favored a more pragmatic–and thus empirical–approach to economic modeling. Despite their relative influence at the time (Mitchell founded the National Bureau of Economic Research in the United States), their view did not prevail and was buried under a landslide of classical economic work. As Hodgson (1991:211) suggests, this was–at least partially–a probable consequence of the lack of methodological and analytical coherence in their work. For the greater part of the century, these contributions were to some extent forgotten. Only a few academics like Weber, Schumpeter (Scott, 1995:2), Galbraith, and Myrdal (Swedberg, 1991: 260) tried either to reconcile it with the classical tradition or build upon it.

It would not be until the early 1970s that the renewed interest of some economists in the role of institutions would give rise to a new body of theory in the area. Of particular importance seem to have been the works of Coase (1972), North and Thomas (1973), and Williamson (1975), which analyzed the structure of institutions as a function of transaction costs. In later works, these theorists–particularly North–developed ideas about other fundamental concepts of neo-institutionalist economics, like property rights and rent-seeking, and their effects on the institutional structure of society (see North, 1990, 1995). However, despite their apparent departure from orthodox General Equilibrium Economics, neo-institutionalist economists borrow extensively from traditional economic assumptions. With some important exceptions (mainly "bounded rationality" theory and recent cross-disciplinary efforts), the central presumption of neo-institutionalist economists is still of rational individuals that make fully informed, self-interested decisions that maximize their happiness (or utility). Even in the more flexible accounts, rational choice institutionalists consider institutional emergence and change a result of fully rational decision-making (for a clear example see Knight, 1992).

Under this line of thought, compliance with institutions is enforced through what Scott (1995:35) has termed a "regulative approach." For these theorists, institutions can only influence human preferences through clear written rules, enforced by a third party. In their view, only positive regulation allows calculated and conventionalized exchanges to take place, because it renders outcomes predictable. For them, rules reduce uncertainty, lower transaction costs and ultimately maximize utility, because they foster a stable environment (Peters, 1999:47).

The problem with this view, however, stems from its extreme reliance on both utility-maximizing rationality and written rules. Firstly, it is impossible to explain why individuals sometimes make decisions that might not maximize their utility. Secondly, it is not clear why some individuals comply with social expectations even in the absence of written rules. Accordingly, historical and sociological institutionalists have traditionally attacked the rationalist account on grounds that it minimizes the influence of extant institutions and social conventions in the process of preference formation (Hodgson, 1988:4–5; Peters, 1999:15). Political scientists and sociologists consider this is a serious mistake that leads to false assumptions when it comes to describing human and organizational behavior, because important environmental influences are discarded across the board.

Despite these insufficiencies–as Hall and Taylor (1996:951) have noted–the rational choice school has made substantial contributions to neo-institutionalist theory by highlighting the prominent role that individual, self-interested decisions play in political life. It seems plausible to accept that a limited degree of rationality is present in most political choices, even if it that rationality is–as will be argued later in this work–circumscribed by structural and social factors.

1.3. *"Cognitive Institutionalism" or the Sociological Approach*

Although the origins of the sociological study of institutions can be traced back to the early-twentieth-century works of Cooley, Hughes, Durkheim, and Weber (Scott, 1995:8), modern institutionalist sociology appears to have emerged in the organizational theory studies of the 1950s. These not only incorporated the early sociological tradition but also introduced organizational components. It was through research like that of Parsons and Selznick (DiMaggio and Powell, 1991[a]:2), that institutional mechanisms connecting society, organizations, and individuals were initially delineated. Both Hall and Taylor (1996:946), and DiMaggio and Powell (1991:11) agree that it was in the late 1970s, with John Meyer's work, that sociological neo-institutionalism emerged.

In both its original and new forms, sociological institutionalism has regarded institutions as the basic "building blocks" of social and political life (DiMaggio and Powell, 1991[a]:2). They criticize the rational choice approach on grounds that it tends to divorce decision-making from cultural and social influences (Peters, 1999:9). For sociologists, rational choice institutionalism relies so much on self-interest that it leaves no room for any noticeable impact of larger societal structures on the individual (March and Olsen, 1984:21–6). The sociological tradition certainly sees institutions as the result of human agency but not through purely rational design (DiMaggio and Powell, 1991[a]:8). Individuals are considered actors who are embedded in their social environment and, as such, comply with the institutional structure (Granovetter, 1985). They are behaviorally influenced through the internalization of the role(s) assigned to them (Hall and Taylor, 1996:948). In the opinion of sociological institutionalists, actors cannot be said to choose freely, given the array of institutions that influence their behavior. For example, Zucker (1983:2) has described the process by which certain social relationships come to be taken for granted, simply because the participants share common cognitions. As March and Olsen have suggested (1989:21–2), this does not mean that decisions are not intelligent or unreasoned. It means that institutional rules and routines are so much codified into organizations, that individuals intelligently take decisions approved as legitimate by their social group (even if those decisions may not be in the self-interest of that individual). In short, options are limited by cognitive boundaries. In support of this view, DiMaggio and Powell describe how some theorists believe that choices cannot even be understood outside certain cultural and historical frameworks. In their own words: "institutions do not just constrain options: they establish the very criteria by which people discover their preferences. In other words . . . the most important costs are cognitive" (DiMaggio and Powell, 1991[a]:11).

To ensure compliance to institutions, the sociological school relies on what Scott has termed the "cognitive approach" (Scott, 1995:40–5). In this approach, institutions curb human behavior through internalized cognition that is sustained and changed by on-going interaction. Patterns of conduct are internalized and thus unconsciously enforced, according to what is acceptable to society. Berger and Luckmann (1967) emphasize how decisions are influenced more by the creation of shared knowledge and by belief systems than by the enactment of formal rules. Hence, in the sociological view, preferences are endogenous (motivated by the institutional environment itself) and behavior relies more on the acceptance of roles than on the rational calculation of consequences (March and Simon, 1958). It follows that individuals–and organizations–move along culturally determined lines. According to Hall and Taylor (1996:947), sociologists break down the "conceptual divide between 'institutions' and 'culture' because the two shade into each other." That cognitive frameworks take precedence over rational choices is in sum the basis of sociological institutionalism.

The main criticism against sociological institutionalism is that it situates itself at the other extreme of rational choice. Individual rationality is sometimes presented as being so constrained by cognitive factors that it completely ceases to be free. Certain accounts give the impression of a world governed by institutions rather than by people. This by no means faithfully reflects the complexity of the social world. As expressed by Hall and Taylor (1996:949), "sociologists frequently posit a world of individuals or organizations seeking to define and express their identity [only] in socially appropriate ways." What follows is a criticism of radical constructivism. Certainly, socially constructed decisions are essential to understanding of individual behavior. Action indeed seems to be a result of socially contrived factors, but not exclusively. Self-interested rationality–even if constrained and limited–does play a part in human action and in decision-making processes, just as structures play an essential part too. Although most sociological institutionalists would not deny these facts *per se*, they would argue that the degree to which preference formation relies on rationality is low if compared to socially constructed influences.

In fairness though, modern sociological institutionalist accounts have moved away from radical constructivism and have acknowledged the importance of individual choice. One example is acceptance, by the majority of institutionalist sociologists, of the concept of "bounded rationality" (Peters, 1999:97–111), originally developed by economists. It follows that sociological institutionalism–like the other two schools–has been promoting an exchange of ideas that is leading to the acceptance of a more general concept: that of a somewhat mediated rationality. This accepts the possibility of individuals acting self-interestedly, but within the limits set by socially constructed cognitive frameworks, and by the inert and path-dependent political and organizational structure. We shall soon examine "mediated rationality" more closely.

1.4. Theoretical Limits and Possibilities

After reviewing the basic characteristics of the three main approaches to new institutionalist theory, two points seem to stand out. Firstly, that no approach is by itself capable of fully explaining the complexity of modern political behavior. Secondly, that there is a need to complement the existing institutional models, in order to theorize more accurately about the phenomena assumed to determine institutional operation at the individual and social levels.

Our immediate objectives then, must be: (a) establish accurate definitions that could help us disentangle some of the confusion fomented by the different institutionalist interpretations; and (b) to analyze the different stages of institutional development, in order to draw more comprehensive theoretical conclusions about each one of them. The exercise that follows will not be so much about amalgamating theoretical currents, but rather about finding connections that may show that they are not fully at odds.

2. TOWARDS A MEDIATED RATIONALITY CONCEPT OF INSTITUTIONS

Any study of institutions must address four fundamental questions. Firstly, what institutions are and how they influence the behavior of individuals. Secondly, how and why institutions emerge. Thirdly, how and why institutions persist. Fourthly, how and why institutions change. In the rest of the chapter, these questions will be carefully analyzed. Let us start with the first.

2.1. *What is an Institution and How Institutions Influence Behavior*

This section has two objectives. Firstly, it will establish how it is that institutions influence human behavior, and secondly it will introduce a working definition of the term "institution." The way in which institutions influence behavior is relevant to our study because the efficacy of institutions depends precisely on their capacity to control individual action in society. The definition of the term is important because it will accurately identify our object of study.

2.1.1. *Institutions and Behavior: Introducing Mediated Rationality*

Most neo-institutionalist theorists agree that institutions influence individual action and thus political outcomes. Influence over human behavior in fact appears to be *the* essential characteristic of institutions (Giddens, 1979). However, problems arise around two central questions: (i) which specific institutional mechanisms influence human behavior, and (ii) how.

Concerning point (i), while some authors favor exogenous mechanisms such as regulations and rules, others prefer endogenous ones such as values and roles. In this book I want to propose that we human beings act under a mix of both types; a mix that I have called "Mediated Rationality."

Under Mediated Rationality principles, individuals are seen as having free rational capacity (endogenous), within the limits set by (a) their social environment, and (b) the political structures under which they live (both exogenous). These external factors limit rationality because they directly or indirectly control important aspects of decision-making, like the amount and type of information that reaches individuals, scales of values, educational opportunities, or political opinions, among many others. In other words, the influence of social and political structures is ontological as well as axiomatic. However, at the same time, rational individuals also seem to have the capacity to affect external structures. Individual action in fact changes the environment everyday, and noncompliant individuals often make evident the limitations and insufficiencies of particular institutional structures. Additionally, external influence frequently "expands" original rational capabilities: for example, when foreign values are rationalized as superior and are thus imitated.

In the Mediated Rationality framework, behavior is understood as a dialectical exchange between the endogenous and the exogenous; a matter of rational capabilities that thrive within the realm of certain possibilities. The specific mechanisms that in my view interact to create Mediated Rationality are three: the regulative, normative, and cognitive. This division coincides with the three "pillars of institutions" presented by Richard Scott (1995:34–61). Although I have borrowed the terminology and description of the characteristics of each mechanism from the work of Scott, the classification of the concepts as part of Mediated Rationality is mine.

This takes us to point (ii) that deals with the specific ways in which these mechanisms operate to influence behavior. To address this issue, I shall establish which are the specific social mechanisms that I am labeling as regulative, normative, and cognitive, as well as the precise ways in which each one of them works.

Regulative Mechanisms. These may be written or unwritten regulations. Their distinguishing feature is that they are always enforced by third parties, either through punishment for non-compliance, or rewards for compliance. Punishment may be formal, as in the case of fines or incarceration, or informal, as in the case of shunning or shaming (Scott, 1995:35–7; cf. Axelrod, 1984; Dasgupta, 1997; Hall, 1999; North, 1990). Regulative mechanisms may also offer rewards, such as promotions for performance. Regulative mechanisms thus enforce a specific type of behavior by practically forcing individuals to act in certain ways. Those who decide to violate regulations do so at their own risk, aware that they will be penalized (or not rewarded) by others if caught.

Normative Mechanisms. These are written or unwritten norms that design the "appropriate" ways to reach certain goals (Scott, 1995:37). The defining characteristic of normative mechanisms is that compliance is voluntary and not enforced by external actors as in the case of regulative mechanisms (Peters, 1999:47). At this normative level, the only punishment is moral; it rests upon the conviction of individuals. However, normative mechanisms not only limit but also enable certain types of behavior: those that the individual might find rewarding. In other words, normative mechanisms elicit specific types of behavior through expectations about oneself.

Cognitive Mechanisms. They are made up of cognitive frameworks such as values, roles or beliefs. They are collections of symbolic representations of the world (Scott, 1995:40) and epitomize those decisions that are taken for granted. In consequence, they are enforced through sustained social interaction (Berger and Luckmann, 1967:73–4). Cognitive mechanisms contribute to influence behavior because individuals seldom question the validity of decisions made at the unconscious level.

By introducing these three mechanisms, I hope to go beyond the endogenous influence vs. exogenous influence discussion, because it seems that the three mechanisms–be they endogenous or exogenous–interact with each other at all times, to motivate individual choice. The simultaneous operation of regulative, normative, and cognitive mechanisms is what in my view constitutes Mediated Rationality.

Mediated Rationality is an analytical device that may help bridge some of the basic disagreements between neo-institutionalist schools because, even if authors from different schools tend to stress the importance of one mechanism over the others, none explicitly denies that the three *can* or *may* work in conjunction to determine human behavior. Mediated Rationality is not a concept we must accept by fiat. Important research in Social Psychology confirms the existence of rich exchange and mutual influence between individually- and socially-motivated influences in the determination of action (Howard, 1994; Baron and Pfeffer, 1994; for a summary of these accounts see House and Mortimer, 1990). These studies also indicate that neither rational nor socially-constructed action consistently predominates over the other. One individual can have various motives for behavior, depending on the circumstances (Gray and Stafford, 1988). Even if culture-specific and highly embedded in social conventions, cognitive frameworks are subject to potential change through rational will (Ridgeway, 1994). Therefore, under a Mediated Rationality framework, conduct can only be influenced by targeting the conscious and unconscious levels of human decision-making at the same time, that is to say that only the simultaneous operation of regulative, normative, and cognitive mechanisms can effectively induce specific actions. Given that institutions are often developed precisely to achieve very specific goals, they must be constituted by all three regulative, normative, and cognitive mechanisms to operate efficiently.

It could be argued that Mediated Rationality is a simple return to the idea of "bounded rationality" (Simon, 1982). However, there are clear differences.

Bounded rationality describes how, because of incomplete information, individuals are unable to act in a truly rational manner. Mediated Rationality is a more comprehensive concept that not only deals with information, but also with cognitive formation and unconscious processes that go beyond obtaining practical data.

After identifying specific regulative, normative, and cognitive mechanisms, describing their operation to influence behavior, and establishing their role as necessary components in the effective operation of institutions, we can now move on to the second point of this section: determining a working definition of institutions.

2.1.2. Defining Institutions

In our days, institutions appear to be everywhere: a handshake, a household, social status, Research and Development, the legal system, Church, state, and even no smoking signs are all regarded as examples of institutions (see Dimaggio and Powell, 1991:1–10; Meyer and Rowan, 1991:42; Wallerstein, 2000:234–50). Unfortunately, despite its basic importance, the definition of institutions is still a contentious question for neo-institutionalist theory. The main definitional problem seems to lie in the tendency to conflate the *elements* that constitute an institution with the institution itself. In other words, when defining the term "institution," theorists in general assert that institutions *are* rules, or *are* procedures, or *are* norms. These claims pose two big problems. Firstly, they risk tautology. For instance, claiming that institutions *are* rules, it then becomes impossible to say that they constrain behavior through rules—it would be circular reasoning. The second and more profound problem is that by asserting the prevalence of one mechanism over others, authors fail to recognize the combined regulative, normative, and cognitive nature of institutions that we have already discussed. Rules alone do not seem to be institutions, just as norms or cognitive frameworks do not seem to be institutions either. Under a Mediated Rationality framework, institutions can only *result from a combination* of regulative, normative, and cognitive mechanisms, without being exact synonyms of these components. Accordingly, for the purposes of this book, institutions will be defined as: *systems consisting of a mix of regulative, normative, and cognitive mechanisms, that influence the behavior of participants, thus structuring relations by increasing certainty*. Let us analyze this definition more closely.

That institutions are *systems consisting of a mix of regulative, normative, and cognitive mechanisms* implies that institutions are a complex combination of elements and not one single mechanism operating in isolation. As we have mentioned, in order to influence behavior effectively, institutions must influence humans at different levels of consciousness. A single mechanism often lacks the strength to curb behavior by itself. For instance, an environmental law is often not enough to stop people from polluting. Social condemnation, personal conviction, and the acquisition of new values might also be necessary. This is why, although institutionalized environmental protection minimally requires an appropriate legal framework to function, it needs more than laws and enforcing agencies to function *effectively*.

Secondly, we have suggested that institutions *bind the behavior of participants*. In fact, as extensively discussed in the previous section, control of human behavior seems to be the *raison d'être* of any institution.

Thirdly, we have claimed that institutions *structure relations and create certainty*. These are also two principles commonly accepted by all the main neo-institutionalist schools. Institutions develop precisely to make behavior predictable and controllable. In fact, the expectation of reciprocity is the very reason why actors accept constraint on their own behavior: consciously or unconsciously, they know that the behavior of others will also be curbed. Reduction in uncertainty derived from institutionally-structured relations allows societies to impose order and ultimately to promote cooperation in a traditional Hobbesian way.

3. ANALYZING THE LIFE CYCLE OF INSTITUTIONS

Having defined institutions and the way in which they operate through Mediated Rationality, the peculiarities of the three processes that make up their life cycle can now be analyzed. By studying institutional emergence, persistence, and change, I hope to complete an analytical framework that can be then applied to analysis of informal structures in the next chapter and to an understanding of informal institutions in Mexico in the rest of the book.

3.1. Emergence of Institutions

The goal of this section is to analyze three moments in the emergence of institutions. Firstly, we shall look at the limited options that precede institutional emergence. Secondly, we shall analyze the mechanisms that operate during the actual process of emergence. Finally, we shall study the processes that determine the initial character of institutions, immediately after they have been created.

3.1.1. Limited Options that Precede Emergence of Institutions

Paraphrasing our own definition, institutions are systems that emerge to structure social relations and create certainty. However, when specific social problems arise, controversy frequently follows the definition of "certainty." What generates certainty for one group might create uncertainty for another; what benefits one side might damage another. Thus, contrary to what some theorists suggest (see Linz, 1994; Riggs, 1997; Sartori, 1997), the institutional options available to specific societies at specific times are often very limited. Apart from being a process influenced by a vast array of social, political, economic, and international interests, institutional emergence is also highly path-dependent in historical and cognitive terms. Path-dependency means that institutions do not emerge from a "tabula rasa" (Peters, 1999:47). Any form of collective action tends to be shaped in relation to the existing institutional structure (Skocpol, 1985:22) and also in relation to the values, roles, and perceptions of the individuals of a given society. In fact, March and Olsen (1989:25–7) point out that it is through the existing structure that actors understand public life, fabricate their political goals, and weigh their available options. In consequence, while in rational terms there might be unlimited numbers of institutional alternatives to solve a specific problem, societies' viable options are normally limited. The emergence of institutions is fully determined by a Mediated Rationality framework, because what is rationally "desired" is inherently limited by what is structurally and cognitively "feasible." It follows then that different social contexts generate distinct logics of institutional emergence. Certain patterns of organization are encouraged while others are inhibited (Whitley, 1998:25). It is precisely this complex interaction between structure and agency what precedes and permeates the emergence of an institution.

3.1.2. The Emergence of Institutions

If, as we stated in our definition, institutions are systems, it follows that when being created, they must acquire a tangible form that allows them to function. The two objectives of this sub-section will be to discuss the processes by which (a) consensus on institutionalization is developed in the limiting environment that we just described; and (b) an institution materializes.

As stated by Scott (1999:33), the first step of institutionalization seems to be the conscious decision by certain groups to create an institution that may help them achieve specific objectives. These groups may lead, in which case the institution would be a "top-down" design; or they may be grassroots groups, in which case the institution would be a "bottom-up" creation. In either case, the process of emergence will follow Mediated Rationality principles: the pursued goals will be adjusted to what the structural and cognitive constraints allow. This process of emergence normally involves intense negotiation and re-negotiation of terms in fora that may range from formalized legislative bodies to informal encounters of deliberation.

During the process of establishing new institutions, the original plans of some groups are usually modified to fit the needs or demands of other groups (even if these are less influential); they are also constantly limited by the existing institutional structure. Some demands remain and new ones are developed. This process may not be swift. Some institutions take years or decades to emerge, others a few hours.

Once consensus is reached, an institution needs to materialize in order to actually function. Institutions may materialize in two ways: (i) as organizations, otherwise called formal institutions; or (ii) as policy networks, otherwise called informal institutions. Either form may influence behavior strongly, as we shall see later. Both organizations and policy networks give an objective dimension to institutions that otherwise would remain abstract systems. Institutions may materialize through one or more organizations or policy networks. They also seem able to materialize through a combination of both. For instance, judicial systems (institutions) have materialized through specific regional courts and tribunals (organizations). The institutionalized international system for the prevention of AIDS has materialized both through extensive informal networks of information, field support and research, and through some formally-constituted organizations like UN-AIDS and numerous NGOs.

The materialization of an institution either through an organization or network, in turn has three conditions. Firstly, the establishment of the principles that will co-ordinate the organization(s) or network(s); secondly, the accommodation of the interests of the "losing" groups through additional organizational arrangements. Finally, the organization(s) or network(s) must be justified before the general population. Only after these steps are complete, can the formal or informal institution be said to have emerged and be ready to operate. I shall now describe briefly how these three processes that I propose take place in the case of formal institutions (i.e. organizations). In the next chapter, I shall address the case of informal institutions.

Establishing the principles that co-ordinate the formal institution. The consensus-building process of creating an institution concludes with the development of specific agreements to establish such structure. The agreements that create formal institutions reflect the positions taken during the consensus-building stage, and normally benefit some groups more than others. It could be said that new institutions are often "appropriated" by one or more groups. This happens because the distribution of resources and power gives some groups advantage over others in the design of the new institutions. Groups with greater influence will determine many of the characteristics of the new institutions, in order to protect their interests. Many authors support this point. For instance, Sened (1991) holds that institutions arise from the desire of actors to impose their will on others, given that those actors can manipulate the political structure in their favor. This affirmation is close to the "distributional theory of institutions" presented by Knight (1992), in which certain groups exercise influence to create institutions that, in their view, will secure their position. Both Axelrod (1984) and Weingast (1996) provide accounts of emerging institutions that are designed to serve the interests of the actors that promoted their creation. For Krasner (1988), political systems are arenas where interests compete, while defending and regenerating ruling interests. Similarly, Selznick (1949) affirms that although conflicting interests are usually present in policymaking, some actors benefit more than others from the resulting institutional structures.

To ensure that the initial agreements of a formal institution are kept, "appropriating" groups frequently favor formalization through written accords. To be able to manipulate the rules of any structure in one's favor is in fact the essence of appropriation. In the case of formal institutions, regulative mechanisms are used to enforce and perpetuate the original agreement. Without the formalization of principles, "appropriating" groups would lack an important element of control. In fact, the formal appropriation of the institution is essential to powerful groups because, as Hall and Taylor argue (1996:952), the initial design of institutions determines the successive relative power of all its participants. The agreements establishing the institution normally refer to rules of membership, representation and franchise, as well as to the rights and obligations of participants. Further legitimacy of formal institutions is sometimes achieved through official state recognition of the formalizing agreement, for example in a law or by decree.

Accommodation of the interests of the "losing" groups. In parallel, if the formal institution is to emerge, arrangements must be made by the "appropriating" actors to compensate the groups affected by its creation. This compensation may take the form of additional formal or informal commitments that may attenuate the effects of the institution, or solve another problem those groups may have. In whatever form, recompenses must often be introduced to dissuade the "losing" groups from systematically blocking the emerging institution. As Burton, Gunther, and Highley (1991:13–20) assert: at this point, public decision-making becomes a matter of "negotiated stability."

Justifying formal institutions before the general public. Public institutions often require the acceptance of at least some sectors of the general population to operate properly. March and Olsen (1989:25–7) show how institutions derive a good deal of structure and meaning from the society in which they are embedded. A formal institution regarded as inefficient, useless, or harmful will most likely fall under close public scrutiny and will be attacked, eventually leading to its change or dissolution. If the population, on the other hand, perceives benefits in the institutional arrangement, they will probably encourage its establishment. Social legitimacy requires consistency between the beliefs of the people and the characteristics of the institution. In an extreme yet illustrative example, it would be difficult to conceive a Catholic tribunal being established in Iran to judge criminal acts, but Muslim tribunals do in fact exist in that nation. To further promote compliance, appropriating groups sometimes make use of legitimizing mechanisms such as the approval of professional associations or from the mass media. Examples of "awareness" and "endorsement" campaigns abound everyday in Western electronic media.

When an institution finally materializes, its initial stages of operation will determine many of its future features. Through repeated functioning, routines are consolidated, and new values and agreements may develop to address unforeseen circumstances. This process of consolidation of mutual agreement has important implications for the subsequent distribution of resources and power. This process of initial consolidation also has significant repercussions on the short- and long-term persistence of the new institutional structure, which we shall now analyze.

3.2. Persistence of Institutions

For an institution to operate properly after emergence, it must persist. It is only through persistence that an institution becomes functional and can meet its objectives. In this section I shall argue that institutional persistence requires two conditions: (i) legitimacy and (ii) what I have termed "stabilizing change." Analysis of these follows.

3.2.1. Legitimacy

It appears that once an institution has emerged, the specific transmission mechanism that allows its consolidation and initial persistence is legitimacy. But what provides a new institution with legitimacy? For Hall and Taylor (1996:949), two sources of legitimacy are state recognition and cultural authority (such as the endorsement of a professional association). Other sources of legitimacy may be adherence to moral or legal rules; consistency between internal beliefs and external objectification (Scott, 1995:45–7); longevity (Singh, 1990); the adoption of similar organizational structures (isomorphism) (DiMaggio and Powell, 1991); the capacity to inculcate values; and effective control of behavior (Peters, 1999:109). The creation of routines, procedures and the approval of the mass media are also seen as sources of legitimacy.

Legitimacy and institutional persistence are connected insofar as social actors perceive that a given institution might help solve a certain problem. An institution provides participants with certainty and patterns for action; with information about social co-ordination on specific issues (Krasner, 1988:82); it equips them with data about others but also about themselves; about how to act in certain circumstances and how not to act. Once actors find an institution legitimate, they will probably embed their own ideas into the new institutional structure, in ways that provide them with daily information. The new structure becomes necessary, thus assuring its initial persistence.

Legitimacy can be–and often is–promoted by the "appropriating" groups benefited by the persistence of a certain institution. Powerful groups normally have access to (or even direct control of) numerous legitimizing channels like the mass media. They can thus publicize the advantages of a given institution both to the actors involved and the general public, even if those "advantages" not always benefit the rest of the population.

So far, however, we have talked only about the short-term persistence of a new institution. What determines institutional persistence in the long run? What mechanism ensures legitimacy of an institution? To answer these questions, we must study the second condition of persistence: stabilizing change.

3.2.2. Stabilizing Change

For numerous authors, long-term institutional persistence may often be a function of inertia and organizational rigidity. Genschel (1997:46–9), for example, affirms that organizational structures tend to be rigid for three reasons: sunk costs, uncertainty about possible alternatives, and the political conflict caused by the potential change. Hall and Taylor (1994:15) favor the second reason. Krasner (1988:81) also supports this view by explaining how organizations create internal and external interests that are difficult to change. Heiner (1983:585) and Shepsle (1986:75) indicate that inertia is common due to natural aversion to risk. Finally, Riker (1980:443) and Steinmo (1993:7) recount how institutions induce distributive biases that put a premium on the indefinite maintenance of the *status quo*. In sum, for all these authors, persistence equals lack of change. From these accounts, one gets the impression that change is unnatural; that it arises unexpectedly and has unidentified sources. An almost arthritic inertia seems to be a permanent condition of institutional life. In my view, this approach fails to catch the dynamic nature of institutions.

If in a constantly changing environment institutions manage to persist, it is precisely because they are able to adapt. Perhaps *dramatic change* is not common, but adaptive change seems to be permanent. To obtain an accurate picture of institutional persistence, I believe it is necessary to explain the possibility of change in terms of the necessity for stable persistence. For this reason, I have developed the concept of "stabilizing change." Let me expand.

Social actors normally comply with institutions because they need them to achieve everyday objectives, regardless of how unfair, uncomfortable, or inefficient these structures might be. However, within a given institutional arrangement, all groups are constantly attempting to enlarge their influence and better their position. "Losing groups" might find for example that, because of changing circumstances, the original agreements upon which the institution was based, no longer offer them sufficient certainty. Thus they will explore ways to change the institution, in order at least to recover the original degree of influence or confidence that they had. Likewise, the values of the general population might evolve, making them find an institution antiquated or useless. In that case, they will probably question the structure and exert pressure to modify it. This situation may not be difficult, since values often differ from one generation to another. Equally, the imitation of foreign structures—one form of what DiMaggio and Powell (1991) have called "isomorphism"—is a common source of shifting cognitive frameworks. On-going processes of strategic action and social change mean that the persistence of institutions does not rely on immobility, but rather on incessant change; on change that can stabilize the relations between the participants of an institution in order to maintain its legitimacy. Institutional stability and persistence are therefore dynamic and not static situations. They are based on the re-negotiation of the premises that allowed the institution to emerge. Re-negotiation might not always be public, but that it takes place seems inevitable.

In recognition of dynamic institutional persistence, some neo-institutionalist authors have adopted a "punctuated equilibrium" approach (cf. Krasner, 1984; Knight, 1992). On this view, long periods of institutional "stasis" (stability) are punctuated by short and dramatic periods of change. The image is one made up of critical junctures that appear as knots in long stretches of institutional continuity (Olsen, 1991:101). The problem with this view is that the motives for change are always unknown; they are exogenous and not built into the model. Few pointers, if any, are given to find out when the dramatic periods of change announced will take place. Both participants and the institution seem to change almost automatically. The combative actors that stage the periods of "punctuated" change suddenly become passive and compliant during periods of stability. Neither the reasons why this happens nor the mechanisms that make the passive actors desire change again are explained. Additionally, nothing is said about the usually highly changing environment (Krasner, 1988:81). As Peters (1999:69) correctly argues, in "punctuated equilibrium" theory, dramatic change comes under situations that are often unexpected by the participants. The cycle of prolonged passivity followed by occasional belligerence to which "punctuated equilibrium" theory confines social change is still an unclear process.

"Stabilizing change," on the other hand, sees a world of institutions that are constantly changing and adapting. Actors seem to be governed by "compliant activism" rather than by "resigned acceptance." Following Hodgson (1988:269), stabilizing change understands institutions as complex systems that reconcile stability with "temporal variety." In sum, under the concept of persistence that I have just presented, institutions need legitimacy to persist, and legitimacy needs "stabilizing change." The following section will analyze precisely what happens when the process of stabilizing change fails and legitimacy is questioned.

3.3. Institutional Change

If the task of institutions is to provide stability and their effectiveness in achieving this goal depends on their persistence, then the topics of institutional breakdown and drastic institutional change necessarily become polemic. What are the mechanisms that bring about drastic institutional change? This is the question that this section will attempt to answer. To do so, I shall first present a brief review of the literature on institutional change. Secondly, I shall identify the motives that lead to dramatic institutional change, which for the sake of this work, I have termed "paradigmatic change." Thirdly, I shall describe in detail five steps that seem to take place when paradigmatic change occurs. By the end of the section I hope to have presented a detailed account of drastic institutional change, as a framework in which to understand the informal processes that will be described in subsequent chapters.

3.3.1. A Brief Review of the Literature on Institutional Change

On the process of institutional change, disagreements between neo-institutionalist theorists orbit around two issues. Firstly, the problem of endogenous versus exogenous change; and secondly, the question whether change is exceptional or inevitable. Let us start with the first matter.

Some authors (e.g. North, 1990; Nelson and Winter, 1982) rely on exogenous-preference models, which hold that change is determined by events outside the institutions. For them, institutions would not change,

were it not for external events that modify the preferences of the participants. The problem with such a view is that while institutions appear to
strongly influence behavior for some time, they suddenly seem to lose all
their constraining power to some random external influence. This view minimizes the possibility of internal contradictions and struggle within the institution, posing a world of perfect institutions that is abruptly destroyed by
external influence.

For a second group of neo-institutionalists, change is built into institutional structures. Explanations vary, but some theorists link change to rationality. For instance, the theory of "institutional entrepreneurs" (cf.
Borman, 1986; Branch, 1988) places privileged access to rational decision-
making upon particular leaders. The theory holds that, in some organizations, certain individuals can identify when the institutional setting is
unfavorable and take steps to change it. The problem with this view is that
the mechanism by which this sudden recognition of institutional inefficacy
strikes these "entrepreneurs" is not clear. No indication is given as to how
or why individuals who accepted an institutional structure for a long time,
suddenly gain a form of "detached rationality" that allows them to question
the institution and push for change. Other authors see endogenous change
as a consequence of some type of collective rationality that is built up
through learning from past mistakes (cf. Hall, 1993; Tolbert and Zucker,
1996). This learning process allows participants to change and adapt the institution periodically, by attempting to solve past contradictions. Although
this body of theory is more comprehensive, it fails to explain dramatic
change. If this constant learning takes place, why would there be a need for
sudden (and in some cases violent) change at all?

In general, the problem with differentiating between endogenous and exogenous change is that the arguments do not explain human behavior adequately. These accounts do not properly reflect that human beings react both
to internal and external stimuli, that is to say that–in Mediated Rationality
terms–both conscious and unconscious motives influence decision-making.
Exogenous-change models underestimate the influence of institutions and the
internal struggles that characterize them. Meanwhile, endogenous-based models overlook that the environment surrounding institutions is always changing,
so institutions (and individuals within them) are affected by it. Mediated rationality could be a way forward because within this framework, change is not
a result of either external or internal factors, but the combined effect of both.

Let us now move to the second issue debated in current neo-
institutionalist literature: the problem of the exceptional versus the inevitable nature of change. Although not a rule, generally those authors that

favor exogenous change also favor the view that change is exceptional. Conversely, those that favor endogenous change tend to defend the inevitability of the process. A third group, attempting to find a compromise, has developed the notion of "punctuated equilibrium" (see Krasner 1988, 74), explained in the previous section. The problem with all these views is that (a) they explain either constant or dramatic change but rarely both; (b) they do not explain the relationship between one intensity of change and the other; and (c) although they identify the *factors* that provoke change, they do not specify the transmission mechanisms through which those factors induce change. Even the theory of "punctuated equilibrium," which aims to incorporate some degree of dynamism, fails to do so fully.

In fairness, most theories of institutional change are not inaccurate, though too static to explain the social world. They explain persistence and rigidity, but weaken at the explanation of the dynamics of change. In many of these accounts, institutions become, as Genschel (1997:44) calls them, the "immovable movers of political life." To see institutional life as a sequence of short-stop-and-long-go cycles is simplistic, because change appears to be at least as common as continuity, if not more (Hall, 1999:136). It is a mistake to study stasis as the normal state of institutions (Zucker, 1988:26).

The challenge is henceforth to develop an explanation of institutional change that recognizes that periods of stability are *dynamic* times that may lead to moments of *even more dynamism*, during processes of change. Stability does not take place on "auto-pilot" (Peters, 1999:71). As suggested in our section on the persistence of institutions, stability is a time of constant change and re-negotiation of the regulative, normative, and cognitive elements that support the institution. Seen this way, change is not an anomaly but a ceaseless process; and drastic change, a latent possibility. How are these two different intensities of change related? What are the causes of drastic change? Potential answers to these two questions follow.

3.3.2. The Origins of Paradigmatic Change

The type of change that occurs during periods of stability has been called already "stabilizing change." However, as suggested, there appears to be another type of change; dramatic in nature and whose impact is more profound. In modern neo-institutionalist literature, Hall (1992, 1993) has recognized this dramatic type of change. In his view, institutional change may be of first, second or third order. It is "third-order change" that he associates with the shift of goals, priorities and hierarchies, and with the creation of new institutions to support often new social objectives. Although he ultimately fails to describe the causal relations between the different types of change, his account is nevertheless valuable. Hall is not alone in emphasizing different intensities of institutional change. Cohen, March and Olsen (1972) developed the "garbage can" model to affirm that, when contradictions arise, organizations attempt to solve them by reverting to familiar responses–to their "garbage can"–, before promoting new core values. This assertion implicitly says that organizations will attempt to solve their problems through stabilizing change before resorting to more drastic types of change.

From these two accounts we may conclude that, although the difference between constant and drastic institutional change is seldom recognized explicitly, there seems to be an implicit acceptance that there is a type of change that may profoundly transform institutional structures. I shall call this latter type of change "paradigmatic change," because–as we shall soon see–it often pursues and eventually involves the substitution of the paradigms that guide decision and policy-making in societies where it takes place. Obviously, such a process of change is no small issue. It often implies that the patterns of relations, and the distribution of resources and influence are radically changed, with obvious social consequences. But, what exactly brings about paradigmatic change in modern societies? In the next paragraphs, I argue that the loss of legitimacy of one or more of the institutions that make up socio-political systems, through a failure of stabilizing change, is the initial cause of paradigmatic change.

As argued before, stabilizing change entails the constant adaptation of the regulative, normative, and cognitive agreements that legitimize a given institutional structure. This adaptation is a necessary response to changes in influence on and within the institution. These environmental changes may range from foreign cultural influence to war. At the same time, internal challenges come from the incessant pressures for change from groups that feel at disadvantage under a certain institutional arrangement, or by the general public, who might question the efficacy of the institution to solve specific problems. After all, as Martin (1994) correctly affirms, "legitimate" structures are usually highly contested and highly questioned ones (see also Stinchcombe, 1968:162). The important fact however, is that a failed process of re-negotiation of institutional terms would constitute a decline in the legitimacy of the institution, through changes in its constituent regulative, normative, and cognitive elements. Indeed, it seems that when public opinion of any of these three institutional mechanisms changes, the institution may lose legitimacy very quickly, and the calls for paradigmatic change increase. As a result, institutions that are legitimate at one time run the constant risk of becoming illegitimate at another. However, to fully understand how it is that paradigmatic change takes place, it is necessary to analyze its advent more closely.

3.3.3. The Mechanisms of Paradigmatic Change

The better to explain the process by which paradigmatic change occurs, I shall now introduce a step-by-step description of how the different factors that provoke paradigmatic change work and interact. Analysis is divided in five steps. For purposes of clarity, each step will be formally separated. However, the process must be seen as a continuum that is inter-meshed in complex ways. This section borrows heavily from the work of Colin Hay. Hay has developed a model of institutional change that is the most dynamic that I have found to date. From Hay's model I have taken the five-step division, the concepts related to the narration and meta-narration of change, the idea that paradigmatic change is usually accelerated by the failure of leading social groups to respond to legitimacy crises, and the mechanism by which institutions are re-established. I have complemented these views with the introduction of my own views about institutional appropriation, about the continuous need for stabilizing change, about the permanent struggle of "losing groups" to appropriate the institutions for themselves, and about the need to legitimize institutions before the whole of the population.

The First Step of Paradigmatic Change. The first step of paradigmatic change is the loss of legitimacy of a given institution, or set of them, through a failure of stabilizing change. This step has been discussed already. If stabilizing change at the regulative, normative or cognitive levels fails, the institution is bound to lose legitimacy and face pressure for change. "Losing groups" or unhappy sectors of society will constantly attempt to create occasions to question the legitimacy of institutions that they perceive to be adverse or useless, in order to change them. If stabilizing change does not take place to counteract these pressures, a loss of legitimacy will ensue. Such attempts to subvert the institutional order, combined with a failure to negotiate stability, may be considered to be the first step of paradigmatic change.

The Second Step of Paradigmatic Change. The second step of paradigmatic change is the identification and narration of contradictions generated by a given institutional structure. Sometimes, the description of a better state of affairs is used in the narration. This is how the de-legitimization of the institution accelerates to the point of potential change. All institutions contain dysfunctional elements (Pierson, 1996:124–7) that engender contradictions, which will eventually become manifest. This arises because institutions are designed to benefit certain groups, but also because perceived institutional success depends on the presence of specific socio-economic conditions that may shift exogenously (cf. Pontusson and Swenson 1996; Hall, 1999:149–50; Lindberg and Maier, 1985; Berger and Dore 1996). As March and Olsen correctly assert, "history cannot be guaranteed to be efficient" (1983:737).

At this point, although both the state and the appropriating groups often attempt to reverse this perception of institutional inefficacy, it is likely that their actions will only be superficial. The underlying causes of the contradictions will not be resolved at first because "solutions" will only be aimed at managing public perception, while maintaining the *status quo* (cf. Offe, 1985:223–6; Hay, 1999:328–9). Policymakers and leading groups might feel confined in their choices of alternative policies by limited resources or by restricted policy-making capacity (see also Skocpol, 1992:42 and March and Olsen, 1983:745 on "institutional stickiness"). Therefore, the perception of institutional and cognitive limitations on the part of state officials is often the main cause for inadequate policy responses (Hay, 1998a:20).

Responses to contradictions at this point begin to take place in a highly contentious and uncertain context, and are thus likely to produce both intended and unintended consequences that may in turn generate further contradictions. These contradictions will be added to the original ones, creating a vicious circle that is hard to break. In effect, once opposing groups collect enough contradictions to make a case, it is probable that political opposition and the mass media alike will give rise to narratives of crisis (Hay, 1998a:23). Narrating crisis is an important step in furthering institutional paradigmatic change, because it is through mass dissemination of the problems that illegitimacy becomes widespread. When the public are bombarded everyday with contradictions, they get a sense of prolonged and inevitable downfall: of a *systemic crisis.*

A systemic crisis takes the definition of social problems out of the hands of the state elite and into the public arena (Hay, 1998a:23). At this stage, the state and "appropriating" groups might still try to alter public perception instead of really solving the contradictions. Slight corrections might be made, but always within the confines of the existing paradigm. As will be described soon, only when it is often too late will governments start to address real underlying contradictions (Hay, 1999:328).

The Third Stage of Paradigmatic Change. From the above analysis we may conclude that there are two types of response to institutional contradictions: (i) those that really address the failures; and (ii) those that only address the symptoms of the emerging crisis, as discursively depicted by the mass media (Hay, 1999:337–8). Most projects include both types of response, because dominant groups often believe that they can reverse the negative tendencies through manipulation of perception. As real and perceived contradictions pile up, they are inter-linked and fused into a meta-narrative of crisis (Hay, 1999:338–9), which constitutes the third stage of paradigmatic change.

Although a necessary condition, the narration of contradictions is frequently not sufficient to promote paradigmatic change (Hay, 1999:324). Competing and contradictory accounts tend to remain uncoordinated, thus having differentiated effects on the population. A unification of all these narratives is necessary if paradigmatic change is to take place. This happens through an exercise of meta-narration disseminated through the mass media. Meta-narration is a process of secondary mediation and abstraction. For instance, a collection of contradictions like the increase of poverty levels, growing trade surpluses of developed nations, and the widening of the technology gap between rich and poor nations can be narrated as a case of a failing global free-trade regime. This in turn may be meta-narrated as a case of a world taken over by multinational corporations that control governments through neo-liberal policies, in order to extract more profit. Specific cases are replaced by abstract cases that link similar (though possibly unconnected) events, at a generic level at which most people can feel identified. This achieves the unification of the independent narratives of crisis, by attributing the cause of all of them to a few actors that can, in turn, be easily identified by everyone. Again, media bombardment turns every detail into a new proof of the existing "emergency." Meta-narration unifies popular feelings because general uneasiness gains individual significance. Individuals become constituted subjects through the story. *Empathy* arises and we all become "compassionate judges and enraged victims" at the same time (Hay, 1996:262–4). In reality, a very small part of the meta-narrative relates personally to us, but the story is often so general that it could be the story of anyone.

This analysis suggests that "losing groups" win the struggle fully to delegitimate institutional structures not when they identify the contradictions or even when they meta-narrate them, but when meta-narration fits individual experience. This is why some institutions often retain their legitimacy, even when everybody knows the reasons why they do not work properly.

At this point, the solution of the original contradictions (even if it is a real solution) will hardly have any effect, because the problem now lies beyond the initial individual contradictions. The people and the media will be waiting for solutions to the "filtered construction of crisis" (Hay, 1999:334) not to the "original construction." This is usually the biggest problem when addressing paradigmatic change: the initial response of policymakers to real problems is often rhetorical; in a way, they only offer solutions along the discursive lines of the prevailing paradigm. After opposing groups manage to meta-narrate systemic crisis, the normal response of policymakers is to go back and attempt to solve some of the original contradictions. In either case, the response is useless because it does not address prevailing perceptions.

In summary, as Hay (1996:255) clearly points out, the ability to impose a new institutional trajectory resides "not only in the ability to respond to crises but in the capacity to identify, define and constitute crisis in the first place." Through meta-narration, institutions start to be re-appropriated. Strategies and structures start to favor the groups in favor of change (Hay, 1999:336) because as Paul t'Hart (1993:41, also quoted in Hay, 1996:2), observes: "those who are able to define what the crisis is all about also hold the key to defining the appropriate strategies for [its] resolution."

The Fourth Step of Paradigmatic Change. After an institution has lost its legitimacy, a search for new institutional alternatives starts. The meta-narration of crisis creates some expectations that, if met, may be the key to the perceived solution of the problems. In short, the fourth step of paradigmatic change is one in which proposals must meet needs. The groups that advance the right proposals and combine them with the necessary degree of power will probably lead the design of the new institution(s)—often to their benefit.

The search for alternatives however is closely contested, charged with ideology and struggle because the resulting paradigm will determine the future power position of most social groups. At this point, even technical judgments about different policy options meet with conflicting data that complicate decision-making (Hall, 1999:159). As Hay (1998:21) argues, the search for new paradigms lies beyond the hands of experts and policy makers. It takes place in a highly politicized public arena, where interests are unpredictable (see study by Barley and Kunda, 1992[1]). Complicating matters further, the struggle to establish a certain paradigm in a state is often influenced by the international community (other states and/or international organizations) (cf. Gourevitch, 1986; Hall, 1999).

At this point however, paradigmatic change *will not* guarantee re-appropriation. If the groups that originally promoted paradigmatic change present no viable proposals, another group may appropriate the institution or the original appropriators might save the day due to a lack of safe alternatives for change. This situation has not been exceptional. For instance, although Keynesianism in the early 1970s was already seen as a highly contradictory model, and its failures were being extensively meta-narrated (cf. Friedman, 1962), the shift to Monetarism did not take place until the monetarists presented viable policy alternatives (Hall, 1993:46). Similarly, in our days, although the neo-liberal paradigm has come under attack, and its contradictions are starting to be meta-narrated, its detractors have not come up with viable alternatives to replace it. Consequently, the paradigm has not been altered.

Even if a new paradigm is adopted, it is improbable that it will solve the contractions of the old. New paradigms regularly address meta-narrated failures and not the original problems. The perceived success of new paradigms often does not result from their efficiency but from two misleading factors. Firstly, the new paradigm will set new goals, priorities and hierarchies. Therefore, "success" is measured through different parameters. Secondly, the emerging paradigm is seen as successful because it frequently provides the stability that was lost during the period of change; it re-establishes some degree of certainty, which is perceived as a good sign.

The Fifth Stage of Paradigmatic Change. Once a new paradigm is established, the process of institutional reconstruction begins. New written and unwritten norms and agreements are created to reflect the new relations of power. Even some of the previous values and beliefs (i.e. cognitive frameworks) may have changed. The process of legitimization studied in the section of institutional emergence is repeated. However, even if the new paradigm swiftly becomes ascendant, it may take longer before its consequences are reflected to any significant extent in the rest of the institutional architecture of society (Hay, 1998[a]:28). This is because even paradigmatic changes at the top fail to affect the web of related norms, routines, and roles that characterize modern political systems. The formal rules that are often modified to re-establish institutions usually represent a small fraction of the universe of written and unwritten precepts that structure societies.

The process of operational change following the establishment of a new paradigm will probably be much slower than the process that animated the paradigmatic change itself (Hay, 1999:327). This explains why, in most cases, even drastic paradigmatic changes fail to show immediate influence on the perceived operation of organizations. A non-specific type of organizational inertia tends to survive paradigmatic institutional change. Disillusionment with the change of regime in many countries clearly illustrates this point. For routines, norms or roles to change immediately, a complete destruction and reconstruction of the institutional and organizational architecture would be necessary. This usually happens in cases of war, revolution, or natural disaster. Even then, if the same personnel run the new organization and the same methods are adopted, old routines are bound to revive. In sum, the translation of a new paradigm into future policy is at best an unpredictable process.

3.3.4. Some Concluding Remarks on Institutional Change

As already explained, political and social structures constantly create contradictions that call for institutional change; social environments vary endlessly in ways that call for institutional change; human values and expectations shift in manners that continually motivate institutional change. In sum, institutional change appears to be inevitable; it seems to be a process that *must continuously happen,* even if at varying degrees.

Of course, depending on the society, change can be functional or dysfunctional. There do not seem to be general rules and hopefully no grand theorizing either. Sweeping radical change resulting from war has in the past helped to promote economic growth by overcoming the inertia of fossilized institutions (cf. Olson, 1982). Sir Henry Phelps Brown (1977) argues in fact that one of the main problems with the British economy is that it missed the "fresh start" of the sweeping institutional change promoted by invasion or revolution (Hodgson, 1988:272). Therefore, we could safely conclude that social change is inevitable, but at the same time offers undisputed opportunities for progress. Analysis of the specific conditions under which this could happen is an exciting topic for future investigation by researchers and policymakers alike.

Chapter Two
Informal Institutions: Becoming Specific

INTRODUCTION

The declared objective of the theoretical section of this project was to link neo-institutionalist theory with policy network theory, in order to understand the operation, social impact, and mutual interrelations of formal and informal structures. Formal institutions have already been analyzed in detail through the general concepts introduced in the previous chapter. It is now time to narrow down the scope of this work and concentrate on the study of informal institutions, which ultimately will be the main object of study for the rest of the book. I shall divide this chapter in five sections. In the first, I shall present a succinct critical review of the literature on informal institutions, with an emphasis on policy network theory. In the second section I attempt to prove that policy networks are in fact informal institutions, and therefore operate as such. In the third section I use a Mediated Rationality approach to introduce a working definition of informal institutions. The fourth section will include a detailed description of the processes of emergence, persistence, and change of informal institutions. Finally, I shall discuss three polemic phenomena that surround the concept of informality: corruption, corporatism, and clientelism.

1. A CRITICAL REVIEW OF POLICY NETWORK THEORY LITERATURE

The modern study of informal institutions can be traced back to critiques of formalist political studies developed in the first half of the twentieth century. Early works on informal group-government relations were developed by

Ernest S. Griffiths (1939), who called attention to the threat that "secretive" negotiations posed to democracy. Also in 1939, Roethlisberger and Dickson described the importance of informal networks of relations in organizations. The trend continued in the second half of the century with authors like Macridis (1955), and Almond and Coleman (1960), who criticized the excessive orientation of political science towards the study of formal statutes. In their view, this concealed essential informal mechanisms and distorted the study of developing countries, where many formal structures were lacking (Peters, 1999:8).

The scarce but constant recognition of a potentially useful analytical role for informality, eventually led theorists from numerous academic disciplines to study this type of relations closer. In Sociology, the explosion in the study of organizational networks elicited works that ranged from the mathematical study of networks (cf. Coleman and MacRae, 1960; Lorrain and White, 1971) to the more structuralist approach (cf. Nadel, 1957; Laumann, Galskeiwicz, and Marsden, 1978; Holland and Leinhardt, 1979). The political sociology strand also made extensive use of the informal network concept. The work of Granovetter (1974, 1985), Stinchcombe (1965, 1968) and more recent writings by Walter Powell (1990), Lynne Zucker (1983, 1986, 1986, 1991) and Anthony Giddens (1979, 1984), made valuable contributions to the topic. On the economic side, Oliver Williamson (1975, 1985, 1991) was the first author to re-explore in the 1970s and 1980s the role of trust-based agreements as instruments that could lower transaction costs. Influential works like that of Robert Axelrod (1984) followed, and encouraged writings in management science like that of Nittin Nohria and Robert Eccles (1992). Political Scientists soon entered the field too. Early terms describing informal relations between government and social groups included "whirlpool," "triangle, "sub-governments," "sloppy hexagon," "webs," "iron triangles" (Dowding, 1995:137–8), "epistemic communities" (Adler and Haas, 1992; Haas, 1990), and "regimes" (Katzenstein, 1978). Meanwhile, Rhodes (1988:77–8) identified as many as six different types of informal community. All these terms attempted to account for a key feature of political life: the flexible interdependence of public and private actors (be they groups or individuals) in policy design, implementation and outcomes.

In recent times, the study of informal forms of organization that bridge the private-public divide has unified many theoretical concepts and in consequence has almost invariably converged in the adoption of the so-called "policy network model", as a legitimate mainstream perspective (Nohria, 1992:1–2). For this reason, and because of its explanatory power, this work will adopt this model as the guiding perspective from which to study informal institutions. I shall now analyze the model further and, in subsequent sections, I shall adapt it to the objectives of this work, hoping to make additional contributions to it on the way.

1.1. The Policy Network Model

Policy network theory has two strong influences: (i) the sociological organizational theory of the 1960s and 1970s; and (ii) the political science literature on subsystems and policy communities developed in the debates between elitists and pluralists in the 1950s and 1960s (Kickert, Klijn, and Koppenjan, 1997:15). Current literature is made up of a robust body of theoretical and empirical contributions, mainly developed in Britain, the United States, Germany, and the Netherlands. However, within these myriad publications, the most influential development to date seems to be the Marsh and Rhodes model of policy networks (see Marsh and Rhodes, 1992[a]).

The Marsh-Rhodes model introduces at least four valuable methodological innovations: (i) it locates the operation of policy networks in the sectoral and sub-sectoral levels of the state; (ii) it connects policy networks with policy outcomes, giving practical use to the concept; (iii) it classifies policy networks along a continuum that runs from exclusive policy communities to inclusive issue networks, unifying under one framework informal collaboration of different types; and (iv) it implicitly differentiates policy networks from state systems. In spite of showing some insufficiencies that have been criticized, the model remains a fundamental landmark upon which a broader study of informal institutions can be built. To introduce concepts that will later strengthen my own argument, I shall now elaborate briefly on some of the above-mentioned methodological innovations of the Marsh-Rhodes model.

(i) The Locus of Policy Networks

The Marsh-Rhodes model states that policy networks are meso-level structures that link public and private actors at either the sectoral or sub-sectoral levels of the state (Daugbjerg and Marsh, 1998:53). In other words, they cut across the public-private divide at levels defined by issues or industries. This assertion is strengthened by studies that identify the presence of sophisticated policy networks at both levels (see Cavanagh, Marsh and Smith, 1995). Examples of sectoral networks are those developed around highly regulated areas such as the oil or chemical industries. Examples of sub-sectoral networks established within these two industries are the gasoline and the agrochemicals sectors (also highly regulated). In either case, and regardless of their general or more specific goals, policy networks must partly operate within the state structure to be able to influence policymaking.

(ii) Policy Networks and Policy Outcomes

On the Marsh-Rhodes model, policy networks represent a pattern of relatively stable relations through which state and private actors negotiate their interdependent interests. Here, the key concept is interdependence (Kickert, Klijn, and Koppenjan, 1997:xviii,6). The groups that have resources that the state perceives to be important for particular goals, will probably be incorporated into the policy-making process and vice versa. Accordingly, these groups will often influence policy outcomes more than those groups that are excluded. Influence in this definition is therefore seen as both "perceptional and relational" (Smith, 1993:72).

(iii) Classifying Policy Networks

The model treats "policy networks" as a generic term that is then broken down into a division that distinguishes between (a) policy communities at one end of the spectrum; and (b) issue networks at another (Hogwood, 1986). The differences between the two types of policy network occur at various levels. Policy communities are more integrated structures, with low numbers of participants, and stable membership (Smith, 1993:7); they negotiate definite issues with specific government agencies. Issue networks, on the other hand, are open structures, with a high and constantly changing number of participants; they are more disputed structures (Peters, 1999:117–8) that develop in areas of lesser importance to the government (Smith, 1993:10).

(iv) Policy Networks and State Systems

Only to conclude the review of the general principles of policy network theory, I shall briefly discuss the relationship between policy networks and the general theories of the state. This is essential, because two potential sources of criticism of the theory are based on this issue. Firstly, it could be argued that some forms of polity could not conceivably accept the operation of policy networks. Secondly, some authors suggest that policy network theory does not hold because it is not applicable in any modern state (see Dowding, 1995:140–1). Let us address both strands of criticism.

On the first point, the compatibility of policy networks with political systems, the study of the state has been traditionally approached from the standpoint of four main theoretical perspectives: Elite, Pluralist, Corporatist, and Marxist theory (Knoke *et al.*, 1996:2; Camp, 1989:6–7). In the case of the first three theories, policy networks are not only accepted, but actually constitute important pillars of their concept of the state. Elite theory, with its emphasis on small governing circles, is particularly prone to talk about network structures (for more on Elite theory see Wright Mills, 1959; Gaetano Mosca, 1959;

Michels, 1960; Nye, 1977; Albertoni, 1982; Marsden, 1983; Pareto, 1984; Yannuzzi, 1993). Corporatist theory, with its endless webs of dependency between actors with unequal power, is so friendly to the inclusion of policy networks that, in effect, the two theories are sometimes confused (for more on theories of state corporatism see Rokkan, 1966; Harris, 1972; Schmitter, 1974; Panitch, 1977; Middlemas, 1979; Schmitter, 1979; Dunleavy, 1982; Olsen, 1983; Streeck, 1983; Hall, 1984; Vogler, 1985; Cawson, 1986; Mann, 1986; Block, 1987; Grant *et al.*, 1988; Cawson *et al.*, 1990; Crouch and Dore, 1990; Jessop, 1990; Smith, 1993; Knoke *et al.*, 1996). Finally, Pluralist theories, by highlighting the constant pressure that interest groups exercise on the government, actually rely to a great extent on the concept of policy networks (for more on Pluralist theories see Truman, 1951; Lindblom, 1977; Heclo, 1978; Jordan and Richardson, 1982; McFarland, 1987; Vogel, 1987; Jordan, 1990[a], 1990[b]; Smith, 1993). The only theoretical approach in which the application of policy network theory is in principle doubtful is Marxist theory. I argue, however, that even Marxism can incorporate it in two ways. Firstly, the concept of the capitalist state, defended by Marxist scholars, logically requires the extremely close interaction of state and capital. This is fertile ground for policy network explanations. Secondly, the emphasis of modern Marxism (like that of Jessop, 1990[a], 1990[b]) on the autonomy of the State, and on disaggregation, clearly fits well with policy network theory as well (Smith, 1993:44). In sum, policy networks do not seem to oppose, but rather to complement and fit into all four general theories of the state. Naturally, the participants, the structure, and the policy outcomes produced by policy networks will vary depending on the type of state where they develop, but this only reinforces the fact that they operate.

As for the second criticism, that policy network theory cannot be generalized as one that can explain the nature of the state, my answer has been implicitly stated already: Policy network theory does not aim to substitute any of the general theories of the state; instead, it complements all of them. In consequence, it can certainly be generalized because it operates at a conceptual level that is very different from that of state theories.

2. POLICY NETWORKS AS INSTITUTIONS

We have now established the theoretical bases of the model that will guide this chapter. However, a first and necessary step to link policy network theory to institutionalist theory is precisely to examine policy networks as institutions. This is an essential pre-requisite to developing the rest of the chapter, since our object of study is precisely institutionalized informality.

I argue that policy networks can indeed be considered institutions of informal nature. I base my assertion on the coincidence of the working definition of institutions introduced in the last chapter and the operational characteristics of policy networks. Recounting, institutions were defined as *the systems consisting of a mix of regulative, normative, and cognitive mechanisms that influence the behavior of participants, thus structuring relations by increasing certainty.* Let us once again break down the definition, to test it against the characteristics of policy networks.

Policy networks as *systems consisting of a mix of regulative, normative, and cognitive mechanisms.* Numerous authors direct attention to the tendency of policy networks to display a complex mix of components that simultaneously constrain and enable human behavior. Policy networks may be viewed as structures in which regulative normative, and cognitive elements play an equally important role (Peters, 1999:117). At the regulative level, individuals are said to join policy networks (and abide by their rules) due to principles of "reciprocity," "interdependence," "access to information," "active communication" or acquirement of "know-how" (Powell, 1990:324-7; Macneil, 1980:13). These are predominantly regulative principles because they all elicit compliance either through fear of exclusion and punishment, or through potential rewards that informal interaction may offer. At the normative level, authors mention factors such as the search for "efficiency," acquisition of "skills and knowledge" and "flexibility" (Macneil, 1980:13; Powell, 1990:324-7; Marsh, 1998[a]:9; Larson, 1992:76). All these concepts might classify as instances in which personal conviction elicits compliance and encourages membership, which would classify them as normative. Finally, at the cognitive level, authors introduce mechanisms like "shared values" and "reputation," which clearly are cognitions that operate at an unconscious level (Powell, 1990:324-7; Marsh, 1998[a]:9; Larson, 1992:76). Most importantly however, most of the above authors seem to agree that the essential mechanism governing policy networks is trust. Given that–as we shall see later–trust synthesizes regulative, normative, and cognitive elements, the assertion seems to further support the view that policy networks operate under a blend of these mechanisms. In short, all these accounts imply that, like institutions, policy networks operate fully under Mediated Rationality principles.

Policy networks and their *influence on the behavior of participants.* If we accept that policy networks operate under Mediated Rationality principles, then it follows that they must have the capacity to influence individual preferences and ultimately constrain or enable human action. According to various works, this seems to be the case. For Jordan (1990a:477-8), "extra-constitutional" structures that link the state to society have enormous influence on policy choice. Peters (1999:119) explicitly adds that informal mechanisms provide strong "patterns of expected behavior," and furnish participants with common values and routines. Knoke, Pappi and Tsujinaka (1996) document the importance of institutionalized informal relations in shaping policy outcomes in the United States, Germany and Japan. Bogason (1996) develops a similar theory for Denmark; Kickert, Klijn and Koppenjan (1997) for the Netherlands; and Wang (1998) for Taiwan and Japan. In sum, policy networks also operate like institutions in this respect.

Policy networks as providers of *increased certainty*. The final characteristic of institutions is that they structure social relations, by providing relative certainty about the probable future behavior of their participants. This is a function that policy networks also seem to fulfill. Indeed, as explicitly stated by Peters (1999:119), informal structures foster "substantial stability" in the social world. In Hay's (1998:33) words, "[n]etworking offers the potential to establish parameters of stability and predictability within an otherwise unstable, disorderly, unpredictable . . . and rapidly changing environment." No further comment seems necessary.

All in all, it appears that policy networks can be safely considered to be institutions of an informal type. They share the objectives and the nature of institutions: to provide order and relative predictability through their influence on human behavior. Their constituent mechanisms also seem to fit the concept of Mediated Rationality, which further grants them institutional status. We could then deduce that, by subsequently describing the operation of policy networks, we would be describing with a certain degree of accuracy the operation of informal institutions that cut across the private-public divide. Analysis of informal institutions of this type is necessary to understanding the case study on Mexico that will be later introduced, so let us now focus on the operation of such structures.

3. DEFINING INFORMAL INSTITUTIONS

Following the analytical structure of the previous chapter, the first step in the study of informal institutions is clearly to define the concept. I shall divide this section into two sub-sections. Firstly, given that both formal and informal institutions seem to operate under Mediated Rationality principles, I clarify the differences between each type of institution. Secondly, I develop a working definition of informal institutions that may further elucidate their particularities, allowing us to move forward in their analysis.

3.1. Mediated Rationality and Informal Institutions

As just substantiated by the study of policy networks, informal institutions operate under the same Mediated Rationality principles that we analyzed in the last chapter. This means that informal institutions, because of their institutional status, also stand beyond stiff distinctions of agency versus structure[1], or internal versus external influences. We could affirm that, just as in the case of formal structures, no decision made within an informal institution could be foreign to a simultaneous mix of external and internal motives of the participants (Smith Ring, 1997:116; Daugbjerg and Marsh, 1998:54).

However, if both formal and informal institutions are governed by Mediated Rationality principles, the real question seems to revolve around the differences between one type of institution and the other. This is to say that, if both formal and informal institutions operate under a mix or regulative, normative, and cognitive elements, we must clearly distinguish each type of institution. In the next lines I shall maintain that the difference between formal and informal institutions lies in the regulative and normative mechanisms that compose each type of institution. In other words, I hold that the cognitive elements of both types of institution are very similar (because the participants are the same in both cases, so obviously values and beliefs are identical), but the regulative and normative spheres show important differences. Let me explain further.

We suggested that regulative mechanisms might be either written or unwritten regulations, enforced by third parties through the fear of legal or social punishment. Similarly, normative mechanisms are written or unwritten principles that dictate appropriate behavior and are self-enforced through moral conviction (Scott, 1995:35–7, 47). Whilst cognitive mechanisms such as roles and values are necessarily symbolic and therefore unwritten, regulative and normative mechanisms (rules and norms) can be either written or unwritten. It follows that the degree of formality presented by the regulative and normative elements of an institution at a given time, directly determines the degree of formality of that particular institution.

Put in different terms, whilst the regulative mechanisms of formal institutions seem to be predominantly written rules, those of informal institutions are mainly unwritten. Equally, whilst written norms frequently govern formal institutions, unwritten norms often support informal ones. In consequence, whilst the punishment for breaking the agreements that support formal institutions tends to be codified in writing, the punishment for breaking the supporting accords of informal institutions is primarily moral and psychological. This is not to say that formal institutions do not rely to some degree on informality, they do. However, the basic agreements concerning objectives, mission, membership, or format of the meetings, tend to be in writing, as opposed to informal institutions, where those same agreements are unwritten. Similarly, in informal institutions, punishment for non-compliance and/or reward for compliance often rely on peer condemnation or recognition (Dasgupta, 1997), instead of being codified in writing. If modern organizations display a complex combination of written and unwritten penalties and rewards, it is precisely because they often comprise, support, and engender a sophisticated combination of formal and informal institutions.

3.2. Defining Informal Institutions

Having distinguished between formal and informal institutions, we can now be more specific and develop a working definition of the latter. In line with the general account of institutions introduced in the last chapter, and aggregating the particularities just studied, we could say that, for the sake of this study, informal institutions will be defined as *systems consisting of a mix of cognitive mechanisms,* **unwritten** *regulative mechanisms, and* **unwritten** *normative mechanisms that influence the behavior of participants, thus structuring relations by increasing certainty.* Let us analyze this definition more closely.

Informal institutions consist *of a mix of cognitive mechanisms, unwritten regulative mechanisms, and unwritten normative mechanisms.* The reason why all these mechanisms are unwritten has just been given. We must now explain how these unwritten mechanisms interact effectively to *influence behavior* and *increase certainty.* In my view, and in that of many other authors (cf. Macneil, 1980:13; Powell, 1990:324–7; Marsh, 1998[a]:9; Larson, 1992:76), both influence and certainty are a function of the high levels of trust frequently found in informal institutions that operate effectively.

Trust synthesizes and acts upon the regulative, normative, and cognitive spheres of human conscience, and thus gives an objective dimension to compliance and certainty under unwritten rules; it constrains and enables the decisions and actions of participants in informal institutions. Although this sub-section cannot attempt to exhaust the study of trust, a closer analysis of the concept, in relation to the ways in which it affects decisions, certainly appears to be in place.

Much has been written about trust. For a comprehensive analysis of trust see Lane and Bachmann (1998). Equally, for a brilliant summary of the different theoretical stances on trust see Lane (1998). Other useful studies include those of Luhmann (1979), Barber (1983), Zucker (1986), Gambetta (1988), Fukuyama (1995), Smith Ring (1997), and Waterhouse and Beloff (1999).

In the eyes of practically all authors, trust is multidimensional and as we have briefly suggested, cuts across cognitive frameworks, rules, and calculation (Bachmann, 1998:300). Most theories agree that individuals and organizations trust each other for three common reasons: "a certain degree of interdependence between trustor and trustee; the assumption that trust provides a way to cope with uncertainty in exchange relationships; and the expectation that the vulnerability arising from the acceptance of risk will not be a source of advantage for one of the parties engaged in a relationship" (Lane, 1998:3). Trust, then, ensures the accomplishment of institutional objectives, by constraining and enabling behavior within pre-specified limits that are acceptable to all participants. This in turn creates certainty not only about the future decisions of other participants, but also about the efficiency of the informal institution itself.

The reason behind the influence of trust on behavior is that it operates at the three levels of Mediated Rationality. At the regulative level, trusted individuals frequently enhance their reputation and increase their opportunities for further networking, whilst untrustworthy individuals are often denied advancement by the enforcement of pre-established unwritten penalties exercised by their own peers (Smith Ring, 1997:117–22). The fear of exclusion or "the shadow of the future," as Axelrod (1984) has called it, is a good example of why the members of an informal institution would avoid breaching agreements based on trust. At the normative level, numerous authors confirm how, particularly during early stages, informal interaction tends to be rooted in strong convictions about the desirability of trusting and being trusted by one's peers. In this case, conviction is not imposed by external agents, but a self-enforced norm, which aims to foster interpersonal understanding (cf. Smith Ring, 1997; Bradach and Eccles, 1989; Zucker, 1986; Barber, 1983; Luhmann, 1979). Even if trust is a predominantly social phenomenon (Lane, 1998:1–2), other personal, self-enforced values such as loyalty, accessibility, availability and predictability have been proven to act as accelerators of the creation of trust (Jennings, 1971). Finally, at the cognitive level, trust is closely tied up with the self-developing identity of humans from infancy. The people and structures in which one trusts become symbolic complexes (Lane, 1998:23) that strongly determine decision-making throughout one's life. Precisely because of its composite nature, trust is a very fragile asset that needs constant renewal and nurture to persist. The construction and maintenance of trust requires frequent and successful transactions (which achieve both effective and equitable outcomes) (Smith Ring, 1997:123–9), in which participants can ascertain the mutual and repeated respect for all unwritten codes of conduct that uphold a particular institution. In consequence, it is difficult for informal institutions to emerge between actors that distrust each other: uncertainty and the probability of opportunistic behavior would be too high to accept. As Lane (1998:20) correctly asserts, the production of trust to some degree depends on a particular combination of trust-encouraging mechanisms that is only present in certain societies. Zucker (1986), Chisholm (1989:192), Hamilton *et al.* (1990), Redding (1990), and Whitley (1998:18) also support this view.

In summary, properly operating informal institutions influence behavior and create certainty because participants perceive and understand that the accomplishment of their objectives, as well as a great deal of their reputation and even their identity depends on their trustworthiness. Breaching informal agreements means damaging trust, an extremely fragile asset that impacts all levels of human consciousness. This is why "negative spirals of distrust" are extremely difficult to reverse (Sydow, 1998:38).

4. ANALYZING THE LIFE CYCLE OF INFORMAL INSTITUTIONS

In line with the analytical process followed in the previous chapter, the following sections will examine the processes of emergence, persistence, and change of informal institutions. The goal will be to note the particularities of informal institutions in relation to these processes.

4.1. Emergence of Informal Institutions

As correctly observed by some authors (e.g. Hay, 1998[b]:45; Smith Ring, 1997:139), formation is one of the most ignored yet most important aspects of network theory and certainly of institutional theory in general. Analyzing this process is essential because informal institutions do not exist *ex ante*; their emergence determines most of their membership and structure. This section will explore why and how informal institutions emerge. To do so, and following the structure of the previous chapter, we shall look at three moments in the emergence process. First, we shall examine how limited policy options and agreements among participants influence the degree of formality with which institutions in general emerge and materialize. Secondly, we shall analyze the conditions that support the materialization of informal institutions. Thirdly, I shall introduce the processes that determine the initial characteristics of informal structures. Finally, I shall briefly explain the interrelationship of emerging informal institutions and formal institutions.

4.1.1. Formality or Informality?

Numerous academic works support the possibility of institutions materializing either in a formal or an informal form at the time of emergence (cf. Rhodes, 1997, 1988; Thomas, 1997; Haas, 1992; Sabatier, 1988; Knoke and Laumann, 1987). The question is: why would a particular institution emerge as an informal structure (i.e. as a policy network) instead of as a formal one (i.e. as an organization)?

Like in the previous chapter, I hold that the particular political, economic, and social context at the time of the emergence of an institution greatly limits the alternatives available to social actors. Therefore, an institution might emerge as an informal structure under two alternative conditions: when participants are either (i) structurally compelled to it or (ii) when they find informality more useful to achieving their objectives. Let us analyze both points.

Informality as the only option. When existing formal structures are so tight and complex that any change to adapt them to new problems would be economically, politically, or ideologically unfeasible, social actors normally *have to* resort to the creation of informal institutions to address their needs. When control over certain institutions is monopolized by certain groups, the state often has to address the interests of competing groups through informal channels. A good example is lobbying in the U.S. Congress or the British Parliament, in which informal consultation takes place everyday with social groups (environmentalists, anti-racists, pro-immigration, and the like) attempting to modify law that currently protects certain interests (industrial production, conservative anti-immigration policies, etc.).

Even if an informal institution is the only option available, it might be blithely accepted though. As we have seen, when founding agreements are rooted in mutual trust, they can convey an enormous amount of information and certainty (Nelson and Winter, 1982:96), so participants can potentially accomplish their objectives with efficiency.

Informality as a choice. In other cases, social actors favor informal institutions because of their advantages over formal ones. Indeed, informal institutions tend to have a degree of flexibility and speed of response difficult to match by formal organizations. Transaction costs are also lower within informal structures that operate through trust (cf. Williamson, 1975; Dasgupta, 1997). Similarly, horizontal communication, common in informal structures, facilitates information flows that increase efficiency and efficacy (Jordan and Richardson, 1982; Chisholm, 1989:30, 115–8; Saward, 1990:588; Ronfeldt, 1993:75). If the existing structures allow it and informality is perceived as a superior alternative, actors will most likely opt in its favor.

In sum, in line with Mediated Rationality precepts, the options available to decide between formal or informal structures are frequently limited, for they are invariably dictated by a combination of the desirable with the feasible.

4.1.2. Conditions that Support the Materialization of Informal Institutions

As stated in the previous chapter, the effective materialization of any institution requires three conditions: (i) the establishment of the basic principles that will co-ordinate such institution; (ii) the accommodation of "losing" interests;

and (iii) its justification before the general population. As we may recall, these elements provide legitimacy to the institution at all levels. Informal institutions are not different. In the lines that follow, I shall describe the three processes, emphasizing some particularities of informal structures.

(i) Establishing the basic principles that will co-ordinate the informal institution.
The founding agreements of informal institutions, like those of their formal counterparts, establish very specific aspects of the emerging structure. We shall briefly analyze three of these aspects that are of capital importance to the rest of this book: (a) the type of emerging agreements that informal institutions rest upon; (b); the possible types of informal structures that may emerge; and (c) decisions about membership.

(a) Since institutions in general often benefit some groups more than others, the agreements that establish informal institutions are often dictated by the "winners" and are in consequence highly biased. By definition, these agreements do not acquire a written form. Rather, they are a collection of commonly created and mutually accepted principles, often enforced through trust. These "rules of the game" govern how participants must behave within the network (Rhodes, 1986). As said before, mutual agreements are established in operational aspects such as the objectives of the institution, the nature and regularity of meetings, or the topics open for negotiation. These agreements eventually become part of the accumulated experience of the participants (Nohria, 1992:11), so they become additional means of selective exclusion (Smith, 1993:61). However, at the same time, they are also one of the sources of the enormous flexibility of informal institutions. When new members join, the agreements are often explicitly and implicitly clarified, and this is the way in which they are transmitted.

(b) The specific type of informal institution that materializes depends on the nature of the relationship between the participants, and on the objectives they pursue. As we saw in section 1.1 of this chapter, the Marsh-Rhodes model states that policy networks can be of two types: policy communities and issue networks. Policy communities are more exclusive constructs in which both resources and aid in policy implementation are exchanged intensively between the state and private actors (Smith, 1993:10; Richardson and Jordan, 1979:74 cited in Marsh, 1998[a]:6). Issue networks develop in areas that are too new, too broad, or too controversial for the state to develop close relationships with social groups (Smith, 1993:10). They have looser membership, and exchange fluctuates in importance given the unequal resources of the participants (Marsh, 1998[a]:16). Although these are two ideal types, located at two opposite extremes, the model opens up the possibility of particular types of policy networks emerging anywhere in the spectrum, as a combination of the two types. In fact, for Smith (1993:65), the number of structures possible "is infinite."

Finally, (c) there are no rules as to which groups are incorporated into informal institutions. It depends on the specific problem that is being resolved. However, the state normally gets involved only in those institutions that help it attain its goals. Endless influences–external and internal to the social groups–count when deciding which groups are convenient for what. External factors such as a change in the economic situation or war may bring into prominence groups previously forgotten. In other cases, the costs of developing policy without the involvement of certain key actors is so high that the state has little option but to include them (Saward, 1990:591–5; Smith, 1993:72). Whatever the case, one point remains true about membership: groups that have no *perceived* valuable resources to exchange will hardly enter an informal relation with the state. Resources exchanged through informal institutions include both tangible and intangible assets: information (Smith, 1993:7), goals (Kickert, Klijn, and Koppenjan, 1997:6), influence, political support, and legitimacy. Tangible resources may include money, goods, or political position.

(ii) Accommodation of the interests of "losing" groups

We argued in our last chapter that, in order for an institution to gain and retain legitimacy, the interests of the groups that are affected during the emergence of such institution must be accommodated through additional organizational arrangements. In this respect, informal institutions may be both solutions to and sources of this question. They are solutions when, as often happens, they become the "additional organizational arrangement" and are developed to accommodate the interests of some "losing" group. However, they can also be sources of exclusion. Due to their restricted membership, informal institutions tend to create themselves some "losing" groups, made up of those actors that are barred from participation. The frequently low profile of these structures makes them particularly prone to exclude radical or highly visible groups (Smith, 1993:61). This exclusion can be dangerous not only for the legitimacy of the network itself, but also for society as a whole, particularly when the excluded groups resort to violence. Thus, as in the case of formal institutions, adequately accommodating "losing" interests is essential to the emergence and persistence of informal structures.

(iii) Justifying informal institutions before the general public

If formal institutions have to be openly justified to gain popular legitimacy, informal institutions often involve forgoing high-profile campaigns, and encouraging discretion amongst its members (Jordan and Richardson, 1987; Grant, 1989). This is probably a result of the frequently sensitive information that is discussed within such structures. Nevertheless, even informal institutions need a degree of public approval to emerge and persist. Informal structures that involve the state and other social groups can never be totally secret. For this reason, such institutions cannot be at odds with the cognitive frameworks (i.e. values, roles, beliefs) of the population. They must fall within the limits of accepted values and objectives of society as a whole. An informal institution that conflicts with the symbolic constructions of the population will most likely become a source of suspicion and doubts and will motivate attacks that could be even stronger than those against formal institutions. For example, if a formal committee on economic promotion fails, it may be perceived only as an inefficient structure. However, if this same committee were informal, allegations of corruption and conspiracy would probably be automatic.

4.1.3. Processes that Determine the Initial Characteristics of Informal Institutions

Like formal institutions, during the late stages of emergence, informal institutions often develop additional characteristics through interaction. As with institutions in general, appropriation manifests itself through the creation of additional agreements that consolidate and expand the original ones. We shall study this process in more depth because it is crucial to understanding the case study that will be presented in the next chapter.

Appropriation. We have seen that institutional appropriation requires ability to determine in general terms the internal rules and policy directions of a given structure. The same applies to informal institutions (Laumann and Knoke, 1987). Appropriation not only takes place when consensus is being built to create the institution, but also during the early stages of operation. Even the structures that accommodate the interests of "losing groups" include actors more powerful than others.

The presence of institutional appropriation in informal institutions—also called "agency capture"—has been strongly confirmed by investigation (cf. McConnell, 1966, Cater, 1964). For most authors, appropriation reflects pre-existing patterns of structured inequality (Marsh, 1998[b]:188–9; Smith, 1993:72–3). In the case of political informal institutions, structured inequality is often reinforced through the state's acceptance of certain groups and the exclusion of others. The incorporation/rejection of certain groups to and from informal structures seems to be a function of at least five factors: size of the group (Ronfeldt, 1993:50), resources available to exchange with the state (Ronfeldt, 1993:50; Smith, 1993:4), quality and constancy of links with other members of the network (Ronfeldt, 1993:50), perception of other members of the network (Smith, 1993:4), and ideology (Berger and Luckmann, 1967; Giddens, 1986; Smith, 1993:4). While the first two factors are fairly self-explanatory, an example cited by Smith (1993:4) illustrates the combined role of links, perception and ideology in determining state recognition and thus the appropriation of informal institutions by specific groups. For him, "the British trade union movement was just as well-resourced–and I would add as large–on 2 May 1979 as it was on 3 May 1979 but with the election of a Conservative government a large part of its political clout disappeared overnight."

An additional way in which the state promotes the appropriation of informal institutions is by playing the role of arbitrator between social groups (Schmitter, 1974). Naturally, it often arbitrates in favor of those groups with which it has ideological affinity (cf. Nordlinger, 1981). In fact, the more centralized political decision-making is, the more the state can: (i) select the participants of the informal institutions in which it also participates; (ii) play the interests of the different groups against each other; and (iii) promote its own goals and those of selected groups (Peters, 1998:32).

Most groups that conflict with the state or with members of the policy network will normally be excluded from the structure. The repeated exclusion of groups and policy options often becomes "en-structured" (Berger and Luckmann, 1967). This does not mean, however, that the state is omnipotent in deciding appropriation. Although it often has more resources to exchange and therefore more power than most groups, public policy-making usually involves intricate consensus building. In fact, as mentioned before, some groups often become prominent *in spite* of state rejection, either through their legitimacy or power (Saward, 1990:591–5) which, in either case, can sometimes be greater than that of the state (Marsh, 1998[a]:9).

In the case of informal structures of the policy network type, appropriation often results in higher influence on policy decisions through increased access to decision-making centers. This access often means more and better information, greater exchange of resources, and even the opportunity of further excluding competition (Scharpf, 1978; Crozier and Friedberg, 1980; Pierson, 1993:601–6; Kickert, Klijn, and Koppenjan, 1997:215). Access through appropriation of policy networks appears to occur through what I see as concentric "circles of power." For Kadushin (1979:130), circles of power represent the "dense parts" of policy networks. This could also apply to systems of networks. They are concentric because the further a circle is from the core, the less direct influence it has on decisions. In other words, the concept of circles of power implies that some actors are "more central" than others. The quality of the connections of particular members determines their proximity to the core, and therefore their influence on policy decisions.

The concept of "circles of power" is inherently supported by Useem (1984:26–75) through his description of an "inner circle" of actors that have privileged leadership of the higher echelons of business and society and therefore enjoy preferential access to decision-makers. In practical terms, this preferential access often translates itself into repeated leadership of business associations and non-profit organizations, as well as into their role as *de facto* advisers of their respective governments in economic matters (*ibid.*, pp. 70–80).

This does not mean that circles of power are cliques of unanimous thought. Although members are unified in general ideological terms (Field and Higley, 1973:9), extensive discussion often takes place (Kadushin. 1979:133). Naturally, the closer concentric circles are to the core, the closer their ideological identification with that core will be, the fewer ideological differences they will have, and the higher their influence on policy decisions. Although full informal systems tend to include a broad spectrum of social groups, those that are less identified with the core will probably be located in the outer circles. They would still be part of the system indeed, but at a distance that makes their influence minimal.

To conclude this discussion about circles of power, I will only add that the mechanism that allows them to function is the degree of relative power between the various participants (Simon, 1994:279; Cook *et al.*, 1994:414–6). Although the exact definition of power is extremely polemic (Dahl, 1994:307–8), in this context power is understood as "non-sectional" or "positive-sum" power (Scott, 1994:ii) of the type advanced by Steven Lukes (1986:11–17). Under this definition, power is not imposition, but rather the potential to influencing outcomes. Power is institutionalized in the system to ensure fulfillment of agreements (Parsons, 1986:103), and not forced upon others in the traditional Weberian sense (Weber, 1986:28–33; cf. Spencer, 1994:140–9). The question here is not "who can affect whom?" or "who can control who?," but rather "who can get what?" (Lukes, 1986:9–11). Put in the terms introduced by Galbraith (1986[a]:223–6; 1986[b]:29–39), "compensatory power" in this case gives way to "conditioned power," which is gained through persuasion. Following this interpretation of power, the circles closer to the core would have better access and thus more influence. Actors located in those closer circles are able to secure policy decisions favorable to their interests. To achieve this, they do not have to control anyone directly (as traditional definitions of power would suggest). Rather, they are simply better placed to benefit from public decisions *more* than others.

The Development of Additional Agreements. After an informal institution starts to operate, additional agreements often consolidate and expand the original ones. As suggested in the last chapter, this process also takes place within formal structures, but changes might be more difficult to introduce due to the written accords that support them. Consolidation and adjustment tend to be more common in informal structures.

Often, not even the "appropriators" of the institution know exactly what is required to consolidate the structure. However, once they start operating, informal institutions frequently go through four processes that further define many of their features: (i) functional connections are developed; (ii) interaction between members becomes more frequent (Smith, 1993:62); (iii) consensus is developed (Jordan, 1990b:327); and (iv) some further recruitment may take place (Hay, 1998[b]:45–7). Let us briefly look at each one of these processes.

(i) During materialization and consolidation, informal institutions go through a process of connection to specific access points in the state. This happens because the state is not a monolithic actor (Mann, 1984), but a collection of agencies (Smith, 1993:49). Authority and decision-making are dispersed (Daugbjerg and Marsh, 1998:65–6) and may not be co-extensive with the boundaries of state ministries (Knoke *et al.*, 1996:10). However, the important point is that these scattered, semi-independent centers, where the institution initially connects, eventually become the loci where the informal structure will permanently operate (Heclo, 1978; Katzenstein, 1978; Scharpf, 1978: 346; Richardson and Jordan, 1979:74; Wicks and Wright, 1987).

(ii) In emergent informal institutions, government agencies and private groups get involved in constant interaction. Some initial resources might be exchanged but, more importantly, repeated contact causes other values to develop: shared perceptions, participation patterns, interaction rules (Kickert, Klijn, and Koppenjan, 1997:6), internal codes of conduct, modes of network governance, internal hierarchies (Hay, 1998[b]:47) and new objectives. These values are negotiated and re-negotiated heavily during this period, leading to the creation of a more "dense structure" (Dasgupta, 1997).

(iii) Once the core values of the informal network are created, ideological consensus starts to appear, further consolidating the institution. Without sufficiently shared attitudes, the institution cannot solidify (Jordan, 1990b:327). This initial consensus in turn becomes the long-term ideology that defines solutions to problems and even the problems themselves (Therborn, 1980:15–8). Ideology often privileges the appropriating interests further and promotes a more active exclusion of opposed groups. At this point, other forms of non-network type of co-ordination may be instituted to strengthen the ideology. For example, hierarchical control of some sort and/or formal rules of exclusion.

(iv) Finally, the core values and the ideology of the informal institution are reinforced by the consecutive recruitment of partners that provide strategic resources and conform to the leading ideology (Hay, 1998[b]:45–7). Members that cease to conform are expelled, sometimes despite their resources. At this point, the institution is practically consolidated, through both structural (Krasner, 1988:83) and personal ties (Granovetter, 1985). It is this dialectical relationship in Mediated Rationality terms (i.e. satisfaction of the conscious and unconscious expectations of participants) that provides informal institutions with stability.

4.1.4. Relation between Formal and Informal Institutions

Once an informal institution emerges, it does not operate in isolation, but is closely linked to the extant formal structures in dialectical terms. Informal institutions may either be (a) one way to compensate for the insufficiencies of the formal edifice (as when they accommodate the interests of "losing" groups); or (b) structures that enable individuals to take advantage of the formal edifice. In other words, informal institutions substitute for the deficiencies of formal ones, but also complement them by enabling actors to grasp opportunities. Having implicitly explained point (a) in previous sections, let us have a closer look at point (b).

Social co-ordination through informal institutions is enabling because valuable resources are exchanged through these structures: information, trust, obligations (Smith Ring, 1997:115–6), friendship, and/or funds (Laumann *et al.*, 1978:458). Additionally, the state frequently exchanges some degree of "non-sectional" power for assets like support or information (Smith, 1993:59). This means that informal institutions are not only structures of exchange but strategic alliances of collective action, where common agendas of mutual advantage are discussed, either to solve a problem or to take advantage of an opportunity created by the formal structure (Hay, 1998[b]:42; Knoke *et al.*, 1996:19–20).

This account is a first step towards regarding networks as dynamic structures, because it portrays institutions that are internally responsive to environmental (external) changes, and vice versa. Additionally, this view also implies that there is no clear hierarchy of importance between formal and informal institutions. None is subordinated to the other. They operate in dialectical conjunction and, in fact, stabilize each other. More research is required to expand on the relationship between these two degrees of institutional formality. This is a fascinating area of institutional research that directly pertains the issue of governance. Although deeper inquiry into the nature of this formal-informal dialectical relation is beyond the scope of this project, all along the book and in the last chapter of this work I present some basic points for further investigation on the topic. For now, let us move on to study the process of institutional persistence.

4.2. Persistence of Informal Institutions

In the last chapter we saw that if an institution is to function, it must persist over the time necessary to fulfill its objectives. It was also affirmed that persistence is a function of legitimacy, which is in turn maintained through stabilizing change. Stabilizing change was defined as the flexible re-negotiation of the original terms of institutional emergence, in order to adapt them to internal and external changes. In neither of these respects are informal institutions different. Given these consistencies, we shall in this section analyze the particular factors that determine legitimacy and stabilizing change in the case of informal institutions. This will help us understand the process of persistence better and will create a more specific theoretical framework to apply to the empirical part of this work.

4.2.1. Legitimacy

In line with a Mediated Rationality approach, the legitimacy of informal institutions is created and maintained through regulative, normative, and cognitive mechanisms. We also saw that, in the case of informal institutions, the mechanism that best represents this Mediated Rationality character is trust. Trust maintains legitimacy because it cuts across all levels of human consciousness and synthesizes them. When the participants of an informal institution (or society in general) begin to distrust such structure, its legitimacy will most likely decline rapidly. Trust being such a fragile asset, it is evident why informal structures tend to be more vulnerable to breaches and, therefore, to change and dissolution.

If the fragility of trust were not enough, there are other sources through which informal institutions may lose internal (related to the participants) or external (social) legitimacy. These are also located in the regulative, normative, and cognitive spheres of informal institutions. It was said in the last chapter that, over time, social actors only see institutions as legitimate if they regard them as useful to their personal or common objectives. A perception of uselessness can come from practically any of the Mediated Rationality mechanisms, rendering informal institutions even more unprotected against change. For instance, the perceived strategic interests and resources of the participating actors may vary (Smith, 1993:66; Knoke et al., 1996:8; Hay, 1998[b]:49); interdependent exchanges within a certain network may become less attractive to the participants (Kickert, Klijn, and Koppenjan, 1997:xviii,6; see also Hanf and Scharpf, 1978; Rogers and Whetten, 1982; Gage and Mandell, 1990; Thompson et al., 1991; Marsh and Rhodes, 1992[a]); society might find the institution outdated or too secretive to fit changing values; or simply, the informal form of organization may lose its advantage in solving specific problems. Instability may be created by participants that will constantly attempt to improve their position within the institution or even by powerful actors that may perceive an opportunity to gain more through change: the corollary is that the legitimacy of informal institutions is extremely hard to maintain, and this is why the process of stabilizing change is crucial.

4.2.2. Stabilizing Change

Stabilizing change is a process of constant adaptation to changing circumstances. It helps maintain institutional legitimacy because it often re-establishes balances of power that informal institutions lose through constant dialectical interaction between environmental and internal change (cf. Nohria, 1992:7; 1998:42–3; Marsh, 1998b:187). In the case of informal institutions, the process of stabilizing change is particularly critical because of extreme vulnerability to internal and external transformations shown by these structures.

In this context, the strategic re-negotiation of positions within informal institutions tends to be arduous because of what I see as an inherent "informality dilemma." This dilemma refers to a contradiction between informality and the *status quo*. Given that the agreements and understandings that hold policy networks together are almost never written, participants are constantly tempted to re-negotiate their position in the institution, with a view to better promotion of their interests. However, in order to preserve the integrity of the institution, the inherently biased core values of the structure often cannot be changed (Peters, 1998:29). In the end, participants run into the "informality dilemma": if they improve their position, the informal institution might disappear. Yet, very frequently, the only possible way to improve their position is precisely to drastically change the institution.

In any case, if an informal institution is to survive and avoid obsolescence, an active process of stabilizing change has to take place. The specific outcome of stabilizing change is not relevant, as long as the actors involved find it equitable and that at least it returns them to their *quo ante* position (Smith, 1993:64). If actors see the initial agreement violated and the balance of power changed, legitimacy might diminish and actors may withdraw participation from the informal institution.

However, it cannot be affirmed that stabilizing change can maintain the power structure in perfect balance indefinitely. Constant re-negotiation may tilt the balance of power in varying directions (Hay, 1998^b:51). Actors still may accept such shifts if they know that the possibilities of future discussion and change are open. All members have an incentive to remain in the institution: the leaders, to protect their privileges; and the disadvantaged groups, to maintain some influence over policy, hoping that a future conjuncture may tilt the power structure in their favor. It is only when these are improbable that actors will definitely leave the institution. In other words, we confirm that when stabilizing change fails across the board, legitimacy is lost, and the room is open for more drastic institutional change to take place.

4.3. Change in Informal Institutions

In the previous chapter, institutional change was divided into two types: stabilizing change and paradigmatic change. This section sets out to analyze the second type. Also in the last chapter, I described the general reasons why paradigmatic change takes place; then I introduced a step-by-step process of how it occurs. In this chapter, however, I shall go one step further and describe the role that informal institutions play during the process of paradigmatic change in a political or economic system, in order to apply it later to the case of Mexico.

The argument I shall put forward is that informal institutions, through sophisticated interaction with formal institutions, largely influence paradigmatic change in political systems. To explain this assertion, I will divide the sub-section in four parts. First, I shall briefly review the literature on change in policy network theory. Secondly, I shall attempt to prove the dialectical relation of influence between informal and formal structures of society, emphasizing the particularities of the relation during periods of change. Thirdly, I shall briefly analyze the role that informal institutions play during each of the five stages of paradigmatic change. Finally, I shall discuss the role that the dialectic interrelation between formal and informal institutions plays during the five stages of paradigmatic change.

4.3.1. A Brief Review of the Literature on Change in Policy Networks

Although many current accounts mention the impact of the process of policy network change on political stability, none that I am aware of relates this impact to the dialectical relation between formal and informal institutions.

Contemporary literature often analyzes policy network change *per se* rather than in relation to other structures. Numerous works dwell upon the issue of the sources of change, and look at exogenous (cf. Shaw, 1996; Smith, 1993:83; Marsh and Rhodes, 1992) and endogenous factors (Peters, 1999:123; Dowding, 1995; Knoke and Kuklinski, 1991). The debate revolves around which source is more influential in triggering change. Endogenous sources are seen as those generated within the network, whilst exogenous sources are considered those generated outside.

In similar fashion, research on the impact of policy networks on the social and political world tends to center on two debates: (i) that of agency versus structure; and (ii) that of the locus of policy network influence. In the first debate, supporters of agency-based models (cf. Wilks and Wright, 1987; Wright, 1988; Wilks, 1989) argue with supporters of structure-based models (Rhodes and Marsh, 1992[a], 1992[b]) whether policy networks produce changes in their members, or if it is members that produce changes in the networks. In the second debate, the discussion attempts to establish the extent to which policy networks influence changes in the operation of the state (cf. Rogers and Whetten, 1982; Hanf and Scharpf, 1978:346; Crozier and Friedberg, 1980; Gage and Mandell, 1990; Thompson *et al.*, 1991; Marsh and Rhodes, 1992[a]; Cavanagh, Marsh and Smith, 1995; Kickert, Klijn, and Koppenjan, 1997:xviii,6; Daugbjerg and Marsh, 1998:53). This second debate also discusses the specific areas where policy networks might influence the state (cf. Heclo, 1978; Katzenstein, 1978; Richardson and Jordan, 1979:74; Wicks and Wright, 1987; Rockman, 1989: 185; Smith, 1993; Jordan *et al.*, 1994; Dowding, 1994[b]; Marsh, 1998[a]:9).

Despite these particular orientations, many authors suggest specific situations of change that may be interpreted as illustrative of the dialectical relation between formal and informal structures: how internal divisions in social groups can affect state policy (Smith, 1993:83–97); or how unexpected events (like violent conflict) and new policy issues prompt the creation of new alliances between the state and private groups (Smith, 1993:88; Knoke *et al.*, 1996:8; Saward, 1990:595). We shall now turn to describe in more detail the features of this dialectical relationship during periods of paradigmatic change.

4.3.2. Paradigmatic Change and the Informal-Formal Relation

As we have seen, a necessary initial condition for paradigmatic change is the loss of legitimacy of institutional structures. This loss of legitimacy, in turn, often takes place when institutions do not adapt to new circumstances due to the failure of stabilizing change. So far, however, we only have a general understanding of this process, not an accurate description of how informal and formal institutions interact while it is taking place. It is this description that we shall develop in the rest of the section.

As mentioned, informal institutions emerge to compensate for the deficiencies of formal institutions, or to complement them in achieving their goals. This means that formal institutions influence the structure, membership, outcomes and persistence of informal structures. However, informal institutions also seem to have an important influence on the formal edifice that they compensate or complement. In other words, while changes in the formal structures of a society affect informal institutions in many ways, the internal changes of informal institutions also affect the organization, membership, and most importantly in terms of paradigmatic change: the persistence of formal structures.

That informal institutions, such as policy networks, can and do affect formal structures, such as organizations, is confirmed by influential authors. Marsh and Rhodes (1992[a]) explain how changes in the structure of policy networks might alter formal hierarchies. Similarly, Knoke and Kuklinski (1991) concede that changes in the membership of policy networks have important consequences for policy outcomes. It is precisely through changing outputs that informal institutions affect formal structures in different ways at different times (Marsh and Rhodes, 1992[a], 1992[b]).

During periods of paradigmatic change, when stabilizing change falters and the legitimacy of institutions is in question, the dialectical relation between the informal and the formal spheres has particular importance for the final result of the process. Indeed, if the legitimacy of the formal institution is threatened, the compensatory and complementary nature of informal institutions might help stabilize the formal structure. Equally, if the legitimacy of an informal structure is declining, certain changes in the formal institutions to which it is attached might reverse or slow the process. In either case, the dialectical relation between the formal and informal structures of society has important influence on policy outcomes, and consequently substantial effects on the political, economic, and social context, as well as on individual lives. It follows that the dialectical relationship between the formal and informal structures must have a leading role in causing but also in controlling dramatic (paradigmatic) social change.

As indicated before, it is unclear which of the two structures–formal or informal–dominates the dialectical relationship. Most likely, dominance is a function of the degree of formality/informality in particular societies or political systems. However, the important point is that the interrelation holds, and its relevance cannot be stressed enough when dealing with profound social change. In the sub-section that follows, we shall study the exact circumstances in which this dialectical relationship underpins stability or accelerates change.

4.3.3. Informal Institutions and the Five Steps of Paradigmatic Change

In the last chapter we introduced five steps that inform the process of paradigmatic change. Being conceptual, they were necessarily general. In this section, I shall attempt to establish in detail how informal institutions contribute to the development of these five stages. This is essential to completing our understanding of this type of structure.

The First Step of Paradigmatic Change. I have suggested that this stage of paradigmatic change is characterized by the failure of "stabilizing change." When this happens, some actors may act strategically to attack extant institutions and decrease their legitimacy. Informal institutions can particularly influence this initial failure of "stabilizing change" for at least two reasons. Firstly, they predominantly rest upon a mechanism both unwritten and fragile: trust. When trust in informal structures is lost, it will most likely induce the internal and external questioning of all the structures related to the informal institution under attack (including, of course, the formal). Secondly, other issues like ideological differences (Smith, 1993:92), or the perception of better options of advancement outside of the network (Gramsci, 1971:235), also contribute to the failure of stabilizing change in informal structures. Again, these failures seem importantly to affect related formal institutions.

The Second Step of Paradigmatic Change. The second step of paradigmatic change refers to the narration of contradictions. Groups that have been excluded, those that feel disadvantaged, and those who can profit from paradigmatic change, engage in campaigns further to undermine institutional legitimacy. This is particularly true if they believe that the political, economic, or social conjuncture will allow them to obtain positional or material benefits. Informal institutions contribute to this process because, as we have seen, they are usually the locus of these disadvantaged groups. Adequate attention to these networks of "losing groups" can either delay or accelerate paradigmatic change.

The Third Stage of Paradigmatic Change. This stage refers to the development of meta-narratives spread by the mass media. Informal institutions tend to be particularly attractive to meta-narration because, in the eyes of the public, they are secretive and enigmatic structures prone to corruption and favoritism. However, the loss of legitimacy through the meta-narration of informal institutions is not automatic. As mentioned in the last chapter, the meta-narration must "fit" the personal situation of the citizens. So, for example, if specific networks are perceived to be contributing to a booming economic situation, any attack against them will be minimized or considered eccentric. Conversely, economic deterioration may cause those same networks to come under scrutiny. As mentioned already, the probable response of the actors who want to maintain the *status quo* within the network will be charged with confusion. Rather than encourage more stabilizing change, they may wrongly believe that their duty is to discourage it. Ideology will also get in the way of adaptation, and might lead to the exclusion of members that favor change. Expulsion or voluntary disengagement may cause further loss of legitimacy of the institution (Azarya, 1988; Chazan, 1988; De Janvry *et al.*, 1995). This will open space for paradigmatic change to continue.

The Fourth Stage of Paradigmatic Change. This stage involves the search for new alternatives to the existing paradigm. As noted before, the groups that are able to offer viable solutions to the meta-narrated crisis will most probably appropriate the new institutions. Here, informal institutions are important at two levels. Firstly, if specific networks decide to support the process of change, the informality of the structure will most likely give them the flexibility to re-direct their objectives and restructure their actions at great speed. This will make those networks particularly likely to re-appropriating some of the new institutional design, should the paradigmatic change finally occur.

At a second level, informal structures play a capital role in building consensus around particular policy alternatives. The search for new paradigms often involves extensive consultation and mobilization of the most diverse social groups. Often, this mobilization can only be achieved through networking, because of the flexibility of informal institutions.

The Fifth Stage of Paradigmatic Change. This is the stage of institutional reconstruction. Not much will be said because we have already seen that, at this stage, informal institutions might be used either to accommodate the interests of "losing groups" or as viable options to achieve certain goals. At this point, the story starts all over again.

4.3.4. The Five Steps of Paradigmatic Change and the Informal-Formal Dialectic

The five steps of paradigmatic change are processes in which the dialectic relation between informal and formal institutions–even if not visible–plays an important role. This is because, at every stage of paradigmatic change, the informal-formal dialectical relation can either (a) retard or even reverse that change; or (b) cause and accelerate it. In the first case, either the informal or formal pillar of a system may "hold" the other while more fundamental modifications to solve the contradictions are implemented. In other words, the dialectical relation may have stabilizing influence.

However, in the second case (b), the illegitimacy of an institution can be accelerated if either the formal or informal "pillar"—whichever is complementary—loses legitimacy as well. In this case, the whole system collapses rapidly because there is nothing to hold it. These effects are particularly true of institutions that materialize through a combination of both formal and informal structures. However, the rule practically seems to apply in every case.

Naturally, describing the operation and influence of the informal-formal dialectic is essential to understanding the operation and change of institutions in countries with high levels of informality. In this type of political system, some sectors of the economy rely almost fully on public-private interaction through informal institutions. This applies specially to countries where wealth is concentrated in a few sectors and hands. In these cases, the economic and political elite are often the same individuals, who have common family and cultural backgrounds, and therefore negotiate through selective networks. Whenever new legislation is introduced in these political systems (as in the case of the legal changes often required by the IMF to countries under structural adjustment programs), consensus is often built through informal agreements with different social groups to face the period of adjustment. In the end, we come back to the same conclusion: informal and informal institutions seem to have a dialectical relation that can stabilize the system in which they operate. I shall attempt to show this through evidence that I present in the next chapter. In my view, the use of this stabilizing mechanism was a strategy often followed in Mexico, with particularly good short and medium-term results.

5. THE THREE C'S AND INFORMAL INSTITUTIONS: CORRUPTION, CORPORATISM, AND CLIENTELISM

Although various authors have identified the potentially developmental, socially beneficial, and economically efficient role of informal modes of organization (see Keefer and Shirley, 2000:88; as well as Chapter 2, Section 1), many others have considered them to be pernicious and undesirable. In the view of some, informal structures involve high degrees of "moral hazard" (Frances *et al.*, 1991:14), meaning that they lack the mechanisms to prevent unlawful behavior. Until recently, numerous informal structures, such as policy networks, stirred up thoughts of "non-transparent and impenetrable forms of interest representation [that] prevent policy innovations and threaten effectiveness, efficiency and democratic legitimacy" (Kickert, Klijn, and Koppenjan, 1997:xviii). These institutions were sometimes seen as closer to the Mafia than to the standards of modern organizations (Hay, 1998[b]:38). Intermittently denigrated, they are at times assessed as sources of policy failure and considered inferior structures, due to what is seen as their inherently secretive, disorganized and corrupt nature (Ronfeldt, 1993:33). In this last section of the chapter, I would like to challenge these negative views. To do so, I shall examine three phenomena closely linked to informality: corruption, corporatism, and clientelism. Through the analysis that follows I hope to prove that, although informal institutions are prone to certain forms of deviant behavior, they also can include mechanisms that can prevent such types of conduct. I shall attempt accurately to identify these mechanisms, for they are essential to understanding why some institutions elicit honest behavior from their members, while others openly allow improper conduct.

5.1. Corruption

Corruption has been defined in many different ways, and its meaning is still heatedly debated in academic circles (cf. Heidenheimer, 1970:3–9). For instance, Tevfik, Price and Charles (1986:108), see it as the "illegitimate use of public power for private benefit." Benson (1978:xiii) adds that such "unethical use of government activity" can also be used for "political benefit." For Brasz (1963:111–7), corruption simply means "the arbitrary use of power." Morris (1992:21) attempts to encompass all these views and affirms that corruption involves "a rational act on the part of a public official, that deviates from the approved ideological promotion of common interest." In other words, corruption for him arises when the behavior of a member of the state is not consistent with the rules set by that same state.

Corruption includes bribery or extortion. Bribery is defined as a dyadic situation in which citizens elicit a certain response from the civil servant through a positive incentive such as money. Extortion, on the other hand, is when a public official manipulates the decisions of a citizen through the use of negative sanctions such as threats (Morris, 1992:25; cf. Rose-Ackerman, 1978). Without attempting to solve this debate, some common elements in the above accounts would lead us minimally to define corruption for the sake of this work as *improper behavior that is used for private benefit in economic or political terms.*

Linking this definition to the study informal institutions, one may realize that whilst some informal institutions foster this type of behavior others do not. For example, both the drug cartels and the freemasonry are institutionalized informal social groups, whose operation, goals, and levels of corruption differ enormously. In consequence, when relating corruption to informality, one must distinguish at least three types of corrupt informal institutions. Firstly, those in which corruption is common and goes unpunished. Secondly, those in which corruption is occasional but is punished. Finally, those in which corruption is an actual objective of the informal institution. Examples of the three types abound. Both the first and second types of corrupt informal institution are customary in some governmental circles (see Rose-Ackerman, 1999). Meanwhile, the Mafia would be a good example of the third type of informal institution (see Gambetta, 1993). For purposes of this study, however, we shall overlook this third type of corruption, which is beyond the focus of this work. Instead, we shall concentrate on the first two types of corrupt informal institution.

The distinction just introduced between common and occasional corruption is essential because it can help us understand that corruption can be controlled. All institutions, formal or informal, appear to be potentially open to corruption, but it is more common in informal structures because their founding agreements are not formally codified and may be imprecise or insufficient. The structural looseness of informal institutions is therefore particularly inviting to corruption, but corruption will only happen if rules or norms against corruption are nonexistent or ambiguous. The high degrees of trust often present in informal structures are not an automatic deterrent against corruption, since trust simply elicits compliance with a given institution, not honesty. The trustworthy and institutionally compliant may well engage in corruption, when honesty is not explicitly enforced. I argue instead that *punishment* may deter corruption.

Indeed, the threat and enforcement of punishment appear to play the central role in the control of the corruption levels of institutions (Ali, 2000:9). In the case of many individuals and societies, strong personal values or convictions might be enough to stop them from engaging in corruption. However, such situation is at best unpredictable. For this reason, the threat of punishment for corruption must be present in informal structures and must follow Mediated Rationality principles. Such threat must target the regulative, normative, and cognitive levels of human consciousness to be fully effective, that is to say that punishment must potentially come from (a) third parties, (b) guilt for the violation of convictions, and (c) guilt for the violation of values, roles, or beliefs. Many informal institutions either do not establish punishment for misbehavior, or do so at only one level of human consciousness, thus opening room for corruption. For example, the violation of religious precepts is less common in theocratic societies than in secular states because moral punishment is often complemented with legal action. Following these principles, an effective strategy of punishment against cases of corruption in informal institutions would have to be based on three conditions: (a) the introduction of a clear definition of "corruption" in the basic agreements of the informal institution; (b) the establishment of unambiguous punishment for corruption, at all levels of human consciousness; and (c) the punctual enforcement of such penalties. Additionally, the modification of certain routines and related institutions might also be necessary to eliminate practices that are already corrupt, or that could encourage corruption in the future (Ali, 2000:5).

Going back to the concept of trust, if losing the trust of one's peers is clearly established as the punishment for corrupt behavior, that warning might be enough to prevent instances of corruption. This is so because, re-calling earlier sections, trust is a mechanism that influences all levels of human consciousness at once. We must note, however, that in this example the loss of trust was explicitly presented as the expected punishment, and not only as a possibility. In addition, any breach of trust would have to be detected, and punishment would have to be duly enforced. Finally, in order to close the dissuasive circle, any procedures that might lead to breaches of trust would have to be changed. The loss of trust is probably one of the most feared punishments for participants in informal structures. Nevertheless, some might not find the threat sufficient, so additional threats including out-right exclusion, economic sanction, legal prosecution, or public exposure might serve as reinforcing instances of dissuasion.

In summary, although informal institutions appear to be structurally open to corruption, their flexibility also allows them to introduce anti-corruption mechanisms with relative ease. These mechanisms, however, must be complex enough to address every aspect of human consciousness. They may also be introduced in conjunction with modifications in some rou-tines within the institution, and even in conjunction with changes in related institutions that might influence the likelihood of corruption. This set of tasks is naturally difficult to implement, but such difficulty explains pre-cisely why the eradication of corruption is often a complex and colossal en-deavor.

5.2. Corporatism

When we talk about corporatism in this book, we refer to the conceptualiza-tion of State Corporatism developed in the Southern European and Latin American contexts. Under this traditional connotation, corporatism may be understood as a theory of unequal dependency between social actors with un-even power, one of them being the state. For Smith (1993:1), corporatism emerges because the complexity of society coincides with the concentration of state power. As a result, as Crouch and Dore (1990:3) describe, "groups receive certain institutionalized or *ad hoc* benefits in return for guarantees by the groups' representatives that their members will behave in certain ways." In other words, corporatism implies selective and conditioned incorporation. In this sense, it appears that the obvious prerequisite for corporatism is a state powerful enough to be in a position: (i) to choose the group it wishes to incorporate amongst various competing options; and (ii) to change its choice if such group stops to or fails to meet the promised standard of behavior.

Evidently, corporatism has advantages for the state, but apparently also for incorporated groups. While their influence lasts, they often enjoy a monopoly of access in their area of interest (Schmitter, 1974:85–6). In other words, corporatism enables the "chosen" groups to gain a regulatory and representative position that they would not otherwise have (Smith, 1993:31; see also Rokkan, 1966; Olsen, 1983).

Corporatism between government agencies and economic actors (either business or trade unions) is seen as the most common form of this phenomenon (cf. Harris, 1972; Panitch, 1977; Middlemas, 1979; Schmitter, 1979; Vogler, 1985; Jessop, 1990). Economic groups are integrated into the state machinery through various channels and at every level (Cawson, 1986; Cawson *et al.*, 1990; Grant *et al.*, 1988). In fact, for some authors, corporatism blurs the state-society divide "due to highly complex patterns of mutual penetration" (Block, 1987:21; Streeck, 1983:265–6), and evolving interactions that "continuously redefine the meaning of the public and private spheres" (Knoke *et al.*, 1996:6; Hall, 1984:21; Mann, 1986:1; Dunleavy, 1982:205). Thus, corporatism could be summarized as a complex system of representation through integration that, nevertheless, maintains an unequal power relation between the "incorporator" (the state) and the "incorporated" (the social groups).

Naturally, corporatism makes extensive use of informal structures, since most of its underlying agreements require operational flexibility. In consequence, the choice of informality as a means to corporatism might be a straightforward decision of the participants, simply because it is an efficient form of organization to reach their objectives. It could also be the only option available, particularly if we consider that formal corporatist arrangements are politically discouraged and even legally prohibited in many political systems. Whichever the case, informality in the end seems to be the most suitable system in which to achieve corporatist goals. The key question for our purposes then becomes: can informal institutions include mechanisms to discourage the development of corporatism?

My answer is yes. As in the case of corruption, informal institutions tend to be the vehicles of corporatist arrangements. However, they can also serve other functions as well, without engaging in corporatist processes at all. This dissuasive capacity seems to depend directly on the inbuilt agreements that the specific institution may have to punish corporatism. Most corporatist agreements tend to develop through informal institutions, but that does not mean that all informal institutions have to allow corporatism. In fact, corporatist arrangements can be prevented, if informal institutions operate under agreements that thwart the phenomenon at the normative, regulative and cognitive levels. Once again, the threats of exclusion, legal action, or political shunning are all examples of specific mechanisms that can be simultaneously invoked to discourage corporatism.

5.3. Clientelism

In the view of Lemarchand (1981:15), clientelism is a system by which individuals with higher power and status–called patrons–, co-opt individuals with a lower level of either of these attributes–called clients–, to offer them some of their resources in exchange for subordination and loyalty. Clientelism differs from corporatism in two respects: (i) the powerful patron may not be the state; and (ii) the client may not have a monopoly of access to the patron. This is a relationship of pure mutual convenience and, although patrons often favor the same clients, the exchange has in principle no long-term implications like corporatism.

Even if not tied to the state, governments and political parties have often used the system. Material resources such as money, houses or jobs are exchanged for electoral backing or professed support for certain policies (cf. Flynn, 1974; Eisenstadt and Roniger, 1981; Kaufman Purcell, 1981). The system is often used by local bosses in many countries, to keep hold of their regions behind a façade of legitimacy (Kaufman Purcell, 1981:192)

It is explicitly accepted that, since clientelism does not necessarily involve repeated interaction between the parties, subordination through clientelism entails low mutual trust, lack of concern for reputation, loose agreements, and sometimes the violation of law (Whitley, 1998:23; Lemarchand, 1981:20–9). In consequence, like corruption and corporatism, clientelism also makes intense use of informal channels. Also as in those cases, *ad hoc* informal institutions are often created to serve clientelistic purposes, and not the other way around. This is to say that, if a given informal institution contains elements or agreements that explicitly punish clientelism, the likelihood of the problem occurring is lower. But, clearly, the converse is also true. This is why I must stress that deviant behavior in informal institutions is often a structural matter, rather than only a problem of randomly deviant agents.

5.4. The Three C's and Informal Institutions

As we have briefly seen, although it is true that informality is a condition for improper relations, it is by no means the only condition, and thus those types of behavior are not inevitable. The threat and enforcement of punishment can–and often does–prevent such devious conduct. Punishment is necessary because the agreements that structure informal institutions do not deter unacceptable behavior automatically.

In summary, there is no basis for the claim that informal institutions are intrinsically fraudulent, obscure, and inefficient. Neither can informal institutions be said inherently to promote breaches in codes of conduct, unless expressly designed to do so. Rather, it seems that when informal institutions allow the emergence of deviant behavior, it is because they fail to punish corruption, corporatism, and clientelism adequately. When properly designed, informal institutions are positive structures that lubricate political and economic life (Frances *et al.*, 1991:16), and actually remain the underlying basis of institutional stability in many countries where Western formalizing traditions are still uncommon (Ronfeldt, 1993:30–3).

6. CONCLUSIONS TO THE THEORETICAL PART

It was said in our introduction that the broad objective of this theoretical part of the book would be to link neo-institutionalist theory to policy network theory, in order to accomplish two more specific goals: (a) to create a framework within which to study institutionalized informality in the Mexican economy during the 20th century; and (b) to confirm the degree to which informal institutions promote political stability. I believe that the general and the two specific objectives have been achieved.

Firstly, analysis of neo-institutionalist and policy network theories confirmed that policy networks can be regarded as institutions of informal nature, that influence behavior with a degree of efficacy equal to that of formal institutions. This in turn allowed us to examine the dialectic interrelation between informal and formal institutions, thus offering a deeper insight into the effect of informal structures on social life.

The connection of these two bodies of theory also allowed us to clarify numerous concepts that pervade current literature in both camps, making it easier to understand the micro and macro-processes at work in the operation of institutions. The concept of Mediated Rationality, as a device to explain individual behavior under institutional influence, was also developed. This concept is offered as a small contribution towards future research, and in no way an exhaustive or inflexible position on the issues of individual behavior and preference formation, which are too broad and complex to be treated in this work.

A theory of institutional change also has been advanced. It is usually taken for granted that an institution that works adequately will continue doing so indefinitely if change is prevented. This is a myopic view. Factors both internal and external to the institution change continuously, so the structure has to adapt if it is to continue functioning. This constant change was conceived as a never-ending circle of adaptation. In this context, two different processes of change were described: (i) stabilizing change, which may legitimately be seen as an adaptive type; and (ii) paradigmatic change, which is best described as a process of dramatic ideological and structural adjustment. The words of Giuseppe Tomasi di Lampedusa in "The Leopard" seem to have been confirmed: "If we want everything to remain as it is, it will be necessary for everything to change."

Finally, the section also made clear that informal institutions–contrary to popular belief–do not inherently allow unethical behavior. Although they do provide a potential locus for unacceptable behavior, they are also receptive to mechanisms that can help prevent it, such as the threat and enforcement of punishment. The difference between a developmental and a pathological informal structure can be strongly attributed to differences in their structural design.

In terms of the first specific objective of this theoretical part, which was the creation of a framework within which to study institutionalized informality in the Mexican economy during the 20th century, I believe the concepts advanced throughout the previous two chapters are comprehensive enough to explain the processes that I shall introduce in the next part.

Concerning the second specific objective, this theoretical section has initially confirmed that informal institutions may be sources of political and economic stability. At the individual level, informal institutions provide certainty in exchange and relations and thus promote a feeling of overall stability. At the societal level, this type of institution also provides stability, because it operates in conjunction with formal structures, and influences their persistence. As we saw, this dialectical relation can support the political system of a country as a whole in periods of dramatic change, thus reversing or retarding processes of institutional breakdown. This positive connection between informal institutions and stability shall further be confirmed and expanded by the case study that I introduce in the following part.

Finally, given the enormous influence of informality in political life, I believe that the study of informal institutions should move towards fostering a stronger predictive power. There is already a substantial literature (cf. Galaskiewicz and Wasserman, 1993; Wasserman and Faust, 1994) attempting to measure numerically the degree of openness, centrality, and the patterns of interaction amongst groups that operate in informal networks. These predominantly mathematical analyses must now be incorporated into and adapted to the political and economic discussion of informality (Peters, 1998:25). Understanding the way in which informal institutions work and react is central to present and future policy-making. In fact, as Keefer and Shirley (2000:88) indicate, both theory and recent comparative studies suggest that institutional development ought to be at the core of development policy. Unfortunately, neither academic literature nor development practitioners have been able to devise concrete guidelines on how nations can achieve an environment of security and predictability. I hold that this can only be done through the measurement of the formal and informal structures that create and maintain trust, co-operation, certainty, and stability. To support this type of approach, the analysis of informal forms of organization must be accepted as fully legitimate, and must move from the purely analytical sphere to more prescriptive approaches that can indicate the best ways to combine informal forms of organization with formal structures, so overwhelmingly favored today. I hope that this theoretical part serves as a small contribution towards crystallizing these goals.

Part Two
Informal Policymaking Institutions in Mexico, 1936–1984

"How will you people sustain yourselves, Mister Under-Secretary?

Yes . . . that's the only way: declare the strike nonexistent . . . destroy them through one clean blow and jail their leaders. It will be as if it hadn't happened. . . . Yes, certainly. And something else, to speak plainly: if you gentlemen appear weak, my associates and I will of course have to remove our capital from Mexico. We need some guarantees. Listen, what would happen, for example, if two hundred million dollars were to leave the country in the space of two weeks? Eh?"

Carlos Fuentes, Mexican Novelist in *The Death of Artemio Cruz*
(1964).

"Twenty good years, years of confidence, social peace, class collaboration; twenty years of progress after Lázaro Cárdenas' demagoguery; twenty years of protection for the company's interests; twenty years of submissive union leaders and broken strikes."

Carlos Fuentes, Mexican Novelist in *The Death of Artemio Cruz*
(1964).

Part Two

Introduction to the Empirical Part

From the early 1940s to the late 1970s, Mexico enjoyed conditions that encouraged political stability and promoted high levels of economic growth through private investment. Recurrent economic crises in the 1970–1982 period abruptly tipped stability, halted economic expansion, and triggered the 1982 global debt crisis.

Various theories in Economics and Politics were put forward to explain this process of deterioration. However, it is noteworthy that the drastic drop in economic performance coincided with the breakdown of a structure that receives frequent positive mention, yet little analysis in current literature. The structure is a complex system of policy networks that linked the Mexican government and the private sector during the period of industrialization. These informal institutions appear to have played a prominent role in the developmental strategy of the Mexican State, constituting a parallel structure of negotiation and exchange. Unfortunately, no single academic work that I am aware of analyzes this system fully. Its origins, operation, and effect remain unclear.

I have called this system of policy networks the "Informal Consultation and Exchange System" (ICES). In line with the stated hypothesis of this book, the objective of this empirical part is to evaluate the influence of informal institutions grouped in the ICES on economic stability in Mexico. The section will use the theoretical framework developed in the last section and will be divided into three chapters. The first will identify and describe the participants in the ICES as well as the processes of emergence and persistence of the system. The period covered by this first chapter is 1936 to 1970, which coincides with the rise and climax of the process of industrialization of the Mexican economy. The second chapter will analyze the period of paradigmatic change in the Mexican economy that extended from 1970 to 1984. This process of change is highlighted in a separate chapter not only because of its breadth, but also because of its direct relevance to testing the model of institutional change introduced in the last section. Although both chapters are supported in the existing literature on the topic, the approach is entirely fresh, since it is has been developed around the ICES. Moreover, numerous interpretations were extracted from original archival documents (some never consulted before), and from interviews that I conducted with key participants in the ICES, including three former Presidents of Mexico (for more on the general method of the book see appendices 1, 2 and 3).

The third and final chapter analyzes the structure of the ICES and connections between its participants. This chapter is mostly constructed from original research. It includes a good deal of previously unpublished information, extracted and re-constructed from both archival records and personal interviews. To my knowledge, this is also the first time the ICES has been graphed and dissected in detail.

An important caveat is necessary at this point. This is not a book on Mexican economic policy or its technicalities. It is not a study of specific social or political events either. The work aims exclusively at theoretical and empirical analysis of the Mexican ICES. Consequently, other events will be examined in relation to the ICES only. Episodes such as the 1968 student movement, the nationalization of banks, or Mexican foreign debt cannot be an object of study in this work. Each of these issues has been, needs to be, and certainly will continue to be sole objects of study in other works.

Chapter Three
The Historical Development
of the ICES

INTRODUCTION

The objective of this chapter is to analyze the basic characteristics of the Informal Consultation and Exchange System (ICES), along with the processes of emergence and persistence of the structure. This will help us understand a good deal about the effect of the system on general economic stability. The chapter starts with a definition of the ICES. In a second section, the ICES is presented as a system of informal institutions that was pervasive in the Mexican political system. Thirdly, I describe participation in the ICES. Finally, I develop an historical account of the institutional features of the ICES from 1936 to 1970.

1. THE INFORMAL CONSULTATION AND EXCHANGE SYSTEM (ICES) IN MEXICO

1.1. What is the ICES?

The ICES was a collection of informal institutions. As established in our theoretical framework, institutions may be formal or informal. The first type materializes through organizations; and in the case of business-state relations, the second type materializes through policy networks. The ICES was a system constituted by at least seven policy networks that operated in the economic policy areas of Mexican government roughly from 1936 to 1984.

The system seems to have had two chief goals: (i) to maintain economic stability; and (ii) to promote industrialization. The prominence of the ICES stems from these two goals being also the main objectives of the

Mexican State after 1934 (Erfani, 1995:59–90; cf. Scott, 1959; Looney, 1978: 9–26; Story, 1986:33–109).

The seven individual policy networks operated mainly around six secretariats and also around the President, but constantly intersected in sophisticated ways to form the ICES. Following the notion of "circles of power," advanced in the last chapter, the system had its core in the President of the Republic: participants closer to the President had more access to direct negotiation and therefore more influence on the decisions in specific areas (Luna Ledesma, 1992:26, 1992ª:28).

The ICES linked the government and the private sector during years of high economic growth and fantastic political stability, operating in conjunction with the formal institutions of the country, in a dialectical relation similar to that described in our theoretical section. All these relations and mechanisms will be further clarified in the following two chapters.

1.2. The ICES and the Mexican Political System

Before analyzing the structure of the ICES, it is necessary to document its pervasiveness in Mexican economic policy areas. Following our theoretical account of informal institutions, I shall attempt to show (a) that an integrated system of policy networks linking the public and private sectors existed in Mexico; (b) that these policy networks influenced behavior through various regulative, normative, and cognitive mechanisms; and (c) that they structured relations and created certainty.

The existence of extensive public-private informal relations in post-1936 Mexico is well documented in established literature. I have confirmed their existence through archival documents and through interviews conducted with prominent politicians and business people. From this information, I corroborated that businessmen and the members of various state agencies indeed maintained extensive relations consolidated into a highly informal system.

Bailey (1986:127) notes how "the most significant contact and negotiation [between government and business in Mexico] was carried on discreetly." Vernon (1964:153–4) goes farther, affirming that "extensive ties between public officials and private interests are part and parcel of Mexican life. . . . Most . . . government policy goes on *sub rosa*, beyond the ken of newspapers and the public." Stevens (1977:235) talks about an "intimate interrelation" of business and government. Vellinga (1989:78) confirms that business participated "directly, and at the highest level, in the decision-making process, without having official representation in the government." Puga (1993:53) talks about "alternative ways of participation that neither impl[ied] the inclusion [of businessmen] in the official party nor their personal presence in government positions." Córdova (1984:40, 55) saw business organizations as "elite sectors" that operated only "at the summit, in a relationship with the state that is exclusive, quasi-secret, in the office."

These relations also constituted a system, a sophisticated collection of policy networks (each created around a specific secretariat or directly around the President) that later intersected around a core, represented by the President himself. The archives of literally every government administration in the 1936–1984 period show this pattern. Conflicts and requests were discussed by businessmen and the Secretaries of State first. They were then taken to the President of the Republic, who acted as a final arbiter (cf. LCR 521.4/2; LCR 545.22/133; MAC 545.22/188; MAC 523/5; MAV 111/3826; MAV 565.4/848; ARC 433/153; ARC 111/3612; ALM 521.8/675; ALM 111/3357; LEA 30/01/74; LEA 28/05/73; López Portillo, 1988:1051; López Portillo, 1988:1163; MMH 10.01.00.00 C2 E4; DGCSPR, 1983).

As noted in claim (b) above, this informal system of policy networks strongly seems to have influenced the behavior of participants through the presence of unwritten regulative and normative mechanisms such as membership agreements and norms of negotiation, as well as through cognitive mechanisms such as pro-industrialization values. As suggested in our theoretical section, these mechanisms were in turn synthesized in the high levels of trust that regulated and at the same time enabled the operation of the system. Specific commitments within the ICES that relied heavily on trust are well documented. For instance, Cisneros (1986:124–5) talks about a "political pact" that rested upon "an implicit commitment" of business to channel their interests through the Executive, and limit their open political participation (see also Garrido and Puga, 1992:132). In exchange, the government would "avoid non-consulted radical change, maintain the general stability of the economy and assure acceptable rates of return on investment," as well as limit its participation in economic activities and supply hard currency to finance foreign capital goods (Quintana and Garrido, 1986:112). It is added that the negotiation and discussion of interests implied "a struggle, but always within the institutional spheres" (Cordova, 1984:55). Naturally, none of these agreements was established in writing, which only confirms the strong influence that trust had on the behavior participants.

Finally, this system of policy networks structured relations and created certainty, as affirmed in claim (c) above. A helpful account was given to me during an interview with Juan Sánchez Navarro, Vice-President of Modelo Brewery (maker of "Corona" beer) and one of the most influential businessmen in Mexico:

> Of course the relationship with the government determined private in-
> vestment! If you had the government against you, you could not do any-
> thing . . . With dignity and always defending our interests, but we still
> needed to maintain a constant dialogue with the different parts of the
> state to get things done" (JSN 21/06/01).

We could infer then that the system structured the channels to be followed
so that, in the end, actors could obtain certainty. The "dialogue" that
Sánchez Navarro narrates also speaks of an intensive exchange of different
resources. Often these resources were ephemeral: money, licenses, political
privileges and support; many others they were highly technical and of truly
national interest. I confirmed highly specialized policy consultation and exchange of statistical data in industrial and financial areas through archival
documents (cf. ABM 22/04/68; ABM 12/02/68; ABM 19/04/71; ABM
09/08/71; ABM 08/09/80; MAC 545.22/1335.5; MAV 708 1/5–8; JLP
Cj2028 E327).

In sum, all sources appear to confirm an informal system that regulated much in private-public relations in Mexico. The system was a collection of policy networks built around specific secretariats. Additionally, the
system was based on agreements that entailed high degrees of trust and mutual enforcement, while at the same time provided valuable channels for exchange of information and resources. I argue that this system is in fact what
I have already defined as the ICES, and that the evidence presented confirms
not only its existence but also its effect on decision-making.

1.3. The Participants of the ICES

To proceed with the analysis of the ICES, it is necessary to identify and describe its participants and introduce the groups and processes that make up
the Mexican political system. The section will be divided in two sub-
sections. Firstly, I shall introduce the public-sector participants; secondly,
the private-sector actors.

1.3.1. Public Sector Participants

The President of the Republic

Traditional accounts of the Mexican Presidency portray an office of near om-
nipotence (see Zaid, 1992; Cordera and Tello, 1981; Carpizo, 1998; Cosío
Villegas, 1974:25–7). These works place the President as the "supreme ar-
biter" of the political system (Leal, 1986[a]:190; Leal, 1986[b], 1986:30;
Vernon, 1964:13; Ramos, 1993:115; Scott, 1959:116; Puga, 1993:57).
Others see him (because in Mexico it has always been a "him") as "the most

important single factor determining the outcome of any program" (Vernon, 1964:11), and even as the main source of stability (Garrido, 1989:417). Even authors who acknowledge limits to presidential power (see López-Portillo Romano, 1994:67; Córdova, 1984:55–61), attribute it to personal benevolence of the individual rather than to specific institutional constraints. Throughout this work, I shall argue against all these views by showing how the real autonomy of the Presidency declined as the economic power of Mexican businessmen increased.

However, even if holding progressively limited power, the President did act as the core of the ICES, if the system is organized in "circles of power." His position was that of coordinator of the system. Although an enormous power was indeed institutionalized through endless formal, informal and even illegal institutions (called by Garrido (1989:421) "constitutional," "-meta-constitutional," and "anti-constitutional" institutions), many authors fail to identify the operation of other institutions that instead of promoting, controlled presidential power. These structures–the ICES being one if tgen–were informal, and that is why their visibility was minimal. Nonetheless, their influence was not mean, particularly when they consolidated and matched the influence of centralized power. Only by acknowledging this widespread web of informal balances could we explain why, if the formal powers of the President appeared to be greater in the 1970s than in the 1930s, his real power and autonomy vis-à-vis private groups were so inferior, as was the case (Hamilton, 1982:283–5).

The process that caused this reduction in relative power will become clearer as the work progresses. However, I shall end this brief description of presidential power by reaffirming that the power of Mexican Presidents had definite limits. These limits would become evident in the 1970s.

The Core Secretariats of the ICES

Naturally, an essential part of the ICES were the different Secretariats of State. Each often represented one of the policy networks that made up the ICES. In practical terms, they were the direct connection between the President and specific areas of the private sector. The most important to the functioning of the ICES were six:

a) The Secretariat of the Presidency (SP). It coordinated the actions of all secretariats to achieve the administration's policy objectives; managed the enormous, unchecked and discretionary budget of the President; and organized his daily schedule. This meant that the Secretariat of the Presidency was at the center of the ICES: it controlled physical access to the President; "transmitted" presidential decisions to the secretariats; and sometimes (though not often, according to archival evidence) directly transferred economic resources to individuals, firms, or social groups.

b) The Secretariat of the Treasury and Public Credit (SHCP) was in charge of collecting tax revenue, as well as regulating financial activity. Its contact with the private sector was through taxing and its close relations with private banks.

c) The Secretariat of Programming and Budget (SPP) in 1977 absorbed the functions of the SP and some of SHCP. It planned expenditure and investment and coordinated policy. It also paid all government bills, so it had some power over firms that depended on government contracts for survival.

d) The Secretariat of Industry and Commerce (SIC) was in charge of promoting (often understood instead as "regulating and controlling") commerce and industry, as well as foreign trade. It set and enforced price controls; enforced payment of fees to chambers of commerce and industry; controlled the granting of import licenses; and played the role of a consumer protection board.

e) The Secretariat of National Patrimony (SEPAFIN) managed the numerous state-owned enterprises and natural resources of the country. Its role in the ICES was to supervise the enormous subsidies and sub-contracts that state enterprises granted to private firms. It also dealt with the distribution of oil, gas, and electricity, which was in the hands of the state.

f) The Secretariat of Labor and Social Provision (STYPS) was in charge of labor relations. It set minimum wages, working benefits, and arbitrated in potential strikes. It was a powerful secretariat in the eyes of businessmen. Although it often participated in the determination, formulation, and implementation of industrial policy, its interference in technical consultation was a function of the profile of incumbent Secretaries. For example, in the 1970s, Porfirio Muñoz Ledo was a labor Secretary often active in macro-economic policy design (PML, 22/05/02).

These secretariats had daily contact with widely differing parts of the private sector, so they had different political clienteles. This is why the ICES operated as a concentrating system, in which otherwise uncoordinated and isolated policies came together.

Other Secretariats

Other government secretariats also participated in the ICES but selectively and temporarily. They were incorporated when (a) the issues had a direct effect on their functions; or (b) when specific firms in their area of expertise were involved in a negotiation within the ICES. Once negotiation was over, they would again be removed from the ICES, simply by not including them in further meetings. The selectively-incorporated secretariats included:

a) The Secretariat of Communications and Transportation (SCT) constantly negotiated with private firms in the electronic media, construction and transportation. It was contacted too when transport or communication infrastructure was required.

b) The Secretariat of Public Works (SOP) managed relations with some construction firms.

c) The Secretariat of Agriculture and Hydraulic Resources (SARH) worked closely with agro-industrialists and construction firms that built rural infrastructure.

d) The Secretariat of Tourism (SECTUR). Given the size of the sector in Mexico, it related in many ways (financing, regulating, co-investing, developing infrastructure) with businessmen that had tourist firms of any type.

The Bank of Mexico (BM)

Founded in 1925, the Bank of Mexico is still today the central bank of the country. It is highly professionalized. Obviously, throughout its long history it has been in close contact with banks, stockbrokerage firms, credit unions, and other financial intermediaries such as insurance or factoring companies. Even if hierarchically subordinated to the Secretariat of the Treasury, its importance made it practically semi-independent. In fact, the Director was appointed by the President and not by the Secretary of the Treasury (King, 1990:10).

The Bank of Mexico was extremely important for at least two reasons to the operation of the ICES. Firstly, it was a daily point of contact between the government and the banking sector. As we shall see later, bankers were the most powerful faction in Mexican business. Existing literature and endless archival records confirm that this relationship was intense and based on exchange of highly technical data and negotiation of law (Concheiro, Gutiérrez and Fragosa, 1979:247; ABM 11/09/67; ABM 09/10/67; ABM 13/11/67; ABM 30/11/67; ABM 11/12/67; ABM 15/01/68; ABM 12/02/68; ABM 22/04/68; ABM 10/12/69; ABM 08/12/69; ABM 19/04/71; ABM 09/08/71; ABM 08/09/80). Secondly, the BM eventually became the ideological stronghold of monetarist-liberal thinkers in Mexico. Accordingly, the BM normally shared ideological views with the private sector, which gradually promoted mutually closer relations (Erfani, 1995:60).

Nafinsa

Founded on 24 April 1934, Nacional Financiera S.A. (Nafinsa), the National Financing Institution, was the main credit agency of the Mexican government. Like the BM, it was hierarchically subordinated to the Secretariat of the Treasury, but often received direct orders from the President, bypassing

the intermediation of the Treasury. That it had close and daily contact with industrialists gave it enormous influence in the planning and implementation of
industrial policy (Villa, 1976:3; Blair, 1964:193–9).

1.3.2. Private Sector Participants

The Mexican private sector is characterized by dramatic variations in firm
size, production activity, and cultural background of its members. In these
circumstances, it is not surprising to learn that it always has been divided in
ideological and operational terms (Guillén, 1985:155; Tirado, 1987: 483;
Rubio, 1990:257). This traditional disunion is probably nowhere more evident than in their organizations of representation.

Despite valuable efforts to classify private organizations in geographi-
cal (cf. Concheiro, Gutiérrez and Fragosa, 1979) and ideological terms
(Saldivar, 1991:54–6), the most accurate classification seems to be that
based on their relationship with the state. Here, private organizations are divided into two categories: (i) "semi-official" and (ii) independent. The former are created by the government whilst independent organizations have
private origins. Let us briefly describe these.

(i) Semi-official organizations

These are represented by the chambers of commerce and industry, equivalent both to the chambers of commerce and the trade associations in Europe.
Chambers are created for each specific industry, and then these chambers
join "confederations of chambers," which represent all the industries at the
national level.

The main feature of these chambers was their relative weakness vis-à-
vis the government due to two factors: (a) their dependent status; and (b)
their poor representation of their membership. These organizations grew
closely linked to the state (Becerril Straffon, 1986:10). Both the 1936 and
1941 Law of Chambers of Commerce and Industry gave the federal government monopoly of authorizing the creation or dissolution of any chamber.
The Law also provided that all chambers were obliged to include a representative of the Secretariat of Industry and Commerce on their governing
board. Although the representative had no vote, she had power of veto over
agreements that could "threaten public order" or "harm common good"
(Alcázar Ávila, 1970:12; Medin, 1990:85). In other words, these chambers
were tightly controlled (Shafer, 1973:132).

The poor representation offered to members had at least five sources:
(1) endless hierarchy of sector, locality, and region diluted effective representation (Hernández Rodríguez, 1992[b]:258); (2) membership was compulsory,

but chambers were seen as inefficient, so their members did not pay dues until forced to do so and did not participate in elections (Lamartine Yates, 1980:95; Hernández Rodríguez, 1992[b]:260); (3) delays in the payment of dues often constrained the activities of the chambers, further reinforcing their perceived inefficacy (JMBN, Coparmex, 1999:38); (4) the extreme diversity of membership (due to differing size and type of production) caused the confederations of chambers to have very loose objectives and conflicts of interest in their representation; and (5) often, the leaders of the confederations were elected on the basis of their proximity to the President of the country. This lack of democracy further weakened their credibility (Alcázar Ávila, 1970:98; Beltrán Mata, 1987:72–3; Basañez, 1981:101). It is to be expected that, as both Derossi (1971:40) and Story (1986:125) confirm, industrialists trusted direct individual action more than unsatisfactory representation of semi-official chambers. Another option was to join independent organizations.

(ii) Independent Organizations

These were the stronger representative groups of the private sector. Through voluntary and direct affiliation, they were encouraged to offer better representation. These organizations were frequently consolidated from their inception around common objectives and interests (Hernández Rodríguez, 1992[b]:258–9). Additionally, they offered useful services to their members. It seems that their distance from the state gave them greater legitimacy and, therefore, more political weight (Concheiro, Gutiérrez and Fragosa, 1979:269–71; Puga, 1982:189). An additional factor in their stronger position might have been the ample resources of their founding members. Independent associations were normally created by powerful business groups (such as bankers and big industrialists) effectively to defend their interests, after realizing the deficiencies of semi-official groups.

I shall now introduce each of the individual organizations, both semi-official and independent that in my opinion played a prominent role in the ICES.

Semi-Official Business Organizations
a) CONCANACO

The National Confederation of Chambers of Commerce (CONCANACO) was founded on 3 November 1917 (Arriola Woog, 1988[a]:49). Its foundation was influenced by conservative groups of the northern city of Monterrey (Story, 1986:129). Despite its high number of affiliates (in 1979 claimed some 400,000), CONCANACO gradually lost importance and legitimacy.

This seems to have been a consequence of its permanently ambiguous relations with the state. Numerous episodes throughout CONCANACO's history document frequent shifts in the confederation's position over innumerable public issues (see Bailey, 1986:128; Tirado, 1987: 484; Concheiro, Gutiérrez and Fragosa, 1979:310; cf. Sánchez Gamper, 1989:62, 75; Alcázar Ávila, 1970:59). This ideological variability seems to have stemmed from the heterogeneity of CONCANACO's membership: small business owners were in favor of government protection, while larger firms openly opposed it. Since 4% of the confederation's membership represents 80% of invested commercial capital in the country, the remaining 96% controls only 20%, and representatives of firms of all sizes and regions have held the presidency (Concheiro, Gutiérrez and Fragosa, 1979:306, 311–4), the organization is highly unpredictable in political terms.

b) CONCAMIN

The National Confederation of Chambers of Industry (CONCAMIN) was founded in September 1918 to defend the economic and political interests of the chambers of industry (Arriola Woog, 1988ª:49). By 1979 it had some 94,000 members (Bailey, 1986:128; Tirado, 1987: 484). Like CONCANACO, the heterogeneity of its membership explains the sometimes ambiguous stance of the Confederation on many issues.

The different tendencies within the CONCAMIN may be identified at different times in its history. On 7 April 1945, it signed a "Pact of National Unity" with the corporatist Mexican Labor Confederation (CTM) to ensure extensive collaboration (Arriola Woog, 1988ᵇ:248; Hernández Rodríguez, 1985:159; Krauze, 1997:55). Yet, in 1964, CONCAMIN presented the "Economic Charter," a document that strongly rejected government intervention in the economy and enshrined private property and free enterprise. The document eventually became the ideological manifesto of the whole of the Mexican private sector (Concheiro, Gutiérrez and Fragosa, 1979:291). Despite these contradictions, CONCAMIN has proven more coherent that CONCANACO. Since industry often required more government protection than commerce, even large firms favored some degree of intervention, making ideological shifts less common. Accordingly, economic policy frequently favored CONCAMIN over CONCANACO, also on grounds (in my view erroneous) that industry was more important than commerce.

c) CANACINTRA

On 5 December 1941, the government authorized the creation of the National Chamber of Transformation Industries (CANACINTRA). The chamber grouped the newer, small and medium-sized firms that developed during the war years, known as the "New Group" (Medin, 1990:86; Arriola Woog, 1988ª:57). This was as much a political move (to create a counterweight to more conservative industrial interests) as it was an act of recognition of a new breed of Mexican businessmen that had new needs and expectations (Concheiro, Gutiérrez and Fragosa, 1979:298–300; Handelman, 1997:102).

CANACINTRA was born as–and continues to be–a part of CONCAMIN (Puga, 1993:77). However, CANACINTRA is by far the most important chamber member of CONCAMIN. In fact, it has *de facto* autonomy due to its membership (around 82,000 firms in the early 1990s) and political stance. CANACINTRA has often opposed CONCAMIN itself (Story, 1986:153–6; Puga, 1993:78). While CANACINTRA defended a strongly "nationalist ideology" based on state-led development (Puga, 1993:143), CONCAMIN favored a more modest degree of state intervention (Alcázar Ávila, 1970:59). For instance, when electricity was nationalized in the 1960s, amidst ferocious complaints from most private groups, the Vice-President of CANACINTRA declared: "we have been waiting 15 years for this day" (Alcázar Ávila, 1970:85). CANACINTRA's support was often rewarded by the government through subsidies and protection (Concheiro, Gutiérrez and Fragosa, 1979:301–4). Since the 1970s, when CANACINTRA considered that government interference had become excessive, its ideology has grown increasingly ambiguous: confrontational at times and favorable to the government at others (Concheiro, Gutiérrez and Fragosa, 1979:294–5, 339; Story, 1986:124).

Independent Business Organizations

a) ABM

The Mexican Bankers' Association (ABM) was constituted on 12 November 1928 (ABM 12/11/28). It grouped all the private banks of the country (Arriola Woog, 1988ª:59). Its members were only differentiated by their size, because their structure and interests were normally the same (Concheiro, Gutiérrez and Fragosa, 1979:247). This gave the association enormous ideological and political homogeneity.

Traditionally, The ABM was the most influential of private organizations, and it remained highly independent of the political bureaucracy. Their close relations stemmed from mutual interest: while the sector was highly regulated, the government also depended heavily on private funds to finance its projects (FitzGerald, 1978, quoted in Erfani, 1995:97; Concheiro,

Gutiérrez and Fragosa, 1979:243). Despite the ABM's not being an official consultation partner of the government, it fulfilled that role more than any other (Shafer, 1973:133; Concheiro, Gutiérrez and Fragosa, 1979:247; Arriola Woog, 1988ª:59). At various points, the ABM even played a mediating role between the government and the rest of the private sector (Camp, 1990:63). As numerous archival records indicate, consultation between the ABM and the government was intensive and based on exchange of highly technical data and opinions about future policy (ABM 11/09/67; ABM 09/10/67; ABM 13/11/67; ABM 30/11/67; ABM 11/12/67; ABM 15/01/68; ABM 12/02/68; ABM 22/04/68; ABM 10/12/69; ABM 08/12/69; ABM 19/04/71; ABM 09/08/71; ABM 08/09/80). Consultation took place particularly through the National Banking Commission, the National Stock market Commission, the Bank of Mexico, and the Secretariat of the Treasury (Concheiro, Gutiérrez and Fragosa, 1979:247). Some powerful bankers however bypassed the ABM and negotiated their specific concerns directly with the President or the Secretaries of State (Vernon, 1964:19).

The influence of the ABM on economic policy-making cannot be understated. Perhaps the most concise proof of its power was offered by David Ibarra, former Secretary of State for Finance and Public Credit, during an interview I had with him: "Only the bankers existed in the negotiations . . . the other groups were secondary . . . only the bankers existed because then you were talking to the owners of capital . . . the rest of the business representatives were 'business politicians,' employees of those owners . . ." (DIM, 04/05/01).

b) AMIS

The Mexican Association of Insurance Institutions (AMIS) was established in 1935 (http://www.amis.com6.mx/amis.nsf?OpenDatabase), to defend the interests of insurance companies. Since the banks owned many of these firms directly and indirectly, the Association normally followed the powerful ABM in its political decisions. Its interaction with the government derived from its being one important part of the financial system, rather than from its capacity to exert real pressure.

c) CMHN

The Mexican Businessmen Council (CMHN) was formed in 1962, largely in response to Mexican support of the Cuban Revolution, the nationalization of electricity, the Mexicanization of mining, and the limitations on foreign investment (Camp, 1990:167). The CMHN is little or hardly known: it is legally autonomous, does not have a president and is formed by the 30 (or so—numbers change constantly) wealthiest firm owners of the country (Story, 1990:71), but also by some leading managers.

The CMHN seems to have awesome behind-the-scenes influence on decisions that affect the interests of its mighty members. The level of contact with government officials unambiguously suggests that (Vernon, 1964:20; Lamartine Yates, 1980:95; Camp, 1990:168). I have confirmed the ready access to the President that these businessmen enjoyed. In an interview with Miguel De la Madrid Hurtado, President of Mexico from 1982 to 1986, he confirmed: "[Big businessmen] occasionally called me. I would see them in groups. But they also had the freedom to ask me for meetings, to tell me their worries, to listen to my opinions . . . and yes, I would meet them" (MMH 24/07/01).

The CMHN is without question the most elitist and unrepresentative of the major organizations. Additionally, unlike the ABM, it often lacks unity in its decisions because membership is homogeneous in terms of wealth, but heterogeneous in specific demands to the government. Nevertheless, it keeps a constant influence probably based on the individual power of its members.

d) Coparmex

The Employers' Confederation of the Mexican Republic (Coparmex), was founded in 1929 by Luis G. Sada and other Monterrey businessmen. It was constituted as an employers' syndicate (Hamilton, 1978:12; Arriola Woog, 1988[a]:39) to protest against the then recently approved labor laws that, in their view, had been timidly opposed by other private organizations (Camp, 1990:163). Conceived as a trade union of employers, it was exempted from the Law of Chambers of Commerce and Industry (Beltrán Mata, 1987:69), so it grew relatively independent of the government.

Coparmex is an exceptional private-sector union that tries to influence general opinion through its high profile (Concheiro, Gutiérrez and Fragosa, 1979:122). Highly militant, for many years it scared off many potential members (Camp, 1990:163–4), particularly those prone to reliance on government favors. However, in the early 1970s, Coparmex's fierce defense of the private sector against excessive government intervention, made it more influential and attractive (Shafer, 1973:133). From 1970 to 1979, the number of affiliates of the confederation rose from 13,000 to 18,000 (Camp, 1990:163; Bailey, 1986:128; Tirado, 1987: 484). The salient feature of Coparmex should not then be its confrontational character but its ideological influence. The confederation has been called by many "the conscience of the private sector" (www.coparmexchiapas.org/porque.shtml). And indeed,

Coparmex's liberalist ideology identified and guided the Mexican private sector during the second half of the 20th century (Coparmex, 1979:35–34). The core idea was that free enterprise and private property were "natural, primary and unbreakable" rights (Alcázar Ávila, 1970:55).

e) CCE

The Business Coordinating Council (CCE) was officially created on 7 May 1975. It initially united six private organizations (CONCANACO, CONCAMIN, Coparmex, ABM, CMHN, AMIS, and the National Agricultural Council). CANACINTRA joined later because, as Carlos Gutiérrez–former President of CANACINTRA–told me during an interview: "At the time of the CCE creation, CANACINTRA was seen as too close to President Echeverría" (CG, 08/06/01). After the nationalization of the banking system in 1982, the ABM was replaced by the Mexican Association of Stockbrokerage Houses (AMCB). In practical terms, the AMCB served the same purposes as the ABM and, in fact, was formed in most cases by the same people.

The CCE was an attempt to establish a political front that, with its 900 thousand members, could help stop the reformism of the Echeverría government (1970–76). A second objective was to influence the choice of the next presidential candidate (Luna and Tirado, 1992:33). A third objective was to steer the economic policy of the country towards the ideological doctrine defended by the private sector. For some, however, the creation of the CCE meant the official entrance of the private sector into open political participation (Concheiro, Gutiérrez and Fragosa, 1979:317–20): it meant the violation of one of the agreements of the ICES. This is illustrative of the difficulty in private-public relations during the mid-1970s.

The CCE had colossal problems of representation from the start. Firstly, all seven organizations have their own members, very different goals, and divergent views about the "right" policies. Secondly, while the CONCANACO and the CONCAMIN contribute 69% of the membership, their vote has the same weight as, for instance, the CMHN, that fields only 30 members. Thirdly, the CONCAMIN, CONCANACO, and CANACINTRA were formed through compulsory membership, whilst membership of the other organizations was voluntary. Finally, national organizations are privileged over local. As a consequence of these factors, behind a façade of strength, the organization lay on weak foundations and has become a political tool that often benefits larger businessmen, with the complicity of the semi-official chambers (Luna and Tirado, 1992:54, 83). In fact, as we shall see later, during the late 1970s and early 1980s, the CCE became an incubator of a new breed of aggressive politicians that favored business interests.

There were two other private groups that, in spite of their low profile, seem to have exercised an enormous ideological influence on the operation of the ICES. The first is the American Chamber of Commerce–Mexico and the second the Monterrey Group.

a) AMCHAM

The American Chamber of Commerce-Mexico (AMCHAM) was created in 1917 (Luna Ledesma, 1992ᵃ:25) as an initiative of a group of American businessmen who, with the help of their embassy, became organized to defend the private mining and oil interests that could be affected by the nationalist ideology of the Mexican Constitution approved that same year (Puga, 1993:81). The importance of the AMCHAM is clear for both obvious and subtle reasons: obvious, because its three thousand members produce 25% of Mexican Gross Domestic Product (GDP) (Story, 1986:127); subtle, because the AMCHAM has enormous ideological influence on Mexican businessmen, who look up to their American counterparts and are thus particularly receptive to their political views (Camp, 1990:118).

The full ideological strength of the AMCHAM was fully felt in the early 1970s. Through many publications, it explicitly invited its members to intensify the defense of private enterprise against the rise of "nationalism" and "statism" (Puga, 1982:195). It is now established as a matter of record that they actively planned many of the conflicts with the government during that period (cf. Green, 1981; Arriola Woog, 1988ᵃ:115; Erfani, 1995:113). However, the actions of the AMCHAM stopped there. They wanted firstly to avoid potentially violent governmental reactions against their interests. But most importantly, they knew well that their greatest effect was ideological, so they concentrated on cultivating that strength.

b) The Monterrey Group

The Monterrey Group is not an officially constituted organization. Nor is it a formalized alliance, but a vast network of economic interests connected through ideological, family, and marriage links in the northern city of Monterrey, Mexico (Vellinga, 1989:110). It consists of about 200 families who through their businesses generate about 25% of Mexico's industrial output (Handelman, 1997:101). The core of the group is the Cuauhtémoc Brewery (maker of "Sol" beer amongst others) and its related firms.

Monterrey, 150 kilometers from the border with the United States, is almost a different country. The city grew through a self-generated process of capitalist-industrial development, which makes it a notable exception in Mexico and certainly in most of Latin America (Vellinga, 1989:91). The existence of conglomerates in the most modern sectors of the economy, distinguish Monterrey from the rest of the nation (Derossi, 1971:56–7). English is widely understood and spoken and many of its businessmen are educated at U.S. universities (Derossi, 1971:51–5). Politically, Monterrey has particular influence in Coparmex and, to a lesser but important degree, in CONCANACO (Story, 1986:129). Unlike other business groups that have supported the one-party rule of the Revolutionary Institutional Party (PRI), Monterrey has traditionally supported the National Action Party (PAN), a right-wing party that in the year 2000 acceded to the presidency for the first time in its history (Handelman, 1997:101; Vellinga, 1989:124).

The Monterrey Group espouses a profoundly nationalistic ideology and rejects the indiscriminate allowance of Foreign Direct Investment (FDI) (Luna Ledesma, 1977:38). Although foreign partnerships are increasing, Monterrey industry is generally 100% Mexican (Vellinga, 1989:103). They also reject state intervention in the economy, so their activities have developed against the background of constant tension with the central government. This opposition to central control does not mean that the Monterrey Group firms did not benefit from government contracts and support. In fact, the two greatest moments of expansion of the Monterrey Group coincided with the heyday of public spending in the 1940s-50s and during the oil boom of the late 1970s-early 1980s (Cerutti, 2000:161; Nuncio, 1982:234–40). However, although Monterrey firms always took the privileges offered by the government (and they were many throughout the years) with a view to winning their support, they always rejected even the slightest transgression against private enterprise. This gave them an ideological authority that, as in the case of the AMCHAM, cannot be overstressed.

Other Business Organizations

As duly considered in our theoretical sections, the government would selectively incorporate into the ICES other private organizations whenever useful or necessary. This selective incorporation took place in two cases: (i) when topics close to their interests were discussed and they could offer valuable technical advice (Puga, 1982:201); or (ii) when policy implementation could benefit from the legitimacy of a specific group. These selectively incorporated organizations include: The Mexico-American Committee of Businessmen, created in 1951 (Luna Ledesma, 1992[a]:25); The Social Union of Businessmen (USEM), created in 1957 with a Catholic social doctrine (Luna Ledesma, 1992[a]:25; Buendía, 1986:15); the National Association of Importers and Exporters of the Mexican Republic (ANIERM) (Puga, 1982:201); and the Coordinating Committee for the International Affairs of the Private Sector (CCAIIP, later CEMAI), created in the 1950s (Shafer, 1973:154, 188).

2. ANALYZING THE LIFE CYCLE OF THE ICES

After the parenthesis of the previous section, we are now able to resume the original course of our argument. In the next two sections I shall introduce the processes of emergence and persistence of the ICES. These sections will be useful to start testing the theoretical framework developed in the first part of the book. Moreover, they will also serve as a step in examining the precise influence of institutionalized informality on economic stability and industrial growth in Mexico, which is the ultimate objective of this book.

2.1 The Emergence of the ICES

In our theoretical section, we analyzed three moments in the emergence of institutions. First, the moment that precedes emergence. We concluded that this first moment seems to be charged with struggles that eventually limit the number of institutional alternatives available. Second, we analyzed the processes of actual emergence and materialization of the institution, characterized by intense negotiation between those actors involved. Finally, we studied the process of consolidation, where many future characteristics of the new institution are established through interaction. This section will follow the same order to describe the emergence of the ICES.

2.1.1. The Creation of Conditions for Emergence of the ICES (1917–1946)

This sub-section will be divided into three periods that coincide with three different political moments in Mexican history: (i) The reconstruction period (1917–1934); (ii) the Lázaro Cárdenas del Río Period (1934–1940); and (iii) the Manuel Ávila Camacho Period (1940–46). Each of these periods fostered the creation of specific pre-conditions for the emergence of the ICES. As we shall confirm, these conditions were successively re-shaped in such a way that, in the end, the most viable structure that could be created to face the challenge of industrialization was the ICES.

(i) The Formation of the Post-Revolutionary Mexican State (1917–1934)

Although informality in the public-private domain goes back a long way in Mexico (Shafer, 1973:126; Cosío Villegas, 1974:16), the Mexican Revolution undoubtedly eliminated all contact between the economic elite and the different governments that emerged during that chaotic period of Mexican history.

The Revolution (as it is commonly called), which lasted from 1910 to 1917, was a violent civil war that caused great loss of life and a generalized disruption of production. Some scholars calculate a reduction from 6% to 10% in the population, a 24% loss in manufacture, and a 50% decrease in agricultural production (King, 1970:9; Handelman, 1997:35). The revolt also translated into a significant distortion of social and political relations, so little can be ascertained about the condition of either formal or informal institutions during or immediately after the conflict, except that they were in chaos.

Both the peace and reconstruction processes, however, offer valuable insights into why policy networks re-emerged and subsequently prevailed in business-state relations. It is essential to look at three elements: (a) the exclusion of business from the emerging state structure; (b) the relative strength of the state vis-à-vis the rest of society; and (c) the economic-growth ideology of the reconstruction era.

a)Exclusion of Business

After armed conflict, peace was achieved through lengthy and difficult negotiation that included all the disparate but influential forces that participated and triumphed in the revolt (Ulloa, 1985). The main interests of each of these groups were incorporated into the new Constitution, and their leaders included in the new government coalition (Kaufman Purcell, 1981:196–7; Hansen, 1971[b]:87). Businessmen, however, were excluded from this process, not only because they were disorganized and relatively weak vis-à-vis victorious groups (Cockcroft, 1990:128), but also because they were seen as ideologically close to the old regime (Knight, 1986[b]:319, 464–5, 498; Luna Ledesma, 1995:79; Scott, 1959:115). In fact, the first organizations that aimed to unify all the revolutionary factions invariably saw themselves as socialist (Cosío Villegas, 1974:40–48). The exclusion of business was formally reflected in the key articles of the newly drafted Constitution. Control of the economy was expressly granted to the state (in articles 25 to 28), and close pacts with peasantry and labor were also formalized through the 27th and 123rd articles (Córdova, 1984:21). This legal and ideological exclusion (that in some cases turned into persecution) set a clear tone for the new revolutionary state: any future deals with business would have to be secured avoiding the formal structure of the Constitution. The private sector accepted this type of relation, but started to search informal channels of communication and negotiation with the public sector (Luna Ledesma, 1995:79). The exclusion of businessmen from formal political structures after a social revolution is not exclusive to Mexico, but that is why this work may help explain the emergence of informality in other political systems too.

b) The Strength of the State

In the chaotic post-Revolution atmosphere, a strong state was seen not as the natural but as the only entity that could pacify the nation. To this end, constitutional delegates gave enormous power of decision and arbitration to what turned out to be a highly centralized executive power that depended upon the strength of the presidency (Cosío Villegas, 1974:22–30). This led to the introduction of discretionary powers and regulations that gradually increased the already great power of the presidency. Granted such presidential power, business was practically at the mercy of government officials in everything from everyday requests like licenses and supply of energy to more lasting issues like entering new sectors of the economy or unfair competition from state-owned enterprises. In these conditions, it is no surprise that businessmen attempted to develop informal channels to negotiate with those public agencies that ultimately could "make or break" their companies (Purcell and Purcell, 1977:192).

c) The Need for Economic Growth

Public aversion of the new state to business seems to have been a two-edged knife, however. The new revolutionary leaders well knew that capital investment and management were necessary conditions if urgent reconstruction of the country were to take place. Without economic growth, living standards could not be raised and the pact with the masses would have lost all legitimacy and eventually all support too. The tension between the need for economic growth and anti-business ideology gave rise to what Basañez (1981:40) has called the "contradictory" nature of the post-revolutionary Mexican state, meaning that it was a theoretically peasant and worker state, which nevertheless needed to assure profits to capitalists in order to ensure its own survival; it had to be both a fierce re-distributor of income and a gentle promoter of capital accumulation. Thus steps were quickly taken to develop the institutional infrastructure that could support the recovery of the economy. The Bank of Mexico–the central bank–was established in 1925, the National Roads Commission in 1926 and, in that same year, investment started to flow back into the country due to the introduction of various laws that protected foreign capital (King, 1990:10). Additionally, Nafinsa, the National Bank for International Trade (Bancomext), the Bank for Urban and Public Works (BUOP), and the National Bank for Agricultural Credit (BNCE) had been created by 1936 (Medin, 1972:126).

In summary, by the early 1930s, Mexico was finally a nation at peace, where at least basic political and economic formal institutions had been created and where a set ideological path could be recognized. In this environment, the new post-revolutionary state faced the need to promote private investment, but was constrained by enormous legal and ideological obstacles in its relations with business. At the same time, capitalist groups were also bound by the exceptional discretionary powers of the state. It was at this time that a decisive figure in the development of the ICES came to power: President Lázaro Cárdenas del Río.

(ii) The Lázaro Cárdenas del Río Period (1936–1940)

Lázaro Cárdenas del Río was perhaps the most forceful President in the modern history of Mexico. His impact on relations with the private sector well illustrates this. His presidency also had a direct effect on the emergence of the ICES. The remainder of this section will explain how his contribution shaped the three conditions of emergence already discussed, and introduced four new ones.

a) Exclusion of Business

Cárdenas fully consolidated the institutional exclusion of business from the state structure in ideological and organizational terms. Ideologically, Cárdenas was openly pro-labor: the number of labor strikes went up from 200 in 1934 to 675 in 1936, and the government's labor tribunals (directly in charge of the Executive through the STYPS) in most cases favored labor (Martínez Nava, 1984:88–90), justified by the amendments to the Federal Labor Law that were introduced in that same year (Juárez González, 1982:61–2). The orientation of education was another source of ideological menace to businessmen: Cárdenas attempted to introduce what he called "socialist education" in public schools (Cárdenas, 1979[a]:135–43). Although the project did not prosper, schools were nevertheless instructed to promote "cooperativism" (*ibid.*). Finally, Cárdenas declared his position in public threat: In Monterrey, in a famous speech on 11 February 1936, after much criticism from representatives of business of constant strikes, Cárdenas reminded them that "those businessmen who are tired of social struggle, can hand over their factories to the workers or to the government. That will be patriotic; not closure" (Cárdenas, 1979[a]:198).

Cárdenas added to legal exclusion enshrined in the Constitution, by formally excluding businessmen from the Party of the Mexican Revolution (PRM) that he created in 1938 (PRI, 2001:1). The PRM supplanted the existing National Revolutionary Party (PNR). The PNR was the party that had taken Cárdenas to the presidency. It had been created in 1929 by triumphant revolutionary generals, to unite the different factions, legitimize their ascent to power and integrate the governing bureaucracy (Leal, 1986[b], 1986:27). The PNR, however, was based on the power of local bosses, thus maintaining the pre-Revolutionary state of affairs. Cárdenas saw the need to create a new party, based on a nation-wide coalition of social sectors to break with the idea of regional powers (Cosío Villegas, 1974:53). To that end, he organized the PRM around three sectors: workers, peasants, and the military; business was left out. Cárdenas was establishing the principle that the claims of businessmen would be subordinated to those of other social groups. As a class, businessmen had to accept the "rules of the game" to survive.

b) Strengthening the Power of the State

Additional laws approved during the administration further consolidated the discretionary power of the state over business. The "Expropriation Law" of 1936 (Cárdenas, 1979:172–3) allowed the government without impediment to nationalize any industry considered of "national interest." This power was used to nationalize the railways in 1937 and the private oil industry in 1938 (Juárez González, 1982:58). The "Tax on Income Law" of 1938 (Cárdenas, 1979:172–3) allowed the government to tax "excessive profits" on grounds that high profits "could only be obtained by firms that . . . carry out monopoly practices" (Medin, 1972:124). Although the law was vilified as "Hitlerist totalitarianism" by the private sector, it was still passed.

c) The Perceived Need for Economic Growth

Although the Cárdenas administration did not seem to have an explicit industrial plan (Gracida and Fujigaki, 1988:15–6), archives show that by 1938 the government had recognized the need for industrialization. The option was seen as a way to counteract potential import restrictions and grasp the export opportunities created by the then imminent "European War" (LCR 564.1/2016). Thus conditions were established to develop the industrial capacity on which production would rely during the war years (Medina Peña, 1995:123). Public investment in economic development doubled and, by the end of the Cárdenas administration, amounted to 37–40% (Wilkie, 1967:127). Additionally, on 30 December 1939, a fiscal decree provided for the granting of five-year tax breaks to firms that entered new industrial sectors (Medin, 1972:121). From 1935 to 1940, industrial establishments had increased by 82%, the value of production and salaries had grown by 90% and invested capital had risen by 123% (Medin, 1972:117; Zabludovsky, 1979:49). Clearly, although the process of industrialization had not consolidated with Cárdenas, he had taken important steps to start it (Erfani, 1995:62; Ramírez Rancaño, 1977:110).

d) Creating Four New Conditions for the Emergence of the ICES

Apart from influencing recognized conditions for the emergence of the ICES, Cárdenas created four others that greatly influenced the characteristics of the system: (i) the formal organization of the private sector; (ii) the co-option of labor; (iii) recognition of the importance of business for national development; and (iv) favors granted to specific business groups. Let us briefly explain each.

(i) *The Formal Organization of the Private Sector.* On 27 August 1936, the Cárdenas government published a new Law of Chambers of Commerce and Industry that classified the chambers as "autonomous" organizations, but "of public interest" (Arriola Woog, 1988ª:52; Juárez González, 1982:51–2). This last detail meant that the state could allow or ban them, choose where their headquarters had to be located, dissolve them if membership went below certain numbers, and intervene in their administration when "public interest" was at stake (Story, 1986:118–9). Although the notion of "public interest" was highly contested by businessmen, the law was nevertheless passed (Juárez González, 1982:55). In practical terms, the law allowed the subjugation and partial semi-incorporation of the private sector into the state. However, it also made membership compulsory for all firms. This was a key point. It meant that, for the first time in history, the whole of the Mexican private sector would be formally organized, and at a speed that would not have been possible without state intervention. In parallel, Cárdenas's policies also promoted business organization for a different reason: The anti-business attitude of the regime strengthened the role of independent organizations like the ABM and the Coparmex.

These effects meant two things for the emergence and future operation of the ICES. Firstly, in one way or another, businessmen were finally organized and ready to start gaining a sense of class in the new post-revolutionary regime. Secondly, from the very start, private groups would enter the ICES either structurally weak and dependent or structurally strong and independent.

(ii) *The Co-option of Labor.* If the ICES was eventually possible, as a system linking business and the state, it was because the labor movement was incorporated into the state apparatus. This gave both government and business the certainty that pacts could be kept without excessive labor intervention. Cárdenas started this incorporation through two decisions: Firstly, by promoting the creation of the Mexican Labor Confederation

(CTM), a unified national front of workers loyal to him (Ayala Anguiano, 1979:206–8); and secondly, by granting the CTM a number of political positions that turned it into a virtual appendix of the government from 1938 onwards (Handelman, 1997:38; Nava García, 1983:148).

(iii) The Recognition of the Importance of Business for National Development. Towards the end of his administration, Cárdenas made strenuous efforts to "heal the wounds" he had inflicted on the private sector (Martínez Nava, 1984:111). Most likely he realized that businessmen were necessary to ensure lasting economic growth. Industrial action was severely restricted through political control of labor leaders. From 1935 to 1938, the number of striking workers fell from 145,000 to only 15,000 (Ayala Anguiano, 1979:222). In an early rehearsal of the ICES, the government consulted private chambers on issues such as railways, export tariffs, and electricity rates (Juárez González, 1982:52–3). Such consultation set a precedent. If definite informal channels did not emerge then, it was probably for two reasons: firstly, because relations, even if increasingly cordial, were never close (Martínez Nava, 1984:100–1)[1]; secondly, because the ideology of important members of the government still left little room for it. For instance, ironic as it may sound, the Secretary of the Economy, Francisco J. Mújica, strongly opposed any deals with business (Martínez Nava, 1984:117; Medin, 1990:12).

(iv) Favors Granted to Specific Business Groups. The distance that Cárdenas kept from businessmen did not stop his favoring some. Hamilton (1978:31) documents how the Legorreta family, owners of Banamex, the biggest bank in Mexico, were so close to Cárdenas that their speech in the 1934 Banking Convention was "visionary," i.e. almost identical with those Cárdenas gave later (see also Cockcroft, 1990:145). The "vision" paid off soon. Banamex was the only private bank that financed the many public projects of the Cárdenas government (Hamilton, 1978:30). Similarly, the 1938 tax on "excessive profits" was only partially applied to bankers. They would pay this tax on foreign exchange and gold sales profits only, which represented a minimal part of their profits (Hamilton, 1982:192–3). Such privilege during the Cárdenas government acted as a precedent for both emergence and subsequent operation of the ICES. Bankers and other influential businessmen preferred direct relations with the President over more formal links. When the ICES emerged, they fought to preserve this as their exclusive privilege. Subsequently, Presidents would continue favoring selected businessmen.

(iii) The Manuel Ávila Camacho Period (1940–1946)

Manuel Ávila Camacho succeeded Cárdenas as President in 1940, inheriting a set of political, economic, and social conditions that his policies would further modify. Ávila Camacho worked mostly on consolidating many of the processes started by Cárdenas, but using a new approach towards business. This approach shaped the future ICES. This section will briefly analyze the impact of Ávila Camacho on each one of the seven conditions that he inherited.

a) The Exclusion of Business

Ávila Camacho invariably kept a respectful distance from businessmen (Krauze, 1997:50; Medin, 1990:12–6; cf. Loyo, 1983). However, he was a strong believer in private property and free enterprise (Perzabal, 1988:22–3; Derossi, 1971:17). He was resolved to continue "healing the wounds" inflicted by Cárdenas on the private sector and, in consequence, took steps to compensate for the formal exclusion of business from the state. He did this through various means and supported by what he called "the policy of national unity" (Medin, 1990:13; Erfani, 1995:62; cf. Loyo, 1983; Monsivais, 1979:306).

Firstly, he removed radical government officials. Secondly, he eliminated the anti-business bias in labor justice, by giving business representation in newly-created "conciliation tribunals" (Niblo, 1999:148). Finally, and most importantly, he promoted consensus in Mexican society on the idea of economic growth through industrialization (Concamin, 1976b:37). Avila Camacho's government actively exalted industrialization as the best way to promote social justice: businessmen rose from antediluvian villains to modern heroes that would fulfill "The Mexican Dream" for all. Many argue that Ávila Camacho reversed the exclusion of business but started that of labor (Erfani, 1995:70).

b) Strengthening the Power of the State

In spite of his pro-business stance, Ávila Camacho did not lag far behind Cárdenas in strengthening the power of both the Presidency and the Mexican State as a whole. Firstly, he subjugated the power of the legislature and the judiciary to that of the executive. Control over the legislature was exercised through the establishment of a sophisticated combination of written and unwritten political rules that made the President the supreme leader of the PRI[2], which was the only party in power. This meant that, because the political careers of legislators were often in the hands of the President, they rarely dared challenge him. These same feeble legislators enabled the President to gradually control the judiciary: they approved laws that allowed him to appoint magistrates and judges, making the judiciary a virtual appendix of the executive. The National Archives contain numerous documents that prove the submissiveness of the legislative and judicial powers to the President[3].

The government also started a gradual process of economic intervention. In 1941, the *Compañía Exportadora e Importadora Mexicana, S.A.* (CEIMSA) was created. This was a state-owned company that monopolized the exports, imports, and distribution of many basic products in order to control prices (Vernon, 1964:164–6). Other state-owned companies were created in the steel and raw material sectors (Zabludovsky, 1979:61–3). A national social security system, managed directly by the executive, was also constituted (Coparmex, 1979:30). Direct economic intervention was a new mode of state power that would gradually strengthen the influence of the President (Hernández Rodríguez, 1985:159). Because of this constant intervention of the state in the economy, the private sector began to realize that a system to constrain the power of the state was necessary to protect their economic interests: the ICES would serve that role.

c) The Perceived Need for Economic Growth

It was Manuel Ávila Camacho who finally gave meaning to the notion of economic growth by introducing import substituting industrialization (ISI). The process was seen as the only remedy to the economic insufficiencies of the country (Córdova, 1984:66; Zabludovsky, 1979:59). Authors agree that Ávila Camacho did not originally plan to introduce ISI in Mexico. However, both domestic and international factors converged to enable the implementation of such strategy (cf. King, 1970:16; Ayala Espino, 1988:248; Vernon, 1971:92; Medina Peña, 1995:122). Firstly, as foreseen by the government, the Second World War (WWII) deprived Mexico of needed manufactured imports. Secondly, war production in developed economies opened up a market for Mexican manufactured consumer goods. Finally, in the ideological arena, archival records prove that structuralist theories had already instilled urgency in promoting manufacture for export (GR C70 EXP16; see also Vernon, 1964:141; Mancera Aguayo, 1993:42; Martínez Nava, 1984:123; López-Portillo Romano, 1994:33; Prebisch, 1991).

Accordingly, Ávila Camacho introduced the first complete framework to industrialize the country: the Law of Transformation Industries (Gracida and Fujigaki; 1988:31). He also started re-servicing foreign debt to regain foreign investor confidence (Sánchez Gamper, 1989:50) and continued assigning growing public investment to industrialization: about 40% of the total (Medina Peña, 1995:130). This strategy was made possible by the huge transfer of European fleeing capital to Mexico during WWII. International reserves increased from US$28 million in 1939 to US$376 million in 1945 (Del Cueto, 1974:140). In these circumstances, from 1939 to 1946 the volume of industrial production grew by 39% and its value by 209%. While industrial production represented only 1.7% of the value of exports in 1939, in 1946 the proportion was 32.5% (Medin, 1990:18). In 1944, for the first time in Mexican history, the GDP share in manufacturing surpassed that of agriculture.

The industrializing project however was not without problems. It was implemented swiftly and was thus highly improvised. It was born in extreme dependency on exports to the U.S. and American technology (Gracida and Fujigaki; 1988:35; Medin, 1990:16–7). These contradictions would eventually take their toll. The relevant point for the ICES, however, is that businessmen were prospering, which created the need for systematic relations with the state because (a) their political weight was growing; and (b) closer relations were necessary to move forward in the process of industrialization.

d) Business Organization

Ávila Camacho passed a new Law of Chambers of Commerce and Industry in 1941 (Alcázar Ávila, 1970:12; Medin, 1990:85). Although he did not relax control over business, he did take into account many of their views, at least in two matters. Firstly, the joint chamber of commerce and industry created under Cárdenas, the CONCANACOMIN, was divided into the two confederations that we analyzed above: CONCANACO and CONCAMIN, as had been long demanded by businessmen. Secondly, the CANACINTRA was created to represent the new industrial interests. In sum, with regard to business organizations, Ávila Camacho continued his policy of "distant attention": always listening, but never getting close. The effect of such relations on the emergence of the ICES is clear: for industrialization to continue, the growing importance of the private sector had to be recognized and the increasing interaction between the government and businessmen had to be structured, but neither process could be made too evident to avoid damaging the worker/peasant coalition that provided the Mexican State its political legitimacy.

e) The Growing Co-option of Labor

Ávila Camacho saw the control of labor as a *sine qua non* of industrialization (Zabludovsky, 1979:60). He continued the co-option that Cárdenas had started, but with economic rather than with political goals in mind (Gracida and Fujigaki; 1988:15).

Co-option was furthered by increasing the number of political positions granted to CTM members (Hansen, 1971[b]:49). For the ICES, this meant that the state would be able to negotiate directly with business, without serious opposition of trade unions. The only condition was *extreme discretion,* to avoid at any cost the impression that the pact with labor was being traded for one with business.

f) The Growing Influence of Businessmen

During the Ávila Camacho administration, contact between the President and businessmen though cordial was irregular (Tirado, 1987: 488; Handelman, 1997:40). The assertion is supported by the many unsuccessful requests for meetings that I found in the National Archives (MAC 545.22/133–1). In fact, contact between government and business seems to have been so scarce that a document signed by the American Chamber of Commerce in 1941, praised a "tradition-breaking" meeting between President Ávila Camacho, the Secretary of the Treasury, and the ABM. The document adds that "Bankers, unaccustomed to a frank and friendly appeal for support from a Mexican President, hailed the meeting as a first step in a broad program of economic progress." (Shafer, 1973:129, 148).

Despite lack of contact between the government and businessmen, the private sector of all trades and sizes was becoming aware of its strength and importance. This is clear in the constant complaints against the lack of consultation that one finds in the archives and newspapers of the time (MAC 545.22/262–1; MAC 545.22/133; *El Universal*, 31/03/44). Indeed, enormous pressure was put on the government to design channels of negotiation that could allow businessmen to participate in the formulation of infrastructure, credit, and industrial policy. This pressure would have been unthinkable even six years before. The power of the private sector was growing, and it was growing fast.

g) The Continuation of the "favored businessmen" Tradition

Like Cárdenas and every other President after him, Ávila Camacho also favored selected businessmen. At least two are openly identified with his administration: Manuel Suárez, owner of the largest asbestos company in Mexico; and Aarón Sáenz, banker and owner of sugar mills (Krauze, 1997:68). The bankers in general also benefited enormously from increased government and private borrowing. The number of banks rose from 72 in 1940 to 142 in 1942 (Solórzano, 1984:19–20). These facts had two implications for the ICES. Firstly, this form of privileged relation became accepted and defended by businessmen. As time went by, rather than favoring one or two businessmen, Presidents would cultivate several. Secondly, since they had a monopoly on government borrowing, bankers kept consolidating their power of access to high officials.

It could be safely concluded that, by the end of the Ávila Camacho administration, the seven conditions that we have been studying had consolidated to a degree that allowed the emergence and materialization of the ICES. These conditions were so constraining that their simultaneous convergence would definitely limit the institutional options available to organize public-private relations at the time. This "point of emergence," was reached after tremendous accumulated negotiation over a period of almost 30 years (1917 to 1946). The struggle had often been hostile, so the compromises were extremely delicate. In other words, as suggested in Section 3.1.1 of our first theoretical chapter, the political, economic, and social environment that preceded the emergence of the ICES, severely limited the feasible institutional options available to accommodate the tangled web of commitments, objectives, interests and perceptions that surrounded Mexican industrialization in the mid-1940s. In this context of limited choice, the ICES would soon emerge.

2.1.2. The Emergence, Materialization and Initial Characterization of the ICES (1946–1958)

My research indicates that the ICES emerged, materialized and started to operate during one single presidential administration, that of Miguel Alemán Valdés (1946–52). Further and important development also took place during the administration of Adolfo Ruiz Cortines (1952–8), who succeeded Alemán. This section will study both periods.

(i) The Miguel Alemán Valdés Period (1946–1952)

Miguel Alemán Valdés became President of Mexico in 1946. By that time, the conditions were ripe for the emergence of the ICES for at least three reasons. Firstly, the continuation of ISI–then definitely established as the development strategy of the Mexican Government–required extensive private-public interaction and thus institutional channels of communication that simply did not exist. Secondly, the government had relaxed business exclusion through closer and more intensive contact. Finally, the co-option of labor had removed a potential (and important) obstacle to closer business-government relations.

In this context, three factors prompted the emergence of the ICES. The first was external. By 1946, with the end of WWII, the dynamism of the Mexican economy was beginning to wane along with the riches procured by trade and foreign investment during the war. Alemán deemed institutionalized collaboration with business essential to continue the process of industrialization. The other two factors were internal. Firstly, as the economy was enlarging, businessmen needed greater security for investment, which the existing legal framework certainly could not provide. Secondly, businessmen judged it necessary to counterbalance the enormous power of the executive, in order to protect their interests against discretionary action. Appealing to the legislature or the judiciary to solve their problems would have been futile, since–as we have discussed–both bodies were politically subordinated to the executive.

Businessmen realized that the only option was to use their economic power and political weight to negotiate, on equal terms with the executive, policy that affected them. Likewise, the government–politically unable to modify laws that supported its alliance with workers and peasants–understood that the accomplishment of its economic objectives would only be possible through the development of negotiation channels that could create confidence in investors: by virtue of mutual convenience, the ICES would soon emerge.

It was said in our theoretical framework that the process of institutional emergence is divided into two steps: (a) consensus on institutionalization and (b) materialization of the institution. Let us study both processes more closely in the case of the Mexican ICES.

a) Consensus on the ICES.

The decision to establish an ICES does not seem to have occurred through specific meetings or on specific dates. However, consensus on the desirability of such a system was reached among private and public actors since the start of the Alemán administration. At all levels of government, starting with the President, the development of closer relations with businessmen was seen as a necessary policy to solve the post-war recession and continue the industrialization of the country (Cypher, 1990:45; Medina Peña, 1995:124–5). The goal at all levels of government became to dilute differences between the public and the private spheres (Luna Ledesma, 1992ª:23), and voluntary contact with businessmen intensified to the point where stable policy networks started to emerge. As briefly suggested already, closer contact was facilitated because the cordiality of the previous and new administrations increased business trust, labor did not object this closeness and, very importantly, because Alemán appointed numerous businessmen and professionals to official positions in the government. His cabinet was made up of 55% lawyers, 20% industrialists, 15% technical university graduates, and 10% military (Zabludovsky, 1984:22). Most members of this cabinet, all around 40 years old, represented a new political generation, the so-called "puppies of the revolution" (*Cachorros de la Revolución*), who were less ideological and more pragmatic than their parents (Medin, 1990:44–6, 94). All these actions harmonized values and objectives (cognitive frameworks, using our Mediated Rationality terms) and, in conjunction with mutual understandings (norms) and legal statutes (regulation such as tax and tariff decrees), created enough trust for institutionalized informality to emerge. A new attitude, common backgrounds, little labor resistance, and a superior common objective–industrialization–in sum facilitated relations between the Mexican government and the business sector, leading to the emergence of an ICES.

Such process of intensified contact is well documented. It is agreed that, during the initial years of the Alemán administration, the promotion of economic development virtually turned into a promotion of businessmen. This connection became inseparable and it also became seen as an obligation of the state to keep it that way (Hernández Rodríguez, 1989:46). Pragmatism and a "case-by-case," "piece-meal" approach to policymaking became the style of government action (Purcell and Purcell, 1977:203–4; Story, 1986:177; Luna Ledesma, 1992ª:17). At the same time, archival records confirm that the different business organizations were consulted and rewarded constantly by those government agencies closest to their area of interest (MAV 111/5230; MAV 708.1/5–8; MAV 708.1/5–8). For instance, in 1946, CONCANACO appointed representatives to 17 public bodies, from railways to tourist promotion boards (Shafer, 1973:152–4; Zabludovsky, 1984:22). In 1947, before modifying the tax system, the Secretariat of the Treasury asked CONCAMIN and CONCANACO to organize a convention at which opinions were gathered (Hernández Rodríguez, 1989:50). The Secretariat of Foreign Affairs even granted one seat to a representative appointed by the private sector in the official delegation that attended the 1947 Havana Conference, where Mexico refused to join the GATT; and businessmen were also consulted when Mexico decided to cancel a bilateral free-trade treaty with the U.S. (Zabludovsky, 1979:164–8). In both cases, the outcome was what Mexican businessmen had demanded (Zabludovsky, 1979:167–71, 184). Contact became so close that Alemán himself once confirmed that, before proposing a law, the government normally "held talks with the directors of business organizations to exchange views, learn their opinions and attempt to obtain their approval" (Medin, 1990:93–4).

At this point it is clear that consensus to create a system to co-ordinate public-private relations in favor of industrialization had consolidated. Materialization of the ICES could now take place.

b) Materialization

After social actors reach consensus to create an institution, a process of materialization follows. As established in our theoretical section (see Chapter 1, Section 3.1.2 and Chapter 2, Sections 4.1.1 and 4.1.2), both structural and cognitive constraints often dictate the degree of formality with which the institution materializes. Then, materialization follows three steps: (i) the establishment of the initial agreements of co-ordination; (ii) the accommodation of the interests of "losing groups"; and (iii) the justification of the institution before the general public. Let us briefly study these processes for the case of the Mexican ICES.

In terms of the formal/informal choice, given the conditions that preceded the emergence of the ICES, an informal structure was the most viable to address the need for channels of negotiation between the public and private sectors. Even if the relation between business and government officials became closer, a wealth of legal, political, and social constraints were still in place. For instance, workers and peasants were not willing to change the Constitution or the structure of the PRI to include businessmen. The Revolution was fresh in the mind of these social groups, so they feared that the open presence of business in the governing coalition would dishonor the "social spirit" of the revolt. Obviously, they also wanted to avoid sharing political position in the legislature with another social group. In other words, a combination of regulative (the Constitution, the PRI's founding treaties, and other pro-labor or pro-peasant laws), normative (implicit agreements within the governing coalition), and cognitive (anti-business ideology) constraints encouraged both the government and businessmen to opt in favor of an informal institution to push forward the process of industrialization.

(i) Unwritten initial agreements supported the emergence of the ICES, confirming what was suggested in our working definition of informal institutions (see Chapter 2, Section 3). Each of the policy networks that made up the system was supported by a combination of *specific* and *general* agreements. *Specific agreements* dictated which issues would be negotiated. The discussion of highly technical issues such as taxing, tariffs, interests rates, credit or infrastructure needs were often the *raison d'être* of the main policy networks. The case of banking, that we have already documented, proves this point. Other archival records (MAV 708.1/5–8; MAV 545.22/53) corroborate the assertion[4]. Despite their specificity, all policy networks were nevertheless based on *general agreements* that dictated membership, frequency of negotiation, hierarchy of participants, and also assured compliance to important principles that we already described at the beginning of the chapter. These were basically that business would (a) channel all its demands peacefully through the executive power; and (b) limit its public political participation. In exchange, the government would (a) maintain general economic and political stability; (b) consult with businessmen on any potential change that could affect their interests; (c) assure through all means possible acceptable returns on investment; (d) limit the participation of the government in productive activities already covered by private firms; (e) supply hard currency and import licenses for machinery and intermediate goods (Cisneros, 1986:124–5; Garrido and Puga, 1992:132; Quintana and Garrido, 1986:112). Additionally, all participants implicitly agreed that the President would be the final arbiter, not only because of the constitutional powers he had secured as absolute, but also because he played a unifying role in an otherwise loose system. All these unwritten agreements were ultimately geared to one objective: industrialization.

As stated in our theoretical section, these agreements could not be said to have functioned fully until repeated interaction within the policy networks had taken place. However, they were early understandings that offered mutual benefits to move forward with the creation of the ICES.

(ii) The second step of materialization, refers to the accommodation of "losing" interests. With the emergence of the ICES, the "winners" or "appropriators" of the institutions for industrial policy-making were obviously the business groups, while the main "losing" groups were organized labor and the peasantry.

Indeed, at least two of the pillars of the ICES were in contradiction with the potential advancement of labor. Firstly, the assurance of profits to businessmen through every possible means; secondly, the maintenance of peace and stability. Alemán believed that productivity–and thus profits–could only rise through wage controls, so he practically "froze" wage increases. Due to high inflation, by 1948 the purchasing power of workers (measured through industrial minimum wage) had already dropped by 40% (Zabludovsky, 1979:148). Concurrently, Alemán was persuaded by businessmen that "peace and stability" included the practical prohibition of strikes. Therefore, to "maintain order," government repression of protests intensified (Medin, 1990:45, 108). For instance, numerous independent factions of the CTM were dissolved through either legal action against their leaders or violent repression against the members, using anti-Communism as an excuse (Monsivais, 1979:307; De la Garza Toledo, 1988:54–55). Additionally, puppet leaders, called "charros," were imposed as heads of the main trade unions (De la Garza Toledo, 1988:60–2; Handelman, 1997:40). The best example is offered by the railway workers' union, in which the government imposed a "charro" leader by convicting Luis Gómez Z., a democratically-elected, anti-governmental leader, on charges of "social dissolution" (Krauze, 1997:124–5; Cockcroft, 1990:215).

In other words, the interests of the "losing" groups in the Mexican case were not truly accommodated, but forcefully repressed. It is true that political positions and bribes kept flowing to most union leaders, but they had to accept them in order to avoid repression. Workers thus became doubly "losers," not only because government control cancelled any real possibility of future betterment, but also because they were vilified as potential enemies of stability whenever they decided to protest.

Another group that eventually became a "loser" with the emergence of the ICES were the rural classes. The export earnings that they generated during the 1950s were used to finance industrialization. However, as we shall later see, these earnings were never pumped back into agriculture and rural production was crowded out by manufactures. The topic of agricultural development in Mexico is too broad to explore it further. However, it appears that–as in the case of urban workers–"losing" rural interests were not accommodated but controlled in clientelistic and corporatist ways. The Mexican State intensively co-opted organizations similar to the CTM (The National Confederation of Peasants (CNC) and the Revolutionary Confederation of Workers and Peasants (CROC) being the most famous) to either reward through bribes and political positions or violently repress the rural masses, and remove them as a potential obstacle to industrial investment and profit. In other words, in the Mexican case, losing interests were indeed pacified but not through accommodation, as much as through repression.

(iii) The third step of materialization has to do with the legitimization of institutions before remaining groups of society whose influence and power could not be neutralized, marginalized, or ignored. The ICES had been skillfully justified before these groups since the times of Ávila Camacho, when industrialization was promoted as a panacea that would solve all the economic problems of Mexico. Alemán, however, went further and institutionalized the strategy through the organization of a new political party to substitute the existing PRM. The creation of the new party, the PRI, was a move to wipe out any remnants of Cárdenas's "socialism." At the same time, it was a strategy to legitimize the "modern" policies of the government (i.e. industrialization) through mass support. The PRI effectively became more an instrument of control than of representation (Stevens, 1977:227, 250). The factor that allowed Alemán to retain support of the lower and middle classes was that economic growth did take place and some of the fruits were shared through the PRI in corporatist and clientelistic ways. After the shaky start of the post-war years, the Korean War (1949–1952) caused a new influx of foreign capital that was fleeing instability in Asia and the U.S. International reserves rose from US$34 million in 1948 to US$297 million in 1951 (Del Cueto, 1974:144; Ramírez Rancaño, 1977:135–6). Demand for Mexican exports also grew exponentially (Medin, 1990:116–7). In the end, between 1946 and 1952, manufacturing production had increased by 56%, an average of 9.3% per year; and real GDP had grown by 41%, an average annual rate of 7% (Del Cueto, 1974:148).

The enormous paradox of the Alemán administration, however, was that the workers and peasants, whose support legitimized industrialization, were the least benefited by the strategy: income distribution data for 1950 confirm that the top 5% of the population received 35% of the income and the top 10% received 45%, whilst the poorest 10% of the Mexicans got only 2.4% of national income (INEGI, 1985:233). Political control had started to create additional "losing" groups that, with the years, would realize that their interests had not been accommodated. In more than one way, the industrializing model was sowing some of the seeds of its own destruction.

Despite the social contradictions that Alemán, the PRI and the very emergence of the ICES generated, we know that the system still materialized and persisted. This is probably due to affected groups not immediately seeing a straight connection between the ICES, political control, and their economic problems. In other words, without the advantage of hindsight, a worker would not have identified the ICES as the direct cause of his falling standard of living, so he would not immediately question the structure. And it surely was by maintaining a discreet status that the ICES would survive in years to come (Tirado, 1987: 488).

c) Acquisition of Initial Operational Features of the ICES

In our theoretical framework, after an institution materializes, two additional processes follow: (i) further appropriation of such institution; and (ii) the acquisition of additional operational features. Concerning appropriation, when an institution emerges, some participant groups may prevail in establishing the operational rules of the structure. The acquisition of additional operational features refers to the process by which the agreements, accords, and understandings upon which the new institution is based, are extended or adjusted through the repeated initial interaction of participants. Let us briefly look at these two processes in the case of the ICES.

(i) In my view, the initial appropriator of the structure was the government, although gradually–after a couple of decades–private groups were able to reverse that appropriation in their favor. I base my assertion on the fact that, at the start, the power of business groups was still relatively low. Even if this power was increasing fast, the government still had awesome power to assert its preponderance, for example through discretionary decisions that could not be appealed because the president controlled the judiciary. More importantly, there were no systems in place to control this power. A good example of the still greater strength of the state vis-à-vis private groups is the "Law on Attributions of the Executive Power in Economic Matters" that Alemán proposed in 1951. The statute extended the discretionary power of the executive over a number of areas like price control, distribution channels, rationing, restrictions on imports and exports, veto over production priorities, and the takeover of unproductive factories (DOF, 30/12/50; Medin, 1990:95–6). The reason offered was that the government needed extraordinary powers to react promptly to any economic disruption caused by the Korean War. However, businessmen saw this explanation as a simple excuse to extend the influence of the state (Medin, 1990:95). Although such Law was fiercely opposed by the whole of the private sector (CONCAMIN even asserted that it was similar to the "Law of National Service of Nazi Germany" (Medin, 1990:96)), the submissive Mexican Congress approved it in the end. It is true that its effects were probably attenuated later through the ICES, but the government had been still able to impose its will.

This exercise of executive power was not only based on imposition, but was also combined with rewards that the Mexican Government could offer submissive businessmen. These rewards included protection against foreign competition (Luna Ledesma, 1992[a]:23); government contracts; the supply of needed infrastructure (Ramírez Rancaño, 1977:138–40); or the sale of heavily subsidized inputs. In sum, although in the future the situation would change, in the early 1950s the combination of imposition and compensation still maintained the Mexican State as the leading actor in the public-private relation.

(ii) Apart from the initial appropriation of the system by the government, many other features that characterized the ICES in its future operation originated at this early stage. I shall introduce seven.

1. *Public Expenditure and the ICES.* The privileged channel through which government financing was negotiated and assigned to the private sector became the ICES. At a time when public investment was expanding greatly, this was no small issue. Most business groups abandoned their "anachronistic liberalism" (Zabludovsky, 1979:228) and accepted with gratitude state intervention that left them rich profits. Even the most conservative groups–like the Monterrey Group–jumped on the wagon[5].

2. *The Banks and the ICES.* Enormous amounts of money were normally channeled through private banks, because legal reserves were used as a source of government financing. This is precisely what put private banks at the center not only of the ICES, but also above the rest of the private sector (FitzGerald, 1978, quoted in Erfani, 1995:97).

3. *The "Financial Axis" and the ICES.* Alemán, a lawyer, established the unwritten principle that the economy had to be managed by technically trained officials at the Secretariat of the Treasury and at the Bank of Mexico (Krauze, 1997:128). This, combined with the enormous power of the bankers, created the most solid of the policy networks that formed the ICES. This policy network

would be known as the "financial axis" and became the stronghold of the monetarist-liberal ideology.

4. *The President and the ICES.* During the Alemán administration, participants in the ICES introduced an unwritten rule that dictated that the President could not be criticized in public. Criticism should be directed towards his secretaries (Zabludovsky, 1979:190–204; Medin, 1990:49). This was more than servility: an attack on the President also could have meant the cancellation of negotiation, which at the time was invaluable for businessmen.

5. *Hierarchies and the ICES.* It is with Alemán that the earliest evidence of a hierarchy within the ICES appears (MAV 545.22/300; MAV 111/62). Issues that were perceived as less important (usually because of the low influence of the firm(s) involved) were delegated by the President and the Secretaries of State to lower levels of government. This created "sub-policy networks" within existent policy networks. This hierarchy within the ICES partially explains why the system was seen as pervasive throughout the Mexican economy.

6. *Foreign Companies and the ICES.* With Alemán, Mexico gradually opened up to foreign investment (Hamilton, 1982:200). Foreign companies that fully invested in Mexico often joined the ICES directly, once they realized that it was common practice. This created yet more sophisticated and complicated connections within the system. Instead, foreign investors that entered the country through joint ventures with Mexicans often relied on the connections of the Mexican partners.

7. *"Favored Businessmen" and the ICES.* As might be expected from his style of government, Alemán not only continued, but actually took to the limit the tradition of favoring specific businessmen. The close contact between some businessmen and Alemán is confirmed through archival documents that show constant meetings and describe complex business deals. This certainly appears to have been the origin of the high levels of corruption often associated with Alemán (see Scott, 1959:251) and the "favored businessmen" network in general. At least four businessmen that eventually became enormously rich are directly linked to Alemán: Antonio Ruiz Galindo, maker of steel office equipment and representative of some foreign firms (General Motors, Siemens); Bernardo Quintana, owner of ICA, the largest construction company in Latin America; Bruno Pagliai, owner of tube factories; and Rómulo O'Farril, owner of "Novedades," a leading newspaper, and of various other trading firms (MAV 111/3826; MAV 111/4489; MAV 136.2/434; MAV 512.2/67; MAV 565.4/848; MAV 546.4/33; MAV 546.6/452; MAV 606.3/235; MAV 111.1/130; MAV 111/3243; Krauze, 1997:101). Emilio Azcárraga Milmo, owner of TELEVISA, the largest TV company in the

Spanish-speaking world, has been often linked to Alemán. In fact, Alemán's son eventually became Vice-President of the Company and one of the main stockholders. However, I cannot prove this relation through first-hand evidence because the file of Azcárraga Milmo in the National Archives (MAV 111/6361) is reported missing.

It could be affirmed, then, that by the end of the Alemán Valdés administration, the ICES had emerged, materialized, and acquired its initial characteristics. With his successor, Adolfo Ruiz Cortines, the system would continue evolving and its features would consolidate.

(ii) The Adolfo Ruiz Cortines Period (1952–1958)

Adolfo Ruiz Cortines became President of Mexico in 1952. Like Alemán in 1946, he inherited a difficult economic situation. An important engine of industrialization–the Korean War–had ended at the start of his government (Medina Peña, 1995:140). Manufactured and agricultural exports (which still represented 51% of the total) decreased by 17% in 1953. This triggered balance of payments crises and the Peso was devalued in 1954[6] (Nafinsa, 1977:401).

With the growth strategy crumbling (Álvarez, 1973:101), Ruiz Cortines decided that strengthening the alliance with the private sector was the quickest way to revive the ailing economy, and thus maintain the legitimacy of the Mexican State, which was by then tied closely to economic growth. However, the new President adopted a more distant attitude towards the private sector (Vernon, 1964:108). The close relations that Alemán had promoted with businessmen had caused endless public scandals of corruption and concentration of wealth (Scott, 1959:251). Ruiz Cortines sought to establish (a) cordial yet transparent relations with the private sector; and (b) some degree of formality in the interaction of businessmen and the government.

Firstly, he stopped all meetings with businessmen that could be interpreted as secretive or leading to corruption. Even the most influential officially had to ask for audience in writing, clearly stating the purpose of their visit. In the National Archives there are numerous documents showing that even Emilio Azcárraga, owner of TELEVISA (ARC 433/153) or Jorge Larrea, with important mining interests (ARC 111/1314), had to follow this format for audience.

Secondly, unlike Alemán, Ruiz Cortines kept his friends away from the government and avoided compromising commitments. The anecdote goes that, on the first day of his presidency, he rejected a new car that automobile dealers gave to every new President in welcome (Krauze, 1997:176).

Thirdly, Ruiz Cortines attempted to make negotiation between the government and businessmen more visible. On 28 July 1954, he set up a collective consultative agency called the "Council for Development and Co-ordination of

National Production" (ARC 565.32/10–8). The Council was formed by distinguished businessmen and most members of the presidential cabinet. Although the Council was able to solve some problems (for example, it closed a deal of co-operation between CONCANACO and CEIMSA, the *bête noire* of businessmen that controlled distribution and prices), in the end it became increasingly inefficient and was discreetly dissolved by the President (Scott, 1959:289). The reasons for the Council's failure were structural: since it only had consultative attributes, the Council lacked the authority to make decisions and execute them. Additionally, the Council also lacked the technical specialization of the ICES: it had diverse membership (small and large firms, manufacturers of very different products) and was consequently overloaded with contradictory interests. For these reasons, both public and private actors gradually returned to traditional informal negotiation through the ICES.

We must not forget, however, that the ICES was still developing and, therefore, not all its routines and fine agreements were fully established. At least seven aspects of the ICES were either modified or introduced during the Ruiz Cortines administration. Let us briefly look at each.

1. *The Continuation of Industrialization and the ICES.* In 1955, the "Law on New and Necessary Industries" was introduced. It was meant to be a new thrust for the process of ISI. The law gave tax holidays to firms that entered areas of production considered to be "strategic" by the Secretariats of the Treasury and Industry and Commerce (Gracida and Fujigaki; 1988:31). The goal was to promote the production of capital goods, which was very low when compared to that of consumer goods[7] (Perzabal, 1988:29–42). The law greatly strengthened the ICES because it gave the government additional discretionary power to decide which sectors were "strategic" and which were not.

2. *Macroeconomic Policy and the ICES.* We have noted that one of the initial conditions for the establishment of the ICES was the assurance of profits through all means possible. During the Ruiz Cortines administration, this agreement was given clear interpretation. Such interpretation rested upon four specific policies: (i) taxes should not be raised or changed (Hansen, 1971[a]:69; Cinta, 1972:177); (ii) the exchange rate should remain fixed and currency exchange should not be controlled (Sánchez Gamper, 1989:65); (iii) public investment had to be directed mainly towards infrastructure for industrial development (Hansen, 1971[a]:63); and (iv) active interest rates had to remain low, and if possible negative (Hansen, 1971[a]:69). All these points would be subsequently negotiated through the ICES.

3. *Technical Consultation and the ICES.* Ruiz Cortines was a strong believer in the need for the specialization of the public sector (Vernon, 1964:115). As the economy was becoming bigger, he believed each agency

had to manage its particular area, without presidential mediation. This boosted the ICES. Archival evidence proves that by the second half of the presidential term, highly technical consultation was taking place around specific agencies (ARC 545.3/106)[8]. This policy established what would later become one of the sacred principles of the ICES: before appealing to the President, businessmen had to negotiate with a particular secretariat that would normally solve their problem. Only if agreements were not reached, would the President intervene.

4. *Labor Control and the ICES.* Ruiz Cortines continued the tight control of labor established by his predecessors. In 1958, he fiercely repressed a teachers' strike, which ended with Othón Salazar, their leader, thrown into jail (Krauze, 1997:200–1). The protests that followed on the part of some factions of the telegraph workers, electrical workers, the oil industry and railway workers were also brutally suppressed (Krauze, 1997:197–9). This "maintenance of stability" that had originally served as a founding condition of the ICES, with Ruiz Cortines consolidated as a condition of survival for the Mexican political system. In subsequent years, labor repression would turn into one of the main issues negotiated with businessmen through the ICES.

5. *Differences in Private Groups' Influence and the ICES.* We have mentioned that private groups entered the ICES either structurally weak and dependent or structurally strong and independent. Ruiz Cortines also consolidated these positions. Archival records prove that semi-official organizations had less and more difficult access to the President than independent groups. The President would meet organizations like CONCANACO (111/3612), CANACINTRA (ARC 111/909) or CONCAMIN (ARC 111/4161; ARC 545.3/2), but only after endless requests and long waits. Meanwhile, the bankers, both as a group and individually, had–if not immediate–considerably swifter access to the President (ARC 111/1476; ARC 111/3822). Distinct "circles of power" were starting to take shape within the system.

6. *Exclusion from Politics and the ICES.* Another general rule of the ICES was that businessmen had to limit their open political participation. An event during the Ruiz Cortines government served to confirm this rule once and for all. During the elections for governorship of the State of Puebla, Rómulo O'Farril, owner of an important national newspaper, decided to run as pre-candidate for the PRI. Not only was the pre-candidacy rejected, but anonymous flyers revealing embarrassing aspects of the private life of O'Farril were suddenly made public. These flyers can be consulted in the National Archives (ARC 544.2/27) and accuse O'Farril of being unfaithful to his wife and being corrupt in the past, amongst other

things. O'Farril–formerly a "favored businessman" with Alemán–was re-minded that he should not break the rules of the ICES. In future, the politi-cal role of businessmen would be limited to consultation about potential political candidates or high government officials (Tirado, 1987:478; Shafer, 1973:186).

7. *"Favored Businessmen" and the ICES.* Ruiz Cortines established two unwritten rules concerning "favored businessmen." First, he made clear that the preferential treatment would continue. Though more prudent than Alemán, Ruiz Cortines nevertheless appears to have been linked to Justo Fernández, an important agro-industrialist who obtained endless benefits through direct requests to the President, evidence of which I found in the National Archives (ARC 462.3/9; ARC 515.1/309; ARC 515.1/781; ARC 553/31; ARC 133.1/494; ARC 136.2/303; ARC 111/3391; ARC 515.1/493). Second, Ruiz Cortines also seems to have established that the President in office had to keep his distance from those businessmen favored by his immediate predecessor. This was probably to avoid the impression that only one person was benefiting or maybe because Ruiz Cortines did not trust the loyalty of previously favored businessmen. The fact is that the archives prove that Ruiz Cortines systematically avoided close relations with the "favored businessmen" of Alemán. The cases of Antonio Ruiz Galindo (ARC 433/26; ARC 548/19), Bernardo Quintana (ARC 437.1/36), and Bruno Pagliai (ARC 135.21/198; ARC 136.2/295) are illustrative. All, after endless requests for meetings and direct privilege, obtained little from the President. This practice of distance from previous "favored businessmen" established by Ruiz Cortines was voluntarily followed by all his successors.

In sum, by the end of the Ruiz Cortines administration, the ICES had finally emerged and gained practically all the features that would character-ize it in the future. A new era in which the ICES would persist, consolidate, and thrive was about to start.

2.1.3. The Persistence and Climax of the ICES (1958–1970)

In our theoretical section, institutional persistence is portrayed as the key to institutional operation. If institutions are to be successful, they must consol-idate and persist over time. The ICES confirms this assertion.

In this section, I shall illustrate how persistence promotes function, by concentrating on three moments of the ICES. Firstly, I shall discuss persist-ence after emergence. Secondly, I shall analyze the issue of long-term persist-ence. Finally, I shall narrate how the system thrived after 1961. Analysis will cover two presidential periods: the Adolfo López Mateos (1958–1964) and the Gustavo Díaz Ordaz administrations (1964–1970).

(i) The Adolfo López Mateos Period (1958–1964)

In our theoretical section, the persistence of an institution after emergence is seen as a result of the immediate benefits perceived by its participants. At the start of the López Mateos administration in 1958, the ICES was proving a useful structure to both private and public actors indeed. Both parties understood the value of interdependence. On the one hand, the private sector already recognized a debt to a state that was promoting its growth; on the other, the state recognized the contribution of business to its own legitimacy and survival. All participants were therefore willing to continue collaborating on the same terms (Hernández Rodríguez, 1989:46).

The problem at this point, however, was long-term legitimacy. The success of industrialization was not reflected in general living standards. From 1940 to 1958, inflation had averaged a constant yearly increase of 11.6% (calculated with data from INEGI, 1985:756). In consequence, real wages had dropped by 22.1% (Gracida and Fujigaki; 1988:23, 30). López Mateos saw that if he did not correct the contradictions of industrialization, the advantages of the strategy would soon be questioned by the whole of the population. Put in our terms, "stabilizing change" was urgently needed. In these circumstances, a new stage in the implementation of ISI was introduced in 1958: *Desarrollo Estabilizador* or "Stabilizing Development."

Much has been written about this strategy, so I will summarize it very briefly. *Desarrollo Estabilizador* aimed to deepen ISI, while maintaining financial stability. The model relied on foreign capital to substitute low indigenous savings. The main assumption was that the rapid growth of the economy would allow for repayment of foreign loans (Cypher, 1990:62–3). These foreign funds would be used to increase government spending which in turn would raise aggregate demand. Public spending would be channeled through the private sector, so investment would be promoted. Additionally, low taxes would be imposed, so profits would be reinvested, creating a virtuous circle of investment and saving. These increased savings would raise legal reserves in the central bank. These could then be pumped back selectively into the economy to substitute foreign loans and promote strategic areas. Finally, for all this to work, monetary stability was vital. The exchange rate would anchor the strategy (given the high dependence of Mexican production on imports) and would be fixed, thus controlling one possible source of price instability. Inflation would also be kept low through the combined management of credit and interest rates; through price controls; and through extensive subsidies in raw and intermediate inputs supplied by state-owned enterprises (Ayala Espino, 1988:331; Reynolds, 1977:1005; Villa, 1976:87; Villarreal, 1988:95; King, 1970:37; Mancera Aguayo,

1992:108). The architect of *Desarrollo Estabilizador* was Antonio Ortiz Mena, the new Secretary of the Treasury. As we shall see, he would play a leading role in the consolidation of ICES.

The new strategy renewed trust of the private sector. In one respect, it complied with all the basic agreements and objectives of the ICES. At the same time, it ensured the continuation of industrialization under the conditions demanded by businessmen. The strategy also showed immediate results for the general population. Inflation fell from 10.5% in 1958 to 3.6% in 1959 to–0.4% in 1963 (Nafinsa, 1977:218–9). Likewise, real wages increased by 40% in the same period (calculated with data from Basañez, 1990:171). This meant that purchasing power started to recover fast. The process of "stabilizing change" renewed confidence in the process of industrialization as a whole and preserved its legitimacy.

"Stabilizing change," however, was not only required at the economic level. In political terms, the Mexican State was also suffering an enormous legitimacy crisis. The main source of political dissatisfaction was the general perception that post-revolutionary regimes had favored business at the expense of the middle and lower classes. While government rhetoric and even the educational system promoted communitarian values, labor had been savagely repressed; the emerging and expanding young middle classes could not find enough jobs; and in general terms, the government seemed to be too close to capitalists and too far from the rest of the population. Then came the Cuban Revolution in 1959. This further ignited nationalistic and socialist fervor in Mexico, particularly amongst the young.

López Mateos felt that the only way to control the nation was to appear publicly close to those demands: he immediately supported the Cuban Revolution. Between June and July 1960, he had declared at least twice that "the [Mexican] Constitution was leftist" and that his government was "of the extreme left within the Constitution" (Arriola Woog, 1988[b]:252–3; Martínez Nava, 1984:132). Though the telephone industry had been already "Mexicanized" by purchasing all shares from foreign investors (Story, 1986:68), the government also nationalized the electric industry, purchased one of the biggest steel companies, took control of two cinema chains, and increased its levels of spending (Ramírez Rancaño, 1977:151–2; Nava García, 1983:198).

This "dirigiste economy," as it was called by a political analyst of the time (cf. Ballvé, 1958), scandalized businessmen. Even if the new economic policy had renewed their trust, these political decisions were–in their eyes–profoundly contradictory. Their confidence was shaken. Businessmen directly threatened to lower investment and engage in capital flight as a consequence of the "adventurous assertions of high public officials" in favor of Cuba (Martínez Nava, 1984:132–4; see also Concheiro, Gutiérrez and Fragosa, 1979:122). In an additional display of opposition CONCANACO, CON-CAMIN and Coparmex published a famous one-page letter in all the national newspapers on 24 November 1960. The letter was entitled: "Which Way Mr. President?" For the first time after the emergence of the ICES, businessmen felt powerful enough to attack the President directly and shake the informal system to the core. In this letter, they criticized what they saw as excessive government intervention in the economy. They directly inquired if there would be any further nationalization. Finally, they demanded that the government clearly show that Mexico was "a free economy" with "free enterprise" because, in their view, these were the "foundations of all other liberties" (*Excelsior*, 24/11/60; see also Alcázar Ávila, 1970:88; Martínez Nava, 1984:143).

Many basic rules of the ICES had been violated by both sides: the government was not consulting certain policy decisions with businessmen, nor was it maintaining social "order." As a consequence, businessmen were not respecting the President. Although archival records prove that during that time contact between businessmen and government officials continued, such interaction obviously was not effective (ALM 545.2/5; ALM 111/3357; ALM 135.2/433; ALM 135.2/291; ALM 534.9/7; ALM 433/304; ALM 437.1/109). However, things were about to change.

According to Juan Sánchez Navarro, one of the most influential Mexican business leaders and author of the "which way . . ." letter, from the day of its publication, López Mateos's attitude changed dramatically. During an interview, he gave me his impressions of the day the letter was published:

> It was very peculiar . . . We were in an airplane [with the President]. He was sitting alone in the front seat . . . In the middle of the flight, he started reading the newspaper. And we thought: "oh God, this plane will fall!" . . . He kept quiet the rest of the trip, thinking . . . Then we arrived to Poza Rica, and in Poza Rica the President changed . . . He changed his attitude towards businessmen and in relation to Marx-Leninism (sic) . . . From then on, the López Mateos government changed . . . and the best three and a half years of López Mateos were when he changed. It was a change that made possible the most prosperous era of Mexico (JSN, 21/06/01).

This change is not an exaggeration from the author of the letter. It was confirmed through a public, apologetic response to the letter given by the Secretaries of the Treasury and Industry and Commerce. Both gave an assurance that the government would always limit its intervention (Martínez Nava, 1984:145–6), which implied that the government would soon change its policies.

With the new economic strategy showing its first concrete results, social unrest had decreased. López Mateos apparently decided that further
confrontation with the private sector would only be counterproductive. He
seems accordingly to have resolved that it was time to engage in a different
type of "stabilizing change," only this time to reverse conflict with the private sector. During a speech to the Organization of American States (OAS),
he condemned Communism and justified his support for Cuba in terms of
respect for sovereignty. Problematic unions (oil, telegraph, and railways
workers; as well as pilots and teachers) continued to be fiercely repressed.
Their leaders were thrown into jail and the protesters violently controlled
(De la Garza Toledo, 1988:130). Additionally, López Mateos suppressed
guerrilla groups (the National Liberation Movement, MLN), and affirmed
that he would fight against "left or right" if it endangered the Constitution
(Ramírez Rancaño, 1977:157). "Order" had been re-established as apparently had negotiation; the President recovered his stature and the ICES appeared to be operating again. All this can be confirmed both through public
declarations of businessmen themselves, who were swift to announce that
confidence and negotiation had been fully re-established (Krauze, 1997:269;
Martínez Nava, 1984:148–54), and also by macroeconomic figures, which
confirm rising levels of investment. In fact, between 1960 and 1964, GDP
grew at an average of 7.5% per year (INEGI, 1985:311).

An undeniable fact, however, seems to be that during this time the autonomy of the state vis-à-vis the private sector had reached definite limits
(Hamilton, 1982:283–5; see also Cosío Villegas, 1974:72–3; Martínez Nava,
1984:21). It had become clear that economic growth was the prime guarantor
of continued political survival for the PRI-based political system. This dependence of the post-Revolutionary regime on economic growth in effect limited its
power over the private sector. At the same time, however, businessmen still depended heavily on the government for their growth, so they favored cordiality
over clash. This close interdependence is what finally consolidated the ICES.

In these conditions, the system came to the forefront as an important
structure in maintaining political and economic stability. Even if the ICES perpetuated an undemocratic, unrepresentative, and unaccountable regime, it was
a structure that also served the interests of the business elite because, at least, it
provided patterns for economic decisions (a degree of certainty), allowed them
to obtain profits (confidence of returns on their investments), and enabled them
to control the enormous power of the Mexican State (protected their property).
The reasons why the ICES remained informal, we have already seen: flexibility
and discretion, but at this point also the unwillingness of the regime to change
a legal framework that had perpetuated its power, and even the unwillingness

of union and peasant leaders to change a system that benefited them personally (even if it did not benefit their membership).

However, leaving ethical considerations aside (since the purpose of this section is not to judge the ICES but to describe its historic development), I argue that the early clashes between López Mateos and the private sector were–contrary to traditional accounts–the result of a system that was consolidating, and not of one that was crumbling. The evidence I have gathered points towards a novel process of "stabilizing change" that neither the government nor businessmen had witnessed before. The ICES was a relatively new structure, so the routines and agreements were not fully internalized by the participants yet. In my view, both sides were still adjusting to an unprecedented kind of collaborative relation that had never been tested to the degree it did in the late 1950s.

After López Mateos decided to strengthen relations with the private sector, collaboration thrived. In a system in which–as we have seen–legal (formal) institutions discouraged rather than encourage private investment, the confidence-creating role of informal co-operation cannot be understated. Obviously, the success that the economy and the political system enjoyed at the time cannot be attributed exclusively to the ICES. As stated in our theoretical framework, formal and informal institutions seem to maintain a dialectical interrelation through which they both support each other. In the case of Mexico, the ICES was able to recover and flourish after a shaky start with López Mateos, precisely because the formal economy started to work properly. Equally, the formal economy continued to grow because the ICES was thriving. Stable and prosperous international conditions also contributed to foster internal growth and stability.

The fact is that after 1961 the ICES became a mechanism that produced intensive consultation and exchange between the public and private sectors in Mexico. Different resources started to flow back and forth through all the policy networks of the system: information, economic resources, data, specific privileges, plans, and projects. Similarly, all the particular characteristics of the system that we studied before, consolidated fully through this increased interaction.

Foreign investment also started to flow more actively into the country (Erfani, 1995:81). The main forms of investment were the purchase of small companies and joint ventures with larger firms (Gracida and Fujigaki; 1988:41). This was attractive for big Mexican companies because it meant that they could grow exponentially over short periods. Very large Mexican corporations started to emerge. These firms, along with 250 or so major multinationals, also started to use the ICES to negotiate directly with the

President (Leal, 1986[b], 1986:37; Shafer, 1973:195), further boosting the importance of informal relations.

The early apogee of the ICES became evident through numerous events. By 1961, CONCANACO was already working closely with CEIMSA, the state distribution company; CONCAMIN and the ABM were openly asking their members to cooperate with the state (Vernon, 1964:170–1; Hansen, 1971[b]:91). In 1963, a new 1% tax on payrolls was swiftly cancelled after business organizations protested against it (Alcázar Ávila, 1970:93–6; Concheiro, Gutiérrez and Fragosa, 1979:287). In 1964, CONCAMIN declared that: " . . . in Mexico, the philosophy of co-ordination between the private sector and the public sector has been the most successful." (Concamin, 1976[b]:47). There was a widespread sense of optimism in the future of the country (Elguea Solís, 1989:172–3).

Additional confirmation of the solidity of the ICES lies in the low level of legislation in economic areas during the period of *Desarrollo Estabilizador* (Lomelí and Zebadúa, 1998:44). Surprisingly, in spite of the growing complexity and size of the economy, confidence seems to have been maintained and even increased without major legal changes. In principle, this could be a consequence of the existence of extensive and binding informal agreements that fostered, and at the same time were maintained by, high levels of mutual trust.

During this time, the practice of favoring specific businessmen continued. I have been able to identify two probable "favored businessmen" of López Mateos. Octaviano L. Longoria, owner of various trading firms, extensively benefited during the administration (ALM 521.8/145; ALM 705/2; ALM 564.2/274; ALM 565.1/69). Another businessman who probably benefited, although I have not been able to confirm more than a very close friendship, was Alejo Peralta, owner of the largest electric equipment firm in Mexico (Suárez, 1992:109, 127–8). Similarly, the practice of respectful distance from the "favored businessmen" of previous Presidents was certainly continued by López Mateos. Antonio Ruiz Galindo and Bruno Pagliai were the best examples of rejection to the granting of privilege (ALM 545.3/89; ALM 133.2/173; ALM 111/2713; ALM 524/117; ALM 563.3/297).

One additional characteristic of the ICES also emerged during this time: the formation of the "nationalist group." During his presidency, López Mateos created the Secretariat of the National Patrimony (SEPAFIN), in charge of managing state owned enterprises and natural resources. A policy network that also included the Secretariat of the Presidency and CANAC-INTRA gradually emerged around SEPAFIN. This policy network held a particular mixture of strong nationalistic and Keynesian views that opposed the monetarist-liberalist views of another important ICES policy network:

"the financial axis." The creation of the "nationalist group" would have strong implications for the future ideological struggle in Mexico, because of the unorthodox economic views of its members (Erfani, 1995:100).

As for the working and rural classes, the consolidation of the ICES unambiguously confirmed their status as the main "losing" groups. López Mateos attempted to re-accommodate their interests through a new Federal Labor Law that extended some privileges (Krauze, 1997:235) and/or through more positions in the government and the legislature. However, their weakness was structural: they had lost capacity to defend their interests due to incorporation maintained through "carrot and stick" repression (Hamilton, 1982:285).

(ii) The Gustavo Díaz Ordaz Period (1964–1970)

Gustavo Díaz Ordaz became President in 1964. At the beginning of his administration, all the main characteristics of the ICES were finally established. After at least four years of intensive operation, these features at last had been understood and accepted by all participants. Díaz Ordaz would reinforce this trend, and the ICES would reach its definite zenith. However, unfortunate political events in 1968 would also initiate a process of change that eventually led to the dissolution of the ICES. This section will analyze this exciting time of contrasts in Mexican history. I shall divide analysis in four parts. First, I shall summarize all the features that characterized the ICES at the start of the Díaz Ordaz government. Secondly, we shall look at the economic situation of the country in the late 1960s. Thirdly, I shall explain the economic and political conditions that made further economic growth possible. Finally, I analyze the economic and political conditions that prompted dramatic change in the ICES.

a) The Features of the ICES

Throughout this chapter, we have followed the process by which the ICES gradually acquired its definite features. Continuous operation finally consolidated the mutual compromises that supported the system. At the time of its climax, during the mid-1960s, the features of the ICES can be summarized in 16 points:

1. The ICES was formed by at least seven main policy networks, based around specific secretariats. The number of networks sometimes increased if the issues under discussion required the incorporation of additional Secretariats of State.
2. Each policy network negotiated technical issues related to its area of interest.
3. All policy networks reported to the President, who acted as an arbiter. Most of the time, however, presidential power was highly constrained by that of businessmen, who had a large influence on economic growth.
4. Because the proper operation of the ICES depended on a combination of servility and cordiality to the President, he could not be publicly questioned or

criticized. This was also a manifestation of the how the power of the President was more formal than real.

5. All issues had to be negotiated inside the particular policy networks before reaching the President.

6. Some policy networks within the ICES had stronger ideological unity. The most notable were (i) the "financial axis," formed by Secretariat of the Treasury-Bank of Mexico-Nafinsa-bankers; and (ii) the "nationalist group," formed by Secretariat of National Patrimony-Secretariat of the Presidency-CANACINTRA.

7. All the policy networks were geared towards the promotion of industrialization through assurance of private profit. Industrialization was the main goal of the Mexican State.

8. Other general issues that concerned businessmen were also negotiated through the ICES. At least in economic matters, the ICES practically substituted the subservient (to the President) legislature. Examples of these issues of general interest were: taxes, state intervention in the economy, public investment, labor policies, exchange and interest rates, supply of currency to buy equipment and intermediate goods, import licenses, trade protection, subsidies, price controls, and prices of government-supplied goods and services (e.g. oil and electricity).

9. Businessmen had to channel their specific demands through the ICES.

10. Businessmen had to refrain from participating openly in politics.

11. The government would guarantee political and economic stability, and ensure prior consultation with businessmen on any changes that might affect stability.

12. Because practically all negotiation between the public and private sectors was carried out through the ICES, the autonomy of the government was largely limited by the demands of the business sector. The ICES turned into a mechanism of control of state action, privilege for a few businessmen, and exclusion of a great majority of the population.

13. Access of businessmen to government officials varied, but it normally depended on the importance that both the President and the Secretaries of State placed on specific groups at specific times. As a rule, private were favored over semi-official groups.

14. Bankers were the most influential private group in the ICES, because public investment was often financed and channeled through the private banks. In exchange, banks accepted stringent regulation.

15. Issues were classified in importance depending on the size and influence of the firm(s) involved. The President dealt with the most important and the lower echelons of government with the least important, creating sub-policy networks within the networks.

16.   The most important foreign firms also participated in the ICES, but always at high levels: Secretaries of State and the President. Smaller foreign firms participated through their Mexican business partners.

b) The Economic Situation of Mexico in the 1960s

In October 1965, The Economist published an editorial in which it affirmed that "taking into account its current level of development, Mexico can easily become, in the short term, the Japan of the Western Hemisphere . . ." (Banco del País, 1965:45). And it was honestly believed. By the mid-1960s, the World was admiring a "Mexican Miracle" of economic development that few countries could match (Ayala Anguiano, 1979:234). Mexico gave the unambiguous impression that it was on its way to the developed world. In 30 years, electric power generation had gone from 0.5 to 7.5 millions of watts; the road network had increased from 5,000 to over 70,000 kilometers; extensive areas of land were given to farmers; the whole of the territory was covered by microwave telecommunications; the Mexico City subway was constructed; Mexico would even organize the Summer Olympic Games in 1968 and the Football World Cup in 1970, two events never organized by a developing country before (Tello, 1979:13; Nava García, 1983:211; Basañez, 1990:45).

Macroeconomic figures also indicated a "miracle." During the Díaz Ordaz government, GDP grew at an average yearly rate of 7.5%, with a figure of 11.7% in 1964. Average inflation had been 2.6%—lower than that of the U.S.; the IMF used the Peso as a reserve currency; and wages had risen over 6% per year in real terms (Krauze, 1997:315; Ortiz Mena, 1992:123; Pérez López, 1992:146). Even in terms of the dependence of the economy on foreign debt, *Desarrollo Estabilizador* had fared fantastically well. In 1965, over 60% of the Mexican foreign debt had an average maturity date of 10 years. During that year, the closest maturity date was three years (Banco del País, 1965:42). Even in 1969, foreign debt had only reached US$4.2 billion and only 10% had a maturity date between one and five years, while 50% had a maturity date of 10 years or more (Moreno and Caballero, 1995:152; Nafinsa, 1977).

These outstanding results were a combination of various economic and political factors that we will analyze in the coming section. However, in spite of all the deficiencies that economic policy may have had (and these we will soon study), it fostered a level of prosperity that Mexico had never known.

c) The Economic and Political Conditions for Growth

The outstanding levels of economic growth that Mexico achieved in the 1960s bolstered the ICES. Likewise, the agreements reached within the ICES further supported confidence in investment. In a dialectical interrelation of the type described by our theoretical section, formal and informal institutions were fostering economic stability.

The Díaz Ordaz government left untouched the *Desarrollo Estabilizador* model started by López Mateos. Even the Secretary of the Treasury, Antonio Ortiz Mena, and the Director of the Bank of Mexico, Rodrigo Gómez, remained in their posts. This fostered a high degree of continuity in macroeconomic policies (Jacobo, Luna and Tirado, 1989:8) and thus high levels of mutual trust between public and private actors. In fact, the combination of the macroeconomic policies of *Desarrollo Estabilizador* and informal negotiation through the ICES, became for businessmen *the essence* of trust, security, and confidence (Hernández Rodríguez, 1989:51). In the words of Miguel Alessio Robles, President of CONCAMIN in 1970–1, "Businessmen have been able to launch projects of great importance due to . . . the continuous and beneficial dialogue between the public and the private sectors, which is an intangible asset that we are mutually obliged to preserve." (MAR 1971).

Additionally, the ICES had consolidated as an effective institution of control of public power. Consultation had become practically obligatory, so the private sector had acquired an undisputed unwritten right of veto over government policy and action (Luna Ledesma, 1992ª:31). Antonio Ortiz Mena, Secretary of the Treasury, quoted in Camp (1990:114–6) conceded: "Our contact with the private-sector leaders was constant when I was in government. We would call them, give them our ideas about a policy, wait for their reaction; then we would analyze these reactions, take them into account, and incorporate them in our final policies." As suggested before, even government spending was virtually controlled by the bankers, because public spending depended on private finance (see FitzGerald, 1978, quoted in Erfani, 1995:97; Hernández Rodríguez, 1989:48).

The international economy was also helping the Mexican economy. Despite early signs of future instability, like the increase of inflation and the competitive devaluations of international currencies, developed economies had been growing favorably during the 1960s. For Mexico, this meant a relatively stable flows of FDI and exports that further supported economic expansion (Banamex, 1978:524–57).

This period of political and economic stability, however, should not be confused with stasis, in the sense introduced by "punctuated equilibrium" theory. This stability was a result of constant negotiation within all the policy networks of the ICES. As confirmed by archival records, intensive "stabilizing change" took place daily regarding specialized issues (ABM 11/09/67; ABM 13/11/67; ABM 15/01/68; ABM 12/02/68; ABM 10/12/69; ABM 08/12/69). Unfortunately, stability would not last for long. The shadows of deterioration were looming over Mexico because, up until then, both the political system and *Desarrollo Estabilizador* had been based on repression, exclusion, and inequality: the patience of Mexican Society had been exhausted and, this time, rhetorical promises would not be enough to pacify them.

d) Political and Economic Limits of the Mexican System

In contrast with the general sense of optimism of both businessmen and members of the government, the majority of Mexicans had reached a limit of forbearance towards the end of the 1960s. This was a peculiar time in Mexican history, because the optimistic economic outlook that we described above turned into widespread pessimism in a matter of months. The next paragraphs will examine the political and economic limits that the Mexican political system had reached. This analysis will serve as an introduction to the next chapter on institutional change.

(i) The Political Limits. As confirmed by Derossi (1971:174–8), by the late 1960s, industrialists and bankers saw themselves as the most influential social group in Mexico. They were not mistaken. The post-Revolutionary regime had resorted to industrial development as the most likely guarantor of political survival. Industrialization became a pretext for repression and an attempt to co-opt all those who disagreed with the strategy or with its mode of implementation. Understandably, many groups of an increasingly complex Mexican society started to complain.

By the 1960s, however, challenges to the government were not coming anymore only from uneducated industrial laborers. Pilots' and doctors' unions started demonstrating in the streets for better salaries, but also for more and better political participation. Even then, the reply from the government was the same as in the past: repression, violence, dissolution, discredit, and jail (Krauze, 1997:236, 296–301). This was the other side of the coin of confidence and trust generated through an exclusive system like the ICES. Given that the government had been clearly unable to properly accommodate the economic and democratic needs of the old and new "losing groups," the urban middle classes decided they had also reached the limits of tolerance (Cockcroft, 1990:239). Proof of this assertion would come from university students.

In July 1968, two large groups of students (one from the National Polytechnic Institute and the other from the National Autonomous University of Mexico) clashed in a sector of Mexico City for old rivalries between the two universities. The police intervened violently, temporarily jailing some students and sending most to hospital. Protests were organized against this excessive response. When protests grew, they were repeatedly met with the same reaction: fierce repression. As government violence grew, so did the protests.

Gradually, students started to express profound dissatisfaction with the authoritarian and undemocratic regime. Endless protests, growing violence, and failure to negotiate followed. Finally, on 2 October 1968, 10 days before the Summer Olympic Games were due to start, the largest demonstration of all took place. Between five and ten thousand students gathered in Tlatelolco, an area of Mexico City. As had become customary during previous demonstrations, speakers started to attack the endless contradictions of the regime. Suddenly, shooting started. Explanations abound. Even today, it is not clear how many died, but at least three hundred students "disappeared." At the time of writing, efforts are still being made to clarify these events (Krauze, 1997:320–51; Poniatowska, 1994; *La Jornada,* 09/07/02).

The impact that the 1968 student killing had for the future of the ICES cannot be exaggerated. Firstly, the responsibility for the killing was attributed to the Secretary of the Interior, and future President, Luis Echeverría Álvarez. As we will see soon, the killing deeply influenced his decisions when he reached the Presidency. Secondly, the event was considered the definite break of the Mexican political system. It was the first time since the 1920s that the state had committed massive murder to maintain "order" and "political stability." Numerous theories were put forward to explain the killing: they ranged from a KGB or CIA plot to the revenge of Díaz Ordaz against students who had mocked his ugliness (Medina Peña, 1995:202; .cf. Krauze, 1997:296). However, more serious accounts recognize that the reaction of the government only showed the exhaustion of a political regime that had dismissed democratic representation, social inclusion, balanced growth, and political adaptation in favor of political survival, privilege for a small minority of businessmen, and repression (Basañez, 1990:37; Medina Peña, 1995:161, 208).

(ii) The Economic Limits. The model of *Desarrollo Estabilizador,* designed to solve the contradictions of industrialization, had itself created numerous inconsistencies. I shall enumerate the most salient.

First, despite its amazing growth, the Mexican economy did not manage to enlarge the internal market. Inequality in income distribution not only had not diminished, but had in fact increased (Carrión and Aguilar, 1972:45; Ward, 1986:15; Handelman, 1997:121). In 1969, the lower 50% of the population received 15% of national income, 39% less than in 1958. Meanwhile, the top 10% received 51%, 11% more than in 1958 (Vellinga, 1989:51; calculated with data from INEGI, 1985:233). There was also great inequality of income between regions (Villa, 1976:152).

Second, economic inequality also caused problems in production. Increasingly, Mexican firms started to produce goods geared to the reduced but affluent middle classes. Meanwhile, products for mass consumption were largely imported, putting pressure on the balance of trade (Looney, 1985:62; Carmona, 1982:53–82; Paniagua, 1987:18; Tello, 1979:27).

Third, furthering inequality, the nation had an inefficient tax system. *Desarrollo Estabilizador* was based on tax exemptions in exchange for investment, so the tax burden was placed on salaries (Erfani, 1995:95). This created an inequitable and manifestly unjust tax system that placed the greatest burden on those least able to bear it and expressly exempting the rich.

Fourth, there were stark differences between small independent and larger firms, linked to multinational interests. This created further concentration of wealth and technology (Cordero and Santín, 1977:21; Cordero and Santín, w/d:52; Carrión and Aguilar, 1972:119–21; Lomelí and Zebadúa, 1998:39). Given that tax exemptions had been handed out indiscriminately (Gracida and Fujigaki; 1988:32), the industrial base was big but inefficient (Tello, 1979:16).

Fifth, tariff protection, originally imposed as a temporary measure, became and an end in itself (Aspra, 1977:121; Rubio, 1990:248), creating highly inefficient firms, never ready to give up the privilege of buying cheap imported intermediate and capital goods (Looney, 1985:21–2; Izquierdo, 1964:287). This created a paradox: firms whose production substituted imports, often refused to use national inputs, because they did not trust quality or price. A proof is that, while industrial output increased 5 times between 1940 and 1965, imports of foreign industrial goods and replacement parts increased 12.5 times (Cockcroft, 1990:161–2). In other words, Mexican industrialization depended heavily on imports. During the 1960s, 46% of all imports were rigidly determined by the industrial structure (Carmona, 1982:211; Guillén Romo, 1984:78; Ayala Espino et al., 1979:68). Some firms depended, for 90% of their machinery needs, on imported technology (Ramírez Rancaño, 1974:29). In fact, between 1965 and 1969, 72% of exports were used to finance machinery imports (Villa, 1976:31). The perverse contradiction, then, was that the more industry grew, the greater balance-of-payment imbalance there would be.

Sixth, the bias towards industrial growth fostered dangerous imbalances in agriculture (King, 1970:38). Whilst public investment in industry increased 15 times between 1952 and 1970, agricultural development only increased roughly 7 times (Nafinsa, 1977:369–70). Additionally, the little investment there was given to large commercial farmers (King, 1970:41). This caused (i) widespread poverty in rural areas; and (ii) additional pressure to import agricultural foodstuffs. The "losing" condition of the rural classes had been confirmed.

Seventh, planning was difficult. Industrialization policies were left uncoordinated and improvised throughout the years (Villa, 1976:29; Saldivar, 1991:88–91). This often led to unwanted and unexpected consequences at all levels.

Eighth, subsidies for industrial firms had increased over the years to a point where they caused colossal losses to the government. Given tax collection was very low, these subsidies created growing financial deficits over the years, and therefore the need for greater public debt (Puga, 1993:60; Beltrán Mata, 1987:88–9; Story, 1986:75–6).

In conclusion, *Desarrollo Estabilizador* promoted internal growth and price stability, but through the development of deep structural imbalances. It promoted inefficient substitution of imports through high dependence on foreign capital and technology. In many respects, the Mexican pattern of capitalist accumulation had reached its limits (Ramírez Rancaño, 1977:188; Ayala Espino *et al.*, 1979:19–20). Although on 9 November 1970 the President of CONCAMIN, Miguel Alessio Robles, affirmed that the Díaz Ordaz administration ended " . . . in a climate of absolute tranquility and unity of the great Mexican family; of confidence in the future of Mexico and collaboration between all national sectors" (Tello, 1979:11), history would prove him wrong. A dramatic process of change that we shall analyze in the next chapter was about to start.

Chapter Four
Institutional Change and the ICES

INTRODUCTION

The process of institutional change is central to the understanding of institutions, because it describes a situation still not fully explained by modern social studies. This chapter aims to highlight the importance of analysis of institutional change by closely studying the process against the background of the Mexican case. Such process of change of the ICES is addressed in a separate chapter, not only because of its extent, but also to reflect the centrality of the process in institutional and political terms. At the same time, this chapter aims to explain a period of modern Mexican history that even today remains exciting because of its inherent complexity.

This chapter will test some of the theoretical concepts introduced in the previous section of this book. Recapping, in the first two chapters of this work I introduced two types of socio-political change: stabilizing and paradigmatic. Stabilizing change refers to the constant renegotiation that allows political institutions–and therefore society as a whole–to adjust to changing internal or external circumstances. Paradigmatic change, on the other hand, is a more infrequent process that involves profound institutional and ideological transformation. We concluded that paradigmatic change starts as a result of the loss of institutional legitimacy through the failure of "stabilizing change." Likewise, we agreed that the dialectical interrelation between formal and informal institutions plays an important role in the process, because it can accelerate or retard the loss of legitimacy of a given institution, or a set of them, within a given political system. Finally, following the Hay model, we introduced five steps through which paradigmatic change takes place. This chapter will look at how all these processes apply to the ICES. The chapter will cover three presidential periods that, in my view, coincide with the five steps of the Hay model: the Luis Echeverría Álvarez period (1970–1976), the José López Portillo period (1976–19782), and the first two years of the Miguel De la Madrid Hurtado period (1982–1984).

1. PARADIGMATIC CHANGE STARTED: THE LUIS ECHEVERRÍA ÁLVAREZ PERIOD (1970–1976)

Luis Echeverría Álvarez became President of Mexico in 1970. During his administration, the imbalances in the Mexican economy deepened and the ICES reached a low point. I believe that the first three steps of paradigmatic change took place in Mexico during his government. Let us analyze these three moments in relation to the ICES.

a) The First Step of Paradigmatic Change and the ICES.

We have said that this first step consists of the loss of the legitimacy of existing social institutions through a failure of "stabilizing change." In my view, this step started the day that Luis Echeverría Álvarez became candidate for the presidency in 1969. At that time, the formal institutions on which the *Desarrollo Estabilizador* model was based had developed the contradictions that we have already analyzed. At the same time, the formal political institutions that supported *Desarrollo Estabilizador* came under attack after the 1968 student killing. On the informal institution side, legitimacy was also at stake. Although the direct participants of the ICES were understandably happy with the results of the system, the rest of the population–and certainly Echeverría himself–perceived the structure as one inevitably linked to *Desarrollo Estabilizador*, and thus severely questioned its elitism (Carrión and Aguilar, 1972:225). General institutional legitimacy was under threat, so "stabilizing change" would have been necessary to restore it.

In my view, at that point, the good relations within the ICES would have allowed for a smooth modification of the *Desarrollo Estabilizador* model of development, in order gradually to adjust it to the new circumstances. This would have required enormous "stabilizing change," but in the end, lost legitimacy could have been recovered. Naturally, businessmen would have attempted to defend their interests, but these included social peace for investment. All in all, "stabilizing change" within the ICES could probably have averted a legitimacy crisis. However, the future President had different ideas.

Echeverría, Secretary of the Interior since 1964, was a gray, uncharismatic bureaucrat who became presidential candidate by direct appointment of President Díaz Ordaz. Echeverría was widely regarded as responsible for the 1968 student killing; an allegation that was never proven, but that even today remains a firm suspicion in the Mexican mind, because of his direct power over the security forces that carried out the massacre. In consequence, both as presidential candidate and then as President, Echeverría became almost obsessed with regaining credibility. As Whitehead (1980:844–7) correctly asserts, none of Echeverría's decisions can be understood without looking at 1968. He decided to adopt the stance of the student protesters and–aided by leftist ideologists (López-Portillo Romano; 1994:85)–became (i) the main narrator of the contradictions of *Desarrollo Estabilizador* and (ii) the main instigator of the failure of "stabilizing change." In other words, he accelerated the first stage of paradigmatic change. Let us briefly analyze these two points.

(i) Candidate Echeverría accentuated the loss of legitimacy of the economic institutions by endlessly blaming *Desarrollo Estabilizador* for inequality in the nation and, ultimately, for the unstable social situation (López-Portillo Romano, 1994:83; Martínez Nava, 1984:165; Elizondo, 1994:166). Once he became President, instead of modifying the model, Echeverría adopted a populist approach to appease dissent and decided that *Desarrollo Estabilizador* had to be eliminated completely (Saldivar 1980:87–96; Newell and Rubio, 1984; Rivera Ríos, 1992:Ch. II; Newell and Rubio, 1984:Ch. III).

(ii) Repeatedly, throughout his government, Echeverría disallowed the possibility of informal "stabilizing change" by canceling informal negotiation, publicly blaming businessmen for Mexico's woes, and promoting what business people regarded as anti-business policies. Concerning informal negotiation, he was convinced that a system such as the ICES was a deleterious remnant of *Desarrollo Estabilizador* and, therefore, had to be abandoned (Saldivar, 1991:79). From the first day of his government, Echeverría started to affront businessmen verbally in private and public (Concheiro, Gutiérrez and Fragosa, 1979:332.;Hernández Rodríguez, 1989:11). The minutes of a meeting with Coparmex in early 1971 are illustrative: asked to strengthen dialogue with the private sector, Echeverría replied: "Do not confuse the elastic forms of social interaction, by pretending that the Chief Executive will have to consult . . . a . . . small . . . private organization [like yours]." (Coparmex, 1971:41–7). The tone and frequency of condemnation gradually intensified to the point of attack against the business sector. At a meeting with bank workers in 1972 Echeverría publicly said: "There are . . . bank owners that have seen . . . their institutions (sic) grow, but [they] only think in their interest, as if they had no country. They . . . brag about their religious or Christian convictions, but if Christ lived again, he would have to throw them out like merchants; to whip them away from the temple" (GM, 14/07/72). Subsequently, Echeverría would continue referring to businessmen as "reactionaries and enemies of the people's progress" (Tello, 1979:153–65); "the little rich" or *riquillos* (Valdés Ugalde, 1982:14); or "the rich and powerful ... [who] call themselves Catholics and beat their chests, but refuse to help their neighbor" (Basañez, 1990:54). In 1976, the President of Coparmex, Andrés Marcelo Sada, was even prosecuted for treason on grounds of verbal attacks against President Echeverría and the Mexican Government (Concheiro, Gutiérrez and Fragosa, 1979:128). Sada had to flee the country until the next President dropped the case (AMSZ 27/06/01), which clearly had been a juridically weak political revenge of Echeverría against one of his main critics. Even after two decades, in an interview given to López-Portillo Romano in 1993 (1994:93), Echeverría called Mexican businessmen: "immature, timid, subservient to foreign interests, and pretentious."

Mexican politicians had traditionally attacked businessmen in public rhetorically to legitimize their "pact with the masses" (Stevens, 1977:236; Bailey, 1986:123; Vellinga, 1989:65; Camp, 1990:33). Yet, these words had always been interpreted as a political sketch. Echeverría, however, became too offensive. Most worrying to businessmen, he started to back his words with action (Tello, 1979:59; Story, 1986:114; Basañez, 1990:49; Mendoza Berrueto, 1998:125; Arriola Woog, 1976:449; Elizondo, 1994:169). In one of his first major moves against business, Echeverría promised to break up informal consultation. He publicly called such system "a shameful pact between private enterprise and the government" (Concheiro, Gutiérrez and Fragosa, 1979:333–4). He broke off any personal contact with businessmen. In interview, he told me:

> Those gentlemen wanted to have the government at their service ... that was just not possible. ... They were used to a very particular type of relationship with government. For instance, at Christmas, they would all cooperate, and their wives would go and present jewels to the wife of the President. Since the first year, comrade–as he called his wife–María Esther and I decided to refuse the gift. Then, the permanent invitations to the wedding of the daughter, to the baptism of the nephew ... Presidents were invited to be godfathers of everyone. I decided to stop all that type of contact, and they did not like that ... (LEA 14/07/01).

Additionally, Echeverría attempted directly to weaken the "financial axis," which was one of the main policy networks around which both *Desarrollo Estabilizador* and the ICES were built (Luna Ledesma, 1992ᵃ:35; see also Valdés Ugalde, 1982:8). To do this, he appointed his personal friend (and future President) José López Portillo–a lawyer–as Secretary of the Treasury (Erfani, 1995:104, 112). He also transferred some of the functions of the Secretariat of the Treasury to the Secretariat of the Presidency, under his direct supervision. By May 1973, Echeverría declared: "the economy is managed from *Los Pinos,*" the presidential residence (Zaid, 1992:11; see also Carpizo, 1998:75). If the "financial axis" did not really break up, it was because López Portillo lacked the expertise to manage the economy, and chose to maintain the same people in the financial agencies. Additionally, he had the ambition to become president, so he did not want directly to affect or confront businessmen, as they were a potentially valuable political clientele.

Echeverría introduced additional policies that removed any remaining possibility of embarking on "stabilizing change" with businessmen. Highly populist, he often promoted wage increases and additional fringe benefits for workers (GM, 24/12/74; GM, 24/08/76). He encouraged the public mobilization of labor to persuade employers to meet these demands. He even used price controls or the opening of the market to foreign products as frequent forms of persuasion (Arriola Woog, 1976:104–6, 459; De la Garza Toledo, 1988:161–2; Valdés Ugalde, 1982:14; cf. Tello, 1979:111; Basañez, 1990:51; Martínez Nava, 1984:185–6). In the same vein, Echeverría increased state intervention in the economy. This was mainly achieved through processes of "Mexicanization," as in the cases of *Heinz* and *Indetel,* where the government put pressure on those multinationals to sell their stock to Mexican investors (GM, 29/10/73; GM, 16/10/74); nationalization, as in the case of the tobacco industry (GM, 04/11/72); or through the direct creation or consolidation of state-owned enterprises and trust funds, examples of which are the creation of *SICARTSA,* a major steel mill, and the strengthening of *CEIMSA* (which became *Conasupo*) (GM, 03/75). Although the private sector was sometimes able to attenuate the intervention plans of the Echeverría government, the effort required to do so was enormous and the results uncertain. The fact is that, by the end of the Echeverría administration, state-owned companies and agencies had more than trebled (Luna Ledesma, 1992[a]:40–1). The real problem was that, while in the past state-owned firms had been complementary to the private sector, under Echeverría they were turned into direct competitors (Concheiro, Gutiérrez and Fragosa, 1979:37–49).

If this were not enough, Echeverría extensively modified the regulatory framework, in order to institutionalize state intervention into private decision-making. For instance, in 1972 he passed the "Law on the Registration and Transfer of Technology" and the "Law on the Use and Exploitation of Patents and Brands." They respectively aimed to regulate the type of technology that could be imported into Mexico, and the maximum amount Mexican firms could pay foreign firms for the use of patents and brands. (GM, 03/11/72). In 1974, the law regulating Nafinsa was modified. Instead of remaining a financing agency for private projects, it was thereafter geared to financing the "Mexicanization" of foreign industries (Villa, 1976:11, 48–50). Additionally, Nafinsa entered in direct competition with private banks by joining the open market for trust funds (Villa, 1976:61, 129). Other reforms were the anti-monopoly law (GM, 30/12/74) and the "Law for the Protection of Consumers" (Tello, 1979:134; Lomelí and Zebadúa, 1998:134). Both statutes gave the government ample discretionary power to punish price-setting strategies or violations of price controls. Last but not least, a new "Law for Human Settlements" was passed in 1976 after a bitter struggle with the private sector. In the opinion of businessmen, the law gave the government extensive expropriatory power over land without sufficient rights of compensation or right of appeal (GM, 26/06/76; Concheiro, Gutiérrez and Fragosa, 1979:109).

Echeverría's foreign policy was another source of alarm for the private sector (Concheiro, Gutiérrez and Fragosa, 1979:122; Valdés Ugalde, 1982:9; Arriola Woog, 1988ᵃ:93–4). First of all, Echeverría took the leading role in the organization of a non-aligned-countries movement against what he regarded as increasing American "imperialism" (Lomelí and Zebadúa, 1998:109; Arriola Woog, 1976:453). Additionally, he strengthened links with the Communist bloc by visiting the USSR, Cuba, and China (GM, 09/08/74; GM, Vol. 53). His visit to Socialist President Salvador Allende of Chile was highly criticized by businessmen, as was Allende's visit to Mexico in 1972 (GM, Vol. 17, pp.212–7; Arriola Woog, 1988ᵃ:84; GM, 30/11/72).

But the events that definitely destroyed business confidence for the rest of the Echeverría administration were the assassinations of two prominent businessmen. The first and most critical was that of Eugenio Garza Sada on 17 September 1973. Garza Sada was the leader of the powerful Monterrey Group. He was murdered during an attempted kidnapping by a Communist organization, the "*23 de Septiembre* League." A few days later, Fernando Aranguren, a close friend of Garza Sada, and prominent businessman from Guadalajara, was also assassinated in a similar situation (Medina Peña, 1995:226; Monsivais, 1979:313).

In the case of Garza Sada, Echeverría personally went to pay his respects to the Garza Sada family. He said Garza Sada had been a man he had "met and appreciated deeply" (GM, 18/09/73). However, the private sector always suggested that the government had either performed or ordered the killing (in order to threaten businessmen). For instance, Ricardo Margain Zozaya,

President of the Consultive Council of the Monterrey Group, affirmed during a public speech at the funeral that the government's anti-business rhetoric had incited radical groups to commit the crime (Arriola Woog, 1988[a]:101–3). Echeverría himself was present during that speech. Officially, three members of the 23 *de Septiembre* group were tried and charged with murder, but current investigation confirms that the government knew about the possibility of such murder in advance, and did not warn or protect the victim (see *Milenio Semanal*, No. 254, 5th August, 2002). According to Basañez (1981:89–92, 126–8), however, it is very unlikely that Echeverría ordered the assassination directly. In a brilliant exposition, the author introduces the idea that some powerful business groups in Monterrey (Alfa) and Mexico City (Televisa) could have benefited more from the murder than the government. However, the case–like most important political issues in Mexico–still remains unclear.

After months of claims and counterclaims, trust between the President (and the government in general) and businessmen had seriously eroded. The legitimacy of the ICES had been destroyed, as had been the possibility of "stabilizing change." If we recall that the legitimacy of the formal political and economic institutions was also in crisis, we may conclude that the first step of paradigmatic change was complete.

In retrospect, if the private sector did not react immediately to attacks by Echeverría, it was because it seemed to be organized for good but not bad relations with the government. The ICES had spoilt them. As the literature and the archival documents show, their first reactions displayed clumsiness, hesitation, and desperation (GM, 28/02/74; GM, 03/06/74; GM, 06/06/74; GM, 07/06/74; GM, 29/04/75; Buendía, 1986:33; Arriola Woog, 1988[a]:117; Erfani, 1995:114; Valdés Ugalde, 1982:7). However, an internal reorganization of the private sector had started to take place even before the murder of Garza Sada. The reorganization accelerated after the murder. A new group of more belligerent and forceful leaders would take power and defy the government as never before (Valdés Ugalde, 1982:10; Uribarri, 1985:46–7).

b) The Second Step of Paradigmatic Change and the ICES.

As stated, the second step of paradigmatic change consists of (i) the narration of contradictions of the previous state of affairs; and (ii) the implicit envisaging of a desired new situation. Echeverría actively embarked on both. Firstly, authors agree that the President spoke of *Desarrollo Estabilizador* as pernicious. He wanted to be perceived as a new Cárdenas (Handelman, 1997:42; Krauze, 1997:369), whose rhetoric was geared to recuperating the "authentic" program of the Mexican Revolution (Valdés Ugalde, 1982:1;

Martínez Nava, 1984:167). On point (ii), he introduced a new economic program, which he called "Shared Development" (or *Desarrollo Compartido*), that sought to address the economic and social problems created by *Desarrollo Estabilizador*.

Desarrollo Compartido was a return to "economic nationalism." It aimed to reduce the concentration of wealth, the penetration of foreign capital, and the growing disequilibria in the balance of payments. It was also said that it would reduce industrial inefficiency and poor agricultural performance (Tello, 1980:Ch. I; Saldivar, 1980:87–91; Basañez, 1981:62–71). In industrial terms, he wanted to promote a second stage of ISI, in order to produce capital goods (Tello, 1979:31–3). Redistribution would be achieved through radical tax reform. Echeverría believed that the state had the right and obligation to take over the redistributive role of private business because of what he saw as their failure to ensure productive investment, job creation, and greater economic activity (López-Portillo Romano, 1994:94; see also Hernández Rodríguez, 1990:738; Ward, 1986:18; Uribarri, 1985:24). In terms of relations with the private sector, Echeverría decided that the government would only support "nationalist firms." Since in his conception only 100% Mexican export firms qualified as "nationalist," most Mexican industry–often in partnership with foreign companies–was left out of the government's programs. Additionally, he attempted to replace the ICES with a more transparent, "semi-public," system of consultation and negotiation (Luna Ledesma, 1984:29, 1992ᵃ:36; Leal, 1986:35). He called it the National Tripartite Commission (CNT). The CNT was "tripartite" because it would also include labor in the discussions.

Desarrollo Compartido also included a political agenda. Echeverría wanted to solve the political legitimacy problems inherited from 1968 without threatening the hegemony of the PRI. To this end, he incorporated enormous numbers of former 1968 student protesters into the government (Basañez, 1981:191), firstly by introducing an electoral reform to lower the age of eligibility of Deputies and Senators, to give participation to younger people. Secondly, the same reform created a system of proportional representation through which smaller parties from a broader ideological spectrum could enter Congress. Finally, he created endless new public agencies to accommodate higher numbers of young people in the most diverse areas of specialization (Lomelí and Zebadúa, 1998:98).

In spite of all these great intentions, *Desarrollo Compartido* soon proved a disaster. The model was based on extremely high levels of public expenditure that simply could not be met through the existing sources of financing. When the government failed to pass a tax reform, due to constant resistance within and outside state bureaucracy, Echeverría was forced change the strategy and borrow colossal amounts of foreign money to finance his programs. In only six years (1970–1976), foreign public debt grew by 4.6 times, going from US$4.2 billion to US$19.6 billion (INEGI, 1985:645). This meant that it went from representing 17% of GDP to 38% (calculated with data from INEGI, 1985:311–2). Domestic debt increased by eleven times in the same period (cf. Concamin, 1976ª:22–3). Additionally, most money was immediately spent. Public sector deficit came to represent 70% of its total income (Luna Ledesma, 1992ª:40–1).

Echeverría had engaged in expansionary economic policy to promote state-led economic growth. However, lack of planning and technical knowledge became evident. From 1972 to 1975, aggregate demand increased by 90.3% against only 18.5% increase in production. Monetary expansion amounted to 86% (Concamin, 1976ª:13). In consequence, inflation went from 3.6% in 1970 to 19.2% in 1976. In this situation, national and foreign businessmen further lost confidence in the Echeverría government and engaged in capital flight. In 1976 alone, US$6 billion was removed from the country (González Soriano, 1983:183). International reserves sank from US$1.6 billion in 1975 to US$740 million in 1976 (Fitzgerald, 1979:1–28). The Peso was devalued for the first time since 1955. In one month (September to October 1976), it went from 12.50 pesos per dollar to 26.05. The devaluation of the Peso (then decided by the President) was illustrative of Echeverría's economics. During his administration, the inflation rate in Mexico was 250% higher than in the U.S. Yet, while the dollar suffered 10 devaluations, he kept the Peso artificially fixed until 1976. On 28 October 1976, an agreement with the IMF to stabilize the Mexican economy was announced (Tello, 1979:174–6). In only six years, Echeverría had managed to destroy years of growth.

The negotiation strategy through the CNT also failed. Rather than a substitute for the highly technical ICES, the CNT became a caricature of a legislative body. Archives show that the CNT discussed issues ranging from environmental to educational policy (GM, 12/03/74). In 1975, Echeverría dissolved the CNT not without some bitter words in his most refined style:

> I believe that we could have talked with frankness . . . [but] I think we must now resign ourselves to remaining incongruent. Those who are great believers should not go out on the streets after the transcendental act of confession to continue harming others; and those who are very revolutionary should not remain so only at the level of political speeches . . . [From now on] I prefer to stay with the great masses of workers and

peasants of Mexico, than with my own feeble collaborators or with the gentlemen in business. Excuse the absence of political nicety of this assertion . . . (Luna Ledesma, 1992[a]:45).

However, Echeverría did not stay with the "great masses" either. *Desarrollo Compartido* was also a social flop. If what Echeverría wanted was to promote job creation and the creation of wealth, he seems to have achieved precisely the contrary. While in 1960–1970, 37% of working-age people found a job, in 1970–1975 only 25% did so, and in 1976 job creation was actually negative (Concamin, 1978:19). At the productive level, the average profit to sales ratio from 1973 to 1975 went down from 6.6 cents per Peso to 5.4. All industrial sectors, without exception, lost (Concamin, 1978:17–9).

Desarrollo Compartido seems to have been flawed from the start. The economic changes that Echeverría attempted to introduce excluded any negotiation with the most influential economic actors. Both businessmen and government officials from the "financial axis" boycotted the program, because they simply did not believe in it. In the end, *Desarrollo Compartido* became a mixture of policies that worsened the imbalances of the previous years and, on top, created new and greater ones. A peculiar moment in Mexican economic history then took place. While Echeverría was still narrating[1] the contradictions of *Desarrollo Estabilizador,* businessmen and many sections of society started to narrate those of *Desarrollo Compartido.* Confusion reigned.

c) The Third Step of Paradigmatic Change and the ICES

We have accepted that the third step of paradigmatic change consists of the meta-narration of contradictions of a certain political model or of its particular institutions. However, towards the end of the Echeverría government, what model could have been meta-narrated: *Desarrollo Estabilizador,* which had already been meta-narrated by Echeverría, or Echeverría's Shared Development that was showing so many contradictions?

As suggested earlier, to understand the private sector in the mid-1970s, one needs to realize that it was a time of generational change. A younger generation of businessmen had been taking over the private organizations of representation and they had very definite views about the changes needed in the Mexican political and economic system. I accordingly argue that this younger generation seized the moment to meta-narrate the contradictions of the whole post-revolutionary regime, rather than just the two specific economic models. Educated in the "official" line where the Mexican political system was seen as perfect, and where order and persistence at any cost were paramount, Echeverría probably could not understand the changing reality, much less react to it.

Indeed, by the early 1970s, businessmen had acquired significantly different characteristics from their predecessors, as a result of both changing values and economic growth (Hernández Rodríguez, 1989:42). The new generation was immensely richer and more powerful than their parents, because for 30 years their firms had monopolized the Mexican market. For instance, at that time, 1% of all industrial firms produced around 66% of total output and accounted for the same proportion of total investment (Cordero, 1987ª:11; Cordero, 1987ᵇ:19, 49; Hernández Rodríguez, 1989:61; Hernández Rodríguez, 1988:67; Bortz and Wilkie, 1990:18–9; Martínez Nava, 1984:19; Cordero, 1974:135; Cordera and Tello, 1981:37; Story, 1986:50–1). Additionally, these younger businessmen had often been educated in the U.S., favored closer ties with foreign firms, privileged written contracts over informal arrangements, and held traditional politicians in very low esteem (Derossi, 1971:63–7, 112, 185). Of common cultural background and, in many cases, with close family ties, this new generation had promoted extensive economic links between themselves and with foreign firms, so their degree of ideological unity was very high and greatly influenced by their foreign counterparts (Hernández Rodríguez, 1989:60; Carrión and Aguilar, 1972:140–1; Ramírez Rancaño, 1976:52).

This younger generation saw the dissolution of the ICES as a necessity because, in their view, the increasing size and complexity of the Mexican economy required written laws to ensure certainty (Vernon, 1964:160–1). Of course, they did not want the Shared Development of Echeverría either, which they saw as intrusive and populist. They favored a combination of the macroeconomic stability of *Desarrollo Estabilizador* with open political participation, and clear law to control the government (Hernández Rodríguez, 1989:62; cf. Orvañanos Zúñiga, 1975:16). In future, they wanted to avoid any possibility of the arbitrary excesses displayed by Echeverría. The problem of the Mexican State had ceased to be one of access and had become one of credibility.

If, as we have said, at the beginning of the chaotic times of Echeverría, businessmen were not organized to face attack, the overall unity of the new generation fostered a swift reorganization. The younger generation of businessmen started to gain positions in the main private organizations. Younger leaders like Andrés Marcelo Sada of Coparmex, Joaquín Pría Olavarrieta in CANACINTRA, Jesús Vidales Aparicio in CONCANACO or Jorge Sánchez Mejorada in CONCAMIN, started constantly to challenge Echeverría

(Tello, 1979:97). In 1975, with the backing of the older generation, they founded the CCE, which despite its insufficiencies was able to unite the private sector as a whole (Luna Ledesma, 1992[a]:47–8). The American Government and the AMCHAM strongly supported this new group of more combative Mexican businessmen through public legitimization of their actions (Puga, 1982:195; Basañez, 1981:86). For example, in 1972, the U.S Government officially complained against the tight controls on foreign investment (Medina Peña, 1995:227). In 1973, the AMCHAM sent its members the so-called "Powell Memorandum," in which he urged them to defend private enterprise against attacks of nationalism (Puga, 1982:195). In 1976, the AMCHAM also published extensively on the blessings of foreign investment (CAMCO, 1976[a]:801–3 ;CAMCO, 1976[b]:806). In that same year, 76 U.S. Congressmen published in the newspapers a letter directed to President Ford, expressing their concern at "the appointment of at least one thousand Communists and foreign radicals to important government positions [in Mexico]," and ended by reminding the President of "the Cuban lesson" (Tello, 1979:143).

Apart from encouraging investment strikes and capital flight, the new generation of businessmen initiated the extensive meta-narration of the political contradictions of *Desarrollo Estabilizador* and of all the contradictions of Shared Development. Manuel Clouthier, one of the most militant members of Coparmex declared: "Free enterprise, by nature, is the conjunction of many values. For historical circumstances, it has a mission to achieve. It is linked to needs and therefore recognizes hunger and marginality; it directly acknowledges the good or bad quality of education and suffers because of ignorance. Free in essence, it recognizes when freedom is threatened ..." (MCDR, Coparmex, 1999:19). It was also argued that the private sector is "the driving force of economic development" and that state intervention only had to be "subsidiary and complementary, never basic." In their view, democracy and economic planning were "contradictory," so they proposed collaboration instead. Eugenio Garza Sada, for instance, thought that the state exclusively had to be "like a bulldozer that removes obstacles and clears the path for development" (Casar and Peres, 1988:112–4). Andrés Marcelo Sada added that: " . . . the system of personal freedoms consecrated by our Constitution has been seriously jeopardized, due to invasion of the private spheres of action by the state. . . . Juridical security has been yielding to discretionary decisions and improvisation" (Coparmex, 20/02/76). In 1976, when Echeverría decreed the expropriation of commercial agricultural land in the north of the country, Coparmex denounced "invasions, thefts of crops, demagogy, unrest and violence . . . lack of definition and rules, [and] the crooked interpretations of [the] law made by . . . officials of the Secretariat of Land Reform, Attorney Generals, and governors of the states." They finished by pointing out the threat that this represented to the "rights and liberties" of Mexicans and demanding the Government "stop anarchy and stop destroying Mexico" (Coparmex, 23/11/76; Coparmex, 16/16/76).

The meta-narration of systemic crisis included the organized dissemination of rumor, jokes, and anonymous campaigns against the government (Luna Ledesma, 1992ª:49–50; Mendoza Berrueto, 1998:132). The rumors included the existence of a "ripper" of women in numerous Mexican cities (end of 1972); the imminent scarcity of food due to lack of production (1972); an imminent scarcity of petrol (1973); the sterilizing vaccines that the government was secretly using in public hospitals to control population (October-December 1974); the inclusion of Marxist-Leninist ideas in free text books distributed by the government (1975); the expropriation of private property for communal purposes (1975); the imminence of a coup d'etat (1976) (Monsivais, 1979:317–20); and the imminent nationalization of the banking system (1976) (Coparmex, w/o specific date, 76). This last rumor was so strong that the government was forced to publish an official denial (GM, 16/08/76).

In sum, businessmen were meta-narrating the contradictions and insufficiencies of the Mexican post-revolutionary system as a whole. They went a step ahead of Echeverría, who simply wanted to change the economic model of development and gain popularity. At this point, even an early rehearsal of the fourth stage of paradigmatic change took place. All parts of society–naturally including businessmen–were offering possible alternatives to the Mexican model of economic and political development (Casar and Peres, 1988:109; Cordera and Tello, 1981:9–12; Servitje, 1976:295–7). The main problem was that most proposals were still either too vague or too risky, so a general consensus on the most adequate alternative could not fully emerge (cf. Ysita Septién, 1964; Rubio, 1990:250; *El Economista Mexicano*, Vol. XV, No. 4, Jul-Aug 1981).

Another reason why new options were not fully considered was that, by the time all these meta-narrative campaigns had been properly organized, the presidential election was near. Most groups set out to attempt to influence the choice of the next candidate. The strong stance of businessmen is related by Buendía, who, basing his description on the minutes of a Coparmex meeting, tells how Manuel Clouthier threatened: "If Gómez Villanueva (then Secretary of Agrarian Reform and close aide of Echeverría) is the new President, then we will undoubtedly rise in arms" (Buendía, 1986:44–7).

Fortunately, the appointment prompted no armed conflict. José López Portillo, Secretary of the Treasury, was designated presidential candidate by Echeverría. This confirms that even Echeverría knew he had lost the battle with the economy and with businessmen (Luna Ledesma, 1992ª:51).

d) Brief Concluding Remarks about Echeverría and the ICES.

Although Echeverría set out to destroy the ICES, he did not succeed completely. The main networks of the system survived, because of the highly technical issues discussed in the system. The most important was the "financial axis." When during an interview I asked Mario Ramon Beteta, Secretary of the Treasury with Echeverría (1975–1976, after López Portillo became presidential candidate), if the policy network had survived, he immediately responded: "Yes. If a channel subsisted it was the Secretariat of the Treasury . . . There was no Secretary of the Treasury that could afford to break relations with businessmen or with bankers . . . And they knew it. When other doors were closed . . . they knew that one of the doors that remained open to listen to them was the Secretariat of the Treasury" (MRB, 03/05/01). The other policy network that not only survived but actually strengthened was "the nationalist group," from obvious ideological convergence with Echeverría.

Another feature that remained from the ICES was the practice of favoring specific businessmen. Despite his clashes with businessmen, Echeverría chose some to benefit during his government. The criterion was that, in his view, they were "nationalistic." One was José Represas, President of Nestlé Mexico who, in spite of heading a multinational, invested heavily in livestock and agriculture, which were areas that Echeverría favored (GM, 30/12/70; 06/02/71; 01/09/74). Another was Manuel Senderos, owner of a conglomerate of different firms that were very close to public projects (GM, 16/02/73; GM, 27/07/73). All this is confirmed by the private archives of the ex-President, which I have consulted. Finally, as always, relations with bankers were the smoothest of all. In fact, even if the bankers criticized Echeverría, their judgments were often measured. This probably due to the fact that even under severe crisis, much of the colossal public spending of the time was channeled through private banks (Saldivar, 1991:122, 176; Martínez Nava, 1984:77–8).

All in all, if blame for the public-private clashes has to be placed, in my view it would have to be on Echeverría. I do not question his intentions; I criticize his failure to understand his times: an unforgivable mistake in a President heading such a centralized political system as the Mexican. It is true that the international situation was difficult. The Bretton-Woods system collapsed; international inflation and interest rates escalated; the World economy slowed down; and protectionism increased (López-Portillo Romano, 1994:88). The domestic situation, as we have seen, was also difficult. Unbalanced economic growth coincided with demographic explosion, rural migration, and rising poverty (Looney, 1985:13). But even under these conditions, nothing justifies the economic disorder, the ideological obstinacy, and lack of political sensitivity of Echeverría (cf. López-Portillo Romano, 1994:94). Explanations vary. They range from his personal weakness of character to his political inability. I tend to favor another explanation: the state under Echeverría became "rentist." For Asdrúbal Baptista (1997), a rentist state is one in which money is obtained through means that do not imply accountability of the government. Echeverría could obtain his funds through foreign borrowing, which rendered him totally unaccountable domestically.

We shall further discuss "rentism" later. Now, suffice to say that, in the end, the excesses of Echeverría made him lose the support of business, but also that of the population as a whole. Paraphrasing Looney (1985:66), the political instinct of Echeverría far outran his political abilities; his economic ambitions outran his economics; and his populism outran by far his popularity. If anything, by letting the financial crisis explode three months before leaving office, Echeverría at least allowed the new government to start afresh in terms of legitimacy (Whitehead, 1980:844).

One last fact remains true: by the end of the Echeverría administration, the Mexican business class had fully consolidated (Valdés Ugalde, 1982:20). Echeverría had tested their strength and he had lost (Philip, 1992:403). Forty years after its own consolidation, the mighty post-revolutionary Mexican State had succumbed to the power of the private sector. The new President, José López Portillo, would certainly keep this in mind.

2. PARADIGMATIC CHANGE CONTINUED: THE JOSÉ LÓPEZ PORTILLO PERIOD (1976–1982)

José López Portillo became President of Mexico in 1976. As we have seen, relations with businessmen were strained and the meta-narratives of the crisis were followed by proposals for change: something resembling the fourth stage of paradigmatic change. However, López Portillo—immensely more charismatic than Echeverría and a more artful politician—would change the situation.

In our theoretical section we stated that the dialectical relation between formal and informal institutions allows for stabilization in times when either is losing legitimacy. In turn, this stabilization (or the lack of it) might help retard (or accelerate) paradigmatic change in a given political system. Perhaps no period in Mexican history illustrates these theories better than the López Portillo administration. In this section, we shall study three moments of that administration: (a) the "re-legitimization" of institutions and the reversal of paradigmatic change; (b) the new climax of the ICES; and (c) the restart of the process of paradigmatic change.

a) Legitimizing the Institutions and Reversing Paradigmatic Change

In the view of López Portillo, the only way out of the economic and political crisis that he had inherited from Echeverría was to "re-conquer" the trust of the–by then–very powerful business class, young and old (Whitehead, 1980:856; Hernández Rodríguez, 1989:62; Acosta, 1982:63; Guillén, 1985:158). Unlike Echeverría, López Portillo understood businessmen. As Secretary of the Treasury, he had been in constant contact with them for at least four years. During his political campaign, he avoided any reference to *Desarrollo Estabilizador*, to Shared Development, or even to the Mexican Revolution. Additionally, in a strategy similar to that of Ávila Camacho after the radicalism of Cárdenas 40 years earlier, López Portillo abandoned the aggressive language of his predecessor and launched a slogan which made clear that the new government would re-accommodate business interests: *La Solución Somos Todos* (The Solution is All of Us) (Arriola and Galindo, 1984:118; Rueda Peiro, 1998:55–6).

Once he became President, López Portillo made a priority of reversing the de-legitimization of the formal and informal institutions of the state. The ultimate goal was to reverse the imminent pressures for a drastic change of the Mexican political system. Government incorporation of the 1968 dissidents put in place by Echeverría had had some pacifying effects. However, López Portillo went further and addressed the political concerns of both dissidents and businessmen. Firstly, he passed a number of laws to reduce the discretionary power of the President. Secondly, he further facilitated both the creation of opposition parties and their potential election to Congress (Luna Ledesma, 1992[a]:52–3). This was received with satisfaction on the part of younger businessmen.

At the same time, López Portillo took particular care in reviving the informal alliances with the private sector, which he saw as a key source of micro-economic confidence (Mirón and Pérez, 1988:35). Before entering office, he asked prominent businessmen to approve his cabinet (Basañez, 1990:67). As soon as he was in office, he promised allegiance to some of the basic principles of the ICES that Echeverría had violated: limited state intervention in the economy and the control of public expenditure. Additionally, he established individual production agreements with the 140 most important firms of the country, even opening areas of "exclusive public interest" to private investment (Luna Ledesma, 1992ª:64). Through these agreements, the government expressly committed itself to solving the specific problems of each firm, in exchange for the firm's meeting certain investment and production goals. López Portillo grouped all these policies under an umbrella program called "Alliance for Production" (Hernández Rodríguez, 1988:119). As in the past, López Portillo virtually "privatized" decision-making through the intensive use of informal channels of negotiation (Luna Ledesma, 1992ª:52; Concheiro, Gutiérrez and Fragosa, 1979:323). To underline this renewed closeness with the private sector before the rest of society, López Portillo blamed the economic disaster created by Echeverría on the constant clashes with businessmen. Again, like Ávila Camacho and Alemán 35 and 30 years earlier, the interests of business were portrayed as the interests of the rest of the Mexican society (Valdés Ugalde, 1987: 433; Valenzuela Feijóo, 1986:183). After the "new Cárdenas," a combination of a "new Ávila Camacho and Alemán" was needed to recover business trust.

Having reconstructed personal relations with businessmen, López Portillo immediately introduced changes to the formal economy in order further to strengthen business confidence. Firstly, he controlled public spending and monetary expansion, reducing inflation from 41.2% in 1977 to 15.7 in 1978 (INEGI, 1985:756). Secondly, he conducted a partial but immediate liberation of price and quality controls on commerce. Thirdly, the plans to create or enlarge state-owned enterprises that might interfere with private firms were immediately stopped. Fourthly, he introduced a large program to finance the expansion of Mexican industry. Finally, written agreements with labor were reached to limit wage rises in exchange for more political posts and control of dissident unions. For 1977, the maximum rise agreed was 10% (Looney, 1985:71–80; Luna Ledesma, 1992ª:63; Mirón and Pérez, 1988:36–9, 70; Whitehead, 1980:853; Rueda Peiro, 1998:66). López Portillo even solved the controversy about the expropriation of agro-industrial land carried out by Echeverría, by paying an inflated price for the land to the original owners (Hernández Rodríguez, 1988:109).

In the end, López Portillo had simply re-edited *Desarrollo Estabilizador,* but without openly saying so (González, 1980:12). If the younger generation of businessmen—that only a few months earlier wanted to annul informal channels—did not complain, it was due to pure self-interest. Indeed, most of their firms had been included in the "Alliance for Production" agreements, which in many cases included lucrative government contracts. For them, profit came before ideology, and high profits were surely in sight.

López Portillo was able to reconstruct the ICES, and used the system as a platform to gain time and regain the legitimacy of the formal institutions, which for structural reasons take longer to react. As early as 1977, the private sector considered that the "crisis of confidence" had ended. In their view, "analyzing the Mexican economic situation in 1977, it is clear that the country presents a situation that is very different from a year ago . . . Economic activity has recovered in an extraordinary manner" (Concamin, 1978:34–49). Even the previously bellicose Andrés Marcelo Sada (AMSZ, 1978:16), President of Coparmex, admitted in 1978: "we must recognize that trust in general, and in the permanence of our institutions, has been recovered."

b) A New Climax for the ICES

With firm evidence of a more stable macro-economic situation, confidence increased, and businessmen decided to forget what seemed to have been a fleeting nightmare with Echeverría, and start investing again. The convergence of particularly propitious international and national conditions would dramatically speed the process of recovery.

Western banks had high liquidity due to (a) the flood of dollars coming from Arab oil-producing nations (so-called petrodollars); and (b) the expansive monetary and fiscal policies in developed countries. This made them willing lenders at very low rates, particularly to countries like Mexico that had just confirmed the discovery of immense oil reserves, at a time when oil prices were the highest in history (Lomelí and Zebadúa, 1998:190). The flow of international financial resources to Latin America went from representing 12% of the total in 1966–70 to 70% in the end of the 1970s (Guillén Romo, 1990b:65, 72). Moreover, in 1978 the government introduced a new financing method through Treasury Bonds that gave it additional liquidity (Suárez González, 1993:31).

With widely available funds, López Portillo decided (a) to take off the straitjacket of the IMF stabilization agreement signed by Echeverría; and (b) to develop the oil industry to its full potential to take advantage of high international prices. In 1978 the debt with the IMF was paid in full through internationally syndicated private loans (Whitehead, 1980:850; Pérez López, 1987:32). As for the oil industry, it deserves a particular mention, given its enormous impact.

After the economic crisis caused by Echeverría, it was almost natural for many officials to turn to the enormous proven oil reserves of the country in order to restart economic growth. López Portillo was one such official. Even conservative Secretaries–like Miguel de la Madrid (the future President)–and influential "favored businessmen"–like Bernardo Quintana–believed prices would remain high for some years to come. This, not to mention nationalist

Secretaries–like José Andrés de Oteyza–who saw oil as the only way out of the eternal financial dependence of the country (cf. Menocal, 1981:35, 87, 131–5; Hernández Rodríguez, 1988:130). The development of the oil industry was seen as a race against time in which the quicker oil infrastructure was developed, the more the country would gain (Morales, Escalante and Vargas, 1988:64–91). Extensive foreign borrowing and immediate investment in the oil industry followed.

From 1978 to 1981, the Mexican oil industry experienced the largest expansion in its modern history (Morales, Escalante and Vargas, 1988:93). By 1981, public expenditure in the oil sector already represented 40% of the total and tax revenue collected from *Petróleos Mexicanos* (PEMEX), the state-owned oil monopoly, rose to 25% of the total (López-Portillo Romano, 1994:129). The value of oil exports increased from US$1 billion in 1977 to US$16 billion in 1982, and more dramatically: while in 1970 oil only accounted for 2.8% of Mexican exports, in 1981 it had increased to 74.5% (Nafinsa, 1984:262; Bortz and Wilkie, 1990:20). This awesome growth, however, generated its own contradictions. Already through the percentages here presented, one can identify the crowding-out of the rest of the economic sectors by the oil industry—a clear case of "Dutch Disease." Additionally, investment was disorganized, ill-planned, and risky. For instance, by 1981, PEMEX already owed 87% of its assets and its accumulated debt was larger than that of the rest of the public sector. Such debt also represented a fifth of the total foreign debt (Krauze, 1997:392).

In financial terms, the oil expansion also created deep imbalances. Firstly, the Peso became dangerously overvalued due to a combination of the high and swift inflow of foreign funds and the over-expansion of domestic demand (López-Portillo Romano, 129–131; Levy and Székely, 1983:232–40; Newell and Rubio, 1984:213). Secondly, the ratio of foreign debt to GDP went from 38% in 1976 to 85% in 1982 (calculated with data from INEGI, 1985:311-2, 645). In absolute terms, Mexico's debt went from US$19.6 billion in 1970 to more than US$67.5 billion in 1982 (INEGI, 1985:645; Nafinsa, 1984:242). In other words, it seems that the biggest problem was that the growing oil revenues were not used to decrease the dependence of the country on international capital, but paradoxically to increase its capacity to borrow.

Concerning the ICES, it was practically back to its climax. The massive oil expansion had generated equally mammoth contracts for private firms. Without a formal system of tenders, the Mexican government allocated practically all the contracts though informal channels. Most top businessmen had plenty of reasons to be satisfied. López Portillo placed particular interest in pandering to Monterrey firms, the biggest and potentially more confrontational of the country. *Alfa* and *CYDSA* of the Monterrey Group had their heyday. *Cementos Mexicanos* (CEMEX), the largest cement producer in Mexico, also from Monterrey, saw its sales go up fourfold and its profits increased by eleven times between 1977 and 1981 (Cerutti, 2000:180–2). It is fair to mention that some private organizations were warning the government about the overheating economy. On various occasions during 1979, Coparmex asked for "austerity" (Arriola and Galindo, 1984:120–2; Lomelí and Hernández, 1980:202). However, in the euphoria of the oil boom and with industrialists receiving 71% of total government subsidies, these isolated voices were not listened to (García Hernández, 1980:33). Economic prosperity was reaching big and small firms alike (González Soriano, 1983:185). In 1979, the CCE even agreed formally to join the Alliance for Production in full (Buendía, 1986:96).

At this point, we might reflect upon the new spirit of the ICES because it had obviously changed. Whilst before it had been a system in which the exchange of information and control was equally important than the exchange of economic resources, López Portillo had modified the situation. The massive amounts of money that the government was pumping into private hands was the real reason why the ICES had revived. Of course, it was still based on the same general and specific underlying agreements supported by trust. However, trust and control were now subordinated to greed. The government was becoming too rich and powerful again, and the ability of the private sector to balance that power was becoming limited. However, businessmen were willing to overlook the increased power of the government in exchange for higher profits. As we shall soon see, under these new conditions, the ICES would not survive for long. On 2 December 1980, the President of CANACINTRA, José Porrero Lichtle, merrily announced that "the country will not fall into a crisis like that observed in the last year of the Echeverría government" (*Excelsior,* 02/12/80). He was right: it would be much worse.

c) The New Start of Paradigmatic Change

Already by mid-1979, with rising inflation, soaring public debt and growing public expenditure, the business sector had serious doubts about the solidity of the oil-led development strategy of the Mexican State (Arriola and Galindo, 1984:120–2). In its view, urgent changes were required. However, obstinacy on the part of López Portillo and an intense ideological struggle between monetarist and nationalist members of the cabinet prevented any adjustment. With the legitimacy of the oil-led model of development and its related institutions in question, and with the prospects of "stabilizing change" shaky, the process of paradigmatic change was kicked off again for the second time in less than nine years. The rest of this chapter will analyze how, this time, all the five steps would be taken.

(i) The First Step of Paradigmatic Change

By late 1979, the loss of institutional legitimacy and the failure of "stabilizing change" were becoming increasingly evident. Inebriated by a booming economy[2], strong relations with the private sector, and the increasing prosperity of a good part of society, López Portillo started to break, almost unconsciously, the implicit agreements with businessmen that had originally allowed him to revitalize and re-legitimize the economy. For instance, the reduction of production bottlenecks was approached through a policy of state-enterprise creation, sometimes invading economic sectors where private firms were operating (Casar and Peres, 1988:84). At the same time, the foreign debt was getting out of hand and started to threaten future macroeconomic stability. By 1979 the debt-to-exports ratio was 87.3%, excessively high by any standard (Bailey and Cohen, 1987:11). Equally, the deficit in the balance of payments (BOP) went from US$1.1 billion in 1977 to US$3.4 billion in 1979 (González Soriano, 1983:193). Also in 1979, the U.S. had fallen into recession and the international non-oil markets were weakening. Oil prices rose but so did interest rates, putting enormous pressure on the servicing of the Mexican foreign debt. Wishfully thinking, the Mexican government publicly announced that imbalances were temporary and that while oil prices would remain high, interest rates would soon fall (López-Portillo Romano, 1994:122). In the view of businessmen, the strategy was becoming highly risky and contradictory. Criticism intensified.

As for the lack of "stabilizing change," in October 1980 top bankers and businessmen met the President to ask for an adjustment of the exchange rate, given the differential rates of inflation between Mexico and the U.S. (López-Portillo Romano, 1994:148–9). The devaluation did not take place mainly because, as López Portillo's Chief of Advisers–José Antonio Ugarte–personally confirmed to me during interview (JAG, 06/05/01), the President did not want to face the political consequences of devaluation.

Although the pressure for change continued, "stabilizing change" still did not take place. Manuel Clouthier, then President of Coparmex, declared that "there were always warnings about public sector expenditure being too high and generating dangerous levels of inflation . . ." (Coparmex, 1984:19). As López-Portillo Romano confirms (1994:78, 105), apart from presidential stubbornness, another reason why adjustments, i.e. "stabilizing change," were not taking place was the fierce ideological intra-cabinet fighting that constantly led to political stalemate. It is well documented how out of seven members of the economic cabinet, two were fully liberalists, two fully nationalists, and three had mixed views. López Portillo's motive was to keep a wide ideological representation that could balance decisions. The problem was that the opposing positions often generated lethargic decision-making and constant inactivity instead of balance. This was the case with discussions like the public budget of 1980 and 1981, the decision to join the GATT, or the way to spend the resources generated by oil exports (López-Portillo Romano, 1994:106–20; Looney, 1985:26–7, 90–1; Story, 1986:192). Businessmen, who normally supported the ideological position of the Secretariat of the Treasury and the Bank of Mexico, often felt frustrated when López Portillo opted–as he frequently did–to follow a middle way between the liberal and nationalist postures. In their view, the little change that was taking place was simply not enough to face the new challenges and, therefore, they started to lose confidence in the decisions of the government.

(ii) The Second Step of Paradigmatic Change

In 1980, both national and international agencies (including the World Bank and private consulting companies) had optimistic forecasts for the Mexican economy in 1981 and 1982 (López-Portillo Romano, 1994:135). Reality, however, was different. Both years would turn out to be among the darkest in Mexican economic history. The contradictions of economic policy not only became evident but also, as our theoretical framework predicted, gave rise to even more contradictory public policies that started to be widely narrated. This was a time of confusion and a deep sense of systemic crisis. Radicalism, violent ideological clashes, and a definite break of the ICES would show as the most salient consequences.

As we have seen, during 1979 and 1980, businessmen had already seen certain risks and inconsistencies in economic policy. However, in 1981 these perceptions worsened because the international situation changed dramatically. For a country like Mexico, then almost fully dependent on the right combination of international factors, the changes had disastrous impact. Firstly, with the election of Ronald Reagan to the Presidency of the U.S., the international financial markets changed dramatically. The new American economic policy known as "Reaganomics" meant tax cuts, military expansion, and monetary contraction. This in turn entailed higher federal borrowing, higher interest rates, and lower aggregate demand (López-Portillo Romano, 1994:141). These policies affected Mexico in three ways: (a) the era of cheap financing had clearly ended, and additional funds would have to be contracted for at higher cost; (b) exports to the U.S. would fall, due to the restrictions on consumption; and (c) higher interest meant enormous increases in the service of the already huge Mexican foreign debt.

A second international factor that hit the Mexican economy was the fall in oil prices. Through permanent energy-saving policies, developed countries consumed 8% less energy and 24% less oil in 1981 than in 1980. Additionally, there were discoveries of oil fields around the world, new sources of energy were developed, and Saudi Arabia had record production that year (Basañez, 1990:65). In the end, to remain competitive, Mexico would have had to drop the price of its oil by about 10% in June 1981 (calculated with data from Morales, Escalante and Vargas, 1988:156). However, once again, the refusal of the government to lower the price caused an immediate drop of 700 million barrels in exports. At the end of 1981, oil income was US$13 billion, US$7 billion lower than originally forecasted (Morales, Escalante and Vargas, 1988:161–3). The difference in 1982 was of equal magnitude (Guillén Romo, 1990[b]:78).

As if this were not enough to make the whole economic strategy crumble, the government never adjusted its spending. For the President and his confused economic cabinet, the country only had a "cash flow" problem. If additional finance could be found, in order to wait for the price of oil to rise again, growth would still be possible (Hernández Rodríguez, 1989:63; Cypher, 1990:117). Again, the situation had been misread. More debt, at higher interest rates, was contracted (Lomelí and Zebadúa, 1998:192). Only in 1981, Mexico increased its external debt by US$22.4 billion and an additional US$2.6 billion during the first half of 1982 (Bailey and Cohen, 1987:2). The difference was that instead of paying the 6.5% LIBOR of 1977, the new credits were charged at the 18.8% rate of 1981 or the 21% of the U.S. prime rate for that same year (Bailey and Cohen, 1987:11; Mirón and Pérez, 1988:137; Erfani, 1995:144). After only a few months, by late 1982, Mexico's accumulated foreign debt would reach US$85 billion (Mirón and Pérez, 1988:140). Even with the somewhat irresponsible behavior of international private banks that kept lending to Mexico in spite of well-documented bleak perspectives, it would have been the government's responsibility to maintain some economic common sense and limit its borrowing.

Other internal factors aggravated the financial disaster. Even after this international shake up, López Portillo refused to adjust the value of the Peso. In his own words, "a President that devalues, becomes devalued" (Mirón and Pérez, 1988:136). Public expenditure kept increasing and in fact, in 1981, was 18.4% higher than originally predicted. The public sector deficit doubled during that year, reaching 17% of GDP (Tello, 1984:81). At the same time, soaring domestic interest rates (39.2% p.a. in average), created problems in servicing the domestic debt as well (Nafinsa, 1984:241). The race for the presidential succession also started in 1981. Most members of the cabinet, worried only about how to save themselves and/or reach the presidency, started manipulating information and data in their favor, further complicating the already difficult process of economic response and planning (López-Portillo Romano, 1994:136).

The numerous erroneous economic decisions seem to have been caused as much by miscalculation as by the President's concern to preserve his reputation with a population that had put all its hope in the oil boom (Mendoza Berrueto, 1998:136). Many social projects, including housing, electrification, and introduction of potable water were already underway and could not be stopped, so public investment had to be kept flowing (Cypher, 1990:97). López Portillo saw himself committed to businessmen and the people to generate growth, jobs and welfare, even if the conditions to do so did not hold (Lomelí and Zebadúa, 1998:63; López-Portillo Romano, 1994:124). In his words, "the choice was: we either contract debt and keep the country growing, or surrender and start laying Mexicans off. . . . we opted, under my responsibility, for the debt process" (Luna Ledesma, 1992[a]:55).

Naturally, under this financial mismanagement, the overvaluation of the Peso was an incentive for firms and individuals alike to purchase dollars or property abroad, and protect themselves against potential (and probable) future devaluation. Capital flight accelerated towards the end of 1981 (Tello, 1984:81). The process reveals a new facet of the perverse economic process that was taking place in the Mexican economy at the time, and of the extreme distortion of the ICES.

Through an informal agreement with the bankers, arranged within the ICES, most foreign debt was channeled through private banks. Funds were demanded by the private sector, arguing that they were necessary to renew equipment, buy essential imports, and service the considerable debt they themselves had acquired in foreign currency (Mirón and Pérez, 1988:64). Most foreign debt acquired by López Portillo was absorbed by the private sector. In fact, in 1981, the public sector would have required only US$6 billion dollars to make ends meet. The rest of the debt was used to finance industrial expansion, and maintain a fixed exchange rate and freedom of exchange, which were all conditions that—as we have seen—supported the ICES and maintained confidence in investment. However, in reality, the ICES seems to have been used by the private sector only as a means to ensure the maintenance of a parallel and profoundly dishonest financial mechanism known as the "circular debt mechanism." Mexican banks would obtain the foreign funds from the government and channel them to the many industrial firms they owned or with which they had close ties (Buendía, 1986:197). These firms, rather than invest the money, would buy dollars and invest them abroad. Most of the time, the money was invested in the same Swiss or American banks that would lend additional money to the Mexican government (Mirón and Pérez, 1988:140). In 1981 alone, US$11 billion are thought to have been "recycled" in this way (Tello, 1984:76; Ros, 1987:73). In other words, the government ultimately financed the totality of capital flight. Jacobs and Peres (1983:110) concluded that during 1981 the state acquired 64.4% of the debt and only used 35.1% of it. The banks not only encouraged these actions, but also operated them with significant profit (Tello, 1984:65). If it is true that the mechanism is a grave case of dishonesty, it also shows the absence of public control and inefficient public management at the time (Rueda Peiro, 1998:72). Additionally, even if it cannot be ethically approved, such a system is an understandable economic and strategic reaction to the extreme inconsistencies displayed by economic policy. In the case of the ICES, it is only confirmation that the system had been artificially revived through transfers of money, but that by then it relied very little on the trust that had characterized it twenty years earlier.

In September 1981, Miguel De la Madrid was appointed as the presidential candidate of the PRI. De la Madrid being a long-time member of the "financial axis," his appointment was expected to generate enthusiasm among businessmen. However, in a situation of perceived systemic crisis that included macroeconomic chaos, extremely poor expectations for the economy, unreliable in-cabinet information, and an unfavorable international environment, massive capital flight accelerated; firms stopped production and intensified speculation. Society as a whole, including businessmen, further narrated this sense of crisis. In October 1981, José Luis Coindreau, President of Coparmex, expressed a "profound and fundamental disagreement" with De la Madrid's plans for future government, which in their view were too interventionist. Other members of the same organization complained that he had started his campaign without "first consulting businessmen" (Buendía, 1986:133). In other words, not even the future government inspired confidence.

A number of additional decisions accelerated the narration of contradictions and the perception of crisis. In November 1981, the mighty Alfa Group from Monterrey announced suspension of payments on US$2.3 billion of its foreign debt. The government was forced to bail it out (Arriola and Galindo, 1984:125; Bailey and Cohen, 1987:13). In critical need of fresh funds, Mexico was forced to sell oil to the U.S. at a fixed price and in higher amounts than those allowed by Mexican oil exporting law (Morales, Escalante and Vargas, 1988:165). On 17 February 1982, the Bank of Mexico announced it decision to abandon the exchange market and let the Peso float, given the low currency reserves. The rate went from 17 pesos per dollar to 150 on the black market (Arriola Woog, 1988[a]:177; Tello, 1984:84). The surest proof of the breakdown of the government lies in López Portillo's concealing the decision to devalue from his Secretary of the Treasury, David Ibarra Muñoz, until the last minute (Gil Villegas Montiel, 1984:196). In March 1982, the President decided unilaterally to grant wage rises of 10, 20, and 30% offsetting the potential stabilizing effects of devaluation and fuelling inflation beyond control (López-Portillo Romano, 1994:173; Tello, 1984:90; Hernández Rodríguez, 1988:232–3; Ros, 1987:79). In April, the government recognized for the first time serious foreign debt and internal financial problems (Tello, 1984:97). Yet, on 21st July, it nationalized through acquisition the biggest national air carrier, Compañía Mexicana de Aviación (Tello, 1984:99). However, the narrative of crisis accelerated when strict price controls were introduced and enforced, closing down important commercial stores, the property of the richest men in the country, for violating those controls (Hernández Rodríguez, 1988:223). CONCANACO published a document blaming the government for both inflation and devaluation. CANACINTRA demanded a fixing of the exchange rate to restore some degree of certainty in the economy (Tello, 1984:86). CONCAMIN complained about price controls in the light of increased public expenditure (Tello, 1984:99). At the same time, José Luis Coindreau from Coparmex asserted that López Portillo had created a "fictitious economy," so the next government would have to follow a "policy of economic realism" (Arriola and Galindo, 1984:126). In the "Atalaya 82" conference, attended by the top Mexican businessmen, the President of the CCE said, "the main mistake of the current government is not having controlled inflation, which has provoked a large deficit in the external sector" (Tello, 1984:82; Buendía, 1986:135; Mirón and Pérez, 1988:150). José María Basagoiti, President of Coparmex in 1983, would confirm that the "confidence crisis" started in February 1982, "after suffering so many problems in every firm, so many doubts and so much distrust" (Basagoiti Noriega, 1983[a]:11). López Portillo himself publicly deplored the number of "complaints, problems, criticisms, attacks, questionings, rumors, jokes, gossip, provocations [that] strive to weaken [the government] and take advantage of the circumstances . . . to reach political positions, strength, economic privileges, and speculative profits . . ." (Luna Ledesma, 1992[a]:67–8).

The narrative of crisis advanced by businessmen also found resonance in society as a whole, which is one of the conditions set forth in our theoretical framework for paradigmatic change to continue. The middle classes that had not speculated against the Peso felt betrayed after a devaluation that the government promised would not happen. A week before the February 1982 devaluation, López Portillo had said he would defend the Mexican economy "like a dog" (Krauze, 1997:394). He did not and, even today, he is called "the dog." In August 1982, yielding to the pressure of businessmen, the government freed the prices of various goods (Tello, 1984:100). The price of bread and tortillas went up 100%, and petrol increased by 50%. This ignited the flame of further short-term inflation, panic, and immediate purchase of dollars—this time by the population as a whole (Looney, 1985:120; Mirón and Pérez, 1988:134).

In an attempt to stop capital flight and dollar purchase, the government established a *de facto* exchange control in August 1982, by introducing differential exchange rates for productive and private purposes. Dollar-denominated deposits in Mexican banks would be paid in pesos. These measures further promoted public attacks by businessmen and chaos. The Monterrey Chamber of Commerce said the exchange policy was "absurd." On 7 August, CCE, CONCAMIN, and CONCANACO published a joint letter in the national press affirming that such measures would "not solve the economic crisis, nor will they stop capital flight; rather they will increase the financial problems of business, with consequential effects on the reduction of jobs and production derived from the closure of factories. Additionally, they will foster corruption in the assigning of currency for imports" (Tello, 1984:102). Even the normally discreet bankers openly defied the policy. On 15 August the Bankers' Association published a letter in national press stating that it was not obligatory to convert dollar deposits to pesos (Tello, 1984:109). But this time, López Portillo replied. In mid-August, during a speech, he publicly reminded businessmen how "the hard currency that has entered the country lately . . . has its origin in the public sector . . . It does not come from a private sector that is not competitive" (Arriola and Galindo, 1984:130). The month of August passed amid an ocean of mutual accusation, narration and counter-narration of crisis (Arriola and Galindo, 1984:127–8). With international banks refusing to lend additional funds to Mexico (Tello, 1984:98), and the economy and capital flight out of control, López Portillo reverted to a decision he had been considering for some time: the nationalization of the private banking system and all its related industrial, financial, and commercial assets[3], along with the establishment of a generalized exchange control. He announced the decision during his State of the Nation Address on 1 September, 1982 (Tello, 1984:129).

The decision eliminated any trace and hope of cordiality or negotiation that could have been left between the private and public sectors. As López-Portillo Romano, son and adviser to his father, and one of the five people that drafted the nationalization decree told me in interview, "After nationalization, political contact between the government and businessmen broke off. Some talked to us individually but, in general, it broke off" (JRLPR 20/10/00). The ICES had dissolved. Extensive meta-narration would follow, continuing the now unstoppable process of paradigmatic change in Mexico.

Even most of López Portillo's favored businessmen like Bernardo Quintana, who was confirmed to me as such by José Ramon López-Portillo Romano; Bernardo Garza Sada, from the Alfa Group of Monterrey (cf. Basañez, 1990:67; Mirón and Pérez, 1988:148); or Manuel Espinosa Yglesias from Bancomer, the second largest bank in Mexico (cf. Brannon, 1986:33; Carrión and Aguilar, 1972:147; Tello, 1984:67–8), seem to have reduced their contact with the President considerably after the nationalization.

(iii) The Third Step of Paradigmatic Change

In the third step of paradigmatic change, the contradictions of a political system and its related institutions are consolidated into a meta-narration that abstracts and conceptualizes failures. Meta-narration develops a story with which most of the population can identify. This is precisely what happened in Mexico after the nationalization of the banking system and the generalized exchange control.

During and after the announcement of the nationalization decree, López Portillo justified his decision by citing the "circular debt mechanism" and how much it had damaged the country. In his view, private banks had betrayed the privileged legal and personal treatment that they had historically received from the government and that had allowed them to prosper (Tello, 1984:21–6; cf. FitzGerald, 1978). As published literature and archival records confirm, they always had open access to the highest levels of state; they had been both judges and beneficiaries of the policies that affected them; and they had always enjoyed high profits due to their role as favored financial intermediaries (ABM 14/07/80; Pérez López, 1987:5; Tello, 1984:43, Carrión and Aguilar, 1972:147; Cypher, 1990:120–6). Therefore, to the eyes of López Portillo, their behavior had not only been inexplicable, unjustified, rapacious, and unethical, but also highly anti-patriotic.

For businessmen, the nationalization of the banks had been the final proof that the Mexican political system had to be changed. Once again, they had found themselves unable to control the enormous legal power of the state. This in turn also confirmed to them that informal mechanisms of control, such as ICES's, were not sufficiently strong (Casar and Peres, 1988:115). They would set out formally to ensure that the power of the state could be controlled and that a new pro-business ideology could be instituted to make those changes last. Intensive meta-narration started. On 3 September 1982, The CCE published a manifesto severely criticizing the government and its policies. They also justified speculation because it had been based on a "lack of trust" in the government. They finished by saying that the nationalization of the banks was "a definitive blow to private enterprise and a clear sign that the country has entered Socialism" (Tello, 1984:131; see also Maxfield, 1989:222; Cornelius and Craig, 1988:20). On 5 September, the President of the CCE declared that "the business sector in genuine mobilization, is putting pressure to organize a national business strike for the coming 8th of September" (Tello, 1984:136–8). Although the strike was suspended, the mobilization continued.

The legality of the nationalization decree was strongly questioned, and some banks announced that they would appeal against the measure (Tello, 1984:151). Manuel Clouthier, President of the CCE, started public meetings of protest that he called "Mexico in Freedom" (Buendía, 1986:123). Big business groups devised different strategies to discredit the government, which were highly effective amongst smaller firms (Tello, 1984:170). López Portillo even claims that businessmen established a *Fondo para el Desprestigio* (Fund for Discredit) to attack him and his administration on meta-narrated charges of statism, populism, and corruption (López-Portillo Romano, 1994:184).

Indeed, the contradictions of the López Portillo government were being meta-narrated as a case of excessive state intervention and authoritarian rule that had allowed a deliberate plan on the part of López Portillo to enrich himself through borrowed money. The meta-narrative indicated that most of the borrowed foreign resources had ended up in the hands of the President and his close aides. An "example" of this corruption was the mansion that López Portillo had built on a prominent hill just outside Mexico City, which was highly visible and came to be known as "The Hill of the Dog." Other corruption scandals and rumors were circulated, like that of López Portillo acquiring a castle in Spain. Even the rumor that he was Spanish and had become Mexican was meta-narrated as a case of a "new conquest" that deeply hurt Mexican nationalist pride.

In spite of support of nationalization by some private organizations like CANACINTRA, and the relatively good financial results that the nationalized banks offered in the first months of operation (Tello, 1984:169–174–7), most social groups were disillusioned with the government. Businessmen resented the fracture of the mutual trusting relation and their being publicly affronted (Hernández Rodríguez, 1990:745; Garrido and Puga, 1992:134; Luna Ledesma, 1992ª:66; Mirón and Pérez, 1988:165). The middle classes were seeing their standard of living drop by the hour (López-Portillo Romano, 1994:184; Loaeza, 1989:357–8; Mirón and Pérez, 1988:181). The lower classes, peasants and workers, had simply believed and ceded too much, only to see their real wages drop and their unions weaken by the constant suppression of strikes (Bailey and Cohen, 1987:23).

For these reasons, the process of meta-narration had powerful effects. The loss of personal credibility suffered by López Portillo himself affected the legitimacy of the nationalization of the banks, which in turn reinforced the legitimacy crisis of the President (Gil Villegas Montiel, 1984:198). Younger and even more radical business leaders felt encouraged to join private organizations of representation, particularly Coparmex, CONCANACO, and the CCE (Acosta, 1982:66–76; Arriola Woog, 1988ª:179). Vociferous provincial groups strengthened the protests and meta-narration of government failure, particularly in the North of the country (Arriola and Galindo, 1984:136). As José Luis Coindreau, President of Coparmex would admit, the private groups started to form "a generation of new leaders . . . that later entered politics." (JLCG, Coparmex, 1999:27). These new leaders would trigger a search for values, procedures, and a political program to guarantee the effective participation of businessmen in future decision-making, their mobilization to prevent statism, and the creation of civil organizations that could make private ideology prevail and endure (Luna Ledesma, 1992ª:69; Hernández Rodríguez, 1989:62; Hernández Rodríguez, 1988:163–75; Lomelí and Hernández, 1980:210; Cordero, 1987:164–5).

Miguel De la Madrid, already elected as President, asked businessmen to stop the protests, which meant that he saw and felt the effects of meta-narration. He confirmed this to me in interview: "I told them that in my view we had to protect the peace and stability of the country, and that the big agitation they were creating against the government would only make things worse. I asked them to stop the agitation and wait for the change of government so that then, with legal authority, I could see what could be done and what could not" (MMH 24/07/01). This time, the older businessmen and the bankers accepted the offer and asked the younger generation to stop the protests and wait for the imminent process of negotiation. The CCE-led protests were cancelled by the board of the organization, mainly made up of older businessmen against the wishes of the younger members (Mirón and Pérez, 1988:167–8; Arriola and Galindo, 1984:136). This division of opinion would set the stage for the emergence of two separate currents of private leaders: one that wanted to change business-government relations, and the other, the younger and more radical, that wanted to change business-state relations. As we shall soon see, this meant that meta-narration was suspended, but only temporarily.

At the same time, the "financial axis" quickly regrouped. Jesús Silva Herzog, Secretary of the Treasury appointed on recommendation of elected President De la Madrid, named financial conservatives as directors of the newly nationalized banks (Hamilton, 1986:162–3). The government also established agreements with the IMF, the U.S. government, and the international banks to obtain additional credit and stabilize the economy. The agreements required specialized management of the economy to meet the stringent conditions of the creditors. The need for economic experts speeded the reorganization of the "financial axis" (Tello, 1984:105), which in turn would strongly influence the ideological appropriation of the new institutions that would emerge.

In the end, the economic strategy of López Portillo left the nation with a huge mortgage. Despite the US$48.4 billion that entered the country through oil exports, Mexico acquired roughly US$55 billion in foreign debt before interest (Morales, Escalante and Vargas, 1988:178). By the time López Portillo stepped down the total debt was US$92.4 billion, making Mexico the second largest debtor in the world. (Handelman, 1997:125). Paradoxically, the first government that had legally limited its capacity to borrow, through the 1978 "General Law on Public Debt" (Lomelí and Zebadúa, 1998:178) was the one that trebled the total foreign debt incurred by all previous Mexican governments (Pérez López, 1987:41–3).

As for the "Alliance for Production," it became what Reynolds (cited in Purcell and Purcell, 1977:199) called an "Alliance for Profits"; a relationship based exclusively on temporary earnings (see also Basañez, 1990:63; González and Alcocer, 1980[b]:97). In other words, the ICES had temporarily revived, but based exclusively on the conjunctural profits that the fictitious economic boom was giving to business. Support and cordiality vanished once the abundance of economic resources dried up (Luna Ledesma, 1992[a]:51). López Portillo would end his government as had Echeverría: negotiating an agreement with the IMF; discredited with most of Mexican society; and with a nation searching for alternatives of change, in the early fourth step of paradigmatic change.

3. PARADIGMATIC CHANGE CONCLUDED: TWO YEARS OF THE MIGUEL DE LA MADRID HURTADO PERIOD (1982–1984)

Miguel De la Madrid became President of Mexico on 1 December 1982. During his first three years in office, two processes of particular importance to our study took place. Firstly, paradigmatic change fully consolidated in Mexico.

Secondly, the ICES re-emerged with a structure similar to that it had in the past, but designed to pursue different goals. This section ends our historical study; in the rest of the chapter we shall analyze these two processes.

a) Paradigmatic Change Continued: The Third Step Re-starts

Even if meta-narration of the contradictions of the Mexican State had been suspended, Miguel de la Madrid inherited a country on fire. Financially traumatized, the middle class seriously questioned the ability of the government to run the nation (Kouyoumdjian, 1988:79; Puga and De la Vega, 1990:240). International agencies and the U.S. were urging the new government to put the economy in order (Garrido and Puga, 1992:133). Naturally, businessmen were also demanding political and economic reforms that would remove any possibility of repetition of the recent economic past (Cordero, 1987:166; Casar, 1992:295).

As we have seen, the Mexican private sector at the time was divided in two camps: those that wanted to modify relations with government and those that wanted to modify relations with the state. Whilst the former favored limiting state action through negotiation, the latter wanted to modify the bases of state autonomy through profound legal and political changes (Hernández Rodríguez, 1986:247). For the first group, a revival of the ICES was necessary. The second group, on the other hand, rejected the idea of any further informal dealings. They wanted more than a simple reconciliation with the government (Tirado, 1987: 491). In their view, what was needed was a profound replacement of political structures to ensure the formal representation of business interests (Luna Ledesma, 1992ª:70; Garrido, 1989:418; Valdés Ugalde, 1987: 452).

The trouble was that in late 1982 De la Madrid was not sending any clear signal that could incline either business faction to trust him. Formed in the rhetoric and values of the PRI, De la Madrid had projected a highly ambiguous position throughout his presidential campaign. Despite constantly promising that he would strengthen relations with businessmen, on two occasions he criticized "employers without social conscience" and "false businessmen" (Buendía, 1986:137–40). He also defended in public his allegiance to "revolutionary nationalism" (Bailey, 1986:125), which he said would "determine the actions" of his government (Martínez Treviño, 1983:81–2). In the eyes of businessmen, this meant returning to more of the same (Coparmex, 1984:27).

Shortly before his presidential inauguration, De la Madrid saw that his attitude was turning businessmen against him. It was then that he decided that he had no choice but to send clearer signals of a definite change (Garrido and Quintana, 1988:54). He told me in interview that he had attempted to get closer to the private sector because "it is they who create wealth; without the private sector it is impossible to govern, and when I entered government there was an unpropitious climate; very hostile towards my government" (MMH 24/07/01).

The priority then became to overcome mistrust. This was attempted through highly conciliatory behavior with most organizations and through policy that aimed to show ideological convergence with the private sector (Bailey, 1986:122; Casar, 1989:68 and 1992:296; Hernández Rodríguez, 1986:247). First, De la Madrid legally limited the capacity of the state to intervene the economy, by promoting reforms to articles 25, 26. 27, 28 and 73 of the Constitution (Hernández Rodríguez, 1990:745, 1986:248; Hamilton, 1986:166; Mendoza Berrueto, 1998:213).

Second, De la Madrid abandoned the verbal criticism and superior attitude of his predecessors, and treated businessmen with respect and on equal terms (Mendoza Berrueto, 1998:150–1; Elizondo, 1994:176; Velasco, 1988:279; Acosta, 1982:63).

Third, De la Madrid cancelled the oil-led strategy of development by drastically reducing investment in the state-owned oil monopoly PEMEX (Morales, Escalante and Vargas, 1988:181–96).

Fourth, the government designed a highly favorable scheme to compensate former owners of nationalized banks. The former owners of the three largest banks were paid 118 billion pesos instead of the 47 billion that their businesses costed before the nationalization (Tello, 1984:168). Payment would be tax-free and could be sold in the stock market, which made it immediately liquid (Mirón and Pérez, 1988:173). Likewise, the government would allow 34% of private investment to the nationalized banking system (Saldivar, 1988:124; Hernández Rodríguez, 1990:745). De la Madrid also agreed to return all non-banking assets, which included a total of 339 industrial, commercial, and financial firms to its former owners (Hernández Rodríguez, 1990:747; Hernández Rodríguez, 1986:252; Tello, 1984:17). Under this scheme, the largest bankers recovered their stockbrokerage businesses (Puga and De la Vega, 1990:249; Casar, 1992:298). De la Madrid promoted a law prohibiting nationalized banks from investing in other financial companies (Hernández Rodríguez, 1990:749), ruling out the possibility of competition with the now private stockbrokerage houses. Government controls of stockbrokerage businesses were relaxed, so the private sector came back to the financial industry under better conditions than before. This would be confirmed years later. Between 1986 and 1987, profits of nationalized banks grew 215%, while those of private financial firms increased by over 1000% (Hernández Rodríguez, 1990:749–50).

Fifth, De la Madrid initiated a privatization program that, albeit small, was highly encouraging for businessmen (López-Portillo Romano, 1994:223–4). During the post-revolutionary period, the number of state-owned companies had gone from 15 in 1934 to 391 in 1970 to 1, 155 in 1982 (Mendoza Berrueto, 1998:214). The state not only owned hotels, airlines, and a telephone company, but also a fashion house, bicycle factories, movie theatres and three nightclubs (Salinas de Gortari, 2000:406; Mancera Aguayo, 1993:43). A program for early retirement of civil servants was also started in an effort to reduce the size of the government (Rubio, 1990:254).

Sixth, De la Madrid used a combination tight control, ideological persuasion, and patronage to limit minimum wage rises (cf. López-Portillo Romano, 1994:189–93). Despite regular strikes against his new policies, labor conflicts were consistently addressed only in relation to their impact on production and on business-state relations. Both independent trade unions and those opposed to the government were repressed while "white unions" (organized by the bosses) were actively promoted (Hamilton, 1986:169; Basañez, 1990:86; Ortega and Solís, 1990:228–31). Given that prices controls were relaxed (Hernández Rodríguez, 1990:744), these policies led to a decline in minimum wages of 22% in 1983 and 9% in 1984 in real terms (López-Portillo Romano, 1994:218).

Seventh, De la Madrid appointed a homogeneous cabinet, mainly recruited from the financial groups. Thirteen out of eighteen Secretaries of State belonged to the financial sector (López-Portillo Romano, 1994:194). No radical economists were included (Ros, 1986:82). The ideological homogeneity of the cabinet was aimed at (a) avoiding the ideological clashes (and consequent policy stalemate) that had characterized previous administrations; and (b) giving certainty to businessmen by proving that the "financial axis" was in control of the economy (Hamilton, 1986:170; Puga and De la Vega, 1990:247). Numerous businessmen were also appointed either as advisers or as public officials (Garrido and Puga, 1992:140).

Eighth, De la Madrid introduced FICORCA, a mechanism to protect private firms against exchange rate fluctuation (Luna Ledesma, 1992[a]:70; Hernández Rodríguez, 1986:253; Rueda Peiro, 1998:86). Through FICORCA, the public sector acquired the dollar-denominated debts of private firms, and these were allowed to pay the government in pesos. In October 1983, 1,200 firms were registered and US$12 billion of private foreign debt were rescheduled (López-Portillo Romano, 1994:215; Basave et al., 1995:VII).

Ninth, the so-called "Moral Renewal" program was established by the government to fight corruption in the public sector. The "Law on the Responsibilities of Public Officials" was created and the Constitution was amended, in order to prevent and punish corruption more severely (Luna Ledesma, 1992ª:79).

Finally, De la Madrid introduced a complete emergency macroeconomic program to stabilize the economy. Its three objectives were: (i) to generate a surplus in the BOP; (ii) to reduce the public sector deficit; and (iii) to lower inflation. The policies espoused to achieve these objectives were: (i) the constant adjustment of prices of public goods and services according to inflation; (ii) an increase from 10 to 15% in the federal consumption tax (IVA); and (iii) a drop in real public investment (Casar, 1992:300). Additionally, the Peso was constantly devalued to stabilize the exchange market and help the BOP (Heath, 1999:23; Guillén Romo, 1990ª:55; Hernández Rodríguez, 1990:744). The macroeconomic plan would have an ominous name: PIRE (*Programa Inmediato de Reactivacion Economica*), which in French means "worse."

All these policies in turn were grouped under the umbrella of *Cambio Estructural* (Structural Change) (Guillén Romo, 1990ª:112; Hernández Rodríguez, 1990:743). Structural Change confirmed the perceptions of both factions of the Mexican private sector. To the moderate groups, it confirmed their perception that a new version of the ICES was possible, so they attempted to establish it. However, to the more radical groups, the policies confirmed what they saw as the intention of the government to reactivate corporatism and state intervention, so yet stronger attempts to reform the Mexican State were initiated through increased activism in opposition parties—mainly the right-wing PAN (cf. López-Portillo Romano, 1994:223; Luna Ledesma, 1992ª:73; Hernández Rodríguez, 1986:249). The moderate faction of the private sector thus started working closer to the government to establish a new ICES. Meanwhile, the radical faction reactivated the third step of paradigmatic change, through a process of meta-narration of the contradictions of the Mexican political system (cf. Casar, 1992:302; Maxfield, 1989:216–7).

While the re-establishment of an ICES would be a process that took slightly longer, the meta-narration started immediately. Aided by the PAN and the Catholic Church, the more belligerent business leaders grouped in the CCE, CONCAMIN, and Coparmex conducted a harsh campaign against what they saw as "excessive" state intervention (Maxfield, 1989:223). The 107% inflation rate for 1983 was meta-narrated as a consequence of deficits in state-owned enterprises. Deficits were in turn were presented as a result of the intervention of the government in private business (Casar and Peres, 1988:108). The economic crisis in general was reduced to the corruption and inefficiency of public officials, who were characterized as "interventionist, authoritarian, wasteful, and fraudulent" (Mirón and Pérez, 1988:173; Tirado, 1987: 492). These businessmen saw themselves as the defenders of liberal and democratic tradition, so they demanded fair elections and a free market economy (Mirón and Pérez, 1988:163; López-Portillo Romano, 1994:188). In the eyes of these businessmen, the only solution to all these problems was to take power (Luna Ledesma, 1992[b]:267–8; Hernández Rodríguez, 1990:754).

De la Madrid, however, repeatedly resisted efforts to transform the presidential system and was far from allowing any form of real democracy[4] (Bailey, 1986:133; Villa, 1990:659). In his view, any economic change would have to be made within the existing political system. Through the PRI, confrontational businessmen were branded as "agitators" and were reminded that private organizations were not legally allowed to engage in politics (Hernández Rodríguez, 1986:263; Story, 1990:73–4; Story, 1986:137). The option of these businessmen then became definitely to break with the government and formally challenge the political system. From that moment on, this faction of business in fact became a political opposition movement rather than a business pressure group. Their aim was to articulate and mobilize the middle classes in their favor, and they achieved it. Great numbers of bureaucrats, social movements, intellectuals, political parties, and international organizations joined these businessmen with enthusiasm, in their fight for more democracy (Luna Ledesma, 1992[a]:70; Cordero, Santín and Tirado, 1987:200). Profoundly disillusioned with the government and fearful of further drops in their purchasing power, the middle sectors fully identified their personal situation with the meta-narratives of crisis put forward by the more aggressive businessmen (Valdés Ugalde, 1987:438–40; Tirado, 1987: 492; Tello et al., 1983:54). Consistent with our theoretical framework, paradigmatic change could continue because as Hernández Rodríguez (1986:265) asserts, businessmen articulated the isolated contradictions of the political system and turned this narrative into societal–and not only private sector–demands.

Manuel Clouthier, then President of the CCE, embarked on a tour to the U.S. in April 1983 along with John Gavin, U.S. Ambassador to Mexico. Clouthier meta-narrated the Mexican political system by warning American businessmen about the "real danger of leftists taking power in Mexico," but also announced the emergence of a "new political model" pushed by the private sector (Buendía, 1986:178). He himself took charge of the model. After leaving the CCE presidency, he joined the opposition party PAN, and in 1988 ran for the presidency (cf. Luna Ledesma, 1992[a]:99). Other businessmen also ran for office because they wanted to restore the power of the legislature (Garrido and Puga, 1992:142).

Meanwhile, the more moderate factions of the private sector, represented by CONCAMIN, CANACINTRA, and the ex-bankers, were attempting to re-establish an informal system of consultation and exchange to negotiate future economic and political change (Maxfield, 1989:223). They saw an ICES as the best way to influence policy in the short term. In their view, participation in political action through formal channels would be counterproductive in the short run and ineffective in the long. The changes that affected them were taking place there and then, so immediate negotiation had to be restarted, and only an informal structure could offer such flexibility. Given the willingness on the part of the government also to recreate the ICES, they agreed it was the best way forward. Additionally, to the eyes of moderate businessmen, not only had De la Madrid taken enough steps to assure stability and refrain from intervention in private business, but also the agreements with the IMF ensured that economic policy would be closely monitored (Luna Ledesma, 1992[a]:70).

If an ICES did not re-emerge immediately, it was because a key piece of the system was missing: the private bankers. Indeed, the bankers had been essential to the operation of the "financial axis," which in turn was one of the most important policy networks of the ICES. Without bankers, the system simply could not operate. Moreover, the bankers also played the role of brokers between smaller firms and the state. This connection had also been broken after nationalization (Camp, 1990:191). However, as the ex-bankers regrouped around the Mexican Association of Stockbrokerage Houses (AMCB) and recovered their central role in the economy, an ICES slowly started to re-emerge (cf. Luna Ledesma, 1992[a]:95; 1987:472).

As this was happening though, the economic policy of De la Madrid was crumbling. Although 1983 had been a difficult year, the IMF praised Mexico as an "exemplary case of economic restructuring and a model for other developing countries to follow in their processes of adjustment" (Bailey and Cohen, 1987:29; Basañez, 1990:81–2). Even the Center of Economic Studies of the Private Sector, a think-tank funded by Mexican businessmen, asserted that economic policy for 1983 was "favorable and allows us to foresee a brighter future" (Guillén, 1985:163). 1984 confirmed the "bright" expectations. Real GDP increased by 3.4% and inflation was down to 59.2% from 107% in 1983 (Kouyoumdjian, 1988:82). Industrial expansion and non-oil exports led growth, which was seen as highly beneficial (Ladman, 1986:147). However, already by 1983, Mexico had become a net exporter of capital due to the servicing of the enormous foreign debt (Guillén Romo, 1990[b]:75). If in 1982 Mexico's debt-to-GDP ratio was 49.4%, from 1983 to 1985 it averaged 56.2% (Bailey and Cohen, 1987:19). The debt was growing and not falling.

To make matters worse, the extreme contraction of monetary circulation and credit, along with extreme under-valuation of the Peso and the tight controls on wages, were beginning to cause social unrest. In the second half of 1984, Mexico, the "model debtor," decided to abandon its IMF adjustment targets, arguing potentially disastrous social consequences (Bailey and Cohen, 1987:30–1). De la Madrid was deeply worried about the effects of the austerity program on the 1985 mid-term elections. In his view, if the PRI lost the election, structural change could not have continued, so he decided to sacrifice short- for long-term stability and freed public spending in the last half of 1984 (López-Portillo Romano, 1994:211–2; Bailey and Cohen, 1987:32–5; Ladman, 1986:145).

The combined results of the net outflow of resources and expansionary policies were disastrous. Even though GDP grew by 2.7% in 1985, inflation rose to 63.7% and unemployment went from 8.5 to 10.7%. The Peso was devalued by 114% during the year and foreign debt reached the US$100 billion mark by year's end. To make matters worse, the price of oil dropped by 11% and non-oil exports fell by 9.2% (Ladman, 1986:148–51; Kouyoumdjian, 1988:83). The PIRE had honored its French meaning and led to a worsening economic situation.

In fact, the stabilization program had been politically and economically misplanned: Politically, both the IMF and government had overestimated the capacity of the Mexican State to control a society that was growing ideologically and civically more sophisticated. Economically, since both the IMF and government had also misdiagnosed the roots of the crisis. All along, they had thought Mexico suffered only a short- to medium-term liquidity problem (Guillén, 1985:159). In consequence, "solutions" had only aimed to introduce short-term policies to correct external accounts and financial liquidity (Guillén Romo, 1997:88). In reality the country was suffering aggravated structural indebtedness and productive inefficiency (Bailey and Cohen, 1987:17; Guillén Romo, 1997:117–8). The problem was structural and not conjunctural. All along, the economic strategy had attacked superficial and not underlying contradictions. Instead of helping Mexico out of her crises, the PIRE had pushed the country to the brink of defaulting on its debt. Changes were required, and they were required soon.

b) The Fourth Step of Paradigmatic Change

New economic failure made very clear that the model of development had to be changed. At all levels, society started to search for new alternatives to address the predicaments of the Mexican economy. In terms of our theory, the fourth stage of paradigmatic change had been inaugurated.

Indeed, the now obvious inadequacy of the stabilization program further fuelled the meta-narration of the Mexican political system by the confrontational business groups. This time though, they progressively moved from highly abstract and ideological to pragmatic discourse, oriented to the solution of specific national problems (Cordero, Santín and Tirado, 1987:197). During 1984–5, the most belligerent factions of the private sector did not shy away from making their voices heard (Cordero, Santín and Tirado, 1987:19). They favored widespread economic, political, and social liberalization and this time they could offer a precise program of political and economic reform. In the mid-1980s, a neo-liberal consensus had consolidated around the academic and political circles of the U.S. and Britain. In contrast with the early 1980s, business groups could now offer credible and viable policies that were being tested in the developed democracies of the Americas and Europe. This new *Weltanschauung* favored economic neo-liberalism over statism. Mexicans, tired of recurrent crises, were willing to give the neo-liberalists a chance. In their view, nationalists had had their chances and had failed to deliver: the struggle over new institutional alternatives was–as posited by our theoretical framework–highly contended. This time, however, the clash was not between ideologically different alternatives, but between different degrees and methods of liberalization. The new struggle was between business factions that aimed to acquire formal power in order to swiftly move forward with economic liberalization, and the more moderate businessmen, who favored a gradual economic liberalization in close collaboration with government.

In the view of moderate businessmen, liberalization "from within" was quite possible for various reasons. Firstly, the De la Madrid administration was made up of high numbers of young *técnicos* or technocrats, who shared background with the whole of the business sector, but ideology only with the moderate faction (Garrido, 1989:437; Carrión and Aguilar, 1972:182; Puga and De la Vega, 1990:241). Secondly, this new generation of public officials was convinced that the private sector should become the engine of growth and competitiveness (López-Portillo Romano, 1994:222). Thirdly, the President himself decided that a nationalistic strategy (in which he had strongly believed) could no longer be implemented. In an interview with López-Portillo Romano (1994:207), he admitted that, given the combination of national and international factors, the only "viable strategy" was a move towards more neo-liberal policies. In short, for many businessmen, a "negotiated transition" seemed to be a more sensible option than engaging in open political struggle. In the eyes of these moderate businessmen, solving the economic crisis through negotiation and collaboration with government technocrats would still achieve the changes demanded by the belligerent business faction, but with a lot less confrontation, risk, or instability. Thus moderate businessmen decided openly to withdraw their support from the younger, more confrontational factions of business, and started collaborating with the government. At this point, in late 1984, even some confrontational businessmen decided to attenuate their political activism and also sought to re-open negotiation with the government (Luna Ledesma, 1992:82). Some powerful financial conglomerates and big exporting firms were included in this last group. In the end, they seemed willing to accept some state intervention, as long as it was ideologically acceptable (Cárcoba, 1991:25). The rejection of the radical business wing by more moderate business people was made evident by Carlos Abedrop, one of the most distinguished ex-bankers. In interview, he said: "Thank you, *Maquío* (Manuel Clouthier, the belligerent head of the CCE) for what you did for us, but we thank you even more for what you did not do because we did not let you" (Luna Ledesma, 1992ª:84).

In early 1985, most organizations of business representation started to purge the more radical wing from leadership and replaced it with more moderate leaders (Cordero, 1987:161; Casar, 1992:309), such was the case of CONCAMIN, CONCANACO, and the CCE (cf. Camp, 1990:168–75). Belligerent businessmen, not finding resonance to their political aspirations in most private sector organizations, sought refuge in Coparmex and/or resigned from their positions and joined political parties, the most favored being the PAN (Luna Ledesma, 1992ª:100–1). Others went on to form radical social movements, like Alfredo Sandoval (Coparmex President 1984–1986), in the past linked to the Anti-Communist Front of Universities, who became President of Integrative Human Development (DHIAC), a Catholic, pro-free-enterprise movement that staged various civil disobedience demonstrations against the government (Luna Ledesma, 1992ª:103–4).

With government and business having reached consensus on the advantages of negotiating a neo-liberal economic program, 1985 turned out to be the great turning point in recent Mexican economic history (López-Portillo Romano, 1994:225; Mancera Aguayo, 1993:44). In that year, Mexico accelerated economic liberalization. Financial markets were deregulated; privatization was extended; and in November, the government announced the decision to join GATT (Ladman, 1986:149–50; Rueda Peiro, 1998:87). Tax law was reformed to reduce red tape and broaden the taxpayers' base; the Peso was resolutely devalued to encourage manufactured exports; laws were modified to allow larger amounts of FDI in ever more economic sectors; and price controls were relaxed. The government had initiated what would be a painful process fully to align the country with the Washington consensus (Guillén Romo, 1997:91–8).

Paradoxically, in the end, the change of paradigm was not negotiated with the more extreme and confrontational faction of business, but with the more moderate groups. This was of course possible because internal bureaucratic currents, the middle classes, the U.S. Government, and the international financial institutions, such as the IMF and the World Bank, favored the more gradual change. As contemplated by our theory, the appropriating groups of the new neo-liberal institutions were not necessarily those that more actively meta-narrated the contradictions of the statist model, but those that offered the most viable solutions to that meta-narration.

c) The Fifth Stage of Paradigmatic Change

With a consensus to conduct economic policy along neo-liberal lines, formal and informal relations were modified or created to support such decision. The CCE, that by late 1985 had adopted a collaborative position with government, was in practice recognized as the political representative of the business sector by the President (Garrido and Puga, 1992:140). Other organizations that ideologically fitted the new neo-liberal model of development, namely the Mexican Business Council for External Affairs (CEMAI) and the Mexican Association of Stock Brokerage Houses (AMCB), also started to gain prominence (Luna Ledesma, 1992[a]:95). These new relations, as in the past, started to foster the creation of new policy networks that formed a structure closely similar to that which had operated in the past. This new ICES, however, had significantly different objectives. Whilst the former ICES had emerged to promote industrialization in a highly protected economic environment, the new version was designed to support a new economy open to the world and mainly geared towards financial operations. After 1985, privatization and the outstanding growth of the stock market, caused by financial liberalization, encouraged the emergence of a new generation of financial entrepreneurs that built enormous fortunes (Garrido and Puga, 1992:145; Basave et al., 1995:vii; Dávila Flores, 1990:109). The mechanism by which these entrepreneurs prospered was quite straightforward: through privatization, they bought public monopolies that normally became private monopolies, so they could often issue stock at very high prices (Luna Ledesma, 1992[b]:275). The new ICES developed channels that further promoted this type of finance-based economy.

d) Concluding Remarks

Because of the notably financial orientation of the Mexican economy from 1985, industrialization ceased to be the prime objective of the Mexican Government (Luna Ledesma, 1992[a]:95). Accordingly, our historical account of the effect of the ICES on industrialization must stop here, since the process had virtually ended. However, it is noteworthy to mention that, despite its differences, the Financial ICES seems to have had a stabilizing impact similar to that of the Industrial ICES in the Mexican system. Although inflation reached an average yearly increase of 106% and economic growth only averaged 0.9% in the 1985 to 1987 period (with a GDP drop of −4.2% in 1986)(calculated with data from INEGI, 1985:311; Gutiérrez Garza, 1990:28), no major business-government conflicts ensued. In fact, the growth of the stock market serves as evidence of business confidence: From May 1985 to October 1987, the Mexican stock market index rose from 4,596 to 373,216 points. In other words, it grew 81 times (Dávila Flores, 1990:118). Equally dramatic was the volume of stock traded, which rose from 2.5 million shares in 1983 to 39.5 million in 1988 (Dávila Flores, 1990:118). Some structure parallel to the formal economy must in principle have been supporting the confidence that generated this growth. Obviously, the macroeconomic situation could not have achieved it by itself, given the poor performance of the economy on those years. I argue that, just as it had happened half a century before, the structure was the ICES.

Chapter Five

The Structure of Informality in Mexico

INTRODUCTION

Despite its relevance, institutionalized informality in economic policy-making in Mexico is an understudied topic. Existing analysis is often tangential and brief, revealing little about the operation and features of Mexican policy networks. This chapter precisely examines these structures through the schematic study of what I have denominated the Informal Consultation and Exchange System (ICES).

The ICES was a system constituted by at least seven policy networks that operated in the economic areas of the Mexican government from 1936 to 1984. The system linked the public and private sectors through the exchange of information and resources. This relation seems importantly to have influenced industrial policy-making as well as economic and political stability. The ICES was a sophisticated informal system, so the accounts that have classified it as a "pact," a "commitment" (see Cisneros, 1986:124–5), an "alternative way" (see Puga, 1993:53), or more generally as "negotiation" (Bailey, 1986:127), in my view fail to capture its complexity.

In this section, I shall dissect the different components of the ICES to explain their characteristics. My analysis is the result of data extracted from three sources: existing literature, private and public archival documents, and interviews with participants in the ICES (for methodology see appendices 1, 2 and 3). The chapter is divided into three sections. Firstly, through a series of diagrams, I present the different policy networks that constituted the ICES. Secondly, I show in tabular form the characteristics of the connections between the participants in the system. Finally, I offer some conclusions about the structure of the ICES.

1. A GRAPHIC INVESTIGATION OF THE ICES

The structure of the ICES needs to be analyzed more closely in order to clarify and support some of the assertions made in previous chapters. Through a series of diagrams, I shall attempt to illustrate the structure of the system, the position of its participants and their interrelations. To my knowledge, this is the first time that a system like the Mexican ICES is comprehensively examined.

Naturally, changes in personal ties or the organization of government occasionally altered the pattern or strength of the connections. However, the diagrams that follow summarize positions and links that, according to my research, were institutionalized, unequivocal, and somewhat permanent, particularly during the 1950s and 1960s, when the system yielded its best results.

The graphic representation of the ICES will consist of ten diagrams. The first shows the position of participants in three "circles of power" that constituted the system. As discussed in Chapter 2, the circle in which a participant operated was a measure of influence within the system. Diagrams 2 to 8 depict the main policy networks that made up the ICES. Diagram 9 examines the strength of the connections between the various policy networks. Diagram 10 is a full graphic representation of the ICES that aims to present its complexity. Detailed analysis will follow each diagram. All diagrams are my own in terms both of the information presented and the design.

1.1. Relative Power and the ICES: The "Circles of Power"

Diagram 1 shows the position of the different participants of the ICES in different "circles of power." Circles of power, as defined by this work, are concentric regions that determine the "centrality" of particular actors in relation to the core of a system. An actor's centrality would in turn determine his ability to influence policy outcomes, by virtue of his privileged access to decision-makers. More influential actors are therefore located in the first concentric circle of power, closest to the core. The second concentric circle contains participants who are less influential than those in the first circle but more than those in the third, and so on.

The core of the system is the President because, even if as we have suggested, his power was often limited by that of businessmen, he still had at least four advantages over them. Firstly, he was the only one who held a complete picture of both the positions of the participants and the interests negotiated in the ICES. Secondly, he had legal access to enormous amounts and types of resources to exchange in the system. Thirdly, the Secretaries of State, who were the first instances of negotiation, directly reported to him. Finally, he controlled both the legislature and the judiciary. These four factors granted the President the power to act as a coordinator in most decisions, but also as a final arbiter

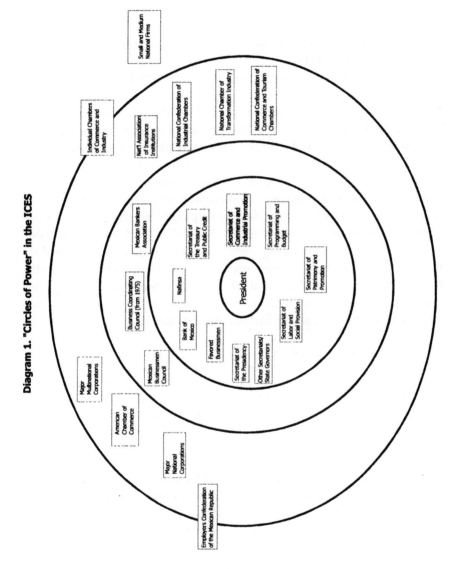

Diagram 1. "Circles of Power" in the ICES

if necessary. In either case, he had large maneuvering power to persuade business groups about a certain decision or compensate them if so required.

The first concentric circle of power was constituted by different Secretaries of State; the General Director of the Bank of Mexico; the General Director of Nafinsa; some state governors; and by "favored businessmen," who acted in practice as advisers to the President. Both the amount and quality of access of all these actors was very high, since they represented the closest aides of the President.

In the second circle of power we find private groups with high political influence: the bankers represented by the Mexican Bankers Association (ABM), the Mexican Businessmen Council (CMHN), and the Business Coordinating Council (CCE). The members and heads of these groups met the President frequently and their opinions were taken very seriously before making policy decisions. All three groups were highly representative of big capital in Mexico, so their influence stemmed from the economic importance of their select membership. Bankers were important for three additional reasons. Firstly, they financed public spending and were intermediaries for foreign loans (ABM 11/08/80; ABM 11/09/72; ABM 15/01/68). Secondly, they heavily were involved in industry through either interlocking directorates or direct ownership (Cordero and Santín, w/d). Finally, they were a vital channel of resource and information exchange, as confirmed by Antonio Ortiz Mena, former Secretary of the Treasury and close ally of the banking sector during industrialization:

> The state and the banking system are interrelated in two ways. Firstly, bankers have always given their point of view to the state and, in turn, the government takes their views into account. Secondly, they are an excellent conductor or conduit of views from the private sector as a whole. In many cases, bankers served as mediators to persuade the whole of the private sector about the desirability of certain government policies (cited in Camp, 1990:190–1).

The CMHN, which gathered the 30 or so richest men in the country, also had fantastic clout through the economic weight of its members. This translated into influence over other private organizations, which saw the CMHN members as points of potential access to high government officials (Camp, 1989:190–3). Finally, the CCE became the political representative of Mexican business only after 1975, when it was created (Arriola Woog, 1988[a]:61). They had constant access to the President. Many of the CCE's Presidents were also members of either the AMB or the CMHN, which increased their influence (ABM/LP; Concheiro, Gutiérrez and Fragosa, 1979:261).

The third circle of power was constituted by the National Confederation of Industrial Chambers (CONCAMIN), the National Confederation of Commerce and Tourism Chambers (CONCANACO), the National Chamber of Transformation Industry (CANACINTRA), and the Mexican Association of Insurance Institutions (AMIS). Except for the AMIS, these were all government-sponsored and held a semi-official status. As suggested in Chapter 3, these groups often had limited independence and influence, because their very existence depended on the President or his Secretaries of State (Hernández Rodríguez, 1991; Shafer, 1973:191–4). Although law obliged the government to consult these organizations during design and implementation of policy (Arriola Woog, 1988ª:52–3; Martínez Nava, 1984:65), such consultation was in practice infrequent, selective, and depended on the discretionary decisions of public officials (MAC 543.22/133–1; MAC 545.22/188; ARC 111/3612; ARC 111/909; MAV 111/3024). When these organizations attempted to contact the President to offer their views, they were frequently unsuccessful. As a matter of record, they negotiated with Secretaries and under-Secretaries of State only, and sporadically paid "courtesy visits" to the President. During these visits, their demands and problems were discussed in very general terms only, so substantial negotiation was carried out back in the office of the Secretary or under-Secretary. During the late 1960s and the 1970s these groups were consulted more intensively (LEA 22/09/71; López Portillo, 1988:1090), but presidential contact with bankers and other big businessmen always remained more intensive and fruitful (ABM 13/05/68; ABM 22/06/68). Concerning the AMIS, despite being an independent organization, it frequently played a secondary role behind the bankers. This role may have been at times voluntary, but even when not so, it would have been difficult for the members of the AMIS to go against the will of the mighty ABM in financial matters.

Also in the third circle of power we find multinational and major national corporations. These two tended to be close allies due to their extensive business partnerships. Although law prohibited foreign investment in numerous sectors of the Mexican economy, foreign companies usually were in partnership with local firms, so they participated extensively in national production (Cordero, 1977:28). Other foreign companies operated independently, covering economic sectors that Mexican firms had not entered or those that the government did not consider strategic. The influence of these companies was obviously based on their economic weight.

The American Chamber of Commerce-Mexico (AMCHAM) may also be placed in the third circle of power. As I have suggested, the AMCHAM was a pressure group that attempted to influence policy-making through its ideology (Camp, 1989:140–4; Arriola Woog, 1988ª:113–115), but since the

Mexican State had a nationalist orientation, the AMCHAM's activism could not be public. Accordingly, the AMCHAM attempted to maintain discreet relations with most private organizations and an equally reserved but constant contact with the state. Public officials recognized the potentially destabilizing role of the AMCHAM, so they preferred to keep a cordial relation with the chamber. I locate the AMCHAM in the third circle of power because its influence, interests, and demands were rarely voiced to the President directly. Instead, they were channeled through other participants in either the first or second circles of power. Common intermediaries between the AMCHAM and the President were "favored businessmen," the CCE, the CMHN, or a specific Secretariat of State.

Some organizations in Diagram 1 appear on the limit of the third circle of power, i.e. Coparmex and the industry-specific chambers of commerce and industry—this is to show that they were often marginal to policy-making. In the case of Coparmex, throughout most of its history it was seen as a radical organization with small membership (mainly during the 1960s). Highly ideological and close to the Monterrey Group, it was often excluded from policy negotiation due to its anti-governmental political posture (Coparmex, 1979; cf. Cerutti, 2000; Nuncio, 1982; Luna, 1977). Its limited influence did not stem then from subjection to the government like semi-official organizations, but from overt exclusion. Over time, however, Coparmex came to be seen an effective channel to oppose interventionist public policies. This increased its popularity and clout, and probably repositioned the organization closer to the center of the ICES in the mid-1970s. In the case of the industry-specific chambers, they represented very specialized interests, so they were normally incorporated into the ICES only when discussion was relevant to their economic sector. Otherwise, they fully depended on the mediation of the organizations in the closer circles of power to voice their concerns. Mainly because of their size, notable exceptions to this rule were the national chamber of restaurants and the chambers of the chemical, pharmaceutical, steel, and textile industries, as well as some regional chambers, namely Guadalajara, Monterrey, and Puebla (Bailey, 1986:127).

Finally, outside the third circle of power we find the small and medium-sized national companies, whose political and ideological influence was generally negligible. In fact, their contact with policymakers was frequently indirect, through either the highly unrepresentative chambers that grouped them or the low-level bureaucrats that extorted bribes from them.

1.2. The Policy Networks of the ICES

The ICES was constituted by a collection of at least seven policy networks that interacted vertically and horizontally (see Diagram 9), creating a complex system of negotiation and exchange. On particular occasions, the number of policy networks could increase to negotiate specific issues (by region or economic sector). As already discussed, the center of the system was the President, who acted as a consolidator of information. The rules of the ICES were straightforward: Every policy network represented the interests of specific economic actors, normally determined by the functional area in which the network operated. I identified this mode of operation through archival records and confirmed it through interviews. For instance, the "financial axis" would negotiate, defend, and transmit to the President the interests of the financial elite, while the "nationalist group" would represent the interests of smaller national firms, ideologically and economically in favor of protectionism; other policy networks represented other economic groups.

Most consultation was carried out at the secretariat level but when discussion involved more than one policy network, the President would often intervene (Shafer, 1973:147). During regular meetings with the President, Secretaries discussed conflicting issues and presented requests. Those meetings were rarely public (Cornelius and Craig, 1988:27), but it was there that the President would make most decisions. The President trusted some Secretaries of State more than others, which meant that the former had more influence than the latter on the final decisions reached during those regular meetings. Though rarely, state governors and "favored businessmen" also participated in these meetings. More commonly, the President would meet these two groups separately and individually. "Favored businessmen" acted as economic policy advisers and discussed diverse issues of interest to the President, such as the situation of a specific firm or the relations of the President with a specific businessman or business group. Meanwhile, state governors discussed with the President the demands or concerns of their local business constituencies.

As a consequence of these complex relations, the President often received contradictory information. Secretaries of state frequently exaggerated, hid, or minimized figures and facts either to benefit the groups they favored or to enhance their own reputation (López-Portillo Romano, 1994:145). Another problem was servility, which Camp (1990:107) has called "presidential deference." Neither Secretaries of State nor the private groups spoke frankly to the President. Instead, he actively had to seek out different sources of information to avoid receiving an incomplete or biased perspective. If the President needed to persuade a group about something or hear more about an issue, he would meet with the head (or sometimes the members) of such group and clarify his doubts. All these activities imposed on the President an information and work overload that often led to policy failure. Yet, the President had the opportunity and power to reconsider and shift decisions because, if compensation and persuasion did not work, more forceful measures were readily used. However, if private organizations were properly consulted, even unsatisfactory results could be accepted because the "right of consultation" had been respected (Shafer, 1973:149).

Negotiation and exchange took place on both regular and *ad hoc* bases. Regular negotiation customarily was started by the government, normally with organizations in the first circle of power. *Ad hoc* negotiation was started when business groups disagreed with a particular decision (Shafer, 1973:147). Although *ad hoc* negotiation was more commonly initiated by groups in the second or third circles of power (since they were frequently excluded form regular negotiation), all groups would use this mechanism if they felt ignored. For example, regular negotiation would take place to screen the potential reactions of businessmen to reforms in economic matters, while *ad hoc* negotiation would take place if those reforms were being prepared without previous consultation. Organizations tended to monitor the drafting of law and decrees to ensure that their interests were not affected in the process (Shafer, 1973:147–8). Before and during negotiation of most issues, business organizations usually sought expert advice on the technicalities of the matter and then compared their conclusions with those of government experts (Shafer, 1973:148). Complex bargaining often ensued before reaching a final decision. Topics in which expert advice was frequently contracted included taxes, prices, trade policy, monopolistic practices, government intervention, labor relations, social security, minimum wages, and payment of government contracts. Full pieces of legislation or specific articles were often changed to accommodate business demands. Fine-tuning the amounts or percentages of wage or tax increases was also common (Shafer, 1973:148–9). The resources exchanged during negotiation were diverse and included money, influence, direct privileges, strategic information, and political support.

While the early stages of negotiation of a given law or program usually remained secretive, when the period of implementation approached, new actors and groups were incorporated in the policy-making process. This was considered necessary because, even if a project had to be modified to please the newcomers, public endorsement was vital to secure the legitimacy of the new policy.

We shall now analyze the seven policy networks that in my view constituted the ICES: (i) the "financial axis"; (ii) the "nationalist group"; (iii) the "red tape" policy network; (iv) the "favored businessmen" policy network; (v) the "secretariat-specific" policy networks; (vi) the "republican" policy networks; and (vii) the "multinational" policy network.

1.2.1. The "Financial Axis"
Diagram 2 shows the "Financial Axis." This policy network was constituted by the Secretariat of the Treasury, the Bank of Mexico, the Mexican Bankers

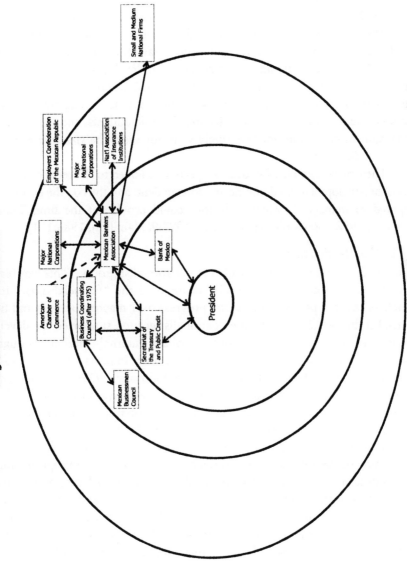

Diagram 2. "The Financial Axis"

Association (ABM), and the Mexican Association of Insurance Institutions (AMIS) (Bailey, 1986:127; Luna Ledesma, 1995:79; Vernon, 1964:12; Carrión and Aguilar, 1972:82; Saldivar, 1991:18). Other groups related to the network were the CMHN and the CCE through interlocking membership with the ABM; Coparmex; the national and multinational firms linked to the ABM; and the AMCHAM (through ideological influence).

The "financial axis" was the stronghold of the monetarist-liberalist officials of the Mexican Government. This "bankers' alliance," as Sylvia Maxfield (1990) calls it, started immediately to develop after the Mexican Revolution. It saw its heyday during the 1960s, when presidents López Mateos and Díaz Ordaz trusted them with the economic management of the country. Macroeconomic stability, balanced public budgets, and the modest expansion of credit and money supply were for them the *sine qua non* of economic development.

Their privileged position over the years was linked to the reliance of the model of development on domestic and foreign debt, and thus on the expertise required to manage it, which only they could provide at the time (Luna Ledesma, 1992ª:28; Cordero and Tirado, 1982:9; Hamilton, 1986:151).

1.2.2. The "Nationalist Group"

Diagram 3 depicts what I have called the "nationalist group." This was historically seen as a "political axis" that opposed the "financial axis." Its members favored political and social progress over macroeconomic and financial stability. Accordingly, the "nationalist group" supported the development of national industry and a robust internal market through government promotion and protection against imports (Rivera Ríos, 1992:Ch. II; cf. Alcázar Ávila, 1970:85; Zabludovsky, 1979:164–8; López-Portillo Romano, 1994:116). The most conservative members of the Mexican business sector in fact regarded the "nationalist group" as the anti-business faction of the government (Bailey, 1986:127).

The "nationalist group" was formed by the Secretariat of National Patrimony; the Secretariat of the Presidency (the Secretariat of Programming and Budget later came to replace both); the Secretariat of Labor and Social Provision; and the semi-official chambers of commerce and industry, predominantly constituted by national firms. National companies depended heavily on trade protection and government subsidies to survive, thus their "nationalistic" views. The only semi-official organization with a historically ambiguous position towards economic nationalism was CONCANACO, thus the dotted connection in Diagram 3.

The "nationalist group" was a result of the high levels of bureaucratic unity around both the President and the post-Revolutionary nationalistic

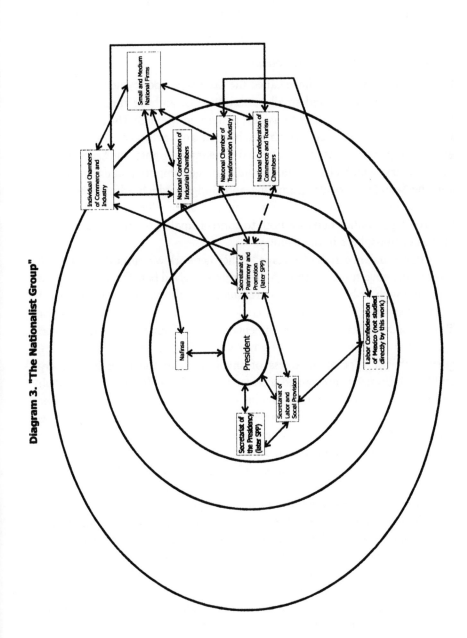

Diagram 3. "The Nationalist Group"

ideal. The policy network reached its climax during the 1970s and staged acrimonious clashes with the "financial axis" over policy decisions (Luna Ledesma, 1992[a]:30). As we discussed, this struggle was one of the main causes of the eventual dissolution of the ICES.

1.2.3. The "Red Tape" Policy Network

Diagram 4 shows what I have called the "red tape" policy network, constituted by medium-size and small national firms, and the three secretariats that predominantly regulated business activity in Mexico: The Secretariat of Industry and Commerce, which established and enforced price controls, granted import licenses, and protected consumers' rights; the Secretariat of the Treasury, which charged taxes and managed import and export duties; and the Secretariat of Programming and Budget, which administered government spending and paid government contractors. The government used the "red tape" policy network both to control smaller firms and to sense the business atmosphere in the country.

Power balance in the "red tape" policy network was almost fully tilted in favor of the government, although firms often received benefits from either cooperating with or bribing the low-level state officials that operated in this network (Derossi, 1971:40). Benefits could include lower or no taxes, import licenses, or swift payment of government contracts. Though the policy network operated at the lower echelons of government (Camp, 1990:107), it was frequently the only point of access of small firms to the state (cf. Bizberg, 1990:711). If small firms wanted access to high-ranking officials, they could obtain it only by either belonging to a big economic group or resorting to intermediaries from the first circle of power (Shafer, 1973:132; for more on this see Cordero, 1974). This complex system of intermediation fuelled the need for the "right connections" and personal contacts if small businessmen wanted to get anything done (Cornelius and Craig, 1988:28; Kaufman Purcell, 1981:204). As a witty businessman cited in Purcell and Purcell (1977:196) affirmed, "Americans have the know-how but we Mexicans have the know-who."

Obviously, corruption in the "red tape" policy network was rife, evident, and even encouraged by bureaucrats through extortion. Business organizations often complained about "corrupt government inspectors and other agents" (Shafer, 1973:128). These included tax collectors who would "overlook" unpaid tax bills in exchange for the right amount of money; inspectors from the Secretariat of Industry and Commerce that enforced or ignored price controls based on the amount of the reward; and General Directors or cashiers at the Secretariat of Programming and Budget who processed the checks of generous contractors faster than others.

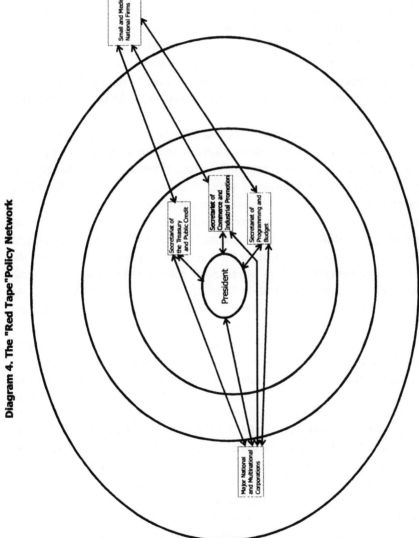

Diagram 4. The "Red Tape" Policy Network

Small and Medium National Firms

Secretariat of the Treasury and Public Credit

Secretariat of Commerce and Industrial Promotion

Secretariat of Programming and Budget

President

Major National and Multinational Corporations

In spite of its peculiarities, the "red tape" policy network was a part of the ICES because, in my view, it served the same purpose as the other networks: exchange of information and resources, even if this happened on very unequal terms.

1.2.4. The "Favored Businessmen" Policy Network

Diagram 5 presents the "favored businessmen" policy network. Directly built around the President, this policy network was highly influential in economic policy-making. "Favored businessmen" were *de facto* economic advisers to the President. The group was formed both by prominent members of the business sector and by not so prominent friends of the President who may have happened to be businessmen. Being "only" a notable businessman did not ensure access to the group of the "favored" (MAV 111/756), one also had to be close to the incumbent President.

The clientele of "favored businessmen" were other prominent members of the business elite. "Favored businessmen" acted simultaneously as points of access, unofficial negotiators and, interpreters of opinion. In exchange, "favored businessmen" had privileged access to policy-making and high-ranking government officials, which allowed them to defend their interests and protected their firms from otherwise commonly unfair decisions on the part of low-level public officials. The most "daring" also used their access to privileged information and contacts to further their personal businesses, not only by obtaining direct benefits (such as government contracts) but also by affecting competitors (Vernon, 1964:150–1; Stevens, 1977:237; MAV 565.4/848). As confirmed by Puga (1993:66), "timely information from the friendly official was an important element in the consolidation of firms."

Each President favored specific businessmen and those favored by previous Presidents were always respected, though rarely trusted or directly benefited by the incumbent President (ARC 433/153). Examples of "favored businessmen" during different presidencies in the 1936–1984 period were Mr. Bruno Pagliai (MAV 111/3826; MAV 111/4489; MAV 512.2/67) and Mr. Rómulo O'Farril (MAV 606.3/235) with President Miguel Alemán Valdés; Mr. Luis G. Legorreta with President Adolfo Ruiz Cortines (ARC 111/3822); Mr. Octaviano Longoria with President Adolfo López Mateos (ALM 521.8/145), and Mr. José Represas with President Luis Echeverría Álvarez (LEA 06/02/71). Favored businessmen had strong ties with the President (due to the direct and individualized relations between the two), but weak with other secretariats (except the Secretariat of the Presidency, in charge of scheduling their meetings with the President).

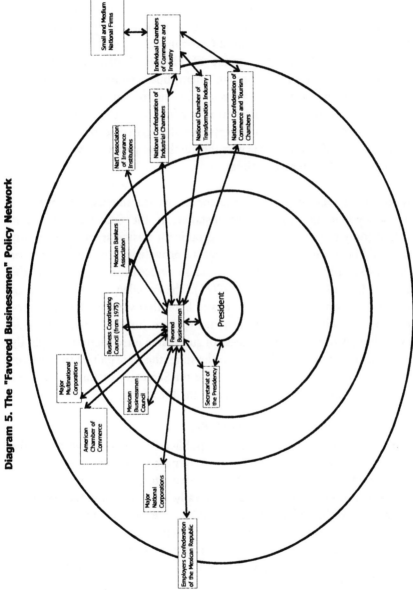

Diagram 5. The "Favored Businessmen" Policy Network

Small and Medium National Firms

Individual Chambers of Commerce and Industry

Nat'l Association of Insurance Institutions

National Confederation of Industrial Chambers

National Chamber of Transformation Industry

National Confederation of Commerce and Tourism Chambers

Mexican Bankers Association

Business Coordinating Council (from 1975)

Favored Businessmen

President

Secretariat of the Presidency

Major Multinational Corporations

Mexican Businessmen Council

American Chamber of Commerce

Major National Corporations

Employers Confederation of the Mexican Republic

1.2.5. The "Secretariat-Specific" Policy Networks

Diagram 6 shows what I call the "secretariat-specific" policy networks. These were based around secretariats not directly involved in economic matters, but that had contact with private firms due to their area of operation.

Given numerous government projects were managed by non-economic secretariats and agencies (Secretariat of Communications and Transportation, Secretariat of Agriculture, Secretariat of Human Settlements, PEMEX, National Commission for Electricity, etc.), many businessmen maintained close relations with officials from those agencies (Concheiro, Gutiérrez and Fragosa, 1979:141–2). If an important matter arose or a firm required attention in those areas, the President would often incorporate the related secretariat into the ICES (cf. Scott, 1959:280). This is why the number of policy networks operating within the ICES increased at times.

Another way in which these policy networks operated was through the occasional introduction of private-sector actors (or interests) to the economic policy-making process. For instance, if the Secretary of Public Education (only to name one) knew a prominent businessman that for any reason could be useful to the government (to provide legitimacy, support, or advice, for example), such Secretary would introduce the businessman to the President (MAC 111/3485; LEA 16/07/71). The President would then introduce the businessman to the Secretaries of State that were in charge of economic matters, who would in turn incorporate him into the economic policy-making process. In this process of successive introduction everybody won: the businessman gained access to the state, the state gained the services or public support of the businessman, and the Secretary of state gained the gratefulness of both the businessman and the President.

1.2.6. The "Republican" Policy Networks

Diagram 7 presents what I call the "republican" policy networks of the ICES. These were formed around the 32 governors of the Mexican Republic.

In the one-party Mexican political system, governors had little autonomy or power vis-à-vis the President. Literally, all state economic resources were granted by the federal government so, like businessmen, governors often had to negotiate support with different Secretaries of State. As Mendoza Berrueto (1998:227), former governor of the state of Coahuila, confirms in his book: "if the governor has a good relationship with the federal officials and bureaucrats, he will be lucky to have some of his projects included in the yearly investment program. Even then, there are cases in which some projects, having been authorized by the Secretary . . . are later suspended, in a discretionary way, by lower-level bureaucrats."

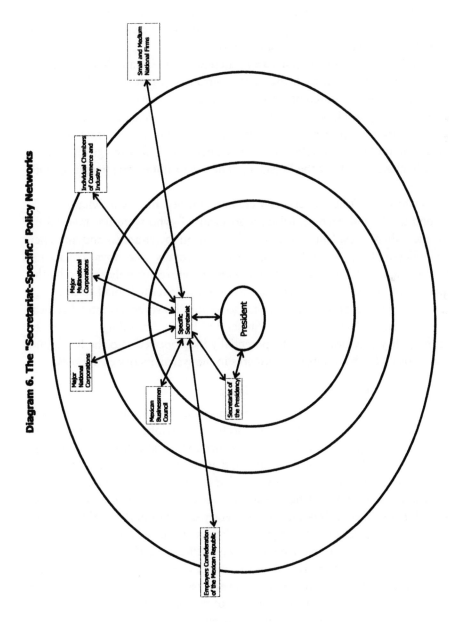

Diagram 6. The "Secretariat-Specific" Policy Networks

President

Specific Secretariat

Secretariat of the Presidency

Mexican Businessmen Council

Major National Corporations

Major Multinational Corporations

Individual Chambers of Commerce and Industry

Small and Medium National Firms

Employers Confederation of the Mexican Republic

Concerning the ICES, states almost operated as federal agencies in charge of regional issues. Governors presented the requests of local businessmen to the President and the Secretaries of State, who then chose to either continue negotiating through the governor or negotiate directly with such businessmen. The decision depended, of course, on the importance that the President (or Secretary) attached to the issue.

When a governor supported a particular businessman, though, the federal government often took the matter seriously (Derossi, 1971:49), since such support was granted only to close friends or businessmen with a heavy economic weight. However, as was the case with businessmen, the influence of a governor on policy-making depended on his or her relation with the President and/or the Secretaries of State. There were "favored governors"— usually close friends of the President. These had immediate access to both the President and the Secretaries of State, so their influence on policy decisions was high. Other governors were not so lucky: there was what I call "-second-level" and even "third-level governors," who were not favored by the incumbent President, and thus suffered from lower access and influence on policy-making. Second-level governors normally were loyal collaborators or friends of past Presidents and were therefore not fully trusted by the incumbent. Third-level governors, additionally, governed small states.

This process of consultation with governors, however, indicates that local versions of an ICES were common (Shafer, 1973:150). Accordingly, 32 "republican" policy networks could be potentially incorporated into the ICES, and that is also why the number of networks in the system increased at times.

1.2.7. The "Multinational" Policy Network

Diagram 8 presents what I call the "multinational" policy network. This was built around the AMCHAM and its objective was to influence government decisions both directly and through the Mexican business elite (PML 22/05/02; Camp, 1990:118). The links in Diagram 8 attempt to show these relations.

Direct lobbying was usually aimed at cabinet members and other opinion leaders like "favored businessmen." As confirmed to me in interview with Porfirio Muñoz Ledo, former Secretary of Labor and Social Provision, direct lobbying was done through "breakfasts or lunches, and all sorts of invitations, in the traditional American way" (PML, 22/05/02).

The AMCHAM rarely had direct contact with the President, so when an interview occurred, it often referred to a persistent problem that had remained unresolved (Camp, 1990:118). The lack of contact between the AMCHAM and the President must be understood as an effort to keep appearances, and not as evidence of animosity between the Mexican State and the foreign firms: A

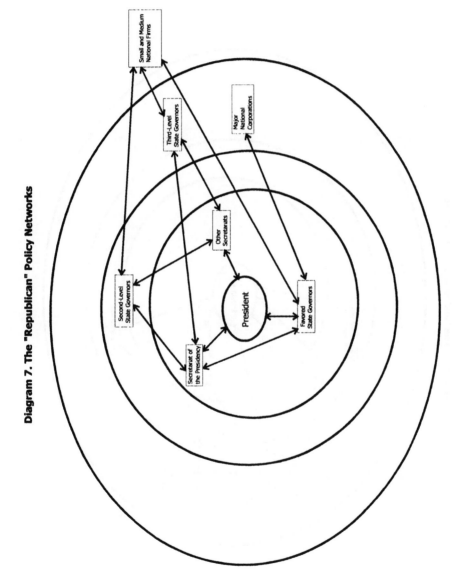

Diagram 7. The "Republican" Policy Networks

Diagram 8. The "Multinational" Policy Network

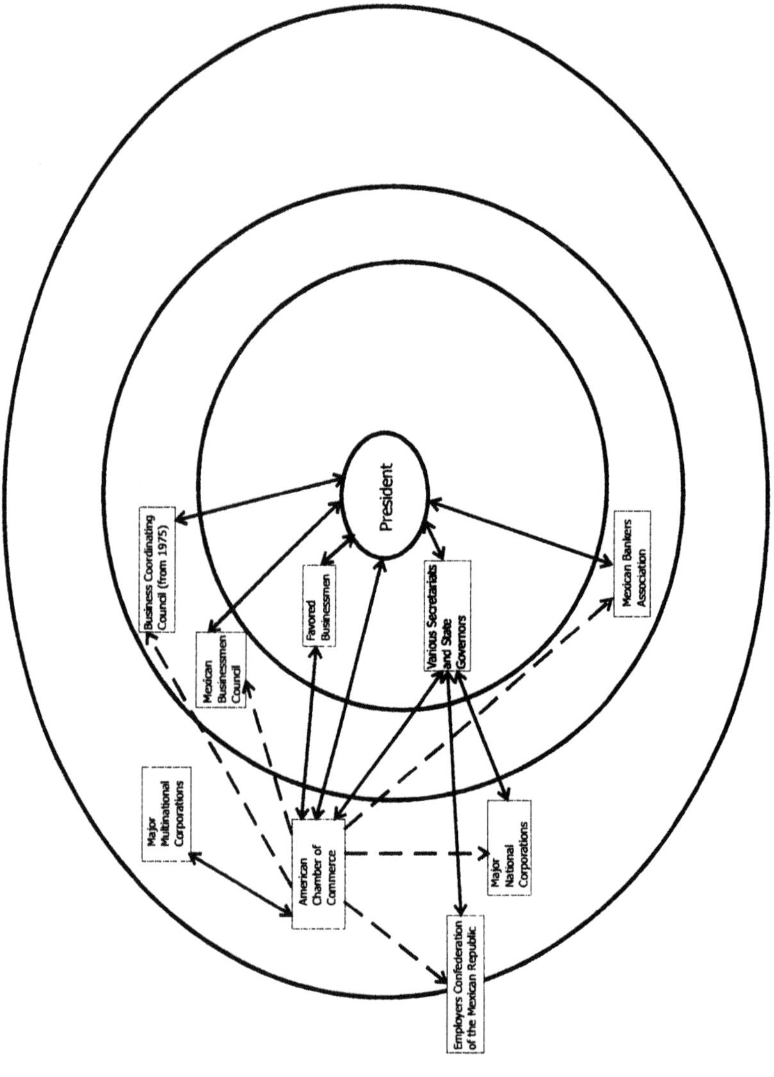

Figure content (labels):
- President
- Business Coordinating Council (from 1975)
- Mexican Businessmen Council
- Favored Businessmen
- Various Secretariats and State Governors
- Mexican Bankers Association
- Major Multinational Corporations
- American Chamber of Commerce
- Major National Corporations
- Employers Confederation of the Mexican Republic

regime rhetorically committed to a nationalist economy had to avoid constant contact between its leader and the representatives of foreign investors, since too much closeness would have been contradictory and publicly unacceptable.

The Secretaries of State normally kept the President well informed about the requests of the AMCHAM though. Close contact at the secretariat level was important because good relations with foreign producers had positive impact on the relation with domestic businessmen (Camp, 1990:120), who saw the confidence of foreign investors in economic policy as a "thermometer" of the situation of the country.

1.2.8. Inter-Policy Network Connections

Diagram 9 summarizes the relations between the policy networks that constituted the ICES. It is an attempt to clarify both their diverse ideological orientation and the impact that such orientation had on policymaking, since the different policy networks often took sides on specific issues and pooled their individual power to influence decision-making. As Valenzuela Feijóo (1986:178) confirms, the Mexican State had "a relationship of unity and opposition with private capital, depending on the agency."

The policy networks of the ICES were grouped in three camps. Firstly, the "financial axis," the "favored businessmen," and the "multinational" policy networks often clustered in support of neo-liberal-style policies. Their ties were very strong in both ideological and operational terms. Secondly, the "nationalist group" and the "red tape" policy networks often joined forces to defend government intervention in the economy.

That the Secretariat of the Treasury was involved in both the "financial axis" and the "red tape" policy network did not imply contradiction: the type of bureaucrat involved in one camp and the other was very different. High-ranking officials, committed to the "financial axis," were highly mobile financial technocrats, with upper-level education, and formed in the different financial agencies of the government. Meanwhile, low-level bureaucrats were unionized, had lower levels of education, and favored state intervention. Ideological disagreement between the two groups was frequently overlooked though, in order to achieve organizational objectives. The weak lines that connect the neo-liberal and nationalist groups in Diagram 9 attempt to represent the often strained and difficult relation between the two. Though contact was unavoidable because both groups participated in similar committees and working groups, it was rarely voluntary since it often involved ideological clash (cf. López-Portillo Romano, 1994).

Diagram 9. Inter-Policy Network Connections

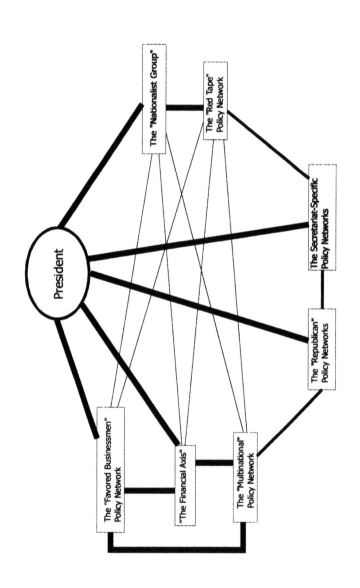

A third clique within the ICES was formed by the "republican" and the "secretariat-specific" policy networks, which were neither committed to liberalism nor to statism, so they supported either, depending on the issue. This attitude probably was a consequence of their intermittent involvement in economic policy-making. But in any case, given the dissimilar social actors that these two groups represented, it would have been impossible for them to adopt an inflexible ideological posture.

Finally, all policy networks obviously had a strong relation with the President, who was—as we already discussed—the coordinator and/or final arbiter in the system.

1.2.8. A General Overview of the ICES

Finally, Diagram 10 shows the ICES in full, as a complex system of relations between numerous actors with different degrees of influence. It incorporates in one design all the policy networks just examined. Because of its intricacy, my aim is not to make this last diagram fully explanatory, but illustrative of the puzzling complexity of informal economic negotiation in Mexico.

2. THE CHARACTERISTICS OF ACCESS IN THE ICES

To complement our graphic analysis of the ICES, in this section I shall examine the connections and resources exchanged between the participants of the ICES and the Mexican Government. As established in our discussion of "circles of power," access to decision-makers was what determined the "non-sectional" power of the different participants, and thus their influence on policy outcomes. The tabular analysis that I introduce now has five columns of information. The first establishes who were the public officials with whom the different participants of the ICES routinely negotiated. The second indicates who were the public officials with whom the participants negotiated only occasionally. The third evaluates the quality of the connections of each participant, by establishing the easiness with which that participant could initiate negotiation. The fourth introduces the frequency with which participants met the President. This fourth point is vital, since the President had access to a wealth of resources of all types to benefit social actors. Those with better access to the President could defend their interests better or get a better compensation if affected by a policy decision. The final column enumerates those resources commonly exchanged between business groups and government.

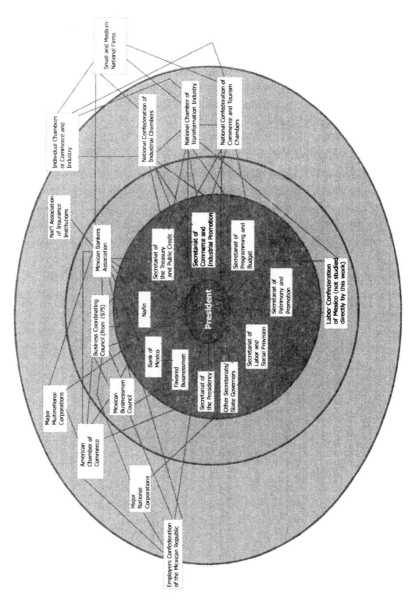

Diagram 10. A General View of the ICES

The diagram contains the following labels:

Small and Medium National Firms

Individual Chambers of Commerce and Industry

National Confederation of Industrial Chambers

National Chamber of Transformation Industry

National Confederation of Commerce and Tourism Chambers

Nat'l Association of Insurance Institutions

Mexican Bankers Association

Business Coordinating Council (from 1975)

Major Multinational Corporations

Mexican Businessmen Council

American Chamber of Commerce

Major National Corporations

Employers Confederation of the Mexican Republic

Secretariat of the Treasury and Public Credit

Secretariat of Commerce and Industrial Promotion

Secretariat of Programming and Budget

Nafin

Bank of Mexico

Favored Businessmen

Secretariat of the Presidency

Other Secretariats/ State Governors

Secretariat of Labor and Social Provision

Secretariat of Patrimony and Promotion

Labor Confederation of Mexico (not studied directly by this work)

President

As briefly mentioned before, the resources exchanged through the ICES included both material and non-material assets such as money, political leverage, influence, strategic information, direct privileges, certainty, legitimacy, and political support. "Strategic information" in turn included privileged data about economic, political, and social policies that imminently would be introduced in the near future. "Direct privileges" included specific favors such as tax exemptions, fee reductions, import licenses, subsidies, or finance at lower rates.

Table 1 summarizes the relational position of the different participants of the ICES, which in turn might explain why and how some were more influential.

3. SOME CONCLUDING REMARKS ABOUT THE STRUCTURE OF THE ICES

The ICES was a complex system constituted by numerous policy networks that differed in their effectiveness to affect policy outcomes. Those that were ideologically closer to the government (and the President) in office also had more influence on policy outcomes. This was evident, for instance, in the decreased importance of the "financial axis" during the government of Luis Echeverría Álvarez. At the time, the nationalist drive of the President made the "nationalist group" relatively more prominent than any other policy network. "Nationalists" were then able to propose and implement policy proposals both that conformed to their ideology and directly benefited their members. In other words, the system constantly promoted different degrees of inequality by excluding some groups. Moreover, the ICES had an inherent bias in favor of macro-negotiations and one equally strong against micro-negotiation. While most large corporations had ready access to policy negotiation, regardless of ideological orientation, small firms were dependent on various levels of representation and intermediation that in the end diluted any impact they could have had on policy outcomes. As Gabriel Zaid, a Mexican economic thinker has affirmed, "the private sector does not seem to see how much it destroys the private sector . . . when it negotiates with the government and forgets small businessmen" (Zaid, 1995:50–1).

It seems then that, even if the ICES was the most viable institutional structure that could have emerged to promote industrialization under the specific conditions and constraints of the Mexican economy, it surely did not turn out to be the best over time. A system like the ICES may have served a useful function during the early industrialization period, but by the late 1960s it had already become a pale substitute for effective democratic representation, checks and balances, and effective multi-party competition.

Table 1: Access Characteristics of the Informal Consultation and Exchange System in Mexico.

Position	Negotiated Directly with	Negotiated Sometimes With	Easy Access to Negotiators?	Met the President	Resources exchanged through ICES (the group gave...in exchange for... from the government)
Favored Businessmen	President	Secretary of State	Yes	Very Often	Legitimacy, political support, business information in exchange for high degrees of strategic information, innumerable direct privileges, certainty, abundant economic resources
Head of Influential Group (CMHN, ABM, CCE)	President Secretary of State	Under-Secretary of State	Yes	Very Often	Legitimacy, political support, business and technical information in exchange for strategic information, direct privileges, certainty, economic resources
Individual Member of Influential Group (CMHN, ABM, CCE)	Secretary of State Under-Secretary of State	President	Yes	Often, with a limit in the number of times	Legitimacy, political support, business information in exchange for privileged information, direct privileges, certainty, economic resources
Head of Less Influential Group (CONCAMIN, CONCCANACO CANACINTRA, AMIS	Secretary of State Under Secretary of State	President Area Director	Not always	Occasionally	Legitimacy, political support, business and technical information in exchange for certainty, direct privileges, a small degree of strategic information, economic resources

Table 1: Access Characteristics of the Informal Consultation and Exchange System in Mexico. (continued)

Position	Negotiated Directly with	Negotiated Sometimes With	Easy Access to Negotiators?	Met the President	Resources exchanged through ICES (the group gave...in exchange for...from the government)
Individual Member of Less Influential Group (CONCAMIN, CONCANACO, CANACINTRA, AMIS)	Under-Secretary of State, Area Director, Area Sub-Director	Secretary of State	No	With difficulty, almost never	Legitimacy, political support, business information in exchange for certainty, some direct priveleges, some economic resources
Head of Copamex	Secretary of State	President	Yes	Occasionally	Some political support, avoidance of public exposure of government errors, business and technical information in exchange for a small amount of strategic information, certainty, direct privileges
Head of the AmCham	Secretary of State, Under-Secretary of	Area Director	Yes	Occasionally, disguised as 'courtesy visits'	International legitimacy, help in relations with U.S. government, business and technical information in exchange for some amount of strategic information, direct privileges, certainty, access to policymakers
Head or President of Major National Firm	Secretary of State, Under-Secretary of State	President, Area Director	Yes	Very rarely, but it was possible if requested	Investment, job creation, some exports, political support, business information in exchange fro control of labor, wages, direct privileges, economic resources, market certaintiy

Table 1: Access Characteristics of the Informal Consultation and Exchange System in Mexico. (continued)

Position	Negotiated Directly with	Negotiated Sometimes With	Easy Access to Negotiators?	Met the President	Resources exchanged through ICES (the group gave…in exchange for… from the government)
Representatives of Major Multinational Firms	Secretary of State Under-Secretary of	Area Director State Governor	Yes	Very rarely, but it was possible if the firm was large enough	Investment, job creation, technology transfer, exports, business information in exchange for control of labor and wages, direct privileges, certainty, economic resources, market protection
Head of Important Sector-Specific Chambers of Commerce or Industry	Under-Secretary of State	State Governor	Yes	Approximately once every three years	Business and technical information in exchange for certainty, direct privileges sector-specific strategic information, economic resources
Head of Less Important Sector-Specific Chambers of Commerce of Industry	Under-Secretary of State Area Director	Area Sub-director State Government Secretaries	Not always	No, but could, happen *exceptionally* if the President was interested	Legitimacy, political support, business and technical information in exchange for certainty, direct privileges, sector-specific strategic information, economic resources
Head of Medium and Small National Firms With Highly-Placed Access Contact	Secretary of State Under-Secretary of State	With whoever the Access Contact arranged	Depended on Access Contact	Depended on Access Contact	Investment, job creation, some exports, political support in exchange for control of labor and wages, direct privleges, certainty, economic resources, market protection
Head of Medium and National Firms Without Access Contact	Middle- and Low-level Bureaucrats	Area Director	No	Never	Economic resources, political support in exchange for specific, direct privileges

Table created by the author

If the ICES persisted it was precisely because the government would not allow any form of representative democracy to develop. In the long run, the country paid the toll through growing inequality.

Another reason that may explain why the ICES remained in operation despite these remarkable contradictions probably is that the Mexican economy was historically concentrated anyway. By privileging big private groups that—as we saw before—produced about 80% of GDP, the ICES maintained the confidence of those firms that literally ran the country, even if they were a select minority. In the highly discretionary Mexican political system, the confidence of big businessmen had to be renewed everyday (Martínez Nava, 1984:79). Creating confidence for big investors was then the contribution of the ICES to Mexican industrialization. This is possibly why Shafer (1973:126) saw "the great development of consultation" as one of the "important institution-building achievements by both government and private enterprise". In other words, in the end, the ICES may not have been equitable, but it certainly was pragmatic in achieving the central objective of the successive post-1940 governments: to legitimize their political monopoly through economic growth, at any price.

Part Three
Empirical and Theoretical Conclusion

"Want of foresight, unwillingness to act when action would be simple and effective, lack of clear thinking, confusion of counsel until the emergency comes, until self-preservation strikes its jarring gong—these are the features which constitute the endless repetition of history."

Winston Churchill, British Statesman. *

"If liberty and equality, as is thought by some, are chiefly to be found in democracy, they will be best attained when all persons alike share in the government to the utmost."

Aristotle, Greek Philosopher.

"The only stable state is the one in which all men are equal before the law."

Aristotle, Greek Philosopher.

"I can retain neither respect nor affection for a Government which has been moving from wrong to wrong in order to defend its immorality."

Mahatma Gandhi, Indian Statesman.

"It is only by not paying one's bills that one can hope to live in the memory of the commercial classes."

Oscar Wilde, Irish Writer.

"We are never deceived; we deceive ourselves."

Johann Wolfgang von Goethe, German Writer and Scientist.

"Where there is no vision, the people perish."

Proverbs 29:18

Chapter Six

Formality, Informality, and the Mexican Experience

INTRODUCTION

The last chapter of our enquiry has four objectives. Firstly, to test the general hypothesis of the project. Secondly, to test some of the theoretical assertions made in our theoretical section, in the light of the information presented by the case study on Mexico. Thirdly, to draw conclusions that may constitute practical advice for future policy-making in Mexico or other countries where informality might be equally extended. Finally, I establish directions for my future research. The chapter will be divided in four sections that follow the same order as these four objectives.

1. TESTING A GENERAL HYPOTHESIS

The hypothesis of this book was that informal institutions have the capacity to promote economic stability. In my view, this hypothesis only partially has been proven correct, since I had failed to consider the equally relevant stabilizing role played by formal institutions. In consequence, I had also failed to recognize the influence that the dialectic interrelation has on economic stability.

To reach this conclusion, we first linked neo-institutionalist theory to policy network theory and confirmed that some informal structures, such as policy networks, may be regarded as institutions. Policy networks influence behavior at different levels of consciousness, allow participants to foresee probable patterns of behavior for themselves and for others, create a basis for stable relations of exchange, and therefore, as institutions, provide some degree of economic stability.

However, we also discovered that informal institutions are necessarily related to formal institutions, since they emerge to either compensate or complement the functions of formal structures. This interrelation between informality and formality is dialectical, and indicated that informal institutions do not have the capacity to operate in isolation. The existence and operation of a dialectical interrelation between formal and informal institutions was further examined through study of the Mexican ICES. Historical and structural analyses confirmed that the ICES always operated in conjunction with the formal economic and political structure. In fact, the exclusion of businessmen from the formal legal framework was what prompted the emergence of the ICES. Its protracted operation was also a response both to the lack of democratic representation and the need to promote the development of the real economy. Even the dissolution of the system was linked closely to the breakdown of the formal economy.

A related point confirmed by our case study was that during crisis or periods of paradigmatic change, informal institutions may provide stability to formal institutions and to the political system as a whole. The examples of the López Portillo and the De la Madrid administrations were illustrative in this respect because the two presidents used the ICES to transmit confidence, while the formal economy adjusted. The possibility of informal institutions providing stability in times of change seems to be rooted in their enormous flexibility, but also in a related characteristic that was only implicitly mentioned in our theory: their speed of reaction. In our case study, informal institutions not only displayed a flexible and loose structure, but also a capacity to transmit information faster than most formal structures.

All in all, the discovery and analysis of the dialectic interrelation between formality and informality allowed us to realize additional features of this type of structure that go beyond those originally predicted.

2. TESTING THEORETICAL ASSERTIONS

In the first part of our enquiry, I made numerous theoretical assertions that require confirmation in light of the complementary information offered by the case study on Mexico. The objective of the section is to help us draw better conclusions about the operation of informal institutions, by analytically comparing our theoretical predictions with empirical evidence. The section follows the same structure as the theory part of the book insofar as it discusses the definition, emergence, persistence, and change of informal institutions. I shall also discuss the applicability of these conclusions to countries other than Mexico.

2.1. *Defining Informal Institutions*

We defined informal institutions as "the systems of relations consisting of a mix of cognitive mechanisms, unwritten regulative mechanisms, and unwritten normative mechanisms, that influence the behavior of participants, thus structuring relations by increasing certainty." After analysis of the ICES, the definition can be confirmed with a particular addition: the institutional status of the ICES as a whole. Let me expand.

The policy networks that constituted the ICES, in my view fulfill the characteristics of our working definition, so they indeed may be seen as informal institutions. However, the investigation of the ICES has shown that the system is not only a collection of policy networks, but an informal institution in its own right. Analysis proves that the ICES fits by itself the definition of informal institutions, and thus may be regarded as an informal institution formed by other informal institutions. The possibility of a "mutual embedding" of informal structures is one we had not foreseen in our theoretical chapters either.

2.2. Emergence of Informal Institutions

In our theoretical part, we established the emergence as a three step process: firstly, a social group agrees on the creation of an institution and the basic accords to support it; secondly, the institution materializes as either a formal institution (an organization) or an informal institution (a policy network); finally, through interaction, additional accords are established. In general, the emergence of the ICES confirmed these predictions but, again, with some caveats.

Concerning the first step, the particularity was that the time over which agreements were established was noticeably long: 10 to 12 years, after which it only took a couple of years to materialize and function. It follows that, at least in principle, emergence follows no time standards.

The accommodation of "losing" groups, admitted as a pre-requisite for materialization of institutions, also showed distinctive features. Accommodation of the interests of labor and the peasantry (the main "losing" groups in Mexico) took place at the minimum level necessary to avoid widespread social unrest. Instead of effective democratic accommodation, the Mexican government granted selective corporatist rewards to these groups and, when these rewards were insufficient and social groups demonstrated against the state of affairs, violent repression was always kept at hand as a ready alternative: a response not predicted by our theory either. The conclusion in this respect simply is that "losing" interests do not necessarily have to be democratically accommodated. When feasible and/or less complicated, the appropriators of an institution may also use a "carrot and stick" approach (through political or financial inducement, first, and then through intimidation and violence if necessary) to appease potential opposition to emergence.

A third point corroborated through the study of the ICES was that institutions may emerge as either organizations or policy networks. In Mexico, those policy networks that emerged and later constituted the ICES were the materialization of institutionalized industrial planning. In many Western democracies, industrial planning was (and is) carried out through specific committees or working groups in either the executive or the legislature, where social groups formally gather to negotiate and implement accords. This may happen directly or through democratically elected representatives. In Mexico, where congressional representation was defective and the executive had legal and political constraints directly to negotiate with businessmen, the institution of industrial policy-making materialized through informal structures instead. In the end, however, the ICES seems to have served the same objectives: represent interests, negotiate change, balance power, and create confidence in investment. Naturally, the effectiveness of one form of negotiation or the other varies, depending on the context where it emerges, but the functional equivalence of the formal and informal structures apparently remains unchanged.

On the emergence of institutions, the final theoretical assertion verified by the case study was one also supported by Hall and Soskice (2001:54–60). In their view, and in mine, an institutional structure that may emerge at a given point in time is specific to its social and historical context. Under specific regulative, normative, and cognitive constraints, I believe that choices concerning the number of structures that may emerge are very limited. In the case of Mexico, the ICES was the only structure that could have emerged after the Mexican Revolution because a formal incorporation of businessmen into the governing coalition or the single-party system was politically impossible. In fact, a hypothetical incorporation of the economic elite into the "Revolutionary Family" would have undoubtedly fuelled further social unrest, by giving some of the leaders of the struggle an excuse to claim the "betrayal" of the ideals of the movement. Therefore, industrialization, at that very particular time, was only possible through the development of the ICES. This is not functionalism, but the realization that social, historical, and cognitive constraints are usually so vast that institutional options to solve specific social problems, at a specific point in time, are very limited and, in most cases, in fact perhaps limited to one.

2.3. Persistence of Informal Institutions

We suggested that the maintenance of legitimacy through stabilizing change is the factor that determines the persistence of institutions. The study of the ICES confirmed this.

The centrality of adaptive change in the persistence of institutions was confirmed by the interesting contrast between the López Mateos and the Echeverría administrations. The beginning of the two governments was marked by a shift to the left that deeply worried businessmen, but while López Mateos used the ICES to promote stabilizing change in the formal economy, Echeverría de-legitimized both the ICES and the formal edifice, causing the disastrous results that we already described. Our case study seems to confirm, with Garrido (1989:445–6), that "the maintenance of stability required the permanent negotiation and re-negotiation of political and economic pacts to keep the system running."

Paradoxically, it appears that if stabilizing change is not evident in most political systems it is because institutions are adjusting and thus operate well. In other words, negotiation and adaptation keep struggle away from the public eye. It is only when institutions cease to operate properly that these struggles become obvious and ensuing demands for change, public.

2.4. Change of Informal Institutions

The case study on Mexico in my view confirmed the validity of the model of paradigmatic change that I developed, based on the work of Colin Hay. To strengthen this assertion, I present in Appendix 4 an example of how paradigmatic change was narrated by an influential businessman.

The stabilizing (and destabilizing) capacity of informal institutions was equally confirmed. The troubled administration of José López Portillo, in which informality played the double role of a retardant and, later, an accelerator of paradigmatic change, illustrated this assertion.

Finally, analysis of the ICES also confirmed that–in line with Mediated Rationality–trust is an essential mechanism in the operation of informal institutions. Trust seems to have been based on a combination of regulative, normative, and cognitive mechanisms that allowed participants to carry out exchange. At the regulative level, stringent punishment was exercised when the rules of the system were broken: public discredit of Mr. Rómulo O'Farril, the businessman that attempted to enter politics in the mid-1950s, provides a good example. Normatively, self-enforced compliance was also common: the public declarations on the part of businessmen and politicians alike offer a good example of what was and was not considered "adequate" behavior in informal negotiation. Finally, common values and the creation of roles around the idea of industrialization also allowed the very existence and daily operation of the system. All throughout Mexican industrialization, in the periods when any of these three elements was missing or violated, trust deteriorated quickly and so did the ICES. The beginning of the

López Mateos, the whole of the Echeverría, and the end of the López Portillo administrations confirm this assertion.

2.5. Informality Beyond Mexico

This work also confirmed to me the operation of informal institutions, in the style of the ICES, all over the World. Numerous works consulted describe equivalent structures in developing and developed countries alike. For example, Shafer (1973:189) describes similar "pragmatic" institutions in other parts of Latin America. Biggart and Hamilton (1992:472) study Asian economies organized through extensive informal business networks. Garrido (1989:441–3) minutely examines the "Dowrehs," which are circles of influence and exchange common in Iran. Ledeneva (1998) analyses *Blat* in Russia: an informal system of exchange of resources and influence. Bachmann (1998:311) also discusses the creation of trust in unstable institutional environments like those of China and India, which suggests the potential existence of ICES-like structures to promote investment.

The examples could continue, but I believe my point has been made. Many of the processes described and the conclusions extracted in this work appear to be applicable to countries like Mexico, in which informal channels either compensate for the ineffectiveness or complement the functions of formal systems of negotiation and exchange.

3. SOME PRACTICAL CONCLUSIONS FOR MEXICO AND OTHER POLITICAL SYSTEMS

This section presents some of the practical conclusions that may be drawn from our analysis of the ICES. In the lines that follow, I shall analyze five issues that, in my opinion, cover those aspects of our analysis that might be useful for future economic policy-making in Mexico and other countries where informal negotiation and exchange may be equally relevant.

3.1. The ICES and Democratic Representation in Mexico

The pervasiveness of informality in Mexico may be explained as a consequence of deficient democratic representation in the country, of which the ICES was simply one manifestation. Deficient democratic representation was deeply rooted in the legal framework that gave birth to the post-Revolutionary Mexican political system. This favored excessive presidential power and concentration of decision-making capacity in the central government. These "centralist" laws, necessary to pacify the country after the Revolution remained unchanged even after political stability consolidated and, in fact, were actually strengthened.

Even if some informal structures, like the ICES, eventually limited to some degree the power of the Mexican State, they were flawed solutions to the underlying problem of poor democratic representation. Most of these informal systems in fact worsened social inequality by increasingly limiting access to decision-makers. For instance, while the ICES favored larger businessmen, it excluded smaller firms from the most dynamic sectors of the economy. In the best of cases, small national firms eventually became inefficient, semi-corporatist, state-dependent units. The case of labor is similar: through the ICES and similar informal arrangements with labor bosses, the Mexican government allowed the marginalization and impoverishment of workers to a degree that, even today, is difficult to understand. In other words, even if informality was the only possible solution to the legal, historical, social, and cognitive constraints of the time, it was far from being the best alternative, confirming that, as March and Olsen assert, "history cannot be guaranteed to be efficient" (1983:737).

But the real problem did not reside in informality or in the ICES as such. Informality was only a viable response to the existing situation. The problem lay in the one-party system that the Mexican State developed, through a Machiavellian combination of corporatism, clientelism, corruption, rewards, rhetoric, and political manipulation of the masses. Control was justified by the government as a way to sustain economic growth, and economic growth was inevitably linked to the ICES, which was an exclusive structure that promoted inequality and generated numerous social contradictions. The ICES disproportionately benefited the business sector, because (a) businessmen profited from their privileged access to decision-makers; and (b) they also were able gradually to control the power of the Mexican State, but only in those issues that concerned them. When businessmen recognized their support as essential in the maintenance of state legitimacy, they took advantage of that position (particularly the larger corporations), used the ICES in their personal benefit, and ended up generating a vicious, self-perpetuating circle of economic segregation.

The few efforts there were to change this situation of inequality never addressed the real problem: ineffective (almost inexistent) democracy. For instance, when in the early 1970s Echeverría attempted to dismantle the ICES as way to end the privileges of the business class, he removed the only source of business confidence and did not replace it with an effective system of democratic representation or judiciary action that could substitute the function of the ICES. Panic, instability, and a crisis ensued. In my view, a more effective solution, albeit more complicated and opposite to the political interests of the PRI, would have been a gradual democratic opening, managed precisely through the extensive informal channels in operation. This would have created confidence in other parts of the system and, more importantly, would have empowered "losing" groups to defend their interests more effectively. Informality still may have been present, but it would have been less marginalizing.

In a nutshell, the main lesson that might be extracted from studying the relation between informal institutions and democratic representation is that inequality may only be avoided if all social groups have equal access to effective channels of political representation, be them formal or informal. Once one group gains privileged access, or one of the channels of access becomes more effective than others, self-perpetuating and increasing inequality will most likely be generated.

3.2. The ICES and Tri-Partism in Mexico

Closely related to democratic representation is tri-partism. Existing accounts of the Mexican post-Revolutionary System suggest that Mexico grew through a series of tri-partite agreements between the government, organized labor, and the private sector. After analysis of the ICES, I would like to challenge this view.

In my opinion, the only operative pact was between the government and business; labor was subordinated all along. Strictly speaking, the Mexican economy was bi-partisan and not tri-partisan. The existence of a tri-partite agreement was rhetorical and superficial, because neither the more frequent interaction between the government and businessmen nor the larger influence of the business sector in decision-making support the existence of effective tri-partism. As Camp (1990:124) confirms, "whatever occasional concessions labor received, it has never been a crucial actor in the broad sweep of government economic policy."

Unequal representation of labor in decision-making was thus a result of at least two factors: (a) differences in access to decision-makers; and (b) co-option and coercion exercised by the government upon organized workers. We have suggested that the ICES offered more effective access than the formal channels used by labor because, in practice, workers favored the Legislative Power over direct negotiation. In their view, having a high number of pro-labor Deputies and Senators assured adequate influence. The miscalculation lay in the Mexican State being dominated by the Executive, so effective access to the President (like that provided by the ICES) was more important than a high number of congressional representatives.

Concerning the co-option and coercion of labor, it was both an ideological and practical way to achieve the goals of the post-revolutionary Mexican regime. Ideologically, when economic growth became a means to political survival for the PRI, businessmen became the most relevant social group (since they had the capital to generate such growth), and labor became a necessary evil that had to be controlled. Pragmatically, the government only had to offer prominent labor leaders congressional and public positions in exchange for acquiescence. In a country where workers had very low schooling and thus job uncertainty, rising to a high political position was not only a matter of personal pride but also a source of social recognition, and previously unimagined income: co-operation with the government was the safest and easiest means of upward social mobility. Many workers joined trade unions in search of political prominence and not to defend their class' interests. Ideology gave way to pragmatism, but given the repressive nature of the regime, union leaders had little choice but to go with the wishes of the government. This pragmatic behavior engendered a vicious circle: the political success of union leaders did not depend on their defense of workers, but on loyalty to the President. In the end, organized labor lost its independence and, with it, its capacity for self-defense.

Two lessons may be drawn form this story. The first is that proximity to the state does not mean influence in the state. Influence seems to be determined by the quality of the channels of access to decision-makers, not by the mere existence of those channels. Second, in certain cases, informal channels may be equally or more effective than the formal, if they offer such better access to decision-makers.

These lessons may also explain the failure of the attempts to establish more visible, formalized instances of tri-partite negotiation during Mexican industrialization. For example, the National Tri-partite Commission that Echeverría attempted to create in the 1970s seems to have failed because it artificially tried to equate the real power of access enjoyed by businessmen with the lower access of the working classes. Businessmen were not willing to see their influence drop, so they continued using informal channels. A better solution would have been to strengthen dialogue in Congress, through democratically-elected representatives of both social classes but, as we have discussed, that was unacceptable to the PRI regime that wished to maintain a monopoly of power.

3.3. The ICES and Deviant Political Behavior

In our theoretical section, we concluded that though informal institutions may structurally accommodate corruption, corporatism, or clientelism they (a) do not inherently encourage these types of conduct; and (b) in fact may possess inbuilt mechanisms to discourage such behavior. In other words, we predicted that, if properly designed, informal institutions might discourage corruption, corporatism, and clientelism. Unfortunately, after assessing the ICES, I cannot confirm this theoretical assertion. The ICES was constituted by a number of policy networks that appear to be less corrupt, corporatist, or clientelistic than others, but perhaps they simply were better at disguising it. The evidence I collected only proves the existence of high degrees of corruption and clientelism in some policy networks, but not low degrees in others.

Archival, bibliographic, and testimonial sources prove that the most corrupt networks in the system were the "favored businessmen" and "red tape" policy networks, where large amounts of economic resources were exchanged. "Favored businessmen," for example, often sold influence and benefited from government contracts and other privileges. Likewise, inspectors of the Secretariats of the Treasury, and Industry and Commerce extracted exorbitant amounts of illegal money from small business owners.

Meanwhile, other policy networks, such as the "financial axis" or the "secretariat-specific" mostly exchanged opinions about technical issues such as desirable rates of interest, credit caps, or specifications for new infrastructure. Morris (1992:83–4) asserts that corruption in the financial sector of the Mexican government was statistically smaller. This is confirmed by a poll applied by Derossi (1971:40), in which businessmen themselves admitted that high level contact between industrialists and public officials were usually kept on equitable, technical, and non-corrupt terms. However, this is not enough evidence to assume that these networks were clean of corruption. On the first argument, a "statistically smaller" level of corruption confirms only that there still was some; concerning the second argument, businessmen who engaged in high-level extortion or bribery would never declare it in a poll that would be published in a book. For my research, I must admit that I was unable to gather enough evidence to measure the levels of corruption in the ICES.

The main conclusion that I can offer then is that, although informal institutions may hypothetically have inbuilt mechanisms to prevent corruption (or for the matter corporatism and clientelism), I could find none in the ICES. This means either that it was a somewhat ambiguous structure in terms of deviant behavior or that I must find a better method to identify these mechanisms. Those networks in which corruption was "statistically smaller" are worthy of further study, if one wishes to derive more concise conclusions about this topic. On the relation between the ICES and corruption, I must declare that I have failed to obtain enough information to test my theoretical assumptions. This naturally represents an exciting challenge for future research.

3.4. Bureaucratic Interests

A final lesson not directly related to the ICES, but largely relevant to our enquiry, is the role that poor bureaucratic accountability played in policy failure in Mexico.

In a country lacking a civil service system and in which presidential power was disproportionately large, politicians and bureaucrats at all levels found incentive in serving the President instead of the people. Just like labor leaders, bureaucrats could not be fully blamed for this decision either: servility and discipline determined upward political and economic mobility in the Mexican political system.

This has been confirmed by two former Presidents. For José López Portillo, ideology normally disappeared in the President's cabinet and struggle resulted from personal and political ambition "combined with the *sui generis* Mexican process of succession in power" (López-Portillo Romano, 1994:125). Miguel De la Madrid also confessed that no member of the cabinet would ever intentionally go against the will of the President because, in his own words, "that would have been suicidal. In the cabinet–he added–it was all about political survival . . . There was a limit to what you could say to the President" (López-Portillo Romano, 1994:127). If this was the attitude of the closest group of friends and collaborators of the President, one may guess that the behavior of lower ranking officials had to be even more servile. This attitude in the government's inner circles may clarify why, as the power of the Presidency increased over the years, decisions grew more erroneous and divorced from social reality.

3.5. Paradigmatic Change in Mexico and the ICES

The role of the ICES in paradigmatic change in Mexico offers interesting lessons in at least three policy-making issues: (i) the role of informal institutions in economic stability and change; (ii) the influence of generational gaps in political and economic change; and (iii) the latent danger of "state rentism." Let us analyze each of these points.

(i) The Role of Informal Structures in Economic Stability and Change

Traditional accounts explain paradigmatic change in Mexico through analysis of international, economic or political factors. These approaches are accepted as pre-eminent by the academic community and the mass media.

Although all these versions undoubtedly identify the contradictions that unchained the process of change, in my view they lack two important elements. Firstly, they fail to acknowledge the influence of informal institutions in the process of change. Secondly, they remain partial diagnoses and thus fall short of explaining comprehensively how the contradictions that they detect, translated into drastic political change.

I believe that the study of the ICES may start to close an important gap in Mexican economic history. This book by no means could be a conclusive document in the area; in fact, it is a start. However, the project has highlighted the importance of informal structures in determining both adaptive and drastic political change. Future policy-making in Mexico and elsewhere should heed more carefully the stabilizing and destabilizing potential effect of informal institutions. Various events in our investigation can help us strengthen this point, the most salient being perhaps the disregard that Luis Echeverría showed for the role of the ICES in economic stability, and the disastrous results that followed. Even if the economic disaster that he created could not be fully attributable to the dissolution of the ICES, it would be difficult to deny that it played a relevant part. The model of paradigmatic change introduced by this work appears to be an important step in integrating under one explanation different narratives of crisi. The model does not aim to be conclusive; it is only a tool to understand change in Mexico and elsewhere, through an interdisciplinary approach that is most appropriate to address an inherently multifaceted phenomenon like social transformation. Naturally, more research is necessary before more accurate prediction can be made, but different disciplines are already making important intellectual inroads that may optimistically allow us to achieve this goal in the future.

(ii) The Importance of Generational Gaps in Political and Economic Change

A second important lesson seems to emerge from the study of the ICES: generational gaps enormously influence the persistence and change of informal institutions and thus of political and economic systems in general.

As suggested before, informal institutions rely on unwritten and cognitive principles, so interpretation of reality and the values that support an informal structure are prone to vary from one generation to another. This is where stabilizing change becomes important, because if an informal institution is to survive over more than a few generations, it must be adapted to new ideas, values, beliefs, and roles. This appears inevitable, because legitimacy has different meanings for different generations.

The case of Echeverría is once again illustrative because his style of government generated enormous clashes with various social groups. These may be interpreted as failure to understand his times and the actors that he had to deal with. It is generally accepted that Echeverría sought to re-create Cardenism, in a country and a political system that were not feasible for such a system anymore. The changes he attempted to introduce lost legitimacy immediately, because values, expectations, interests, and motivations (not to mention social and political structures) were different from those 40 years earlier. He could not understand that both the power and autonomy of the government had diminished, and that younger generations understood notions like stability, adjustment, and change differently than their parents.

As a part of society, generational changes also affected government officials who, in spite of the required loyalty and servility, also held different views of the world and, as in the case of the failed 1971 tax reform, constantly blocked policy that did not meet their values. It is known that in the Mexican political system, about 80% of the officeholders are replaced every 12 years and 90% every 18 years (Cornelius and Craig, 1988:25). Nowadays, with the pervasiveness of information technology, these new generations of bureaucrats and politicians may have even larger axiomatic gaps in relation to past generations. This is a point that economic policy-making must take into account.

(iii) The Danger of "State Rentism"

The "rentist state" is a concept developed by Asdrúbal Baptista (1997) to describe the Venezuelan experience, but it is fully applicable to other countries. In Baptista's own words, a "rentist state" is one that continually receives "income of international origin that is significant in relation to internally-generated income." This internationally-generated income is not generated through domestic work or capital, but through property of a land-related asset (Baptista, 1997:13). In the case of both Venezuela and Mexico, the asset is oil. I can think of copper in the case of Chile, Bauxite in Jamaica, or diamonds in Sierra Leone.

The problem with this international income is not that it exists, but how and by whom it is appropriated. When the state owns the abundant natural resource, as is the case in many developing countries and certainly in Mexico, export income goes directly to the state. This causes tremendous imbalances because, firstly, the government obtains economic resources regardless of the situation of the domestic economy. This means that even if the government does not raise one single pound in taxes, it still has money to invest, reducing its accountability to society. Secondly, the "rent" is often spent by the state infrastructure projects, but rarely in the development of the internal market (Baptista, 1997:140-1). In the end, this "unproductive overspending" creates its own economic contradictions, because aggregate demand increases considerably faster than production, so inflation and contraction may ensue.

During the 1970s, both Echeverría and López Portillo developed "rentist" governments: Echeverría obtained excess funds through foreign borrowing and López Portillo through oil exports and additional borrowing. The contradictions created were those predicted by Baptista, and the country collapsed. The severity of the crash was simply equivalent to the degree of rentism that Mexico reached during those years and accountability for this irresponsibility did not exist, as also predicted by the model.

The relation between institutions and a "rentist state" is that, if properly designed, the former may help prevent this type of excesses. If both Echeverría and López Portillo were able to consolidate "rentist" governments it was because no institutional counterweights were in place to prevent it. The only mechanism of control, the ICES, was not operating properly and other formal counterbalancing institutions simply did not exist.

4. FUTURE RESEARCH

It is my opinion that this book has raised important issues for future research. The most relevant one is normative and prescriptive, and refers to a deeper investigation the dialectical interrelation between formal and informal institutions, and its direct impact on democratic economic governance and economic development around the world. At this point, I consider it necessary to delineate some of its features, since they constitute additional conclusions to this book.

In my view, economic governance should be understood as a system consisting of formal and informal interdependent structures, dialectically operating together, in order to accommodate needs and expectations of the often diverse groups that compose a given society.

Following this definition, a deeper study of the dialectical interrelationship between formal and informal structures would allow us to go beyond traditional economic analysis and explore common patterns of interrelationship that might aid or inhibit economic stability, private investment, and the distribution of income and wealth during periods of economic growth. To formal and informal institutions summarize, any future investigation of the dialectical relationship between should, in my view, rely on some very specific points that I outline below.

1. Informal structures are institutions that develop to complement or compensate for the insufficiencies of a formal structure.

2. The relation between the two types of structure is dialectical and, therefore, they influence, limit, and enable each other in particular ways.

3. The degree to which one type of structure is more influential than the other on policy outcomes is uncertain. It depends to a great extent on degree of formality present in a particular political system. Ideal-types could and should be developed to advance on the study of this issue.

4. The role of informal institutions seems to be that of "stabilizers." Since informality plays a complementary and/or compensatory role, it acts as a powerful factor in accelerating, retarding, and perhaps even managing change of formal structures. This means that a first step to understand the dialectical relationship between formal and informal institutions is to map the informal structures operating in a political system. Only then can their influence on the formal structures be understood and partially predicted.

5. The study of the dialectical relationship between formal and informal structures, although fully applicable to all political systems, might be more suited to understand those countries, developed or not, in which informal structures are rife.

6. Widespread informality does not necessarily equal institutional underdevelopment. Some countries favor particular cultural patterns, and the development of structures based on kinship, friendship, and accumulated social knowledge.

7. Informal structures seem to be as influential and effective as formal structures. Therefore, it is necessary to develop more sophisticated analytical tools to understand their nature, functions, and characteristics.

8. It is also necessary to determine how the interplay between formal and informal structures influences social interaction and its policy outcomes. This is to say that we need to know more about the circumstances in which policy outcomes are beneficial or pathological. This might in turn give us better insights into issues like the relation between informality and corruption that, for the moment, remain unresolved.

In sum, further studies need to be developed to analyze the impact of informality in economic relations in Mexico and beyond. This project started with the objective of clarifying it. Having reached the end of the book, I must admit failure: rather than being able to offer definite answers, it is clear that, in the best of cases, I have only managed to raise better questions.

Appendix One

RESEARCH METHODOLOGY

This project used four sources of information, which were given different weight, in accordance with a hierarchy established from the start of the investigation. The purpose of this hierarchy was to preserve the objectivity of the information collected as much as possible. Maintaining objectivity was particularly critical for a topic like informality that inherently lends itself to biased accounts. In descending order of importance, the four sources of information used were: (a) primary documentary material; (b) secondary documentary material; (c) primary oral material; (d) personal written accounts.

a) Primary Documentary Material

This refers to official documents, minutes, reports of meetings, background papers, directives, and memoranda. Where possible, these documents were used as the main source of information to extract facts and data. These documents were used exclusively for chapters 3, 4 and 5 of the book, given the first two chapters are theoretical.

I had access to these original documents on various dates between 2 January and 7 October 2001. The archives that I accessed were the National Archives (Archivo General de la Nación); the private archives of Luis Echeverría Álvarez, President of Mexico from 1970 to 1976; the private archives of the Employers Confederation of the Mexican Republic (Coparmex); the private archives of the Mexican Bankers Association (ABM); and the private archives of Gonzalo Robles, an influential economic thinker and official of the central bank during the 1940s, which can also be found at the National Archives.

At the National Archives, the period consulted was 1934–1988; the private archives of Luis Echeverría Álvarez were consulted for 1970–1976; the private archives of Coparmex were consulted for the 1940–1990 period;

the private archives of the ABM only exist for the 1967–1981 period, since the rest was lost during an earthquake in 1985; finally, the private archives of Gonzalo Robles were consulted for the 1935–1952 period.

Given that my research deals with informal structures, it was naturally difficult to find official documents that mentioned the topic. However, to my surprise, I found numerous minutes and memoranda of meetings between the government and the private sector. These documents helped clarify not only the existence of this type of relation but, in many cases, even the changing tone of those meetings throughout the years.

The quality of the bibliographic classification of these archives varies. This happens even in the case of the National Archives, where some governmental administrations are fully coded, while others even lack an index of documents. The classification I used to encode the different archival documents is fully explained in the Archival Bibliography section of this book.

b) Secondary Documentary Material

This includes all academic literature published on the topic (books, articles, and theses), as well as newspapers, magazines, and other pamphlets. The full description of all these documents has been included in the general bibliography of the book. This material was used for all five chapters of the project. Chapters 1 and 2 are exclusively based on these sources. Meanwhile, in chapters 3, 4, and 5, this material was used to support historical facts, numerical data, and isolated information about informality in Mexico. For interpretation purposes, primary sources were utilized instead.

The publications consulted covered eight broad areas: neo-institutionalist theory, policy network theory, power theory, legitimacy theory, institutional change theory, 20th century Mexican history, 20th century Mexican economic history, and international economic history.

The publications were consulted mainly in five libraries: Cambridge University Central Library; the Marshall Library of Economics, at the University of Cambridge; the Latin American Studies Library, at the University of Cambridge; the Daniel Cosío Villegas Library of the Colegio de México (COLMEX); and the Central Library of the National Autonomous University of Mexico (UNAM). Over 500 publications were collated, consulted, summarized, and interpreted to complete this project. They were consulted between 1 October 1999 and 31 July 2002.

The use of this material is extensive throughout the book. However, these publications obviously lack the necessary depth in my specific topic of interest. I must note that I did not come across one single publication that fully dealt with the topic of informality in public-private relations in Mexico during the industrialization period. The three authors that came closest to analyzing the topic were, in chronological order, Robert J. Shafer, Roderic Ai Camp, and José Ramón López-Portillo Romano. Even then, their emphasis differs from mine. Therefore, I can safely affirm that this book is the first work that studies the system of economic informality in Mexico in depth.

c) Primary Oral Material

As a third source in the hierarchy of importance, I utilized primary oral material. This was made up of 25 interviews conducted between 20 October 2000 and 22 May 2002. The interviews took place in the cities of Mexico, Monterrey, Guadalajara, and Puebla. The interviewees were three former Presidents of Mexico, five former Secretaries of State, one presidential Chief of Advisers, one Under-Secretary of State, 14 former Presidents of national chambers of commerce or industry, and two distinguished independent businessmen. The full list of interviewees, with their positions and the date of the interview(s) is included as Appendix 2 of this book. Unfortunately, many of the people I could have potentially interviewed already had passed away. Numerous others declined to be interviewed for different reasons.

The selection of the sample was based on the Hoffman-Lange (1987) approach. In the view of this author, there are three methods to select what can be seen as an elite sample. The first method is "positional," insofar as it identifies the formal holders of power within an organization. Sometimes, "positional" members are not the real holders of power, so a second method is suggested. The second method is "reputational," and refers to the individuals who are alluded by others as the real holders of informal power. Finally, the third method is "decisional," and it refers to those actors who are publicly known to participate in decision-making processes, even if they do not hold and official position.

To select my sample, I combined the three methods suggested. In the case of informal relations in Mexico, being extremely concentrated, the same individuals often qualified under the three headings. The total sample came to 64 individuals, out of which 29 have passed away. The possible sample, then, was reduced to 35 individuals. Out of these original 35, 23 accepted to be interviewed and two more were referred as important "reputational" interviewees. This gives a success rate of 71% if we count all the interviewees or 66% if we only consider the original ones. In other words, the interviewed sample was significant.

The majority of the interviewees were approached in writing, through a letter that explained the general purpose of research. The rest were approached by telephone and declared that did not require a letter to accept the interview.

Of the 25 interviews, 21 were recorded on tape and four interviewees preferred not to be recorded, although all four allowed me to take notes and paraphrase them if necessary. Of the 21 recorded interviews, only 12 were fully transcribed and selectively translated into English. The rest were selectively transcribed and translated into English. This was due to the fact that the information obtained through these interviews would not be utilized beyond the clarification of doubts, triangulation of information, and support for some assertions. Similarly, given that the interviews were not going to be utilized for discourse analysis, they were not processed through any computer package like *Sonar Professional, Ethnograph, Nudist,* or *Atlas/ti.* For retrieval, however, simple word processor techniques were extensively utilized.

I decided to minimize the importance of oral accounts in favor of archival and bibliographic material, in order to offset the potential biasing effects that elite-group interviewing inherently carries. Seldon and Pappworth (1983) assert that oral history has numerous limitations in three fronts: the interviewee, the interviewer, and the nature of the interview itself. The authors present more than 25 different problematic points for the recollection of oral information from elite individuals. The most salient for the case of this project were: the unreliability of memory, the deliberate falsification of information for political reasons, unfairness through vindictiveness against former enemies, oversimplification through rationalization of impressions, and role exaggeration to prove influence.

None of the interviewees asked for complete anonymity. At most, some of them asked to remain anonymous for some parts of their answers. I am aware that the lack of anonymity tends to decrease the quality of politically-sensitive responses. However, I was willing to take the risk because the interviews were low in my hierarchy of information sources. However, I must add that the possibility to remain anonymous was always offered to all the interviewees. In my opinion, if many of them did not want to remain anonymous, is simply because they are already retired from public life.

Practically all the interviews lasted about one hour and twenty minutes. This might be due to the fact that the same questionnaire was applied in all cases, although in the cases of the two former Presidents of Mexico I asked additional questions about their specific administrations. The only exceptions to the standard length of the meetings were three interviews. One lasted three hours, another one lasted two hours and twenty five minutes, and a last one lasted only forty five minutes. The interviews were carried out in a semi-structured manner, but attempting to ask every question on the questionnaire. I believe this was achieved. A full explanation of the questionnaire utilized and the interviewing technique is included as Appendix 3 of this book.

d) Personal Written Accounts

The source of information to which I attached the least importance were personal written accounts. This includes memoirs, biographies, and autobiographies. The reason for these sources being last is that these works tend to be unreliable. Even if some are objective, a great majority–particularly those in which the subject of the biography is still alive–are charged with biased information.

Nevertheless, these works were still consulted, in order to exhaust the possible sources of information. All were consulted in Mexico at the Daniel Cosío Villegas Library of the COLMEX, and at the Central Library of the UNAM. The work was carried out between 2 January and 7 October 2001.

Appendix Two

This appendix shows the interviews conducted under the conditions set forth by point c) of Appendix 1. The order of the information here presented is: (a) name; (b) interviewed for his position as . . . ; and (c) date of the interview (dd/mm/yyyy).

INTERVIEWS ON TAPE:

1955 Period
Guillermo Castro Ulloa—President of Canacintra, 20/06/2001

1970–1976 Period

Mario Ramón Beteta—Secretary of the Treasury, 03/05/2001
Porfirio Muñoz Ledo—Secretary of Labor and Social Prevision, 24/01/2002; 22/05/2002.
Miguel Alessio Robles—President of Concamin, 20/06/2001.
Carlos Yarza Ochoa—President of Concamin, 21/09/2001.
Jesús Vidales Aparicio—President of Concanaco and the CCE, 31/05/2001.

1976–1982 Period

José López Portillo—President, 24/12/2002
José Andrés de Oteyza—Secretary of Patrimony and Industrial Promotion, 18/09/2001.
Jorge de la Vega Domínguez—Secretary of Commerce, 25/06/2001.
José Antonio Ugarte—presidential Chief of Staff and Chief of Advisors, 06/05/2001; 17/05/2001.
Joaquín Pría Olavarrieta—President of Canacintra, 12/07/2001.
Andrés Marcelo Sada Zambrano—President of Coparmex, 27/06/2001.

José Luis Coindreau García—President of Coparmex, 02/07/01.

1982–1986 Period

Miguel de la Madrid Hurtado—President, 24/07/2001.
Jacobo Zaidenweber—President of Concamin, 18/07/2001.
Emilio Goicochea Luna—President of Concanaco, 25/09/2001.
Alfredo Sandoval González—President of Coparmex, 16/06/2001.
Jorge Chapa Salazar—President of CCE, 01/10/2001.

CMHN (Mexican Council of Businessmen)

Ignacio Aranguren Castiello—Owner of "La Gloria" food conglomerate, 09/07/2001.
Juan Sánchez Navarro–One of the main owners of Cervecería Cuauhtémoc, makers of "Corona" beer. Also ex-President of Concamin, and Concanaco, and founder of CCE, 21/06/2001.

Other Businessmen

Carlos Rello Lara—Owner of the Pepsi Cola brand in Mexico and former Secretary of Economic Development in the State of Mexico, 22/03/2001.
Carlos Gutiérrez—President of Canacintra (1997–1999) and prominent member of the Chamber since 1980, 08/06/2001.

INTERVIEWS NOT ON TAPE:

Luis Echeverría Alvarez—President (1970–1976), 04/05/2001; 14/07/2001.
David Ibarra Muñoz—Secretary of the Treasury (1982–1986), 04/05/2001.
José Ramón López-Portillo Romano—Son of the President, Undersecretary of Planning and Budgeting, Main Personal Advisor of the President (1976–1982), 20/10/2000.
José María Basagoiti Noriega—President of Coparmex (1982–1984), 14/06/2001.

Appendix Three

METHODOLOGY FOR THE DESIGN AND ADMINISTRATION OF THE QUESTIONNAIRE

This appendix discusses the methodology of the questionnaire used for this research project. I shall explain four aspects. Firstly, the type of questionnaire that was used. Secondly, the potential problems that the particular type of methodology could have created. Thirdly, the way in which those problems were handled. Finally, I present the questionnaire itself.

What type of Questionnaire?

As confirmed by Seldon and Pappworth (1983), a closed questionnaire is not always suitable to extract oral history. The limitations set by a simple "-yes-no" type of question, usually blur the possibility of extracting full accounts of historical or biographical facts. Moreover, with Uwe Flick (1998:76–113), it seems that people who are recounting historical facts, tend to express their points of view with more depth under openly designed interviews. An open conversation may shed light on points or interpretations previously unknown to the researcher. Consequently, the most effective way to approach the type of historical elite interviews that my work required seemed to be through a semi-structured questionnaire, administered through an informal, yet guided and moderated, conversation.

The method to conduct a semi-structured interview is presented by Scheele and Groeben (1988), and Flick (1998:76–113). In their view, subjective information must be elicited through an exploration that encourages a gradual reconstruction of facts and interpretations. This is achieved through what could be called the "open question-confrontational question" method. The method refers to the presentation of an open question about the topic, to let the interviewees narrate their experience. This open question is then followed by a confrontational question that offers alternative interpretations to the one just presented by the interviewee. This serves to double check her/his answers, double check the answers of other interviewees, and gain new insights into pieces of information that the interviewee may have forgotten and/or hidden. I extensively used this technique during the interviews administered.

Additionally, "theory-driven" or "hypotheses-directed" questions were asked (Flick, 1998:84). These questions refer to the theoretical information on the topic or, for the matter, to the theoretical assumptions of the researcher. These questions served the purpose of making the implicit knowledge of the interviewee more explicit and systematic.

Finally, I utilized an additional strategy presented by Flick (1998:91–5) and suggested by other methodology experts[1]. It consists of asking the interviewees for the free narration of known events that happened to a "third person" in relation to the topic. In short, the interviewees are asked to tell a story about someone else, in reference to the topic under scrutiny. The result is that the interviewees usually narrate their own experiences, giving interesting insights about things that they would not say if they were talking in first person. Of course, the identity of the "third person" is not asked, in order to make the strategy work. This strategy was used to end the questionnaire.

My method then considered a second stage called "Structure Laying Technique" (SLT). The SLT requires a second interview, two weeks after the first one. In this second interview, the interviewees are presented with their own statements, and with a set of analytical relationships that link these statements to each other. The interviewees are then asked to remember the first interview, and correct or validate their own views, and the analytical relationships presented. The goal of this second step is, again, to make the interviewees reflect on their original positions in the light of the analysis of alternative interpretations after some time. Whenever possible, this step of the interviewing method was carried out as well. Unfortunately, due to the busy nature of the interviewees, I could only put this second stage in practice on three occasions.

Problems of a Semi-Structured Interview Method

According to Scheele and Groeben (1988), and Flick (1998), semi-structured interviews carry potential problems that must be kept in mind when the method is utilized. In the following lines, I will mention the most relevant problems and then I will present the solutions that I found to each one of them. The potential problems are classified under three headings: (a) problems with the interview approach; (b) problems with the interviewee; and (c) problems with the interviewer.

a) Problems with the Interview Approach

1. The interviewer must be aware that the confrontational questions considered under this method may arise the irritation of some interviewees. Some interviewees may think that the interviewer is challenging their veracity or honesty, or that is taking sides against them.

2. When the SLT step is carried out, some interviewees may consider that the analytical relationships prepared by the researcher between their statements, are oversimplified or inaccurate, giving rise to potential irritation and/or extensive modification of the answers.

3. It may be impossible to know the confrontational questions in advance, given the unknown outcome of some of the interviews.

4. There may not be enough knowledge of the possible confrontational questions during the first interviews, and an extensive menu of possibilities for the last ones, since more opposing views have been heard. This creates a bias in favor of the first interviewees and against the last ones.

5. The influence of external factors that can affect the interview must be taken into account. Issues such as the time of the day (particularly for old people), the place of the interview, the length of the interview, the health of the interviewee on the day of the interview, the state of mind of the interviewee, the sex of the interviewer, and the degree of trust between the interviewer and the interviewee, are all essential factors to take into account.

6. Some people will refuse to be tape recorded or will refuse to be cited. In these cases, the methodological quality of the interview might be questioned, and/or the insertion of these opinions into the final text might be difficult.

7. Transcripts may miss the essence of the interview, making subsequent citations be out of context. This, in turn, will attach equivocal meanings to the words of the interviewees.

b) Problems with the Interviewee

1. Memory might be unreliable, particularly for hard facts and chronological sequences. Accounts are often clouded by personal interpretations and half-truths that have come to be accepted as facts after many years.

2. Falsification of facts may be deliberate, due to the need to serve certain ends, protect certain people, or justify certain decisions.

3. The interviewee might wish to avenge old rows, and therefore may utilize the interview to discuss conflicts or intrigues of personal nature between her/him and other actors, instead of talking about the problem itself.

4. Similarly, if the facts are particularly compromising or dangerous, the interviewee might conceal the truth, and instead concentrate on superficial judgments or trivial happenings.

5. The interviewee might oversimplify events either to conceal certain facts, or to appear as an articulate and clear thinker.

6. Some roles, particularly that of the interviewee, might be distorted during the interview. The person can either try to appear as a hero or keep a low profile in those decisions that eventually proved harmful or painful.

7. The interviewee might lack a full perspective of the many factors influencing one event. Personal qualities or certain decisions might be given more importance that external issues with an effect on the event.

8. Some statements may be made with a double goal in mind, particularly if the finished work will be published. In other words, the interviewee might see the work as a chance to state a given opinion, regardless of its veracity.

9. Many people will speak with the influence of hindsight, rather than with a true willingness to recall the events at the time when they happened. This might lead to the repetition of information already published and a poor amount of new or interesting data.

10. Numerous unproductive topics may be discussed by the interviewee, given the open structure of the interview.

c) Problems with the Interviewer

1. Questioning may be biased, given the accumulated amount of information in possession of the interviewer, in comparison between the first and the last interviews.

2. When interviewing elites, there is always the latent risk of being over-influenced by certain interviewees that may be admired or respected. Deference towards specific interviewees might strongly bias the quality of confrontational questions, and or interpretations on the part of the interviewer.

3. The interviewer might substitute the reading of extant written evidence with interviews, simply because they are more enjoyable and less time-consuming. The problem is that the interviewee might get irritated at the lack of knowledge of the published evidence on the part of the interviewer.

4. The interviewer might not be familiar with the background of the interviewee, thus wasting valuable opportunities for in-depth questioning, and causing the irritation of the interviewee.

Solutions I used to the Problems of the Semi-Structured Interview Method

a) Problems with the Interview Approach

1. I paid particular attention in making the shifts between the open questions, the theory-driven questions, and the confrontational questions. I attempted to make explicitly clear that at no point was the veracity, honesty, or theoretical knowledge of the interviewee being tested. For particularly sensitive

interviewees, I tended to offer a prior explanation of the interview method, without giving away the goals.

2. On the three occasions that SLT was carried out, the interviewee was advised that he could change the interpretations at will. They therefore saw the exercise as one of validation rather than as one of confrontation.

3. The possibility to meet for a second interview was always kept open, regardless of the application of SLT. This made room to make better confrontational questions, once other opinions had been heard, eliminating–at least partially–the informational bias.

4. External factors were dealt with by allowing the interviewee to set the place, date, and time of the interview. Enough room was always given for cancellations or rescheduling of the interview. In sum, I attempted to make the interviewees feel as comfortable as possible, so that they could concentrate exclusively on the interview. Similarly, the approximate duration of the interview was told to the interviewee in advance, and was always respected—at least on my side.

5. In my case, few interviewees refused to be tape-recorded. For those that did, I prepared a taped record as soon as possible, as suggested by Seldon and Pappworth (1983:87). To do this with a degree of accuracy, I reconstructed the question asked and then answered it using the interviewees' words as much as possible. When necessary, I also made comments about the mood with which the question was answered.

b) Problems with the Interviewee

Since my interviews exclusively had a verificatory character, the triangulation of data was a common exercise. I believe this helped me to offset most of the pressing problems related to the interviewee. In the same vein, and following Seldon and Pappworth's suggestion (1983:16–35), I often reminded the interviewees about the academic nature of the work. This knowledge, in my view, could incline them to be more objective. Additionally, interviewees were advised in advance that the information would be triangulated. This also might have made them keep their objectivity to avoid appearing as liars later on in the research. Finally, full confidentiality was guaranteed at all times. Although no one asked for complete anonymity, some interviewees asked for partial confidentiality, when sensitive facts were revealed. Assuring that such confidentiality will be kept, seems to move interviewees to reveal even more information.

c) Problems with the Interviewer

The main exercise I implemented to avoid interviewer-related problems was a good preparation for the interview. Normally, the more information I gathered about the interviewee, the more information the interviewee offered. This, I tried to keep in mind throughout the whole of the fieldwork.

QUESTIONNAIRE

The design of the questionnaire attempted to respect the principles of impartiality, lack of bias, brevity, and clarity that characterize methodologically valid questionnaires in modern social sciences. The questionnaire here presented includes the notes I made for myself.

> Good morning Mister . . . My name is Arnulfo Valdivia-Machuca and I am currently carrying out doctoral research at the University of Cambridge in England. The name of my book is "State and Business Groups in Mexico: The Role of Informal Institutions in the Process of Industrialization," and in reference to this topic, I am here to ask you about your experience with consultation between the private and the public sectors.

> At this point, you have a choice of allowing me to tape record your answers or not. Similarly, I would like to know if it would bother you if I took some notes during our conversation. DO AS ADVISED! IF NO TAPE RECORDER, REMOVE TAPE, AND PUT TAPE RECORDER AWAY!

> During the course of the interview, I will ask you open questions, which you can then answer freely. Occasionally, I may note alternative interpretations that I have come across either in extant literature or in other interviews. I will note that to you when pertinent. Please do not think I am confronting your opinion. It is simply a way to enrich the conversation, and hear your opinion about what others have said about the same event. In no way take it personally, and if it bothers you at all, please let me know immediately.

> Thank you. The interview should last between 60 and 80 minutes. Let us begin.

> 1.   Are you familiar with the workings of any system of consultation or exchange between the public and the private sectors in Mexico? (open question)
> LOOK OUT FOR CONFIRMATION OF THE EXISTENCE OF THE ICES.

> 2.   To the extent of your knowledge, when did these relations develop? (open question)
> LOOK OUT FOR VIEWS ABOUT THE EMERGENCE OF THE ICES.

> 3.   In your view, what was the degree of formality of state-business relations? (open question)

LOOK OUT FOR EXPLANATIONS OF RELATIONSHIP BE-
TWEEN FORMAL AND INFORMAL INSTITUTIONS.

4. What was the state of these relations when you first became ac-
    quainted with them? (open question)
    LOOK OUT FOR INDICATIONS OF STABILITY, POTENTIAL
    PROBLEMS, PERSPECTIVES

5. Did you participate in any way in these relations? (open questions)
    LOOK OUT FOR PROOF OF EXISTENCE AND FUNCTIONING

6. Which would you consider were the turning events that influ-
    enced the functioning of these relations during your time in office?
    (open question)
    LOOK OUT FOR CLUES TO THE FUNCTIONING OF THE
    ICES

7. What was the state of these relations when you left office? (open
    question)
    LOOK OUT FOR CLUES OF POTENTIAL PROBLEMS,
    CHANGE

8. How would you personally assess the impact of these relations on
    economic stability? (open question)
    EVALUATE INFLUENCE DIRECTLY

9. Did the quality of the informal relationships in the framework of
    these relations ever influence your decisions about investing and
    saving in Mexico (FOR BUSINESSMEN)/your perceptions about
    Mexican businessmen (FOR GOVERNMENT OFFICIALS)?
    (open question)
    EVALUATE INFLUENCE INDIRECTLY

10. Do you know if these relations broke down at some point in
    Mexican history? (open question)
    LOOK OUT FOR CHANGES IN THE ICES AND REASONS
    GIVEN FOR THESE CHANGES

11. In your opinion, what made this relationship break down? (IF HE
    THINKS IT BROKE DOWN AT SOME POINT) (open question)
    LOOK OUR FOR A POSSIBLY EXPLICIT CONFIRMATION
    OF CHANGE

12. Can you evaluate these relations? Were they good or bad for the
    country? (open question)
    LOOK OUT FOR PERCEPTIONS ABOUT THE ICES

13. If you had had the power to change the nature of those relations, what changes would have you made? (open question)
     LOOK OUT FOR FURTHER INSIGHT INTO PERCEPTIONS

14. Some scholars say that informality was an initial step because businessmen did not have enough relative power to ask for formality. Once they gained this power, they pushed for formality, but the government did not understand this at the beginning and refused to offer them a formal relationship, until they basically gained it through pressure. Do you agree with this view? (theory-based question)
     LOOK FOR REACTION TO MY OWN THEORY

15. What was the actual role of the Secretary of (MENTION A DIFFERENT SECRETARIAT TO THE ONE THE INTERVIEWEE HEADED, BUT CLOSELY RELATED) in the private-public relations?
     LOOK OUT FOR INFORMATION NOT MENTIONED PREVIOUSLY

SOME CONFRONTATIONAL QUESTIONS WILL FOLLOW SOME OF THE OPEN QUESTIONS.

Thank you very much for your time and help. If you require it, I can give you a copy of the transcript of this interview (IF RECORDED). Would you want one?

After checking the information I may have additional doubts, and it would be very useful if I could contact you in the future. Would you be willing to give me a second interview in the next two weeks to confirm and expand some of the information you just gave me? This is not an exercise to question the validity of the answers that you just gave me. It is an opportunity for you to expand and perhaps offer additional information on the facts that you just narrated.

THANK YOU VERY MUCH.

Appendix Four

A NARRATION OF PARADIGMATIC CHANGE

We affirmed that the model of institutional change defined by Colin Hay had been confirmed by the Mexican case. To strengthen this point, I analyze a speech by Alfredo Sandoval, President of Coparmex in 1985–86 (Sandoval, 1986:17–8). The document presents an example of how Mexican businessmen interpreted the five steps of paradigmatic change:

> The first and second steps of paradigmatic change, in which the loss of legitimacy of ISI is supported through the narration of the model's contradictions was presented by Sandoval in the following terms: "Politics and economics are interrelated; the corporatist-clientelist nature of the first one wraps the second one, and the economic difficulties create commitments in political terms; turning into a vicious circle."

The meta-narration of these contradictions, or third step of paradigmatic change, followed:

> The same vicious circle turned juridical security and the creative confidence of investors into violations to the Constitution, attacks against private property and capital flight. In political terms, the vicious circle of elections-fraud-violence in some places, greatly damages national morale and the relations between Mexicans. Some experts even believe that the social pact is breaking . . . It would seem that there is impotence on the part of the political system and senility in the political model. It is not only the crisis of the instruments used until now . . . we are questioning the very application of the ideological patterns that engendered and oriented [those instruments]. This is why we affirm that, at the national level, we are witnessing the birth of a new historical period.

In the fourth step, solutions to the meta-narrated systemic crisis are offered: "Either we raise the country to put it at the same level of the peoples that are at the forefront of our civilization, adapting technological, scientific, political, and cultural progress to our identity and conditions, and in this way we solve our current difficulties; or we stick to taboos, myths and petrified ideas, and because of our fear of change we isolate the country from the rest of the world, leaving it behind and in poverty."

Finally, for the fifth step, the institutions that in Sandoval's view must emerge are unveiled: "[we must] apply the social market economy system, with the freedom of entrepreneurship for all Mexicans, as the engine and guide of the economy."

Notes

NOTES TO CHAPTER ONE

1. Barley and Kunda made a study in which they proved how the ideological and rhetorical references of managers change dramatically, depending on the state of the profits of their firms.
   * All quotations extracted from http://www.quotationspage.com

NOTES TO CHAPTER TWO

1. Keith Dowding (1994[a], 1995; see also Dowding and King, 1995) has criticized policy networks because he sees them as too structured-centered, and thus as incapable of sufficiently accounting for individual influence. He suggests the use of a rational choice approach (and game-theory) to solve this problem. However, in a Mediated Rationality context, this becomes a secondary debate. As Hay notes: "Only an account of networks capable of acknowledging the dialectical interplay between structure and agency in the practices and processes of networking would seem adequate to the task of capturing the specificity of network modes of coordination" (1998:40). For more on this debate, see also Wilks and Wright (1987); Wright (1988); Wilks (1989); Marsh (1992[a], 1992[b]); and Daugbjerg and Marsh (1998:70).

NOTES TO CHAPTER THREE

1. The national archives contain endless unsuccessful requests for meetings (LCR 111/4037; LCR 562.4/264; LCR 432.1/2; LCR 444.2/414; LCR 521.4/2). Direct contact was very poor between the President and the private sector.
2. The President of the PRI was elected by a "National Council," whose members invariably owed their political careers to the Mexican President. If national councilors wished to obtain political position in the future they had to support the hand-picked candidate of the President.
3. An illustrative example is a telegram in which Deputy Antonio Manero informs the President about the passing of the Law of Industrial Promotion that "I–the Deputy–consulted with you since my entry to this legislature."

He also "begs" the President for an audience to put "to your high consideration other industrial matters" (MAV 545.22/262.1).

4. There are letters in which CONCAMIN (MAV 708.1/5–8) and the Presidents of all the other private organizations (MAV 545.22/53) expose sophisticated technical arguments to clarify their positions in issues that range from taxes to foreign trade.

5. It is documented in the National Archives that in 1949 Alemán granted 3 million pesos to help found the ITESM, one of the leading universities in Mexico. This university was created by Eugenio Garza Sada, head of the Monterrey Group. The university charged (and still does) hefty tuition fees, which in practical terms turn it into a business and not an institution of public education (MAV 565.4/1066).

6. On 17 April 1954, the price of the U.S. dollar rose from 8.65 to 12.5 pesos (Nava García, 1983:195; Erfani, 1995:77).

7. While import substitution of consumer goods had reached 94%, only 30% of capital equipment was substituted in 1955 (Cypher, 1990:76–7).

8. In this particular case, the CONCAMIN informed the President about the details and results of a white paper that they had developed in conjunction with PEMEX, the state-owned national oil company. It was on the technical aspects of a future energy bill.

* All quotations extracted from http://www.quotationspage.com

NOTES TO CHAPTER FOUR

1. The verb "narrate" is here used in the sense introduced by the Hay model of paradigmatic change. In such context, it means to publicize through the mass media the contradictions of a given policy.

2. GDP in 1978 grew by 8.3%, by 9.2% in 1979, and by 8.3% in 1980 (INEGI, 1985:311).

3. This was no mean number of firms. It was calculated that the four largest banks owned around 300 industrial firms of considerable importance, including the top 100 (Ramírez Rancaño, 1976:75–8; see also Bailey, 1986:124).

4. Numerous instances of electoral fraud took place during the De la Madrid administration, the most notable being the governorship elections in the state of Chihuahua (c.f. Krauze, 1997:406–10).

NOTES TO CHAPTER SIX

1. Methodology workshop with Dr. Jackie Scott, Faculty of Social and Political Sciences, University of Cambridge, Easter Term 2000.

* All quotations extracted from http://www.quotationspage.com

Bibliography

Acosta, Jaime (1982). "¿Qué Buscan los Empresarios?", *Contenido*, October 1982, pp. 59–76.

Adler, E. and Peter M. Haas (1992). "Epistemic Communities, World Order and the Creation of a Reflective Research Program", *International Organizations*, Vol. 46, No. 3, pp. 367–90.

Aguilar Villanueva, Luis (1980). "El Sistema Político Mexicano", in Banco Nacional de México (ed.), *México en la Década de los Ochenta*, Vol. 6 (México: Banco Nacional de México), pp. 1–7.

Albertoni, Ettore A. (1982). *Studies on the Political Thought of Gaetano Mosca: The Theory of the Ruling Class and its Development Abroad* (Milano: Giuffrè Editore).

Alcázar Ávila, Marco A. (1970). *Las Agrupaciones Patronales en México* (México: El Colegio de México).

Alcocer, Jorge (1980). "La Bolsa Mexicana de Valores en 1979", in E. González (ed.), *1979, ¿La Crisis Quedó Atrás?* (México: UNAM/ACERE), pp. 110–34.

Ali, Muhammed (2000). *Erradicating Corruption: The Singapore Experience*, Paper presented for the Seminar on International Experiences on Good Governance and Fighting Corruption; February 17, 2000; Bangkok, Thailand.

Almond, Gabriel A. and J.S. Coleman (1960). *The Politics of Developing Areas* (Princeton, NJ: Princeton University Press).

Anda Gutiérrez, Cuauhtémoc (1984). *La Nacionalización de la Banca* (México: IPN).

Aramburu, Marcelo G. (1989). "El Desarrollo de las Industrias de Transformación en México", in F. Becerra Maldonado (ed.), *Antología del Pensamiento Económico de la Facultad de Economía 1929–1989* (México: UNAM), pp. 190–7.

Arriola Woog, Carlos (1988ª). *Los Empresarios y el Estado, 1970–1982* (México: Coordinación de Humanidades de la UNAM y Miguel Ángel Porrúa Editor).

———. (1988b). "Antecedentes", in C. Alba Vega (ed.), *Historia y Desarrollo Industrial de México* (México: CONCAMIN), pp. 233–75.

———. (1976). "Los Grupos Empresariales frente al Estado (1973–1975)", *Foro Internacional*, Vol. XVI, No. 4, April–June 1976, pp. 449–90.

Arriola Woog, Carlos and J.G. Galindo (1984). "Los Empresarios y el Estado en México (1976–1982), *Foro Internacional*, XXV, No. 2, Oct–Dec. 1984, pp. 118–37.

Ashley, Richard K. (1989). "Imposing International Purpose: Notes on a Problematic of Governance", in Ernst O. Czempiel and James N. Rosenau (eds.), *Global Changes and Theoretical Challenges* (Lexington, MA: Lexington Books), pp. 251–90.

Aspe Armella, P. (1993). *Economic Transformation the Mexican Way* (Cambridge MA: MIT Press).

Aspe Armella, P., R. Dornbusch and M. Obstfeld (1983). *Financial Policies and the World Capital Market: The Problem of Latin American Countries* (Chicago: University of Chicago).

Aspra, L. Antonio (1977). "Import Substitution in México: Past and Present", *World Development*, Vol. 5, Nos. 1/2, pp. 111–23.

Axelrod, Robert (1984). *The Evolution of Co-operation* (New York: Basic Books).

Ayala Anguiano, Armando (1979). "Del Carrancismo al Echeverrismo", *Contenido*, Extra 12, Abril 1979, pp. 129–250.

Ayala Espino, José (1988). *Estado y Desarrollo: La Formación de la Economía Mixta Mexicana, 1920–1982* (México: Fondo de Cultura Económica).

Ayala Espino, José *et al.* (1979). "Introducción", in P. González Casanova and E. Florescano (eds.), *México Hoy* (México: Siglo Veintiuno Editores), pp. 19–94.

Azarya, Victor (1988). "Reordering State-Society Relations", in D. Rothchild and N. Chazan (eds.), *The Precarious Balance: State and Society in Africa* (London: Westview), pp. 3–21.

Azcárraga Tamayo, Gastón (1987). "CONASUPO, Ejemplo Latente de lo Nocivo de la Participación del Gobierno en el Comercio", *Decisión*, Año IX, No. 101, June 1987, pp. 141–4.

———. (1976). "El Crecimiento Económico y la Distribución del Ingreso", in Concamin (ed.), *La Industria Mexicana 1976* (México: Concamin), pp. 382–5.

Bachmann, Reinhard (1998). "Conclusion: Trust –Conceptual Aspects of a Complex Phenomenon", in Christel Lane and Reinhard Bachmann (eds.), *Trust Within and Between Organizations: Conceptual Issues and Empirical Applications* (Oxford: Oxford University Press), pp. 298–322.

Bailey, John (1986). "The Impact of Major Groups on Policy-Making Trends in Government-Business Relations in Mexico", in R.A. Camp (ed.), *Mexico's Political Stability: The Next Five Years* (Boulder and London: Westview Press), pp. 119–42.

Bailey, Norman A. and R. Cohen (1987). *The Mexican Time Bomb* (New York: Priority Press Publications).

Balabkins, Nicholas (1988). *Not by Theory Alone: The Economics of Gustav von Schmoller and its Legacy to America* (Berlin: Duncker and Humblot).

Ballvé, Faustino (1958). "Libertad y Economía", *Temas Contemporáneos*, Año 4, No. 48, 1st December 1958.

Banamex (1978). *Exámen de la Situación Económica de México, 1925–1976* (México: Banamex).

Banco del País (1965). *Temas Económicos Mexicanos, Volumen III* (México: Banco del País).

Baptista, Asdrúbal (1997). *Teoría Económica del Capitalismo Rentístico* (Caracas: IESA).

Barber, Bernard (1983). *The Logics and Limits of Trust* (New Brunswick, NJ: Rutgers University Press).

Barley, Stephen R. and G. Kunda (1992). "Design and Devotion: Surges of Rational and Normative Ideologies of Control in Managerial Discourse", *Administrative Science Quarterly*, Vol. 37, pp. 363–99.

Baron, James N. and J. Pfeffer (1994). "The Social Psychology of Organizations and Inequality", *Social Psychology Quarterly*, Vol 57, No. 3, pp. 190–209.

Bartra, Roger (1982). *El Reto de la Izquierda* (México: Editorial Grijalbo).

Basagoiti Noriega, José M. (1983ᵃ). "Seamos Derramadores de Esperanza (Palabras de Apertura)", in Coparmex (ed.), *La Empresa Privada, Esperanza de México. XLIII Asamblea Nacional Ordinaria"* (México:Coparmex), pp. 11–13.

———. (1983ᵇ). "Nuestro Compromiso es con México", in *México: Nuestro Compromiso. XLII Asamblea Nacional Ordinaria de Centros Patronales y Asamblea Nacional Extraordinaria: El Estado y las Garantías Individuales* (México: Coparmex), pp. 85–91.

Basáñez, Miguel (1990). *El Pulso de los Sexenios: 20 Años de Crisis en México* (México: Siglo Veintiuno Editores).

———. (1981). *La Lucha por la Hegemonía en México* (México: Siglo Veintiuno Editores).

Basave, Jorge *et al.* (1995). *Los Grupos Financieros Empresariales en México, 1974-1987* (México: UNAM).

Bates, Robert and B.R. Weingast (1995). *A New Comparative Politics: Integrating Rational Choice and Interpretivist Perspectives*, Harvard Center for International Affairs Working Paper.

Batson, C. Daniel and T. Moran (1999). "Empathy-Induced Altruism in a Prisoner's Dilemma", *European Journal of Social Psychology*, Vol. 29, Issue 7, pp. 909–24.

Becerril Straffon, Rodolfo (1986). "Gran Empresariado y Grupos de Presión", Foreword to M. Buendía, *Los Empresarios* (México: Océano), pp. 9–14.

Beckert, Jens (1996). "What is Sociological about Economic Sociology? Uncertainty and the Embeddedness of Economic Action", *Theory and Society*, No. 25, pp. 803–40.

Beltrán Mata, José A. (1987). *El Empresario Mexicano en la Política* (México: Editorial Pax México).

Bell, Daniel (1965). *The End of Ideology* (New York: Free Press).

Benson, George (1978). *Political Corruption in America* (Lexington: Lexington Books).

Benson, J.K. (1982). "A Framework for Policy Analysis", in D. Rogers, D. Whitten and Associates (eds.), *Interorganizational Coordination: Theory, Research, and Implementation* (Ames: Iowa State University Press), pp. 137–76.

Berger, Peter L. and Thomas Luckmann (1967). *The Social Construction of Reality* (New York: Double Day Anchor).

Berger, Suzanne (1981). *Organising Interests in Europe: Pluralism, Corporatism and the Transformation of Politics* (Cambridge: Cambridge University Press).

Beteta Monsalve, Mario R. (1992). "Don Rodrigo Gómez: Su Estilo, Su Tiempo", in M.R. Beteta Monsalve (ed.), *Rodrigo Gómez: Vida y Obra* (México: Banco de México/FCE), pp. 13–41.

Biggart, Nicole W. and G.G. Hamilton (1992). "On the Limits of a Firm-Based Theory to Explain Business Networks: The Western Bias of Neoclassical Economics", in Nitin Nohria and Robert G. Eccles (eds.), *Networks and Organizations: Structure, Form, and Action* (Boston, MA: Harvard Business School Press), pp. 471–490.

Bizberg, Ilán (1990). "La Crisis del Corporativismo Mexicano", *Foro Internacional*, Vol. XXX, No. 4, April–June 1990, pp. 695–735.

Blair, Calvin P. (1964). "The Nature of Nacional Financiera", in R. Vernon (ed.), *Public Policy and Private Enterprise in Mexico* (Cambridge, MA: Harvard University Press), pp. 193–240.

Block, Fred (1987). *Revising State Theory: Essays in Politics and Postindustrialism* (Philadelphia: Temple University Press).

Bogason, Peter (1996). *New Modes of Local Political Organizing: Local Government Fragmentation in Scandinavia* (Commack, NY: Nova Science).

Bourdieu, Pierre (1999). *Outline of a Theory of Practice* (Cambridge: CUP).

Borman, William (1986). *Gandhi and Non-Violence* (Albany, NY: State University of New York Press).

Bortz, Jeffrey and J.W. Wilkie (1990). "Contexto de la Crisis Mexicana: La Política y la Economía en el México de la Posguerra", in J.W. Wilkie and J. Reyes Heroles González Garza (eds.), *Industria y Trabajo en México, Volúmen 1* (México: UAM-Atzcapotzalco), pp. 17–29.

Braig, Marianne (1992). *Mexiko, Ein Anderer Weg der Moderne: Weibliche Erwerbsarbeit, Häusliche Dienste und Organisation des Alltags* (Böhlau: BV).

Branch, Taylor (1988). *Parting the Waters: America in the King Years, 1954–1963* (New York: Simon and Schuster).

Brannon, Jeff (1986). "The Nationalization of Mexico's Private Banking System: Some Potential Effects on the Structure and Performance on the Financial System", in J.R. Ladman (ed.), *México: A Country in Crisis* (Texas: Texas Western Press), pp. 24–47.

Brasz, H.A. (1963). "Some Notes on the Sociology of Corruption", *Sociologica Neerlandica*, No. 1, Fall 1963, pp. 111–7.

Bruijn de, Johan A. and Ernst F. Ten Heuvelhof (1995). "Policy Networks and Governance", in D.L Weimer (ed.), *Institutional Design* (Boston, Dordrecht and London: Kluwer Academic Publishers), pp. 161–179.

Bryman, Alan (1988). *Quantity and Quality in Social Research* (London and New York: Routledge).

Buendía, Manuel (1986). *Los Empresarios* (México: Oceáno).

Bueno, Gerardo *et al.* (1977). *Opciones de Política Económica en México después de la Devaluación* (México: Tecnos).

Burke, P.J. and D.C. Reitzes (1991). "An Identity Theory Approach to Commitment", *Social Psychology Quarterly*, Vol. 54, pp. 239–51.

Burke, P.J. and D.C. Reitzes (1981). "The Link between Identity and Role Performance", *Social Psychology Quarterly*, Vol. 44, pp. 83–92.

Burton, Michael, R. Gunther and J. Higley (1991). "Introduction: Elite Transformations and Democratic Regimes" in J. Higley and R. Gunther (eds.), *Elites and Democratic Consolidation in Latin America and Southern Europe* (Cambridge: Cambridge University Press), pp. 1–37.

Bush, Paul D. (1987). "The Theory of Institutional Change", *Journal of Economic Issues*, Vol. XXI, No. 3, September 1987, pp. 1075–1116.

Cadena, Daniel (1975). *El Candidato Presidencial 1976* (México: Arana).

CAMCO (1976[a]). "El Impacto de la Inversión Extranjera en la Economía de México", in Concamin (ed.), *La Industria Mexicana 1976* (México: Concamin), pp. 800–3.

———. (1976ᵇ). "Los Requisitos de Capital de Riesgo", in Concamin (ed.), *La Industria Mexicana 1976* (México: Concamin), pp. 804–6.

Cammack, Paul (1990). *New Institutionalist Approaches to Macro-Social Analysis*, mimeo. in University Library, University of Cambridge.

Camp, Roderic Ai (1996). *Reclutamiento Político en México* (México: Siglo Veintiuno Editores).

———. (1990). *Los Empresarios y la Política en México: Una Visión Contemporánea* (México: Fondo de Cultura Económica).

———. (1989). *Entrepreneurs and Politics in Twentieth-Century Mexico* (Oxford: Oxford University Press).

Campbell, John L. (1998). "Institutional Analysis and the Role of Ideas in Political Economy", *Theory and Society*, Vol. 27, No. 3, pp. 377–409.

Campbell, John C.; M.A. Baskin; F.R. Baumgartner and N.P. Halpern (1989). "Afterword on Policy Communities: A Framework for Comparative Research", *Governance*, No. 2, pp. 86–94.

Caporaso, James A. and D.P. Levine (1992). *Theories of Political Economy* (Cambridge: Cambridge University Press).

Cárcoba, Luis G. (1991). "La Modernización Industrial: Objetivos y Perspectivas", in G. Azcárraga Tamayo (ed.), *Los Empresarios y la Modernización Económica de México* (México: Miguel Angel Porrúa), pp. 25–41.

Cárdenas, Enrique (1996). *La Política Económica en México, 1950–1994* (México: El Colegio de México and Fondo de Cultura Económica).

Cárdenas, Lázaro (1979ᵃ). *Palabras y Documentos Públicos de Lázaro Cárdenas, 1928–1970. Mensajes, Discursos, Declaraciones, Entrevistas y Otros Documentos* (México: Siglo Veintiuno Editores).

———. (1979ᵇ). *Palabras y Documentos Públicos de Lázaro Cárdenas, 1928–1970. Informes de Gobierno y Mensajes Presidenciales de Año Nuevo* (México: Siglo Veintiuno Editores).

Carmona, Fernando (1982). *México: Riqueza y Miseria, Dos Ensayos* (México: Editorial Nuestro Tiempo).

Carpizo, Jorge (1998). *El Presidencialismo Mexicano* (México: Siglo Veintiuno Editores).

Carrión, Jorge and A. Aguilar (1972). *La Burguesía, La Oligarquía y el Estado* (México: Editorial Nuestro Tiempo).

Carroll, Glenn R. and Michael T. Hannan (1989). "Density Dependence in the Evolution of Populations of Newspapers Organizations", *American Sociological Review*, Vol. 54, pp. 524–48.

Casar José I. and J. Ros (1989). "Utilidades, Precios y Salarios", in C. Tello *et al.* (eds.), *México: Informe sobre la Crisis (1982–1986)*, pp. 139–149.

Casar, María A. (1992). "Empresarios y Estado en el Gobierno de Miguel de la Madrid: En Busca de un Nuevo Acuerdo", in C. Bazdresch *et al.* (eds.), *México: Auge, Crisis y Ajuste. I. Los Tiempos del Cambio, 1982–1988* (México: Fondo de Cultura Económica), pp. 290–312.

———. (1989). "Los Empresarios y la Administración De De la Madrid: ¿Estrategia Compartida?", in C. Tello *et al.* (eds.), *México: Informe sobre la Crisis (1982–1986)*, pp. 67–81.

Casar, María A. and W. Peres (1988). *El Estado Empresario en México: ¿Agotamiento o Renovación?* (México: Siglo Veintiuno Editores).

Castells, Manuel (1996). *The Rise of the Network Society* (Oxford: Blackwell).

Cater, Douglass (1964). *Power in Washington: A Critical Look at Today's Struggle to Govern the U.S.A.* (London: Collins).

Cawson, Alan (1986). *Corporatism and Political Theory* (Oxford: Blackwell).

———. (1985). *Organized Interests and the State: Studies in Meso-Corporatism* (London: Sage).

Cawson, Alan *et al.* (1990). *Hostile Brothers: Competition and Closure in the European Electronics Industry* (Oxford: Clarendon).

Cavanagh, Michael; D. Marsh and M. Smith (1995). "The Relationship between Policy Networks and the Sectoral and the Sub-Sectoral Levels", *Public Administration*, Vol. 73, No. 4, pp. 627–33.

Cerutti, Mario (2000). *Propietarios, Empresarios y Empresa en el Norte de México, Monterrey: De 1848 a la Globalización* (México: Siglo Veintiuno Editores).

Chazan, Naomi (1988). *Patterns of State-Society Incorporation and Disengagement in Africa*, in Donald Rothchild and Naomi Chazan (eds.), *The Precarious Balance: State and Society in Africa* (London: Westview), pp. 121–48.

Chisholm, Donald (1989). *Coordination Without Hierarchy: Informal Structures in Multiorganizational Systems* (Berkeley: University of California Press).

CIEN (1989). *La Economía Mexicana, 1982–1988* (México: Centro de Información y Estudios Nacionales, CIEN).

Cinta, Ricardo (1972). "Burguesía Nacional y Desarrollo", in D. Ibarra *et al.* (eds.), *El Perfil de México en 1980, Vol. 3* (México: Siglo Veintiuno Editores), pp. 165–99.

Cisneros, Isidro (1986). "El Proyecto Empresarial", in R. Pozas and M. Luna (eds.), *Las Empresas y Los Empresarios en el México Contemporáneo* (México: Grijalbo), pp. 123–50.

Clapham, Christopher (1982). "Clientelism and the State" in C. Clapham (ed.), *Private Patronage and Public Power: Political Clientelism in the Modern State* (London: Frances Pinter Publishers), pp. 1–35.

Clark, Burton R. (1960). *The Open-Door Colleges: A Case Study* (New York: McGraw-Hill).

Clouthier del Rincón, Manuel J. (1983). "Sobreviviremos a Pesar de Todo lo que se Diga", in *México: Nuestro Compromiso. XLII Asamblea Nacional Ordinaria de Centros Patronales y Asamblea Nacional Extraordinaria: El Estado y las Garantías Individuales* (México: Coparmex), p. 79.

———. (1979). "Palabras Pronunciadas por el Sr. Ing. Manuel J. Clouthier del Rincón, Presidente de Coparmex", in Coparmex (ed.), *XXXVIII Asamblea Nacional Ordinaria de Centros Patronales* (México: Coparmex), pp. 13–17.

Coase, Ronald H. (1972). "Industrial Organization: A Proposal for Research", in V.R. Fuchs (ed.), *Policy Issues and Research Opportunities in Industrial Organization* (New York: National Bureau of Economic Research), pp. 59–73.

Cockcroft, James D. (1990). *México: Class Formation, Capital Accumulation, and the State* (New York: Monthly Review Press).

Coindreau, José Luis (1982). "Buscamos un México Mejor pero No Distinto", in *Memoria de la XLI Asamblea Nacional Ordinaria de Centros Patronales* (México: Coparmex), pp. 11–21.

Cohen, Michael, J.G. March and J.P. Olsen (1972). "A Garbage Can Model of Organizational Choice", *Administrative Science Quarterly*, Vol. 17, pp. 1–25.

Coleman, James S. and D. MacRae (1960). "Electronic Processing of Sociometric Data for Groups up to 1000 in Size", *American Sociological Review*, No. 25, pp. 722–7.

Coleman, James R. (1990). *Foundations of Social Theory* (Cambridge, MA: Belknap Press of Harvard University Press).

Coleman, William D. and G. Skøgstad (1990)."Policy Communities and Policy-making in Canada: A Structural Approach", in G. Skøgstad and W.D. Coleman (eds.) *Policy Communities and Public Policy in Canada* (Toronto: Copp Clark Pittman), pp. xiv, 338.

Collier, Ruth B. and D. Collier (1991). *Shaping the Political Arena: Critical Junctures, the Labor Movement, and Regime Dynamics in Latin America* (Princeton, NJ and Oxford: Princeton University Press).

Collins, Robert M. (1981). *The Big Business Response to Keynes, 1929–1964* (New York: Columbia University Press).

CONABIO (1999) (Comisión Nacional de la Biodiversidad [National Comission for Biodiversity]). http://www.conabio.gob.mx/biodiversidad/pob.htm pp.1–10.

Concamin (1978). *La Industria Mexicana 1978* (México: Concamin).

———. (1976ª). *La Industria Mexicana 1976* (México: Concamin).

———. (1976ᵇ). *Memoria del VII Congreso Nacional de Industriales, Tomo 1* (México: Concamin).

Concheiro, Elvira, A. Gutiérrez and J.M. Fragosa (1979). *El Poder de la Gran Burguesía* (México: Ediciones de Cultura Popular).

Cook, Karen S. *et al.* (1994), "The Distribution of Power in Exchange Networks: Theory and Experimental Results", in J. Scott (ed.), *Power: Critical Concepts, Volume 1* (New York: Routledge), pp. 388–416.

Coparmex (1999). *70 Años, 1929–1999* (México: Coparmex).

———. (1984). *55 Años por la Libertad* (México: Coparmex).

———. (1979). *Coparmex: Su Origen y Desarrollo, Hacia los Próximos 50 Años* (México: Coparmex).

———. (1978). *XXXVII Asamblea Nacional Ordinaria de Centros Patronales* (México: Coparmex).

———. (1971). *Franco Diálogo entre Gobierno y Empresarios* (México: Coparmex).

Cordera, Rolando and C. Tello (1984). "México: Opciones y Decisiones", in H. Aguilar Camín *et al.* (eds.), *México Mañana* (México: Océano/Nexos), pp. 173–86.

———. (1981). *México, La Disputa por la Nación: Perspectivas y Opciones del Desarrollo* (México: Siglo Veintiuno Editores).

Cordero, Salvador (1987). "Los Empresarios y el Sistema Político en México", in R. Pérez Miranda and E.A. Albertoni (eds.), *Clase Política y Élites Polítcas* (México: UAM/ Plaza y Valdés), pp. 156–67.

———. (1987ª). "Presentación", in S. Cordero, R. Santín, and R. Tirado (eds.), *El Poder Empresarial en México I* (México: Terra Nova), pp. 9–15.

———. (1987ᵇ). "Concentración Industrial, Grupos Económicos y Capital Financiero del Sector Privado Nacional", in S. Cordero, R. Santín, and R. Tirado (eds.), *El Poder Empresarial en México I* (México: Terra Nova), pp. 17–49.

———. (1977). *Concentración Industrial y Poder Económico en México*, Cuadernos del CES del Colegio de México, No. 18.

———. (1974). *La Burguesía Industrial en México*, B.A. Dissertation, Faculty of Social and Political Sciences, UNAM, mimeo. in the Daniel Cosío Villegas Library of *El Colegio de México*, Mexico City.

Cordero, Salvador and R. Santín (w/d). *Origen, Formación y Estructura de los Grupos Industriales en México*, mimeo. in the Daniel Cosío Villegas Library of *El Colegio de México*, Mexico City.

———. (1977). *Los Grupos Industriales: Una Nueva Organización Económica en México*, Cuadernos del CES, No. 23 (México: Centro de Estudios Sociológicos del Colegio de México).

Cordero, Salvador and R. Tirado (1982). "Introducción", in S. Cordero and R. Tirado (eds.), *Clases Dominantes y Estado en México* (México: UNAM), pp. 9–15.

Cordero, Salvador, R. Santín, and R. Tirado (1987). "El Proyecto Empresarial: ¿Alternativa de Proyecto Nacional?", in S. Cordero, R. Santín, and R. Tirado (eds.), *El Poder Empresarial en México I* (México: Terra Nova), pp.149–200.

Córdova, Arnaldo (1984). *La Formación del Poder Político en México* (México: Serie Popular Era).

Cornelius, Wayne and A.L. Craig (1988). *Politics in México: An Introduction and Overview* Reprint Series 1, 2nd edition (San Diego: Center for U.S.-Mexican Studies, University of California, San Diego).

Cosío Villegas, Daniel (1974). *El Sistema Político Mexicano* (México: Cuadernos de Joaquín Mortiz).

Covarrubias, Alfonso (1980). "Clima para la Inversión", in Banco Nacional de México (ed.), *México en la Década de los Ochenta, Vol. 7* (México: Banco Nacional de México), pp. 168–177.

Crawford, Sue E. and E. Ostrom (1995). "A Grammar of Institutions", *American Political Science Review*, Vol. 89, No. 3, September 1995, pp. 582–600.

Crouch, Colin and R. Dore (1990). "Whatever Happened to Corporatism?", in C. Crouch and R. Dore (eds.) *Corporatism and Accountability* (Oxford: Clarendon Press).

Cyert, Richard M. and J.G. March (1963). *A Behavioural Theory of the Firm* (New Jersey: Prentice Hall).

Cypher, James M. (1990). *State and Capital in México: Development Policy since 1940* (Boulder: Westview Press).

Czada, Roland (1998). "Interest Groups, Self-Interest, and the Institutionalization of Political Action", in R. Czada, A. Héritier, and H. Keman (eds.), *Institutions and Political Choice: On the Limits of Rationality* (Amsterdam: VU University Press), pp. 229–256.

Dahl, Robert A. (1994). "The Concept of Power", in J. Scott (ed.), *Power: Critical Concepts, Volume 1* (New York: Routledge), pp. 288–309.

Dasgupta, Partha (1997). *Economic Development and the Idea of Social Capital*, mimeo. in Marshall Library of Economics, University of Cambridge.

Daugbjerg, Carsten and D. Marsh (1998). "Explaining Policy Outcomes: Integrating the Policy Network Approach with Macro-Level and Micro-Level Analysis", in D. Marsh (ed.), *Comparing Policy Networks* (Buckingham and Philadelphia: Open University Press), pp. 52–71.

Dávila Flores, Alejandro (1990). "La Bolsa Mexicana de Valores: ¿Alternativa para el Financiamiento de la Inversión Productiva?", in E. Gutiérrez Garza (ed.), *Los Saldos del Sexenio (1982–1988)* (México: Siglo Veintiuno Editores/ UAM), pp. 109–38.

De Janvry, Alain and E. Sadoulet (1995). "Introduction" in A. de Janvry et al. (eds.), *State, Market and Civil Organisations: New Theories, New Practices and their Implications for Rural Development* (Geneva: International Labour Office), pp. 1–19.

De la Garza Toledo, Enrique (1988). *Ascenso y Crisis del Estado Social Autoritario: Estado y Acumulación de Capital en México (1940–1976)* (México: El Colegio de México).

De Regil, Jorge Alonso (1976). "Las Aportaciones Patronales ante los Organismos Públicos de Seguridad Social. Su Crecimiento. Su Efecto ante el Empleador", in Concamin (ed.), *La Industria Mexicana 1976* (México: Concamin), pp. 377–81.

De Soto, Hernando (1989). *The Other Path: The Invisible Revolution in the Third World* (London: Tauris).

Del Cueto, Héctor H. (1974). *Miguel Alemán: Historia de un Gobierno, 1946–1952* (México: H.H. del Cueto).

Derossi, Flavia (1971). *The Mexican Entrepreneur* (Paris: Development Centre of the OCDE).

DiMaggio, Paul J. (1988). "Interest and Agency in Institutional Theory" in Lynne G. Zucker (ed.), *Institutional Patterns and Organisations: Culture and Environment* (Cambridge, MA: Ballinger), pp. 3–21.

DiMaggio, Paul J. and W.W. Powell (1991[a]). "Introduction", in W.W. Powell and P.J. DiMaggio (eds.), *The New Institutionalism in Organizational Analysis*, (Chicago and London: The University of Chicago Press), pp. 1–38.

———. (1991b). "The Iron Cage Revisited: Institutional Isomorphism and Collective Rationality in W.W. Powell and P.J. DiMaggio (eds.), *The New Institutionalism in Organizational Analysis*, (Chicago and London: The University of Chicago Press), pp. 63–82.

Dornbusch, Rudiger and S. Edwards (1991). *The Macroeconomics of Populism in Latin America* (Chicago: University of Chicago Press).

Dornbusch, Rudiger and S. Fischer (1996). *Macroeconomía* (México: McGraw-Hill).

Dowding, Keith (2001). "There Must Be End to Confusion: Policy Networks, Intellectual Fatigue, and the Need for Political Science Methods Courses in British Universities", *Political Studies*, Vol. 49, pp. 89–105.

———. (1994[a]). "The Compatibility of Behaviouralism, Rational Choice and 'New Institutionalism'", *Journal of Theoretical Politics*, Vol. 6, pp. 105–17.

———. (1994[b]). "Policy Networks: Don't Stretch a Good Idea too Far", in P. Dunleavy and J. Stanyer (eds.), *Contemporary Political Studies 1994* (Belfast: Political Studies Association).

———. (1995). "Model or Metaphor? A Critical Review of the Policy Networks Approach, *Political Studies*, Vol. 43, pp.136–58.

Dowding, Keith and D.S. King (1995). "Introduction" in K. Dowding and D.S. King (eds.), *Preferences, Institutions and Rational Choice* (Oxford: Clarendon Press), pp. 1–19.

Dugger, William M. (1988). "An Institutional Analysis of Corporate Power", *Journal of Economic Issues*, Vol. XXII, No. 1, March 1988, pp. 79–110.

———. (1980). "Power: An Institutional Framework of Analysis", *Journal of Economic Issues*, Vol. XIV, No. 4, December 1980, pp. 897–907.

Dunleavy, Patrick (1982). "Quasi-governmental Sector Professionalism: Some Implications for Public Policy-Making in Britain", in A. Barker (ed.), *Quangos in Britain: Government and the Networks of Public Policy-Making* (London: MacMillan), pp. 181–205.

Eckstein, Harry and D.E. Apter (1963). *Comparative Politics: A Reader* (New York: Free Press of Glencoe).

Eisenstadt, Shmuel N., and L. Roniger (1981). "The Study of Patron-Client Relations and Recent Developments in Sociological Theory", in S.N. Eisenstadt and R. Lemarchand (eds.), *Political Clientelism, Patronage and Development* (Beverly Hills and London: Sage Publications), pp. 271–87.

Elguea Solís, Javier (1991). "La Formación de Empresarios", in G. Azcárraga Tamayo (ed.), *Los Empresarios y la Modernización Económica de México* (México: Miguel Angel Porrúa), pp. 211–232.

———. (1989). "Conclusiones", in J. Elguea Solís (ed.), *La Economía Mexicana y sus Empresarios* (México: Universidad Anáhuac del Sur), pp. 171–184.

Elizondo, Carlos (1994). "In Search of Revenue: Tax Reform in Mexico under the Administrations of Echeverría and Salinas", *Journal of Latin American Studies*, Vol. 26, Part 1, Feb. 1994, pp. 191–219.

Elster, Jon (1991). "Rationality and Social Norms", *Archives Européennes de Sociologie*, No. XXXII, pp. 109–29.

Eraña García, Eugenio (1977). "Palabras Pronunciadas por Don Eugenio Eraña García, Presidente de la Asociación de Banqueros de México", in Coparmex (ed.), *XXXVI Asamblea Nacional Ordinaria de Centros Patronales* (México: Coparmex), pp. 43–50.

Erfani, Julie A. (1995). *The Paradox of the Mexican State* (Boulder: L. Rienner Publishers).

Evans, Peter B. (1996). "Introduction: Development Strategies Across the Public-Private Divide", World Development, Vol. 24, No. 6, June 1996, pp. 1033–7.

———. (1992). "The State as Problem and Solution: Predation, Embedded Autonomy, and Structural Change", in S. Haggard and R. Kaufman, (eds.) The Politics of Economic Adjustment.

Evans, Peter B., D. Rueschemeyer and T. Skocpol (1985). "On The Road Toward a More Adequate Understanding of the State", in P. Evans, D. Rueschemeyer, and T. Skocpol (eds.) Bringing the State Back In (Cambridge: Cambridge University Press), pp. 347–66.

Fernández Velasco, Armando (1977). "Palabras Pronunciadas por Don Armando Fernández Velasco, Presidente del Consejo Coordinador Empresarial", in Coparmex (ed.), *XXXVI Asamblea Nacional Ordinaria de Centros Patronales* (México: Coparmex), pp. 59–66.

Field, G. Lowell and J. Higley (1979). "Elites, Insiders, and Outsiders: Will Western Political Regimes Prove Non-Viable?" in B. Denitch (ed.), *Legitimation of Regimes: International Frameworks for Analysis* (London: Sage Publications, for The International Sociological Association), pp. 141–59.

————. (1973). *Elitism* (London: Routledge and Paul Kegan).

Fisher, Mike (1997). *Qualitative Computing: Using Software for Qualitative Data Analysis* (Aldershot: Ashgate).

Fitzgerald, E.V.K. (1979). *The Fiscal Deficit and Development Finance: A Note on the Accumulation Balance in Mexico*, Working Papers No. 35, Centre of Latin American Studies, University of Cambridge.

————. (1978[a]). "Stabilisation Policy in México: The Fiscal Deficit and Macroeconomic Equilibrium", in R. Thorp and L. Whitehead (eds.), *Inflation and Stabilisation in Latin America* (Oxford: Macmillan and St. Antony's College), pp. 23–64.

————. (1978[b]). "The State and Capital Accumulation in Mexico", *Journal of Latin American Studies*, Vol. 10, No. 2, pp. 263–282.

Flapp, H.D. (1990). "Patronage: An Institution in Its Own Right", in M. Hechter, K.D. Opp and R. Wippler (eds.), *Social Institutions: Their Emergence, Maintenance and Effects* (New York: Aldine de Gruyter), pp. 225–43.

Flick, Uwe (1998). *An Introduction to Qualitative Research* (London: Sage Publications).

Flynn, P. (1974). "Class, Clientelism and Coercion: Some Mechanisms of Internal Dependency and Control", *Journal of Commonwealth and Comparative Politics*, No.12, Vol. 2, pp. 138–56.

Friedland, Roger and R.R. Alford (1991). "Bringing Society Back In: Symbols, Practices, and Institutional Contradictions", in W. W. Powell and P.J. DiMaggio (eds.), The New Institutionalism in Organizational Analysis, (Chicago and London: The University of Chicago Press), pp. 232–63.

Friedman, Milton (1962). *Capitalism and Freedom* (Chicago and London: The University of Chicago Press).

Fuentes, Carlos (1964). *The Death of Artemio Cruz* (London: Secker & Warburg), translated from Spanish by Sam Hileman.

Fukuyama, Francis (1995). *Trust: The Social Virtues and the Creation of Prosperity* (London: Hamish Hamilton).

Gage, Robert W., and M.P. Mandell (1990). *Strategies for Managing Intergovernmental Policies and Networks* (New York and London: Praeger).

Galaskiewicz, Joseph J. (1985). "Professional Networks and the Institutionalization of a Single Mind-Set", *American Sociological Review*, Vol. 50, pp.639–58.

Galbraith, John K. (1986[a]). "Power and Organization", in S. Lukes (ed.), *Power* (Oxford: Basil Blackwell), pp. 211–28.

————. (1986[b]). *Anatomía del Poder* (México: Diana).

Gambetta, Diego (1993). *The Sicilian Mafia: The Business of Private Protection* (Cambridge, MA: Harvard University Press).

————. (1988). *Trust: Making and Breaking Cooperative Relations* (Oxford: Basil Blackwell).

García Hernández, Magdalena (1980). "La Marcha de la Economía en 1979", in E. González (ed.), *1979, ¿La Crisis Quedó Atrás?* (México: UNAM/ACERE), pp. 25–82.

Garret, Geoffrey and B. Weingast (1993). "Ideas, Interests and Institutions: Constructing the European Community's Internal Market" in J. Goldstein and R. Keohane (eds.), *Ideas and Foreign Policy*.

Garrido, Luis J. (1989). "The Crisis of Presidencialismo", in W.A. Cornelius, J. Gentleman, and P.H. Smith (eds.), *Mexico's Alternative Political Futures*, Monograph Series, 30 (San Diego: Center for U.S.-Mexican Studies, University of California, San Diego), pp. 417–34.

Garrido, Celso (1998). "Actor Bancario y Poder Financiero en México. Incertidumbres y Desafíos", in E. Gutiérrez Garza, J.M. Ramírez and J. Regalado (eds.), *El Debate Nacional: Los Actores Sociales* (México: Editorial Diana), pp. 55–86.

Garrido, Celso and C. Puga (1992). "Transformaciones del Empresariado Mexicano en la Década de los Ochenta", in C. Puga and R. Tirado (eds.), *Los Empresarios Mexicanos, Ayer y Hoy* (México: Ediciones El Caballito), pp. 131–150.

Garrido, Celso and E. Quintana (1986). "Relaciones Financieras, Grupos Económicos y Disputa de Poder", in R. Pozas and M. Luna (eds.), *Las Empresas y Los Empresarios en el México Contemporáneo* (México: Grijalbo), pp. 107–22.

Gaudiano, Victor Manuel (1977). "Palabras Pronunciadas por el Lic. Victor Manuel Gaudiano, Presidente de la Confederación de Cámaras Nacionales de Comercio de la República Mexicana", in Coparmex (ed.), *XXXVI Asamblea Nacional Ordinaria de Centros Patronales* (México: Coparmex), pp. 23–28.

Genschel, Phillipp (1997). "The Dynamics of Inertia: Institutional Persistence and Change in Telecommunications and Health Care", *Governance*, Vol. 10, pp. 43–66.

Gereffi, Gary and P.B. Evans (1987). "Transnational Corporations, Dependent Development, and State Policy in the Semiperiphery: A Comparison of Brazil and Mexico", in J.L. Dietz and J.H. Street (eds.), *Latin America's Economic Development: Institutionalist and Structuralist Perspectives* (Boulder and London: Lynne Rienner Publishers), pp. 159–90.

Gerschenkron, Alexander (1966). "Economic Backwardness in Historical Perspective", in *Economic Backwardness in Historical Perspective: A Book of Essays* (Cambridge, MA: The Belknap Press of Harvard University Press).

Giddens, Anthony (1984). *The Constitution of Society* (Berkeley: University of California Press).

———. (1979). *Central Problems in Social Theory* (Berkeley: University of California Press).

Gil Villegas Montiel, Francisco (1984). "La Crisis de Legitimidad en la Ultima Etapa del Sexenio de José López Portillo", *Foro Internacional*, XXV, No.2, Oct–Dec. 1984, pp. 190–201

Godau, R.H. (1975). *México: A Bureaucratic Polity*, Unpublished MA Thesis, University of Texas at Austin, mimeo. at the Daniel Cosío Villegas Library of *El Colegio de México*.

Goicoechea Luna, Emilio (1983). "Filosofía y Trabajo, Nuestro Deber en la Crisis", in *México: Nuestro Compromiso. XLII Asamblea Nacional Ordinaria de Centros Patronales y Asamblea Nacional Extraordinaria: El Estado y las Garantías Individuales* (México: Coparmex), pp. 81–3.

González, Eduardo (1980). "La Coyuntura de 1979 en el Contexto de la Crisis", in E. González (ed.), *1979, ¿La Crisis Quedó Atrás?* (México: UNAM/ACERE), pp. 9–14.

González, Eduardo y J. Alcocer (1980ª). "El Papel del Sistema Financiero en la Reactivación", in E. González (ed.), *1979, ¿La Crisis Quedó Atrás?* (México: UNAM/ACERE), pp. 83–88.

———. (1980ᵇ). "El Comportamiento de las Ganancias en el Sector Monopólico-Financiero de la Economía Mexicana: 1977–1979", in E. González (ed.), *1979, ¿La Crisis Quedó Atrás?* (México: UNAM/ACERE), pp. 89–109.

González Casanova, Pablo (1979). "México: El Desarrollo Más Probable", in P. González Casanova and E. Florescano (eds.), *México Hoy* (México: Siglo Veintiuno Editores), pp. 405–19.

González Casanova, Pablo and E. Florescano (1979). "Palabras Preliminares", in P. González Casanova and E. Florescano (eds.), *México Hoy* (México: Siglo Veintiuno Editores), pp. 9–16.

González Prendes, José F. (1986). "Mensaje de Bienvenida", in Coparmex (ed.), *Modernización o Crisis y Autoritarismo, XLIX Asamblea Nacional Ordinaria* (México: Coparmex), pp. 2–4.

González Soriano, Raúl (1983). *Ensayos Sobre Acumulación de Capital en México* (Puebla: Universidad Autónoma de Puebla).

Goulet, Denis (1983). *México: Development Strategies for the Future* (Notre Dame and London: University of Notre Dame Press).

Grabher, Gernot (1993). "The Weakness of Strong Ties: The Lock-in of Regional Development in the Ruhr Area", in Gernot Grabher (ed.), *The Embedded Firm: On the Socioeconomics of Industrial Networks* (London and New York: Routledge), pp. 255–76

Gracida, Elsa y E. Fujigaki (1988). "El Triunfo del Capitalismo", in E. Semo (ed.), *México un Pueblo en la Historia: Nueva Burguesía (1938–1957)* (México: Alianza Editorial Mexicana), Vol. 5.

Granovetter, Mark (1992). "Economics Institutions as Social Constructions: A Framework for Analysis", *Acta Sociologica*, Vol. 35, pp. 3–12.

———. (1985). "Economic Action and Social Structure: The Problem of Embeddedness", *American Journal of Sociology*, Vol. 91, pp. 481–510.

———. (1974). *Getting a Job: A Study of Contacts and Careers* (Cambridge, MA: Harvard University Press).

Grant, Wyn P. (1989). *Pressure Groups, Politics and Democracy in Britain* (London: Philip Allan).

Grant, Wyn P., W. Paterson, and C. Whitson (1988). *Government and the Chemical Industry* (Oxford: Clarendon).

Gray, Louis N. and M.C. Stafford (1988). "On Choice Behaviour in Individual and Social Situations", *Social Psychology Quarterly*, Vol 51, No. 1, pp. 58–61.

Graziano, Luigi (1976). "A Conceptual Framework for the Study of Clientelistic Behaviour", *European Journal of Political Research*, No.4, Vol.2, pp. 149–74.

Green, Rosario (1981). *Estado y Banca Transnacional en México* (México: Nueva Imagen).

Griffiths, Ernest S. (1939). *The Impasse of Democracy* (New York: Harrison-Wilton).

Grindle, Merilee S. (1977). *Bureaucrats, Politicians and Peasants in México: A Case Study in Public Policy* (Berkeley and Los Angeles: University of California Press).

Guadarrama, J. (1988). "Prevén Grave Rezago Industrial si Persiste el Estanca-miento en el Desarrollo Tecnológico", *El Financiero*, November 25.

Guajardo Davis, Guillermo (n/d). *Recopilación de los Más Importantes Discursos Pronunciados y Artículos Publicados por el Señor Guillermo Guajardo Davis como Presidente de la Concamin, abril de 1948-marzo de 1950* (México: Concamin).

Guillén, Arturo (1985). "Interpretaciones sobre la Crisis en México", in P.González Casanova and H. Aguilar Camín (eds.), *México ante la Crisis: El Contexto Internacional y la Crisis Económica* (México: Siglo Veintiuno Editores), pp. 153–82.

Guillén Romo, Héctor (1997). *La Contrarrevolución Neoliberal en México* (México: Ediciones Era).

———. (1990[a]). *El Sexenio de Crecimiento Cero: Contra los Defensores de las Finanzas Sanas* (México: Ediciones Era).

———. (1990[b]). "Del Endeudamiento a la Exportación del Capital: La Consecuencia del Ajuste", in E. Gutiérrez Garza (ed.), *Los Saldos del Sexenio (1982–1988)* (México: Siglo Veintiuno Editores/UAM), pp. 62–108.

———. (1984). *Orígenes de la Crisis en México: Inflación y Endeudamiento Externo (1940–1982)* (México: Ediciones Era).

Gutiérrez Garza, Esthela (1990). "Presentación: El Sexenio del Crecimiento Cero", in E. Gutiérrez Garza (ed.), *Los Saldos del Sexenio (1982–1988)* (México: Siglo Veintiuno Editores/UAM), pp. 11–22.

Guzmán de Alba, Luis (1977). "Palabras Pronunciadas por el Licenciado Luis Guzmán de Alba, Presidente de la Confederación de Cámaras Industriales", in Coparmex (ed.), *XXXVI Asamblea Nacional Ordinaria de Centros Patronales* (México: Coparmex), pp. 31–40.

Haas, Peter M. (1992). "Epistemic Communities and the Dynamics of International Policy Coordination", *International Organization*, Vol. 46, pp.1–35.

———.(1990). *When Knowledge is Power* (Berkeley: University of California Press).

Hall, John A. and G. John Ikenberry (1990). *The State* (Milton Keynes: Open University Press).

Hall, Peter (1999). "The Political Economy of Europe in an Era of Interdependence" in Herbert Kitschelt and others (eds.), *Continuity and Change in Contemporary Capitalism*, pp. 135–163.

———. (1993). "Policy Paradigms, Social Learning, and the State: The Case of Economic Policymaking in Britain", *Comparative Politics*, April 1993, pp. 275–296

———. (1992). "The Movement from Keynesianism to Monetarism: Institutional Analysis and the British Economic Policy in the 1970s", in S. Steinmo, K.A. Thelen and F. Longstreth (eds.), *Structuring Politics: Historical Institutionalism in Comparative Analysis* (Cambridge: Cambridge University Press), pp. 90–113.

———. (1986). *Governing the Economy* (Oxford: Polity Press).

Hall, Peter A. and D. Soskice (2001). "An Introduction to Varieties of Capitalism", in P.A. Hall and D. Soskice (eds.), *Varieties of Capitalism: The Institutional Foundations of Comparative Advantage* (Oxford: Oxford University Press), pp. 1–68.

Hall, Peter and R.C.R., Taylor (1998). "The Potential of Historical Institutionalism: A Response to Hay and Wincott". *Political Studies,* Vol. XLVI, pp.958–62.

———. (1996). "Political Science and the Three New Institutionalisms". *Political Studies,* Vol. XLIV, pp. 936–957.

Hall, Stuart (1984)."The State in Question?", in G. McLennan, D. Held, and S. Hall (eds.), in *The Idea of the Modern State* (Milton Keynes: Open University Press), pp: 1–28.

Hamilton, Nora (1986[b]). "State-Class Alliances and Conflicts: Issues and Actors in the Mexican Economic Crisis", in N. Hamilton and T.F. Harding (eds.), *Modern México: State, Economy and Social Conflict* (London: Sage Publications), pp. 148–74.

———. (1982). *The Limits of State Autonomy: Post-Revolutionary Mexico* (Princeton: Princeton University Press).

———. (1978). *The State and Class Formation in Post-Revolutionary Mexico,* Department of Political Science, University of Southern California, mimeo. in the Daniel Cosío Villegas library of *El Colegio de México.*

Hamilton, Gary, W. Zeile and W.J. Kim (1990). "The Network Structures of East Asian Economies", in S. Clegg and G. Redding (eds.), *Capitalism in Contrasting Cultures* (Berlin: de Gruyter).

Handelman, Howard (1997). *Mexican Politics: The Dynamics of Change* (New York: St. Martin's Press).

Hanf, Kenneth and F.W. Scharpf (1978). *Interorganizational Policy Making: Limits to Coordination and Central Control* (Sage: London).

Hansen, Roger D. (1971[a]). *La Política del Desarrollo Mexicano* (México: Siglo Veintiuno Editores).

———. (1971[b]). *Mexican Economic Development: The Roots of Rapid Growth* (Washington, D.C.: National Planning Association).

Hardy, Cynthia, N. Phillips and T. Lawrence (1998). "Distinguishing Trust and Power in Interorganizational Relations: Forms and Façades of Trust", in Christel Lane and Reinhard Bachmann (eds.), *Trust Within and Between Organizations: Conceptual Issues and Empirical Applications* (Oxford: Oxford University Press), pp.64–87.

Harris, Nigel (1972). *Competition and the Corporate Society: British Conservatives, The State and Industry, 1945–1964* (London: Methuen).

Hart, Oliver (1990). "Is 'Bounded Rationality' an Important Element of a Theory of Institutions?", *Journal of Institutional and Theoretical Economics,* No. 146, pp. 696–702.

Hay, Colin (1999). "Crisis and the Structural Transformation of the State: Interrogating the Process of Change", *British Journal of Politics and International Relations,* Vol. 1, No. 3, October 1999, pp. 317–344.

———. (1998[a]). "'Punctuated Evolution' and the Uneven Temporality of Institutional Change: The 'Crisis' of Keynesianism and Rise of Neo-Liberalism in Britain", Paper presented to the Eleventh Conference of Europeanists, Omni Harbor Hotel, Baltimore, Maryland, 26–28 February 1998.

———. (1998[b]). "The Tangled Webs We Weave: The Discourse, Strategy and Practice of Networking", in David Marsh (ed.), *Comparing Policy Networks* (Buckingham and Philadelphia: Open University Press), pp. 33–51.

———. (1996). "Narrating Crisis: The Discursive Construction of the 'Winter of Discontent'", *Sociology*, Vol. 30, No. 2, May 1996, pp. 253–77.

Hay, Colin and D. Wincott (1998). "Structure, Agency and Historical Institutionalism", *Political Studies*, Vol. XLVI, pp. 951–7.

Heath, Jonathan (1999). *Mexico and the Sexenio Curse: Presidential Successions and Economic Crises in Modern Mexico* (Washington, D.C.: The CSIS Press).

Hechter, Michael, K.D. Opp and R. Wippler (1990). "Introduction" in M. Hechter, K.D. Opp and R. Wippler (eds.), *Social Institutions: Their Emergence, Maintenance and Effects* (New York: Aldine de Gruyter), pp. 1–9.

Heclo, Hugh (1978). "Issue Networks and the Executive Establishment", in A. King (ed.) *The New American Political System* (Washington, D.C.: American Enterprise Institute).

Heidenheimer, Arnold J. (1970). *Political Corruption: Readings in Comparative Analysis* (New York: Holt, Rinehart and Winston).

Heim, John P. *et al.* (1990). "Inner Circles or Hollow Cores? Elite Networks Policy Systems", *Journal of Politics*, No.52, pp. 356–390.

Heiner, Ronald A. (1983). "The Origin of Predictable Behavior", *American Economic Review*, Vol. 73, No. 4 (September 1983), pp. 560–95.

Hernández Laos, Enrique (1985). *La Productividad y el Desarrollo Industrial en México* (México: Fondo de Cultura Económica).

Hernández Rodríguez, Rogelio (1992ª). "La División de la Élite Política Mexicana", in C. Bazdresch *et al.* (eds.), *México: Auge, Crisis y Ajuste. I. Los Tiempos del Cambio, 1982–1988* (México: Fondo de Cultura Económica), pp. 239–66.

———. (1992ᵇ). "Problemas de Representación en los Organismos Empresariales", in C. Puga and R. Tirado (eds.), *Los Empresarios Mexicanos, Ayer y Hoy* (México: Ediciones El Caballito), pp. 247–266.

———. (1991). "Los Problemas de Representación en los Organismos Empresariales", *Foro Internacional*, Vol. XXXI, No. 3, January–March 1991, pp. 446–471.

———. (1990). "La Conducta Empresarial en el Gobierno de Miguel de la Madrid", *Foro Internacional*, Vol. XXX, No. 4, April–June 1990, pp. 736–764.

———. (1989). "Las Relaciones entre el Empresariado y el Estado. La Génesis de un Conflicto", in J. Elguea Solís (ed.), *La Economía Mexicana y sus Empresarios* (México: Universidad Anáhuac del Sur), pp. 11–69.

———. (1988). *Empresarios, Banca y Estado: El Conflicto durante el Gobierno de José López Portillo, 1976–1982* (México: FLACSO/Miguel Angel Porrúa).

———. (1986). "La Política y los Empresarios Después de la Nacionalización Bancaria", *Foro Internacional*, Vol. XXVII, No. 2, October–December 1986, pp. 247–265.

———. (1985). "Empresarios, Estado y Condiciones Laborales Durante la Sustitución de Importaciones", *Foro Internacional*, Vol. XXVI, No. 2, October–December 1985, pp. 157–71.

Hindess, Barry (1989). *Political Choice and Social Structure* (Aldershot: Edward Elgar).

Hirsch Rosemberg, Samuel (1989). "Desarrollo Económico y Desarrollo Empresarial Hacia una Nueva Estrategia", in J. Elguea Solís (ed.), *La Economía Mexicana y sus Empresarios* (México: Universidad Anáhuac del Sur), pp. 141–161.

Hjern, Benny and D.O. Porter (1980). "Implementation Structures: A New Unit of Administrative Analysis", *Organisational Studies*, Vol. 1, pp. 45–72.

Hodgson, Geoff (1991). "Institutional Economic Theory: The Old versus the New" in Geoff Hodgson (ed.), *After Marx and Sraffa: Essays in the Political Economy*, pp. 194–213.

Hoffman-Lange, Ursula (1987). "Surveying National Elites in the Federal Republic of Germany", in G. Moyser and M. Wagstaffe (eds.), *Research Methods for Elite Studies* (London: Allen & Unwin), pp. 27–47.

Hofstede, Geert (1991). *Cultures and Organizations: Software of the Mind* (London: McGraw Hill Book Company).

Hogwood, Brian W. (1987). *From Crisis to Complacency* (Oxford: Oxford University Press).

———. (1986). "If Consultation is Everything then Maybe is Nothing", *Strathclyde Papers in Government and Politics*, No. 44.

Holland, Paul W. and S. Leinhardt (1979). *Perspectives on Social Network Research* (New York: Academic).

Hollingsworth, J. Rogers (2000). "Doing Institutional Analysis: Implications for the Study of Innovations", *Review of International Political Economy*, Vol. 7, No. 4, pp. 595–644.

House, James S. And J. Mortimer (1990). "Social Structure and the Individual: Emerging Themes and New Directions", *Social Psychology Quarterly*, Vol. 53, No. 2, pp. 71–80.

Howard, Judith A. (1994). "A Social Cognitive Conception of Social Structure", *Social Psychology Quarterly*, Vol. 57, No. 3, pp. 210–27.

Huerta, Rogelio (1980). "Estados Unidos y la Coyuntura Internacional", in E. González (ed.), *1979, ¿La Crisis Quedó Atrás?* (México: UNAM/ACERE), pp. 15–24.

Huerta, Arturo and E. Caballero (1980[a]). "La Estrategia Gubernamental: Planes y Programas Económicos", in E. González (ed.), *1979, ¿La Crisis Quedó Atrás?* (México: UNAM/ACERE), pp. 135–64.

———. (1980[b]). "Algunos Aspectos de la Política Económica en 1979", in E. González (ed.), *1979, ¿La Crisis Quedó Atrás?* (México: UNAM/ACERE), pp. 165–74.

Hughes, Everett C. (1936). "The Ecological Aspects of Institutions", *American Sociological Review*, Vol. 1, pp. 180–9

Ikenberry, G.John (1988). "Conclusion: An Institutional Approach to American Foreign Economic Policy", in G.J. Ikenberry, D.A. Lake, and M. Mastanduno (eds.), *The State and American Foreign Economic Policy* (Ithaca, NY and London: Cornell University Press), published in *International Organization*, Vol. 2, No. 1, pp. 615–23.

Immergut, Ellen M. (1992). "The Rules of the Game: The Logic of Health Policy-making in France, Switzerland, and Sweden", in S. Steinmo, K.A. Thelen and F. Longstreth (eds.), *Structuring Politics: Historical Institutionalism in Comparative Analysis* (Cambridge: Cambridge University Press), 57–89.

———. (1990). "Institutions, Veto Points, and Policy Results: A Comparative Analysis of Health Care", *Journal of Public Policy*, Vol. 10, pp. 391–416.

INEGI (1985). *Estadísticas Históricas de México, Volumen 1 y Volumen 2* (México: INEGI).

Izquierdo, Rafael (1964). "Protectionism in Mexico", in R. Vernon (ed.), *Public Policy and Private Enterprise in Mexico* (Cambridge, MA: Harvard University Press), pp. 277–89.

Jacobo, Edmundo; M. Luna and R. Tirado (1989). "Introducción General", in E. Jacobo, M. Luna and R. Tirado (eds.), *Empresarios de México: Aspectos Históricos, Económicos e Ideológicos* (Guadalajara, México: Universidad de Guadalajara), pp. 7–26.

Jacobs, Eduardo and W. Peres (1983). "Tamaño de Planta y Financiamiento", *Economía Mexicana*, No. 5, pp. 79–110.

Jennings, Eugene E. (1971). *Routes to the Executive Suite* (New York: McGraw-Hill).

Jensen, Hans E. (1987). "The Theory of Human Nature", *Journal of Economic Issues*, Vol. XXI, No. 3, September 1987, pp. 1039–73.

Jepperson, Ronald L. (1991). "Institutions, Institutional Effects, and Institutionalization" in W.W. Powell and P.J. DiMaggio (eds.), *The New Institutionalism in Organizational Analysis*, (Chicago and London: The University of Chicago Press), pp. 143–63.

Jessop, Bob (1990ª). "The Capitalist Stateand the Rule of Capital: Problems in the Analysis of Business Associations", *West European Politics*, No.6, pp. 139–62.

———. (1990ᵇ). *State Theory: Putting Capitalist States in their Place* (Cambridge: Polity Press).

Johnston, Russel and P.R. Lawrence (1988). "Beyond Vertical Integration: The Rise of Value-Adding Partnership", *Harvard Business Review*, July–August 1988, pp. 94–101.

Jordan, A. Grant (1990ª). "Policy Community Realism versus 'New Institutionalism' Ambiguity", *Political Studies*, Vol.38, pp. 470–84.

———. (1990ᵇ). "Sub-Governments, Policy Communities and Networks: Refilling the Old Bottles", *Journal of Theoretical Politics*, No. 2, pp. 319–38.

———. (1981). "Iron Triangles, Woolly Corporatism and Elastic Nets: Images of the Policy Process", *Journal of Public Policy*, Vol. 1, pp. 95–123.

Jordan, A. Grant and J.J. Richardson (1987). *Government and Pressure Groups in Britain* (Oxford: Clarendon).

———. (1982). "The British Policy Style or the Logic of Negotiation?" in J.J. Richardson (ed.), *Policy Styles in Western Europe* (London: George Allen and Unwin).

Juárez González, Leticia (1982). "El Proyecto Económico Cardenista y la Posición Empresarial (1934–1938)", in S. Cordero and R. Tirado (eds.), *Clases Dominantes y Estado en México* (México: UNAM), pp. 47–62.

Kadushin, Charles (1979). "Power Circles and Legitimacy in Developed Societies" in B. Denitch (ed.), *Legitimation of Regimes: International Frameworks for Analysis* (London: Sage Publications, for The International Sociological Association), pp. 127–40.

Kanel, Don (1988). "The Human Predicament: Society, Institutions and Individuals", *Journal of Economic Issues*, Vol. XXII, No. 2, June 1988, pp. 427–34.

———. (1984). *Corporatism and Change: Austria, Switzerland and the Politics of Industry* (Ithaca, NY: Cornell University Press).

Katzenstein, Peter J. (1978). *Between Power and Plenty: Foreign Economic Policies of Advanced Industrial States* (Madison: University of Wisconsin Press).

Kaufman, Robert R. (1990). "Stabilization and Adjustment in Argentina, Brazil and Mexico", in J.M. Nelson (ed.), *Economic Crisis and Policy Choice: The Politics of Adjustment in the Third World* (Princeton, NJ: Princeton University Press), pp. 119–169.

Kaufman Purcell, Susan (1981). "México: Clientelism, Corporatism and Political Stability", in S.N. Eisenstadt and René Lemarchand (eds.), *Political Clientelism, Patronage and Development* (Beverly Hills and London: Sage Publications), pp. 191–216.

Keefer, Philip and M. Shirley (2000). "Formal versus Informal Institutions in Economic Development" in C. Menard (ed.), *Institutions, Contracts and Organizations: Perspectives from New Institutional Economics* (Cheltenham and Northampton, MA: Edward Elgar) pp. 88–107.

Keohane, Robert O. and E. Ostrom (1994). "Introduction", *Journal of Theoretical Politics*, Vol. 6, No. 4, pp. 403–28.

Khan, Mustaq H. (1998). "Patron-Client Networks and the Economic Effects of Corruption in Asia" in M. Robinson (ed.), *Corruption and Development* (London: Frank Cass), pp. 15–39.

Kickert, Walter J.M., E.H. Klijn and J. Koppenjan (1997). *Managing Complex Networks: Strategies for the Public Sector* (London: Sage).

King, Timothy (1970). *México: Industrialization and Trade Policies since 1940* (London: Oxford University Press).

Kiser, Larry L. and E. Ostrom (1982). "The Three Worlds of Action: A Metatheoretical Synthesis of Institutional Approaches" in E. Ostrom (ed.), *Strategies of Political Enquiry* (London: Sage), pp. 179–222.

Knight, Alan (1998). "Populism and Neo-Populism in Latin America, Especially Mexico", *Journal of Latin American Studies*, No. 30, pp. 223–48.

———. (1991). "Mexico's Elite Settlement: Conjuncture and Consequences" in J. Higley and R. Gunther (eds.), *Elites and Democratic Consolidation in Latin America and Southern Europe* (Cambridge: Cambridge University Press), pp. 113–45.

———. (1986[a]). *The Mexican Revolution, Volume 1: Porfirians, Liberals and Peasants* (Cambridge: Cambridge University Press).

———. (1986[b]) *The Mexican Revolution, Volume 2: Counter-Revolution and Reconstruction* (Cambridge: Cambridge University Press).

Knight, Jack (1992). *Institutions and Social Conflict* (Cambridge: Cambridge University Press).

Knoke, David. (1992). "Networks of Elite Structure and Decision Taking", *Sociological Methods Research*, No. 22, pp. 23–45.

———. (1990). *Policy Networks: The Structural Perspective* (Cambridge: Cambridge University Press).

Knoke, David and J.H. Kuklinski (1991). "Network Analysis: Basic Concepts", in G. Thompson, J. Frances, R. Levacic and J. Mitchell (eds.), *Markets, Hierarchies and Networks* (London, Thousand Oaks and New Delhi: Open University Press).

Knoke, David and E.O. Laumann (1987). *The Organizational State* (Madison: University of Wisconsin Press).

Knoke, David, F.U. Pappi and Y. Tsujinaka (1996). *Comparing Policy Networks: Labor Politics in the U.S., Germany and Japan* (Cambridge: Cambridge University Press).

Kouyoumdjian, Armen (1988). "The Miguel De la Madrid Sexenio: Major Reforms or Foundation for Disaster?", in G.D.E. Philip (ed.), *The Mexican Economy* (London and New York: Routledge), pp. 78–94.

Krasner, Stephen D. (1988). "Sovereignty: An Institutional Perspective", *Comparative Political Studies*, Vol. 21, pp. 66–94.

———. (1984). "Approaches to the State: Alternative Conceptions and Historical Dynamics", *Comparative Politics*, 16: 223–46.

———. (1983). "Overviews", in S.D. Krasner (ed.), *International Regimes* (Ithaca, NY: Cornell University Press), pp. 1–22.

———. (1978). *Defending the National Interest: Raw Materials, Investments and the US Foreign Policy*.

Krauze, Enrique (1997). *La Presidencia Imperial: Ascenso y Caída del Sistema Político Mexicano (1940–1996)* (México: Tusquets Editores).

Labourdette, André (1992). *Théorie des Organisations* (Paris: Presses Universitaires de France).

Ladman, Jerry R. (1986ª). "Introduction", in J.R. Ladman (ed.), *México: A Country in Crisis* (Texas: Texas Western Press), pp. xi–xii.

———. (1986ᵇ). "The Roots of the Crisis", in J.R. Ladman (ed.), *México: A Country in Crisis* (Texas: Texas Western Press), pp. 1–11.

———. (1986ᶜ). "The Deepening Crisis", in J.R. Ladman (ed.), *México: A Country in Crisis* (Texas: Texas Western Press), pp. 144–169.

Lamartine Yates, Paul (1980ª). "El Sector Privado en México", in Banco Nacional de México (ed.), *México en la Década de los Ochenta*, Vol. 6 (México: Banco Nacional de México), pp. 87–110.

———. (1980ᵇ). "Los Sectores Público y Privado", in Banco Nacional de México (ed.), *México en la Década de los Ochenta*, Vol. 8 (México: Banco Nacional de México), pp. 266–275.

Landé, C. (1977). "Introduction", in S. Schmidt *et al.* (eds.), *Friends, Followers and Factioms* (Los Angeles and Berkeley: University of California Press), pp. xiii–xxxviii.

Lane, Christel (1998). "Introduction: Theories and Issues in the Study of Trust", in Christel Lane and Reinhard Bachmann (eds.), *Trust Within and Between Organizations: Conceptual Issues and Empirical Applications* (Oxford: Oxford University Press), pp. 1–27.

———. (1995). *Industry and Society in Europe: Stability and Change in Britain, Germany and France* (Aldershot: Edward Elgar).

———. (1989). *Management and Labour in Europe: The Industrial Enterprise in Germany, Britain and France* (Aldershot: Edward Elgar).

Lane, Christel and R. Bachmann (1995ª). *Risk, Trust and Power: The Social Constitution of Supplier Relations in Britain and Germany* (Cambridge: ESRC Centre for Business Research, University of Cambridge).

———. (1995ᵇ). *Cooperation in Vertical Inter-Firm Relations in Britain and Germany: The Role of Social Institutions* (Cambridge: ESRC Centre for Business Research, University of Cambridge).

Larson, Andrea (1992). "Network Dyads in Entrepreneurial Settings: A Study of the Governance of Exchange Relationships", *Administrative Science Quarterly*, March 1992, pp. 76–104.

Lasso Gómez, Pablo (1989). "El Modo de Producción Mexicano en el Contexto: Persona-Empresa Cultura-Sociedad", in E. Jacobo, M. Luna and R. Tirado (eds.), *Empresarios de México: Aspectos Históricos, Económicos e Ideológicos* (Guadalajara, México: Universidad de Guadalajara), pp. 411–27.

Lasswell, Harold (1936). *Politics: Who Gets What, When, How?* (New York: Whittlesey House).

Laumann, Edward O., and D. Knoke (1987). *The Organisational State* (Madison: The University of Wisconsin Press).

Laumann, Edward O., L. Galskeiwicz, and P.V. Marsden (1978). "Community Structure as Interorganizational Linkages", *Annual Review of Sociology*, No. 4, pp. 455–84.

Leal, Juan F. (1986ª). *La Burguesía y el Estado Mexicano* (México: Ediciones El Caballito).

———. (1986ᵇ). "The Mexican State, 1915–1973: A Historical Interpretation", in N. Hamilton and T.F. Harding (eds.), *Modern México: State, Economy and Social Conflict* (London: Sage Publications), pp. 21–42.

Ledeneva, Alena V. (1998). *Russia's Economy of Favours: Blat, Networking and Informal Exchange* (Cambridge: Cambridge University Press).

Leff, Enrique (1979). "Dependencia Científico-Tecnológica y Desarrollo Económico", in P. González Casanova and E. Florescano (eds.), *México Hoy* (México: Siglo Veintiuno Editores), pp. 266–85.

Lehmbruch, Gerhard (1998). "The Organization of Society, Administrative Strategies, and Policy Networks", in R. Czada, A. Héritier, and H. Keman (eds.), *Institutions and Political Choice: On the Limits of Rationality* (Amsterdam: VU University Press), pp. 61–84.

———. (1984). "Concertation and the Structure of Corporatist Networks?" in J.H. Goldthorpe (ed.), *Order and Conflict in Contemporary Capitalism: Studies in the Political Economy of Western European Nations*, (Oxford: Clarendon Press), pp. 60–80.

Lehner, Franz (1998). "The Institutional Control of Organized Interest Intermediation: A Political Perspective", in R. Czada, A. Héritier, and H. Keman (eds.), *Institutions and Political Choice: On the Limits of Rationality* (Amsterdam: VU University Press), pp. 211–227.

Lemarchand, René (1981). "Comparative Political Clientelism: Structure, Process and Optic", in S.N. Eisenstadt and R. Lemarchand (eds.), *Political Clientelism, Patronage and Development* (Beverly Hills and London: Sage Publications), pp. 7–31.

Lomelí, Leonardo and E. Zebadúa (1998). *La Política Económica de México en el Congreso de la Unión (1970–1982)* (México: COLMEX/IILCD/IPN/FCE).

Levi, Margaret (1991). "Are There Limits to Rationality?", *Archives Européennes de Sociologie*, No. XXXII, pp. 130–41.

Levy, Daniel and M. Székely (1983). *México: Paradoxes of Stability and Change* (Epping: Bowker).

Lindblom, Charles E. (1977). *Politics and Markets: The World's Political Economic Systems* (New York, NY: Basic Books).

Linz, Juan J. (1994). "Presidential or Parliamentary Democracy: Does it Make a Difference?" in J.J. Linz and A. Valenzuela (eds.), *The Failure of Presidential Democracy* (Baltimore, MD: Johns Hopkins University Press), pp. 3–87.

Loaeza, Soledad (1989). "The Emergence and Legitimization of the Modern Right, 1970–1988", in W.A. Cornelius, J. Gentleman, and P.H. Smith (eds.), *Mexico's Alternative Political Futures*, Monograph Series, 30 (San Diego: Center for U.S.-Mexican Studies, University of California, San Diego), pp. 351–65.

Lomelí, Benjamín and F. Hernández (1980). "Los Empresarios en la Coyuntura Política Actual", in E. González (ed.), *1979, ¿La Crisis Quedó Atrás?* (México: UNAM/ACERE), pp. 200–16.

Looney, Robert E. (1985). *Economic Policymaking in México: Factors Underlying the 1982 Crisis* (Durham: Duke University Press).

———.(1978). *Mexico's Economy: A Policy Analysis with Forecasts to 1990* (Boulder, CO: Westview Press).

López del Bosque, Isidro (1978). "Palabras Pronunciadas por el Sr. Isidro López del Bosque, Consejero de la Confederación Patronal de la República Mexicana", in Coparmex (ed.), *XXXVII Asamblea Nacional Ordinaria de Centros Patronales* (México: Coparmex), pp. 21–6.

López Portillo, José (1998). "We Urgently Need a New World Economic Order, A New Bretton Woods", *Executive Intelligence Review*, September 25, 1998.

———.(1988). *Mis Tiempos: Biografía y Testimonio Político*, Volumes 1 and 2 (México: Fernández Editores).

López-Portillo Romano, José Ramón (1994). Economic Thought and Economic Policy-Making in Contemporary México: International and Domestic Components, unpublished D.Phil. Dissertation, University of Oxford.

Lorrain, François And H.C. White (1971). "Structural Equivalence of Individuals in Social Networks", *Jorunal of Mathematical Sociology*, No.1, pp. 49–80.

Loyo, Aurora (1983). *La Unidad Nacional* (México: M. Casillas).

Luhmann, Niklas (1979). *Trust and Power* (Chichester: Wiley).

Lukes, Steven (1991). "The Rationality of Norms", *Archives Européennes de Sociologie*, No. XXXII, pp. 142–9.

———.(1986). "Introduction", in S. Lukes (ed.), *Power* (Oxford: Basil Blackwell), pp. 1–18.

Luna Ledesma, Matilde (1995). "Entrepreneurial Interests and Political Action in México: Facing the Demands of Economic Modernization", in R. Roett (ed.), *The Challenge of Institutional Reform in Mexico* (Boulder and London: Lynne Rienner Publishers), pp. 77–94.

———.(1992[a]). *Los Empresarios y el Cambio Político: México, 1970–1987* (México: Ediciones Era, Instituto de Investigaciones Sociales UNAM).

———.(1992[b]). "La Estructura de Representación Empresarial en México. La Década de los Noventa y los Cambios en las Estrategias Corporativas", in C. Puga and R. Tirado (eds.), *Los Empresarios Mexicanos, Ayer y Hoy* (México: Ediciones El Caballito), pp. 267–285.

————. (1987). "¿Hacia un Corporativismo Liberal? Los Empresarios y el Corporativismo", *Estudios Sociológicos*, Vol. V, No. 15, September–December 1987, pp. 455-76.

————. (1984). "Los Empresarios y el Régimen Político Mexicano. Estrategias Tripartitas de los Años Setenta", *Estudios Políticos*, Nueva Época, Vol. 3, No. 1, January–May 1984, pp. 28–30.

————. (1977). *El Grupo Monterrey en la Economía Mexicana*, mimeo. in the Daniel Cosío Villegas Library of *El Colegio de México*.

Luna, Matilde and R. Tirado (1992). *El Consejo Coordinador Empresarial. Una Radiografía* (México: UNAM).

McConnell, Grant (1966). *Private Power and American Democracy* (New York: Knopf).

McFarland, Andrew (1987). "Interest Groups and Theories of Power in America", *British Journal of Political Science*, Vol. 17, No. 1, pp. 129–47.

Macneil, I.Robert (1980). *The New Social Contract* (New Haven, CN: Yale University Press).

Macridis, Roy C. (1955). *The Study of Comparative Government* (New York: Random House Publishers).

Mahar, Cheleen, R. Harker and C. Wilkes (1990). "The Basic Theoretical Position" in R. Harker, C. Mahar and C. Wilkes (eds.), *An Introduction to the Work of Pierre Bordieu* (Basingstoke: Macmillan), pp. 1–25.

Mancera Aguayo, Miguel (1993). "The Mexican Economy Since 1955", *Voices of Mexico*, April–June 1993, pp. 41–6.

————.(1992). "En el XX Aniversario de su Fallecimiento", in M.R. Beteta Monsalve (ed.), *Rodrigo Gómez: Vida y Obra* (México: Banco de México/FCE), pp. 88–112.

Mann, Michael (1986). *The Sources of Social Power: A History of Power from the Beginning to A.D. 1760* (Cambridge: Cambridge University Press).

————.(1984). "The Autonomous Power of the State: Its Origins, Mechanisms and Results", *Archives Européenes de Sociologie*, No. 25, pp. 185–213.

March, James G. (1981). "Decisions in Organizations and Theories of Choice" in *Perspectives on Organization Design and Behavior*, pp. 205–44.

March, James G. and H.A. Simon (1958). *Organizations* (New York: Wiley).

March, James G. and J.P. Olsen (1989). *Rediscovering Institutions: The Organizational Basis of Politics* (New York: Free Press).

————.(1984). "The New Institutionalism: Organizational Factors in Political Life", *The American Political Science Review*, Vol. 78, pp. 734–49.

————.(1976). *Ambiguity and Choice in Organizations* (Bergen: Universitetsforlaget).

Marin, Bernd (1990). *Generalised Political Exchange: Antagonistic Cooperation and Integrated Policy Circuits* (Boulder: Westview Press).

Marsden, Peter V. (1983). "Restricted Access in Networks and Models of Power?", *American Journal of Sociology*, No. 88, pp. 686–717.

Marsh, David (1998²). "The Development of the Policy Network Approach", in David Marsh (ed.), *Comparing Policy Networks* (Buckingham and Philadelphia: Open University Press), pp. 3–17.

————. (1998b). "The Utility and Future of Policy Network Analysis", in David Marsh (ed.), *Comparing Policy Networks* (Buckingham and Philadelphia: Open University Press), pp. 185–197.

Marsh, D. and R.A.W. Rhodes (1992a). *Policy Networks in British Government* (Oxford: Oxford University Press).

————. (1992b). "The Implementation Gap: Explaining Policy Change and Continuity" in D. Marsh and R.A.W. Rhodes (eds.), *Implementing Thatcherite Policies: Audit of an Era* (Milton Keynes: Open University Press).

Martin, Joanne (1994). "The Organization of Exclusion: The Institutionalization of Sex Inequality, Gendered Faculty Jobs, and Gendered Knowledge in Organizational Theory and Research", *Organizations*, Vol. 1, pp. 401–31.

Martínez Cabañas, Gustavo (1989). "La Industria Establecida y las Nuevas Industrias", in F. Becerra Maldonado (ed.), *Antología del Pensamiento Económico de la Facultad de Economía 1929–1989* (México: UNAM), pp. 184–9.

Martínez Nava, Juan M. (1984). *Conflicto Estado Empresarios en los Gobiernos de Cárdenas, López Mateos y Echeverría* (México: Editorial Nueva Imagen).

Martínez Treviño, Felipe P. (1983). "El Futuro de la Empresa Privada en la Doctrina del Nacionalismo Revolucionario", in Coparmex (ed.), *La Empresa Privada, Esperanza de México. XLIII Asamblea Nacional Ordinaria* (México: Coparmex), pp. 61–82.

Marván Laborde, Ignacio (1997). *¿Y Después del Presidencialismo? Reflexiones para la Formación de un Nuevo Régimen* (México: Océano).

————. (1990). *Governing Capital: International Finance and Mexican Politics* (Ithaca and London: Cornell University Press).

Maxfield, Sylvia (1989). "International Economic Opening and Government-Business Relations", in W.A. Cornelius, J. Gentleman, and P.H. Smith (eds.), *Mexico's Alternative Political Futures*, Monograph Series, 30 (San Diego: Center for U.S.-Mexican Studies, University of California, San Diego), pp. 215–36.

Mayer, Robert R. (1982). *Social Science and Institutional Change* (New Brunswick and London: Transaction Books).

Medin, Tzvi (1990). *El Sexenio Alemanista: Ideología y Praxis Política de Miguel Alemán* (México: Ediciones Era).

————.(1972). *Ideología y Praxis Política de Lázaro Cárdenas* (México: Siglo Veintiuno Editores).

Medina Peña, Luis (1995). *Hacia el Nuevo Estado: México 1920–1994* (México: Fondo de Cultura Económica).

Méndez, José L. (1998). "Los Pequeños y Medianos Empresarios como Actores Políticos en México", in E. Gutiérrez Garza, J.M. Ramírez and J. Regalado (eds.), *El Debate Nacional: Los Actores Sociales* (México: Editorial Diana), pp. 142–72.

Mendoza Berrueto, Eliseo (1998). *El Presidencialismo Mexicano: Una Tradición ante la Reforma del Estado* (México: FCE/El Colegio de la Frontera Norte).

Menocal, Nina (1981). *México Visión de los Ochenta* (México: Editorial Diana).

Meyer, John W. and B. Rowan (1991). "Institutionalizing Organizations: Formal Structure as Myth and Ceremony" in W.W. Powell and P.J. DiMaggio (eds.), *The New Institutionalism in Organizational Analysis*, (Chicago and London: The University of Chicago Press), pp. 41–62.

———. (1987). "Self and Course: Institutionalization and Its Effects" in G.M Thomas, J.W. Meyer, F.O. Ramírez and J. Boli (eds.), *Institutional Structure Constituting State, Society and the Individual* (Newbury Park, Beverly Hills, London and New Delhi: Sage Publications), pp. 242–260.

Meyer, John W., J. Boli and G.M. Thomas (1987). "Ontology and Rationalization in the Western Cultural Account" in G.M Thomas, J.W. Meyer, F.O. Ramírez and J. Boli (eds.), *Institutional Structure Constituting State, Society and the Individual* (Newbury Park, Beverly Hills, London and New Delhi: Sage Publications), pp. 12–37.

Michels, Robert (1960). *Political Parties Sociological Study* (London: Peter Smith Publishers).

Middlemas, Keith (1979). *Politics in Industrial Society* (London: Andre Deutsch).

Migdal, Joel S. (1994). "The State in Society: An Approach to Struggles for Domination" in J.S. Migdal, A. Kohli and V. Shue (eds.), *State, Power and Social Forces: Domination and Transformation in the Third World* (Cambridge: Cambridge University Press), pp. 7–34.

Miliband, Ralph (1973). *The State in Capitalist Society* (London: Quartet Books).

Mills, C. Wright (1959). *The Power Elite* (New York: Oxford University Press).

Milner, Helen V. (1997). *Interests, Institutions, and Information: Domestic Politics and International Relations* (Princeton, NJ: Princeton University Press).

Mirón, Rosa M. and G. Pérez (1988). *López Portillo: Auge y Crisis de un Sexenio* (México: Plaza y Janés).

Moe, Terry M. (1990). "Political Institutions: The Neglected Side of the Story", *Journal of Law, Economics and Organizations*, Vol 6., pp. 213–253.

Monsiváis, Carlos (1979). "La Ofensiva Ideológica de la Derecha", in P. González Casanova and E. Florescano (eds.), *México Hoy* (México: Siglo Veintiuno Editores), pp. 306–29.

Montesinos Carrera, Rafael (1992). "El Discurso Empresarial en 1985", in C. Puga and R. Tirado (eds.), *Los Empresarios Mexicanos, Ayer y Hoy* (México: Ediciones El Caballito), pp. 233–246.

Morales, Isidro, C. Escalante and R. Vargas (1988). *La Formación de la Política Petrolera en México* (México: El Colegio de México).

Moreno, María de los Ángeles and R. Flores Caballero (1995). *Evolución de la Deuda Pública Externa de México 1950–1993* (México: Ediciones Castillo).

Morris, Stephen D. (1992). *Corrupción y Política en el México Contemporáneo* (México: Siglo Veintiuno Editores).

Mosca, Gaetano (1959). *Ruling Class* (New York: McGraw-Hill).

Mosk, Sanford (1950). *Industrial Revolution in Mexico* (Berkeley: University of California Press).

Nafinsa (1988). *La Economía Mexicana en Cifras* (México: Nafinsa).

———. (1984). *La Economía Mexicana en Cifras* (México: Nafinsa).

———. (1977). *Statistics on the Mexican Economy* (México: Nafinsa).

Nava García, Francisco (1983). *Bases Históricas de la Economía Mexicana 1810–1982* (México: Editora Latinoamericana).

Navarrete, Ifigenia M. de (1967). *Los Incentivos Fiscales y el Desarrollo Económico de México* (México: UNAM, Instituto de Investigaciones Económicas).

Nelson, Richard R. and S.G. Winter (1982). *An Evolutionary Theory of Economic Change* (Cambridge, MA and London: Belknap Press).

Newell, Roberto and L.F. Rubio (1984). *Mexico's Dilemma: The Political Origins of Economic Crisis* (Boulder: Westview).

Niblo, Stephen R. (1999). *Mexico in the 1940s: Modernity, Politics, and Corruption* (Wilimington, DE: Scholarly Resources).

Nohria, Nittin (1992). "Is Network Perspective a Useful Way of Studying Organizations?", in Nittin Nohria and Robert. G. Eccles (eds.), *Networks and Organizations: Structure, Form, and Action* (Boston, MA: Harvard Business School Press), pp. 1–22.

Nordlinger, Eric A. (1981). *On the Autonomy of the Democratic State* (Cambridge, MA: Harvard University Press).

North, Douglass (1995). "The New Institutional Economics and Third World Development", in J. Harris, J. Hunter and A. Lewis (eds.),*The New Institutional Economics and Third World Development* (Routledge: London), pp. 17–26.

———. (1990). *Institutions, Institutional Change and Economic Performance* (Cambridge: Cambridge University Press).

North. Douglass and P. Thomas (1973). *The Rise of the Western World* (Cambridge: Cambridge University Press).

Nuncio, Abraham (1982). *El Grupo Monterrey* (México: Editorial Nueva Imagen).

Nye, Robert (1977). *The Anti-Democratic Sources of Elite Theory: Pareto, Mosca, Michels* (London and Beverly Hills, CA: Sage).

O'Donnell, Guillermo A. (1978). *Burguesía Local, Capital Transnacional y Aparato Estatal: Notas para su Estudio*, mimeo. in the Daniel Cosío Villegas Library of *El Colegio de México*.

Offe, Claus (1991). "Introduction: The Puzzling Scope of Rationality", *Archives Européennes de Sociologie*, No. XXXII, pp. 81–3.

Okuno-Fujiwara, Masahiro (1998). "Toward a Comparative Institutional Analysis of the Government-Business Relationship", in M. Aoki, H.K. Kim and M. Okuno-Fujiwara (eds.), *The Role of Government in East Asian Economic Development: Comparative Institutional Analysis* (Oxford: Clarendon Press), pp. 373–406.

Olsen, Johan P. (1983). *Organized Democracy: Political Institutons in a Welfare State, The Case of Norway* (Oslo: Universitetforlaget).

Ortega, Max and A.A. Solís (1990). "Estado, Capital y Sindicatos, México 1983–1988", in E. Gutiérrez Garza (ed.), *Los Saldos del Sexenio (1982–1988)* (México: Siglo Veintiuno Editores/UAM), pp. 221–36.

Ortiz Mena, Antonio (1992). "La Relación entre el Gobierno Federal y el Banco de México", in M.R. Beteta Monsalve (ed.), *Rodrigo Gómez: Vida y Obra* (México: Banco de México/FCE), pp. 113–36.

Orvañanos Zúñiga, Jorge (1975). "Palabras Pronunciadas por el Señor Lic. Jorge Orvañanos Zúñiga, Presidente de la Confederación Patronal de la República Mexicana, en la XXXIV Asamblea Nacional Ordinaria de Centros Patronales", in *XXXIV Asamblea Nacional Ordinaria de Centros Patronales* (México: Coparmex), pp. 13–23.

Ostrom, Elinor (1990). *Governing the Commons: The Evolution of Institutions of Collective Action* (Cambridge: Cambridge University Press).

Oteyza de, José A. (1979). "'Podrán Bailar sin Codazos ni Pisotones', Predice Oteyza", *Proceso*, No. 127, 9 April 1979, pp. 6–7.

Palma, Gabriel (1994). "The Latin American Economies from 1950 to 1990", in L. Bethell (ed.), *The Cambridge History of Latin America*, Vol. 6, pp. 159–249.

Paniagua, Rafael (1987). "Coacciones y Límites de la Intervención del Estado en México", in J. Lechuga Moreno (ed.), *El Dilema de la Economía Mexicana: Ensayos de Interpretación* (México: UAM/Ediciones de Cultura Popular), pp. 17–37.

Panitch, Leo (1977). "The Development of Corporatism in Liberal Democracies", *Comparative Political Studies*, No. 10.

Pánuco-Laguette H. and M. Székely (1997). "La Distribución del Ingreso y la Pobreza en México", in V. Bulmer-Thomas (ed.), *El Nuevo Modelo Económico en América Latina: Su Efecto en la Distribución del Ingreso y en la Pobreza*, pp. 225–266.

Pareto, Vilfredo (1984). *The Transformation of Democracy* (New Brunswick: Transaction Books).

Parsons, Talcott (1986). "Power and the Social System", in S. Lukes (ed.), *Power* (Oxford: Basil Blackwell), pp. 94–143.

———. (1951). *The Social System* (New York: Free Press).

Perzabal, Carlos (1988). *Acumulación de Capital e Industrialización Compleja en México* (México: Siglo Veintiuno Editores).

Phelps Brown, H. (1977). "What is the British Predicament?", *Three Banks Review*, No.116, pp. 3–29.

Philip, George (1992). "El Poder Presidencial en México", in C. Bazdresch *et al.* (eds.), *México: Auge, Crisis y Ajuste. I. Los Tiempos del Cambio, 1982–1988* (México: Fondo de Cultura Económica), pp. 403–13.

Pierson, Paul (1996). "The Path to European Integration: A Historical Institutionalist Perspective", *Comparative Political Studies*, Vol. 29, pp. 123–63.

———. (1993). "When Effect Becomes Cause: Policy Feedback and Political Change", *World Politics*, Vol. 45, July 1993, pp. 595–628.

Pigou, Artur C. (1978). *Keynes's "General Theory": A Retrospective View* (London: McMillan). First published in 1950.

Pérez López, Enrique (1992). "El Desarrollo Estabilizador: Lecciones del Pasado", in M.R. Beteta Monsalve (ed.), *Rodrigo Gómez: Vida y Obra* (México: Banco de México/FCE), pp. 137–68.

Peters, Guy (1998). "Policy Networks: Myth, Metaphor and Reality" in David Marsh (ed.), *Comparing Policy Networks* (Buckingham and Philadelphia: Open University Press), pp. 23–32.

———. (1999). *Institutional Theory in Political Science: The "New Institutionalism"* (London and New York: Pinter).

Pfeffer, Jeffrey (1992). *Managing with Power: Politics and Influence in Organizations* (Boston, MA: Harvard Business School Press).

Poniatowska, Elena (1994). *La Noche de Tlatelolco* (México: Editorial Era).

Popper, Karl R. (1962). *Conjectures and Refutations: The Growth of Scientific Knowledge* (New York: Basic Books).

Popping, Roel (2000). *Computer Assisted Text Analysis* (London: Sage).

Powell, Walter W. (1990). "Neither Market nor Hierarchy: Network Forms of Organization", in B.M. Straw and L.L. Cummings (eds.), *Research in Organizational Behavior: An Annual Series of Analytical Essays and Critical Reviews*, Vol. 12, pp. 295–336.

Prebisch, Raúl (1991). *Obras, 1919–1948* (Buenos Aires: Fundación Raúl Prebisch).

Puga, Cristina (1998). "El Futuro de las Organizaciones Empresariales", in E. Gutiérrez Garza, J.M. Ramírez and J. Regalado (eds.), *El Debate Nacional: Los Actores Sociales* (México: Editorial Diana), pp. 119–140.

———. (1993). *México: Empresarios y Poder* (México: Facultad de Ciencias Políticas y Sociales, UNAM y Miguel Ángel Porrúa Grupo Editorial).

———. (1982). "Los Empresarios y la Política en México", in S. Cordero and R. Tirado (eds.), *Clases Dominantes y Estado en México* (México: UNAM), pp. 185–201.

Puga, Cristina and C. De la Vega (1990). "Presentación: El Sexenio del Crecimiento Cero", in E. Gutiérrez Garza (ed.), *Los Saldos del Sexenio (1982–1988)* (México: Siglo Veintiuno Editores/UAM), pp. 237–60.

Purcell, John F.H and S.K. Purcell (1977). "Mexican Business and Public Policy", in J.M. Malloy (ed.), *Authoritarianism and Corporatism in Latin America* (Pittsburgh: University of Pittsburgh Press), pp. 191–226.

Putterman, L. and D. Rueschmeyer (1992). *State and Market in Development: Synergy or Rivalry?* (Boulder and London: Lynne Rienner Publishers).

Ramírez, Carlos (1988). "1983–1988: Informe de la Crisis", *El Financiero*, Nov. 25, pp. 54–56.

Ramírez Brun, J. Ricardo (1980). *Estado y Acumulación de Capital en México: 1929–1979* (México: ENEP Aragón).

Ramírez, Miguel D. (1994). "Public and Private Investment in Mexico, 1950–90: An Empirical Analysis", *Southern Economic Journal*, Vol. 61, No. 1, pp. 1–17.

Ramírez Rancaño, Mario (1977). *Crecimiento Económico e Inestabilidad Política en México* (México: UNAM).

———. (1976). "Los Empresarios Mexicanos: Las Fracciones Dominantes", *Problemas del Desarrollo, Revista Latinoamericana de Economía*, Año VI, No. 24, Nov. 1975–Jan 1976, pp. 49–82.

Ramírez Rancaño, Mario (1974). *La Burguesía Industrial: Revelaciones de una Encuesta* (México: UNAM/Editorial Nuestro Tiempo).

Ramos, Jaime (1993). *Los de Arriba: La Cultura y Ejercicio del Poder entre los Mexicanos* (México: Editorial Planeta Mexicana).

Redding, Gordon R. (1990). *The Spirit of Chinese Capitalism* (Berlin: de Gruyter).

Repetto, Fabián (1998). "Notas para el Análisis de las Políticas Sociales: Una Propuesta desde el Institucionalismo", *Perfiles Latinoamericanos*, No. 12, Junio 1998, pp. 53–84.

Reynolds, Clark W. (1977). "Porque el Desarrollo Estabilizador fue en realidad Desestabilizador: Algunas Consecuencias para el Futuro", *El Trimestre Económico*, Vol. 44, No. 176, pp. 997–1023.

———. (1970). *The Mexican Economy: Twentieth Century Structure and Growth* (New Haven: Yale University Press).

Rhodes, R.A.W. (1997). *Understanding Governance: Policy Networks, Governance, Reflexivity, and Accountability* (Buckingham: Open University Press).

———. (1990). "Policy Networks: A British Perspective", *Journal of Theoretical Politics*, Vol. 2, No. 3, pp. 293–317.

———. (1988). *Beyond Westminster and Whitehall* (London: Unwin Hyman).

———. (1986). *The National World of Local Government* (London: Allen and Unwin).

———. (1981). *Control and Power in Centre–Local Government Relations* (Farnborough: Gower/SSRC).

Rhodes, R.A.W. and D. Marsh (1992). "New Directions in the Study of Policy Networks", *European Journal of Political Research*, Vol. 21, Nos.1 and 2, pp.181–205.

Richardson, J.J. and A.G. Jordan (1979). *Governing Under Pressure* (Oxford: Martin Robertson).

Ridgeway, Cecilia L. (1994). "Structure, Action, and Social Psychology", *Social Psychology Quarterly*, Vol. 57, No. 3, pp. 161–2

Riding, Alan (1985). *Vecinos Distantes: Un Retrato de los Mexicanos* (México: Joaquín Mortiz/Planeta).

Riggs, Fred W. (1997). "Presidentialism versus Parliamentarism: Implications for Representativeness and Legitimacy", *International Political Science Review"*, Vol.18, No.3, pp. 253–78.

Riker, William (1980). "Implications from the Disequilibrium of Majority Rule for the Study of Institutions", *ASPR*, Vol. 774, No. 2 (June 1980), pp. 432–46.

Rivera Ríos, Miguel A. (1992). *El Nuevo Capitalismo Mexicano: El Proceso de Reestructuración, 1983–1989* (México: Era).

Rockman, Bert A. (1989). "Minding the State —A State of Mind? Issues in the Comparative Conceptualization of the State", in J.A. Caporaso (ed.), *The Elusive State: International and Comparative Perspectives* (Newburg Park, CA: Sage), pp. 173–203.

Roethlisberger, Fritz J. and W.J. Dickinson (1939). *Management and the Worker* (Cambridge, MA: Harvard University Press).

Rogers, David L. D.A. Whetten (1982). *Interorganizational Coordination: Theory, Research, and Implementation* (Ames: Iowa State University Press).

Rokkan, Stein (1966). "Votes Count but Resources Decide", in R.A. Dahl (ed.), *Political Oppositions in Western Democracies* (New Haven, CT: Yale University Press).

Ronfeldt, David F. (1993). *Institutions, Markets, and Networks: A Framework about the Evolution of Society*, mimeo. prepared for The Ford Foundation, Daniel Cosío Villegas Library of *El Colegio de México*.

———. (1989). "Prospects for Elite Cohesion", in W.A. Cornelius, J. Gentleman, and P.H. Smith (eds.), *Mexico's Alternative Political Futures*, Monograph Series, No. 30 (San Diego: Center for U.S.-Mexican Studies, University of California, San Diego), pp. 435–51.

Ros, Jaime (1987). "Mexico from the Oil Boom to the Debt Crisis: Responses to External Shocks, 1978–85", in R. Thorp and L. Whitehead (eds.), *Latin American Debt and the Adjustment Crisis* (Oxford: McMillan Press and St. Antony's College), pp. 68–116.

———. (1986). "Del Auge Petrolero a la Crisis de la Deuda: Un Análisis de la Política Económica en el Período 1978–1985", in R. Thorp and L. Whitehead (eds.), *La Crisis de la Deuda en América Latina* (México: Siglo Veintiuno Editores), pp. 69–109.

Rose-Ackerman, Susan (1999). *Corruption and Government: Causes, Consequences, and Reform* (Cambridge: Cambridge University Press).

———. (1978). *Corruption: A Study in Political Economy* (New York: Academic Press).

Rosenberg, Morris (1979). *Conceiving the Self* (New York: Basic Books).

Rosenau, James N. (1997). *Along the Domestic-Foreign Frontier: Exploring Governance in a Turbulent World* (Cambridge: Cambridge University Press).

———. (1992). "Governance, Order, and Change in World Politics" in J.N. Rosenau and E.O. Czempiel (eds.), *Governance without Government: Order and Change in World Politics* (Cambridge: Cambridge University Press), pp. 219–49.

Rosenstein-Rodan, Paul N. (1943). "Problems of Industrialisation of Eastern and South-Eastern Europe", in *Economic Journal*, Vol. 53, pp. 202–211

Rubio, Luis (1990). "El Sector Privado en el Pasado y en el Futuro de México", in J.W. Wilkie and J. Reyes Heroles González Garza (eds.), *Industria y Trabajo en México, Volúmen 1* (México: UAM-Atzcapotzalco), pp. 243–62.

Rueda Peiro, Isabel (1998). *México: Crisis, Reestructuración Económica, Social y Política 1982–1996* (México: UNAM and Siglo Veintiuno Editores).

Rueschemeyer, Dietrich and P.B. Evans (1985). "The State and Economic Transformation: Toward an Analysis of the Conditions Underlying Effective State Intervention", in P.B. Evans, D. Rueschemeyer, and T. Skocpol (eds.) Bringing the State Back In (Cambridge: Cambridge University Press), pp. 44–77.

Ruiz Galindo Jr., Antonio (1987). "Modernización del Sector Público", in *Memorias del Congreso Nacional de Empresarios 1987: Modernización Integral de México* (México: Coparmex), pp. 81–92.

Ruiz Massieu, Armando (1996). *El Gabinete en México: Previsión Histórica y Propuestas de Discusión* (México: Océano).

Sabatier, Paul A. (1988). "An Advocacy-Coalition Model of Policy Change and the Role of Policy-Oriented Learning Therein", *Policy Sciences*, Vol. 21, pp. 129–68.

Sada Zambrano, Andrés Marcelo (1978). "Palabras Pronunciadas por el Sr. Ing. Andrés Marcelo Sada, Presidente de la Confederación Patronal de la República Mexicana", in Coparmex (ed.), *XXXVII Asamblea Nacional Ordinaria de Centros Patronales* (México: Coparmex), pp. 15–19.

———. (1977[a]). "Palabras Pronunciadas por el Sr. Ing. Andrés Marcelo Sada, Presidente de la Confederación Patronal de la República Mexicana", in Coparmex (ed.), *XXXVI Asamblea Nacional Ordinaria de Centros Patronales* (México: Coparmex), pp. 13–19.

———. (1977[b]). "Informe del Ingeniero Andrés Marcelo Sada, Presidente de la Confederación Patronal de la República Mexicana", in Coparmex (ed.), *XXXVI Asamblea Nacional Ordinaria de Centros Patronales* (México: Coparmex), pp. 75–81.

———. (1977[c]). *Palabras del Ing. A.M. Sada en la Asamblea del Centro Patronal de Jalisco*, mimeo. in Coparmex Archives.

Saldivar, Américo (1991). *Ideología y Política del Estado Mexicano (1970–1976)* (México: Siglo Veintiuno Editores).

———. (1988). "Fin de Siglo", in E. Semo (ed.), *México un Pueblo en la Historia* (México: Alianza Editorial Mexicana), Vol. 7.

Salinas de Gortari, Carlos (2000). *México: Un Paso Difícil a la Modernidad* (México: Plaza y Janés Editores).

Salisbury, R.H., J.P. Heinz, R.L. Nelson, and E.O. Laumann (1992). "Triangles, Networks and Hollow Cores: The Complex Geometry of Washington Interest Representation", in M.P. Petracca (ed.) *The Politics of Interests* (Boulder, CO: Westview Press), pp. 130–149.

Sánchez Gamper, Phillippe A. (1989). *Del Conflicto al Consenso: Los Empresarios y la Política de Inversiones Extranjeras en México, 1944–1970*, B.A. Dissertation, mimeo. at the Daniel Cosío Villegas Library of *El Colegio de México*.

Sánchez Navarro, Juan (1955). *Ensayo Sobre una Política de Inversiones Extranjeras en México* (México: Concanaco).

Sandoval González, Alfredo (1986). "La Nueva Era del Mundo no es Una Ficción; Ya Está entre Nosotros", in Coparmex (ed.), *Participar para Modernizar a México, XLVI Asamblea Nacional Ordinaria* (México: Coparmex), pp. 15–19.

———. (1985). "Condiciones de la Recuperación Económica de México y la Libertad", in Coparmex (ed.), *Reto de México: Cambio para la Recuperación, XLVI Asamblea Nacional Ordinaria* (México: Coparmex), pp. 1–2.

Sartori, Giovanni (1997). *Comparative Constitutional Engineering: An Inquiry into Structures, Incentives and Outcomes* (New York: New York University Press).

Saward, Michael (1990). "Cooption and Power: Who Gets What from Formal Incorporation", *Political Studies*, Vol. XXXVIII, pp. 588–602.

Scharpf, Fritz W. (1989). "Decision Rules, Decision Styles and Policy Choices", *Journal of Theoretical Politics*, Vol. 1, No. 2, pp. 149–76.

———. (1978). "Interorganizational Policy Studies: Issues, Concepts and Perspectives", in K. Hanf and F.W. Scharpf (eds.) *Interorganizational Policy Making: Limits to Coordination and Central Control*, pp. 345–70.

Scheele, Brigitte and N. Groeben (1988). *Dialog-Konsens-Methoden zur Rekonstruktion Subjektiver Theorien* (Tübingen: Francke).

Schlicht, Ekkehart (1990). "Rationality, Bounded or not, and Institutional Analysis", *Journal of Institutional and Theoretical Economics*, No. 146, pp. 703–19.

Schmitter, Philippe (1990). "Sectors in Modern Capitalism: Models of Governance and Variations in Performance" in Renato Brunetta and Carlo Dell'Aringa (eds.), *Labour Relations and Economic Performance* (Houndmills, England: McMillan), pp. 3–39.

———. (1974). "Still the Century of Corporatism?", *Review of Politics*, No. 36, pp. 85–131.

Schmitter, Phiippe and G. Lehmbruch (1979). *Trends Toward Corporatist Intermediation* (Beverly Hills, CA and London: Sage).

Scott, John (1994). "General Commentary" in J. Scott (ed.), *Power: Critical Concepts, Volume 1* (New York: Routledge), pp. i–xvii.

Scott, W. Richard (1995). *Institutions and Organizations* (Thousand Oaks, London and New Delhi: Sage Publications).

———. (1991). "Unpacking Institutional Arrangements" in W.W. Powell and P.J. DiMaggio (eds.), *The New Institutionalism in Organizational Analysis*, (Chicago and London: The University of Chicago Press), pp. 164–182.

Scott. W. Richard and J.W. Meyer (1991). "The Organization of Societal Sectors: Propositions and Early Evidence" in W.W. Powell and P.J. DiMaggio (eds.), *The New Institutionalism in Organizational Analysis*, (Chicago and London: The University of Chicago Press), pp. 108–40.

Scott, Robert E. (1959). *Mexican Government in Transition* (Urbana: University of Illinois Press).

Searing, Donald D. (1991). "Roles, Rules and Rationality in the New Institutionalism", *American Political Science Review*, Vol. 85, pp. 1239–60.

Secretaría de Industria y Comercio (1917). *Algunos Documentos Relativos al Primer Congreso Nacional de Industriales* (México: Secretaría de Industria y Comercio).

Seldon, Anthony and J. Pappworth (1983). *By Word of Mouth: Elite Oral History* (Cambridge: University Press).

Selznick, Phillip (1957). *Leadership in Administration: A Sociological Interpretation* (Evanston, IL: Peterson Row).

———. (1949). *TVA and the Grassroots* (Berkeley: University of California Press).

Semo, Ilán (1988). "El Ocaso de los Mitos", in E. Semo (eds.), *México un Pueblo en la Historia* (México: Alianza Editorial Mexicana), Vol. 6.

Sen, Amartya (1988). "The Concept of Development", in A.B. Chenery and T.N. Snirvasan (eds.), *Handbook of Development Economics, Vol. 1* (Amsterdam: North Holland), pp. 9–26.

Sened, Itai (1991). "Contemporary Theory of Institutions in Perspective", *Journal of Theoretical Politics*, Vol. 3, pp. 379–402.

Servitje, Lorenzo (1976). "Rentabilidad e Inflación", in Concamin (ed.), *La Industria Mexicana 1976* (México: Concamin), pp. 295–8.

Shafer, Robert J. (1973). *Mexican Business Organizations: History and Analysis* (Syracuse: Syracuse University Press).

Shapiro, Helen and L. Taylor (1990). "The State and Industrial Strategy", *World Development*, Vol. 18, No. 6, pp. 861–78.

Shaw, Eric (1996). *The Labour Party since 1945: Old Labour, New Labour* (Oxford: Blackwell).

Shepsle, Kenneth A. (1986). "Institutional Equilibrium and Equilibrium Institutions", in H.F. Weisberg (ed.), *Political Science: The Science of Politics* (New York: Algora Publishing), pp. 51–81.

Shepsle, Kenneth A. and B. Weingast (1987). "The Institutional Foundations of Committee Power", *American Political Science Review*, Vol. 81, pp.85–104.

Short, J. (1985). *American Business and Foreign Policy: Cases in Coffee and Cocoa Trade Regulation, 1961–1974* (New York, NY and London: Garland Publishing).

Silva Herzog, Jesús (1967). *El Pensamiento Económico, Social y Político de México. 1810–1964* (México: Instituto Mexicano de Investigaciones Económicas).

Simon, Herbert (1994). "Notes on the Observation and Measurement of Political Power", in J. Scott (ed.), *Power: Critical Concepts, Volume 1* (New York: Routledge), pp. 275–87.

———. (1982). *Models of Bounded Rationality*, Vol. 2, (Cambridge, MA: MIT Press).

———. (1957). *Administrative Behaviour*, 2nd Edition (New York: McMillan). Original work published 1945.

Singh, Ajit (1999). Lecture for the "Industrial and Financial Economics" course of the MPhil. Degree in Development Studies at the University of Cambridge, England (24 November, 1998).

Singh, Jitendra V. (1990). "Introduction", in Jitendra V. Singh (ed.), *Organizational Evolution: New Directions* (London: Sage), pp. 11–17.

Skocpol, Theda (1993). "The Potential Autonomy of the State", in M.E. Olsen and M.N. Marger (eds.), Power in Modern Societies (Boulder: Westview Press), pp. 306–13.

———. (1992). *Protecting Soldiers and Mothers: The Political Origins of Social Policy in the United States* (Cambridge, MA and London: The Belknap Press of Harvard University Press).

———. (1985). "Bringing the State Back In: Strategies of Analysis in Current Research", in P.B. Evans, D. Rueschemeyer, and T. Skocpol (eds.) Bringing the State Back In (Cambridge: Cambridge University Press), pp. 3–37.

Skvoretz, John and D. Willer (1991). "Power in Exchange Networks: Setting and Structural Variations", *Social Psychology Quarterly*, Vol. 54, No. 3, pp. 224–38.

Smith, Martin J. (1993). *Pressure, Power and Policy: State Autonomy and Policy Networks in Britain and the United States* (London: Harvester Wheatsheaf).

Smith Ring, Peter (1997). "Processes Facilitating Reliance on Trust in Inter-Organizational Networks", in M. Ebers (ed.), *The Formation of Inter-Organizational Networks* (Oxford: Oxford University Press), pp. 113–45.

Snidal, Duncan (1994). "The Politics of Scope: Endogenous Actors, Heterogeneity and Institutions", *Journal of Theoretical Politics*, Vol. 6, No. 4, pp. 449–72.

Sober, Elliott and D.S. Wilson (1998). *Unto Others: The Evolution and Psychology of Unselfish Behavior* (Cambridge, MA. and London: Harvard University Press).

Solís, Leopoldo (1993). *La Realidad Económica Mexicana: Retrovisión y Perspectivas* (México: Siglo Veintiuno Editores).

———.(1992). "La Labor Promocional del Banco de México en Tiempos de Rodrigo Gómez", in M.R. Beteta Monsalve (ed.), *Rodrigo Gómez: Vida y Obra* (México: Banco de México/FCE), pp. 184–202.

———.(1970). "El Sistema Financiero en 1980", in D. Ibarra *et al.* (eds.), *El Perfil de México en 1980, Vol. 1* (México: Siglo Veintiuno Editores), pp. 73–87.

———.(1967). "Hacia un Análisis General a Largo Plazo del Desarrollo Económico de México", *Demografía y Economía*, Vol. 1, No. 1.

Solórzano, María del Carmen (1984). "Breve Hojeada a la Historia Bancaria de México", *Estudios Políticos*, Nueva Época, Vol. 3, No. 1, January–May 1984, pp. 15–21.

Spencer, Martin E. (1994). "Weber on Legitimate Norms and Authority", in J. Scott (ed.), *Power: Critical Concepts, Volume 1* (New York: Routledge), pp. 140–51.

Steinmo, Sven (1993). *Taxation and Democracy: Swedish, British and American Approaches to Financing the Modern State* (New Haven: Yale University Press).

Stevens, Evelyn P. (1977). "Mexico's PRI: The Institutionalization of Corporatism?", in J.M. Malloy (ed.), *Authoritarianism and Corporatism in Latin America* (Pittsburgh: University of Pittsburgh Press), pp. 227–58.

Stinchcombe, Arthur L. (1968). *Constructing Social Theories* (Chicago: University of Chicago Press).
————. (1965). "Social Structure and Organizations" in J.G. March (ed.), *Handbook of Organizations* (Chicago: Rand McNally), pp. 142–93.
Story, Dale (1990). "El Sector Industrial Mexicano y la Reestructuración Iniciada por el Gobierno", in J.W. Wilkie and J. Reyes Heroles González Garza (eds.), *Industria y Trabajo en México, Volúmen 1* (México: UAM-Atzcapotzalco), pp. 67–89.
————. (1986). *Industria, Estado y Política en México: Los Empresarios y el Poder* (México: Editorial Grijalbo).
Streeck, Wolfgang (1991). *From National Corporatism to Transnational Pluralism* (South Bend, IL: Kellogg Center, Notre Dame University).
Streeck, Wolfgang and P.C. Schmitter (1985). *Private Interest Government: Beyond Market and State* (Beverly Hills, CA: Sage).
Suárez, Luis (1992). *Alejo Peralta: Un Patrón sin Patrones* (México: Editorial Grijalbo).
————. (1983). *Echeverría en el Sexenio de López Portillo* (México: Editorial Grijalbo).
Suárez González, Eduardo (1993). "The Mexican Financial System", *Voices of Mexico*, January–March 1993, pp. 30–6.
Swedberg, Richard (1991). "Major Traditions of Economic Sociology", *Annual Review of Sociology*, No. 17, pp. 251–276.
Sydow, Jörg (1998). "Understanding the Constitution of Interorganizatonal Trust", in C. Lane and R. Bachmann (eds.), *Trust Within and Between Organizations: Conceptual Issues and Empirical Applications* (Oxford: Oxford University Press), pp. 31–63.
Székely, Gabriel (1983). *La Economía Política del Petróleo en México, 1976–1982* (México: Centro de Estudios Internacionales de El Colegio de México).
T'Hart, Paul (1993). "Symbols, Rituals and Power: The Lost Dimensions of Crisis Management", *Journal of Contingencies and Crisis Management*, Vol 1, No. 1, March 1993, pp. 36–50
Tello, Carlos (1984). *La Nacionalización de la Banca en México* (México: Siglo Veintiuno Editores).
————. (1979). *La Política Económica en México 1970–1976* (México: Siglo Veintiuno Editores).
Tello, Carlos *et al.* (1983). *México 83: A Mitad del Túnel* (México: Océano/Nexos).
Tevfik, F. Nas, A.C. Price, and C.T. Weber (1986). "A Policy-Oriented Theory of Corruption", *American Political Science Review*, No. 80, March 1986, pp. 107–19.
Thelen, Kathleen (1991). *Union of Parts: Labor Politics in Germany* (Ithaca: Cornell University Press).
Thelen, Kathleen A. and S. Steinmo (1992). "Historical Institutionalism in Comparative Politics", in S. Steinmo, K.A. Thelen and F. Longstreth (eds.), *Structuring Politics: Historical Institutionalism in Comparative Analysis* (Cambridge: Cambridge University Press), pp. 1-32.
Therborn, Goran (1980). *The Power of Ideology and the Ideology of Power* (London: Verso).

Thomas, Craig W. (1997). "Public Management as Interagency Cooperation: Testing Epistemic Community Theory at the Domestic Level", *Journal of Public Administration Research and Theory*, Vol. 7, pp. 221–46.

Thompson, Grahame, J. Frances, R. Levacic and J. Mitchell (1991). *Markets, Hierarchies and Networks* (London, Thousand Oaks and New Delhi: Open University Press).

Thorp, Rosemary and L. Whitehead (1987ᵃ). "Introduction", in R. Thorp and L. Whitehead (eds.), *Latin American Debt and the Adjustment Crisis* (Oxford: McMillan Press and St. Antony's College), pp. 1–7.

———.(1987ᵇ). "Review and Conclusions", in R. Thorp and L. Whitehead (eds.), *Latin American Debt and the Adjustment Crisis* (Oxford: McMillan Press and St. Antony's College), pp. 318–54.

Thurber, James A. (1991). "Dynamics of Policy Subsystems in American Politics" in A.J. Cigler and B.A. Loomis (eds.), *Interest Groups Politics* (Washington D.C.: Congressional Quarterly), pp. 319–43.

Tirado, Ricardo (1987). "Los Empresarios y la Política Partidaria", *Estudios Sociológicos*, Vol. V, No. 15, September–December 1987, pp. 477–97.

Todaro, Michael P. (1997). *Economic Development* (Reading MA: Addison Wesley).

Tolbert, Pamela S. and L.G. Zucker (1996). "The Institutionalization of Institutional Theory", in S.R. Clegg, C. Hardy and W.R. Nord (eds.), *Handbook of Organization Studies* (London: Sage), pp. 175–90.

Trew, Tony (1979). "Theory and Ideology at Work", in R. Fowler *et al.* (eds.), *Language and Control* (London: Routledge), pp. 94–116.

Truman, David (1951). *The Governmental Process* (New York: Knopf).

Turner, Ralph H. (1991). "The Use and Misuse of Rational Models in Collective Behavior and Social Psychology", *Archives Européennes de Sociologie*, No. XXXII, pp. 84–108.

Ulloa, Berta (1985). *Revolución Mexicana: 1910–1920* (México: Secretaría de Relaciones Exteriores).

United Nations Organization (1949). *Economic Survey of Latin America* (New York: UNO).

Uribarri, Gabriel A. (1985). *Tiempo de Echeverría* (México: Martín Casillas Editores).

Urquidi, Víctor (1970). "Perfil General: Economía y Población", in D. Ibarra *et al.* (eds.), *El Perfil de México en 1980, Vol. 1* (México: Siglo Veintiuno Editores), pp. 1–13.

Useem, Michael (1983). *The Inner Circle: Large Corporations and Business Politics in the United States and the United Kingdom* (Oxford and New York: Oxford University Press).

Valdés Ugalde, Francisco (1987). "¿Hacia un Nuevo Liderazgo Sociopolítico? Ensayo sobre la Convocatoria Social de los Empresarios", *Estudios Sociológicos*, Vol. V, No. 15, September–December 1987, pp. 433–454.

———.(1982). *Una Aproximación al Análisis de las Relaciones entre Empresarios y Gobierno en México, 1970–1976*, mimeo. in the Daniel Cosío Villegas Library of *El Colegio de México*.

Valenzuela Feijóo, José (1986). *El Capitalismo Mexicano en los Ochenta. ¿Hacia un Nuevo Modelo de Acumulación?* (México: Ediciones Era).

Vallina Lagüera, Eloy (1978). "Palabras Pronunciadas por el Sr. Eloy Vallina L., Consejero de la Confederación Patronal de la República Mexicana", in Coparmex (ed.), *XXXVII Asamblea Nacional Ordinaria de Centros Patronales* (México: Coparmex), pp. 37–41.

Velasco Fernández, Ciro (1979). "El Gasto Público en los Setentas", *Investigación Económica*, No. 150, Octubre–Diciembre 1979.

Velasco, Leticia C. (1988). "El Sector Industrial en los Ochenta, Desde la Perspectiva de sus Dirigentes Empresariales", in C. Alba Vega (ed.), *Historia y Desarrollo Industrial de México* (México: CONCAMIN), pp. 277–93.

Vellinga, Menno (1989). *Industrialización, Burguesía y Clase Obrera en México* (México: Siglo Veintiuno Editores).

Vergara, Rodolfo (1993). "Decisiones, Organizaciones y Nuevo Institucionalismo", *Perfiles Latinoamericanos,* Vol. 2, No. 3, December 1993, pp. 119–44.

Vernon, Raymond (1971). *The Dilemma of Mexico's Development: The Roles of the Private and Public Sectors* (Cambridge, MA: Harvard University Press).

———.(1964). "Introduction", in R. Vernon (ed.), *Public Policy and Private Enterprise in Mexico* (Cambridge, MA: Harvard University Press), pp. 1–17.

Vidal, Gregorio (1998). "Corporaciones, Grandes Empresarios y 'Modernización Económica'", in E. Gutiérrez Garza, J.M. Ramírez and J. Regalado (eds.), *El Debate Nacional: Los Actores Sociales* (México: Editorial Diana), pp. 87–118.

Villa, Manuel (1990). "La Política en el Gobierno de Miguel de la Madrid", *Foro Internacional,* Vol XXX, No. 4, April–June 1990, pp. 659–76.

Villa, Rosa O. (1976). *Nacional Financiera: Banco de Fomento del Desarrollo Económico de México* (México: Nacional Financiera, S.A.).

Villarreal, René (1988). *Industrialización, Deuda y Desequilibrio Externo en México: Un Enfoque Neoestructuralista (1929–1988)* (México: Fondo de Cultura Económica).

Vogel, David (1987). "Political Science and the Study of Corporate Power: A Dissent for the New Conventional View", *British Journal of Political Science*, No. 17, pp. 385–408.

Vogler, Carolyn (1985). *The Nation State: The Neglected Dimension of Class* (Aldershot: Gower).

Walker, Jack L. (1983). "The Origin and Maintenance of Interest Groups in America", *American Political Science Review*, No. 77, pp. 390–406.

Wall, Grenville (1975). "The Concept of Interest in Politics", *Politics and Society*, No. 5, pp. 487–510.

Wallerstein, Immanuel M. (2000). *The Essential Wallerstein* (New York: The New Press).

Ward, Peter (1986). *Welfare Politics in México: Papering over the Cracks* (Londond: Allen & Unwin).

Waterhouse, Lorraine and H. Beloff (1999). *Trust in Public Life* (Edinburgh: Edinburgh University Press).

Weingast, Barry R. (1996). "Political Institutions: Rational Choice Perspectives", in R.E. Goodin and D.H. Klingemann (ed.), *A New Handbook of Political Science* (Oxford: Oxford University Press), pp. 167–90.

Wang, Huei-Huang (1998). *Technology, Economic Security, State, and the Political Economy of Economic Networks: A Historical and Comparative Research on the Evolution of Economic Networks in Taiwan and Japan* (Lanham, New York and Oxford: University Press of America).

Weber, Max (1986). "Domination by Economic Power and by Authority", in S. Lukes (ed.), *Power* (Oxford: Basil Blackwell), pp. 28–36.

Weimer, David L. (1995). "Institutional Design: Overview", in D.L Weimer (ed.), *Institutional Design* (Boston, Dordrecht and London: Kluwer Academic Publishers), pp. 1–16.

Wendt, Alexander E. (1987). "The Agent-Structure Problem in International Relations Theory", *International Organisation*, Vol. 41 (summer), pp. 335–71.

Whitehead, Laurence (1980). "Mexico from Bust to Boom: A Political Evaluation of the 1976–1979 Stabilization Programme", *World Development*, Vol. 8, pp. 843–64.

Whitley, Richard (1998). *Contrasting Capitalisms: The Institutional Structuring of Business Systems*, Working Paper No. 376, Manchester Business School.

——. (1996). *The Institutional Structuring of Firms: Strategies and Employment of Practices in Market Economies*, Working Paper No. 303, Manchester Business School.

Wiarda, Howard J. (1997). *Corporatism and Comparative Politics: The Other Great "Ism"* (New York: M.E. Sharpe).

Wilkie, James (1967). *The Mexican Revolution: Federal Expenditure and Social Change since 1910* (Berkeley: University of California Press).

Wilks, Steven (1989). "Government-Industry Relations", *Public Administration*, No. 67, pp. 329–39.

Wilks, Steven, and M. Wright (1987). *Comparative Government-Industry Relations* (Oxford: Clarendon).

Wilson, Frank (1983). "French Interest Group Politics: Pluralist or Neocorporatist?", *American Political Science Review*, No.77, pp.895–910.

Willars Andrade, Jaime M. (1984). *El Petróleo en México: Efectos Macroeconómicos de Política y Perspectivas* (México: Programa de Energéticos, El Colegio de México).

Williamson, Oliver E. (1991). "Comparative Economic Organization: The Analysis of Discrete Structural Alternatives", *Administrative Science Quarterly*, June 1991, pp. 269–96.

——. (1985). *The Economic Institutions of Capitalism* (New York: Freepress).

——. (1975). *Markets and Hierarchies: Analysis and Antitrust Implications* (New York: Free Press).

Williamson, Peter J. (1989). *Corporatism in Perspective: An Introductory Guide to Corporatist Theory* (London, Newbury Park and New Delhi: Sage Publications).

Wright, Maurice (1988). "Policy Community, Policy Network, and Comparative Industrial Policies", *Political Studies*, No. 36, pp. 593–614.

Yanunuzzi, María de los Angeles (1993). *Intelectuales, Masas y Élites: Una Introducción a Mosca, Pareto y Michels* (Rosario: UNR).

Ysita Septién, Fernando (1964). *Programa de Modernización Nacional* (México: Banco de México, S.A.).

Zabludovsky, Gina (1984). "Proposiciones para el Estudio de las Relaciones entre el Estado y Empresarios durante el Período Presidencial de Miguel Alemán",

Estudios Políticos, Nueva Época, Vol. 3, No. 1, January–May 1984, pp. 22–27.

———. (1980). *México: Estado y Empresarios* (México: ENEP Acatlán).

———. (1979). *Las Organizaciones Empresariales en México: Comportamiento Político-Ideológico, 1946–1952)*, B.A. Thesis, Faculty of Social and Political Sciences, UNAM, mimeo. in the Daniel Cosío Villegas Library of *El Colegio de México*.

Zaid, Gabriel (1999). *El Progreso Improductivo* (México: Océano).

———. (1995). *Hacen Falta Empresarios Creadores de Empresarios* (México: Océano).

———. (1992). *La Economía Presidencial* (México: Editorial Contenido).

Zucker, Lynne G. (1991). "The Role of Institutionalization in Cultural Persistence" in W.W. Powell and P.J. DiMaggio (eds.), *The New Institutionalism in Organizational Analysis*, (Chicago and London: The University of Chicago Press), pp. 83–107.

———. (1988). "Where do Institutional Patterns Come From? Organizations as Actors in Social Systems", in L.G. Zucker (ed.), *Institutional Patterns and Organizations: Culture and Environment* (Cambridge, MA: Ballinger), pp. 23–49.

———. (1986). "Production of Trust: Institutional Sources of Economic Structure, 1840–1920", *Research in Organizational Behavior*, No.6, pp. 53–111.

———. (1983). "Organizations as Institutions", in S.B. Bacharach (ed.), *Research in the Sociology of Organizations*, pp. 1–42.

Zúñiga, José A. (1979). "La Economía Nacional Sujeta al Interés de las Empresas Extranjeras", *Proceso*, No. 123, 12 March 1979, pp. 22–3.

ARCHIVAL REFERENCES

ABM refers to *Asociación de Banqueros de México* (Mexican Bankers Association), a private association of representation that operated in Mexico to defend the interests of the financial community, since 1928. All the banks in the country belonged to it. They kindly allowed me to access their private archives from the 1966–1981 period. These appear to be the only surviving archives, given that the previous ones were lost when the building where they were kept collapsed after an earthquake in 1985.

ABM/LP refers to a detailed list of ex-presidents that was given to me by the research department of the Mexican Bankers Association.

ALM refers to Adolfo López Mateos, president of Mexico from 1958 to 1964. These are documents obtained in the National Archives in Mexico City, and the numbers after the initials are the official classification used by the archives. The documents include official letters, memoranda, minutes, telegrams, press publications, invitations, personal letters, and official publications.

ARC refers to Adolfo Ruiz Cortines, president of Mexico from 1952 to 1958. These are documents obtained in the National Archives in Mexico City, and the numbers after the initials are the official classification used by the archives. The documents include official letters, memoranda, minutes, telegrams, press publications, invitations, personal letters, and official publications.

COPARMEX refers to the Private Archives of the Confederation of Employers of the Mexican Republic (COPARMEX) that kindly offered me access to various speeches, minutes, memoranda, press communications and official letters from the period 1960–1986. The numbers next to the "COPARMEX" reference simply indicate the date displayed by the document being used.

DOF refers to *Diario Oficial de la Federación*, which is the official publication of the Mexican government, in which all decisions have to be published to be legally enforceable. The numbers next to the abbreviation refer to the specific date of the issue used.

GDO refers to Gustavo Díaz Ordaz, president of Mexico from 1964 to 1970. These are documents obtained in the National Archives in Mexico City, and the numbers after the initials are the official classification used by the archives. The documents include official letters, memoranda, minutes, telegrams, press publications, invitations, personal letters, and official publications.

GM refers to *"Gobierno Mexicano"*, which is a collection of archival records that Luis Echeverria Alvarez has about his administration (1970–1976). This collection consists of a total of XX volumes, containing minutes, press notes, statements, speeches, and reports of every day of the administration. The appropriate date has been included in the references, given that the collection is precisely arranged in chronological order. All XX volumes were consulted, but only the useful references have been cited throughout the book.

GR refers to Gonzalo Robles, an influential economic thinker and central bank official in Mexico during the 1940s to 1960s. He donated his personal archive, with endless personal and official documents to the National Archives.

LCR refers to Lázaro Cárdenas del Río, president of Mexico from 1934 to 1940. These are documents obtained in the National Archives in Mexico City, and the numbers after the initials are the official classification used by the archives. The documents include official letters, memoranda, minutes, telegrams, press publications, invitations, personal letters, and official publications.

MAC refers to Manuel Avila Camacho, president of Mexico from 1940 to 1946. These are documents obtained in the National Archives in Mexico City, and the numbers after the initials are the official classification used by the archives. The documents include official letters, memoranda, minutes, telegrams, press publications, invitations, personal letters, and official publications.

MAR refers to Miguel Alessio Robles, president of the Confederation of Chambers of Industry in 1970–71. He kindly gave me an important speech that he pronounced in 1971 (date unclear) during the presidential campaign of Luis Echeverria. The speech is important because it summarised the position of the industrial sector on various topics of national importance at that crucial time in history.

MAV refers to Miguel Alemán Valdés, president of Mexico from 1946 to 1952. These are documents obtained in the National Archives in Mexico City, and the numbers after the initials are the official classification used by the archives. The documents include official letters, memoranda, minutes, telegrams, press publications, invitations, personal letters, and official publications.

DGCSPR refers to *Dirección General de Comunicación Social de la Presidencia de la República* or General Directorate of Communications of the Presidency of the Republic. This directorate is in charge of issuing all official statements and news from the office of the president of Mexico. I consulted the specific archives of this agency for the Miguel De la Madrid Hurtado administration (1982-1988).

INTERVIEWEE REFERENCES

The information obtained during the interviews will be referenced with the following initials, followed by the date of the interview (dd/mm/yyyy).

AMSZ	Andrés Marcelo Sada Zambrano.
ASG	Alfredo Sandoval González.
CG	Carlos Gutiérrez.
CRL	Carlos Rello Lara.
CYO	Yarza Ochoa.
DIM	David Ibarra Muñoz.
EML	Emilio Goicochea Luna.
GCU	Guillermo Castro Ulloa.
IAC	Ignacio Aranguren Castiello.
JAO	José Andrés de Oteyza.
JAU	José Antonio Ugarte.
JCS	Jorge Chapa Salazar.
JLCG	José Luis Coindreau García.
JMBN	José María Basagoiti Noriega.
JPO	Joaquín Pría Olavarrieta.
JRLP	José Ramón López-Portillo Romano.
JSN	Juan Sánchez Navarro.
JVA	Jesús Vidales Aparicio.
JVD	Jorge de la Vega Domínguez.
JZ	Jacobo Zaidenweber.
LEA	Luis Echeverría Alvarez.
MAR	Miguel Alessio Robles.
MMH	Miguel de la Madrid Hurtado.
MRB	Mario Ramón Beteta.
PML	Porfirio Muñoz Ledo.

Index